From I Ranch

An Autobiography

By
The Honorable Peter James Gravett
Secretary, California Department of
Veteran Affairs (Retired)
Major General United States Army (Retired)

The Life Story of a Non-Traditional Four
Career Life;
His Journey from a Sharecroppers Son in
the Segregated Jim Crow South to a
Governor's Cabinet Secretary in the West

*"**History with its flickering lamp stumbles along the trail of the past, trying to reconstruct its scenes, to revive its echoes and kindle with pale gleams the passion of former days....**"*

-

Winston Churchill

Published by:

P & B Publishing.

904 Silver Spur Road

Suite 352

Rolling Hills CA 90274

PeterGravett6@GMail.com

Copyright 2018

First Printing, 2018

Rev 1 – 11-2019

Printed in the United States of America

ISBN: 978-1701673601

Book Shepherding/Editing/Formatting – Mike Rounds
www.PublishersHaven.com

CONTENTS

AUTHOR'S NOTE - DEDICATION

I dedicate this book to my parents, the late Clarence and Alice Gravett, for making incredible sacrifices to raise eleven children under austere social, resource constrained and financial conditions. Their vision and determination are inspiring evidence to the resiliency of the indomitable spirit.

When they married the world was not a perfect one, especially in the South of the United States, but they persevered. They were visionary and their vision for a good religious upbringing, a good home environment and educational opportunities for their children was manifested when they pulled up stakes and headed west; pioneers in their day. This venture was to capture what was promised to them by the Declaration of Independence, the "Pursuit of Happiness."

They did not allow the inherent and constant manifestation of institutionalized bigotry which surrounded them to offer a deterrence or cloud their vision in the segregated "Jim Crow" South. They pursued and captured their dream.

I do not have enough in my heart to really thank them for providing for their off-spring by, at times, working two jobs each, mentoring their children, providing a religious centered home environment and setting the example for Gravett families in the future. They were pathfinders and the result is that all of their children found successful paths of their own choosing.

CHAPTER 1 INTRODUCTION

Everyone has a story to tell and they are all different so what follows is my story as best as I can tell it. I always knew that should I eventually write my story the title would chronicle my journey from East Garrison to the Ranch House and even extending far beyond. Both **East Garrison** and the **Ranch House** are located at Camp Roberts, California as will later be described in detail within this treatise. This was important in order for the reader to grasp a full appreciation of the title.

The story does not end at the Ranch House and the reader may suggest it really begins there as that may be considered as the point of departure. This is not a "tell all" book and there are no startling revelations nor are there any exposes'. Additionally this is not intended to be a scholarly work but more a chronology of events in my life as they occurred.

I am writing because many times over the past several years' there have been suggestions by many that I should write my story. These included family members, friends, social acquaintances, colleagues, published authors and various members of organizations to which I belong. These especially included military and veteran organizations members who had often expressed to me that my story was unique and should be shared. Perhaps it was Bishop T.D. Jakes writing in his book *"Destiny"* which finally prompted me to put pen to paper and begin striking the keys on my keyboard. He writes *"The day comes when every person must leave the security of the nest and pursue their destiny.* Perhaps my destiny was to write this book.

My destiny did not emanate from a classroom at the various prestigious colleges and universities attended but from trials experienced growing up, learning from two parents, 10 siblings raised in a three bedroom house and the tribulations of observing my parents sacrifice their entire beings for their children's future. Bishop Jakes continues in his book ...*"education is no replacement for having been in trenches."* It is often said that a picture is worth a thousand words which may be true. However I say that being there or having been there is worth a thousand pictures and I have been there.

It is said that one of the primary methods in learning to write professionally is to read works of others and reading has always been a passion. I prided myself in having read a myriad of works such as Shakespeare and Kipping as well as more contemporaries such as W.E.B. Griffin, Robert Ludlum, Ken Follett, James Patterson, David Baldacci and more recently Tom Brokaw. Bill O'Reilly's published works have also been a favorite.

Personal friends who have also published and I thoroughly enjoyed their ability to keep me engaged include Colonel, US Marine Corps (Retired) Keith Bushey, Moti Shapira, and the late Woodrow (Woody) Hood, Chief Warrant Officer, US Army (Retired) writing under the pseudonym of Sean Ryan Stuart.

I have read many of Ernest Hemingway's "Classics" such as The Sun Also Rises (a favorite) and others.. I also read and study my Bible daily. Reading is indeed learning as evidenced by my academic preparation. Having read has always allowed me stake my place during intellectual encounters.

Condoleezza Rice is also a superb storyteller who is able to masterfully place international governance in perspective. Alex Haley wrote to chronicle black history in America and James Baldwin's words offered words which caused blacks in America to examine where they have been and where they are going.

Henry Louis Gates, Jr. the Alphonse Fletcher University Professor and Director of the Hutchins Center for African and American Research at Harvard University, who is also an award winning author and film maker, excited me with his book, *In Search of Our Roots*, which persuaded me to include the research of my genealogical history in concert with chronicling my story.

To quote Harold Cole, a personal friend and the first President of the 9th and 10th (Horse) Cavalry Association, the Buffalo Soldiers, in his autobiography: We Can – We Will, Ready and Forward; *"I decided to write this book for several reasons. Primarily because I am the last sibling living in my family, and I have the need to leave a legacy, and secondly, no one else can tell my story but me. There is a story in all of us and we owe it to the next generation the opportunity to learn from those who came before."*

While I certainly am not the last living sibling in my family however in recent years two of my siblings passed away, one older and one younger.

When I took on the personal challenge (joy) of this writing it in many ways parallels the words of Harold Cole as it was obvious that I did not want to pen a novel but wanted to tell my story, something that would provide a clue to my son Mark of the life lived by his father and the myriad of opportunities he had received. I had hoped to demonstrate to him that I worked at serving as a living example for him where he could always show pride that I was his father.

Although not intended as a biography of my late wife and Mark's mother, Dorothy Marks Gravett, I clearly understood that it would be of keen interest to him by providing ancestral information from his mother's side, the Marks' family, so I have superficially delved into genealogical records to glean information available. Dorothy hailed from Sandy Hook, Mississippi so the search began there and continued with Mark's birth in California.

Another reason for writing was that a part of me wanted to share events in my life that my siblings and others did not know as I had not shared many of my experiences with them. The reader will decide which path I took. So this was the Genesis of the book.

The reader may early on tend to believe that this work may just be a chronological recap of honors and awards I have been given over a lifetime. Nothing could be further from the truth. While honors and awards are certainly mentioned they provide an introduction of what is to come in my march through life. They will allow the reader to look for benchmarks just how they serve as building blocks for my lifetime of work. The ego was left at the door and the personal judgment will come in the final chapters.

CHAPTER 2 DISCLAIMER

This is not a history of the Gravett family nor is it intended to be. It is not intended to chronicle the life and times of my siblings or my immediate family though many vignettes are mentioned throughout. My siblings each have their own story to tell. In time, perhaps, the entire story of the Gravett family may be penned by another member.

This treatise is intended to share some of my life's experiences; some mundane but perhaps even more of them interesting and exciting. It is for this reason that I say this can be coined as my autobiography and memoirs.

Individuals view life events through various lenses, some even rose colored, and these accounts are primarily through the prisms of mine but also a few others as do the follow-on sources and bibliographies indicate by the acknowledgment of the varied contributors.

A reader with personal knowledge may question or challenge some of the passages in the book such as dates, times, locations, particular actions or even actual authenticity. That is understandable, however, these accounts are as I or others remember them. Information was derived from a variety of sources such as family, friends, institutions, publications, archives and published books and manuscripts, many published by this author.

Measured empirical research was also conducted. Some may offer up differing accounts, some recorded and others transcribed. I apologize in advance for any errors or omissions and I take full responsibility for them. Additionally, I have offered no footnotes but where appropriate I have identified and credited sources.

A CURSORY LOOK BACK

Since I have essentially had four careers; law enforcement, military, business and government, at least two at any given time, it was difficult to separate them in the book and

I have not. They are intertwined and I switch back and forth from one to the other but with the same general timelines. The reader may have difficulty following this milieu but that was the life I lived.

I have been blessed by having been raised by great parents and having wonderful siblings. My life has been filled with service to God, a warm and loving family, genuine friends, public and private educational opportunities, public service, a law enforcement career, a military career, community service, volunteer work, business opportunities, awards and recognitions.

I have experienced government, business and personal domestic and foreign travel while cultivating international friendships, receiving a personal invitation to attend the US President's Inauguration, personal meetings with members of a President's Cabinet, serving as a Member of a Governor's Cabinet and personally meeting Heads of State and being personally gifted by a Country's Secretary of Defense all which will be discussed later.

In this book I have not painted my life as a "rosy" journey because it has not been. Everyone experience some disappointments in their lifetime and I have experienced many, probably more than most. And although I mention a few, it was not my intent to paint a "woe is me" picture because, again, like some people, I have had more successes than disappointments. My intent was to share my successes as I traveled through life and not drag down the reader by describing my failures.

Through the pages in the book I undergo sort of a metamorphosis as one would imagine as I describe parts of my life's activities over seven decades. I learned from family, friends, neighbors and co-workers as well as my formal teachers at all levels of my educational experiences. For example, I morphed from a childhood stutterer in elementary and junior high school to delivering a flawless speech to over 10,000 people gathered in a convention and thousands of military personal arrayed in precision formation of a parade field.

Before handing this manuscript off to the professional editor for review I combed through the pages to ensure accuracy, authenticity and integrity as best I could.

"I can do all things through Christ who strengthens me"
                                        -Philippians 4:13

CHAPTER 3 THE JOURNEY BEGINS

HONORS

I have been inducted into eight Halls of Fame; San Pedro High School Athletic Hall of Fame (along with my brothers and sisters; cumulative we participated there in football, basketball, track and field, baseball, swimming and volleyball). I am recorded in the Long Beach City College Hall of Fame where I received my Associate of Arts Degree, the State of California League of Community Colleges Hall of Fame, the California State University at Long Beach Hall of Fame; I received my Bachelors' Degree there, and a Branch of the US Army; Armor Hall of Fame.

San Pedro High School Athletic Hall of Fame Induction with siblings.

I am the recipient of the Eme' Award, the University of Southern California's (USC) prestigious recognition for being inducted into the African American Graduate Hall of Fame as well as the Boys and Girls Club Hall of Fame where my brothers and I received our penchant for athletics.

The Los Angeles Police Department presented me with its' highest award, the Medal of Valor. Among my more than 20 military awards is the coveted Distinguished Service Medal, the nation's fourth highest award and I am also the recipient of the prestigious Legion of Merit decoration. I have been honored by the governments of

Ukraine, South Korea and Germany as well as the United States.

My name appears on two cornerstones of State of California Veteran Homes which were dedicated while I served in the Governor's Cabinet as Secretary of the California Department of Veteran Affairs. These homes are in Fresno and Redding. I have had the privilege of having a street named in my honor called *Gravett Place* in the City of Santa Clarita, California.

This forth coming surprise honor had not previously been divulged to me by my wife Blanche nor brothers' Phillip, Leon and William who attended the ground breaking and street dedication ceremony. This was for a veterans' village consisting of 83 single family homes on a project in which I was instrumental in developing and constructing.

It was my honor to have been selected to deliver four Commencement addresses; Compton Community College in 1997, Cypress College in 2001, the USC Graduate Center of Public Policy in Sacramento in 2013 and the California State University Long Beach School of Health and Human Services in 2016.

In 1998, a plaque with my name was affixed to a wall in the *Hall of Hero's* at the Pentagon as it was for all US Army African American Generals who had been promoted to that rank in the fifty years following President Truman's signing Executive Order 9981 in 1948. That Order integrated the federal military. The 212 plaques are numerically numbered according to date of promotion, mine being number 200 having received my first General Officer promotion on December 7, 1996.

To the reader please know that I am not a hero as I stand on the shoulders of luminaries such as Henry O. Flipper, the first African American Cadet at West Point, Brigadier General Benjamin Davis Sr., the first African American General, Lieutenant General (later 4 star General) Benjamin Davis, Jr. the second African American General and Major General Harry Brooks, the first African American General to command an Army Division.

It also has truly been an honor to have been selected as the Grand Marshal of several holiday, community, patriotic and Christmas parades in Northern California and Southern California. These include the Martin Luther King "Kingdom Day" Parade in South Central Los Angeles, Korean-American International Day Parade in Korea Town, Los Angeles; Independence Day Parades in Down Town Los Angeles, East Los Angeles, Santa Ana, Huntington Beach, and La Palma; Veterans Day Parades in San Diego, Long Beach and Pacific Palisades; Black History Month Parade in Anaheim and the Christmas Parade in my then hometown of Rolling Hills Estates.

In 2002, I was presented with a replica star of those on Hollywood's Walk of Fame. The brass plated wooden star plaque, identical to those presented to movie and T. V. personalities, was presented by the Honorary Mayor of Hollywood, Johnny Grant, at my military retirement dinner. Johnny had been a personal friend for many years and was the first invitee to my wedding to Blanche.

A few years earlier, Johnny had arranged for me to attend the Academy Awards presentations which was a one in a lifetime opportunity. Since I was attired in my General Officer's Formal Mess Dress Uniform I stood out in the crowd many probably believing I was a doorman or valet. I also received an invitation to attend the Governor's Ball following the event.

For scores of years, Johnny had made numerous overseas trips to entertain our troops in wartime and in peace. In keeping with this tradition I had arranged a helicopter flight for him and the cast of the Saturday Night Live television show on the first leg of their trip with him to Afghanistan to entertain and visit the troops. Our other Hollywood connection was that he had arranged for me to technically consult on scripts involving military and veteran sections of made for TV movies and discussed some for the big screen. I was humbled to have been selected as a speaker at Johnny' memorial service at Hollywood's iconic Pantages Theater.

I have been honored by various veteran organizations at their State Conventions. Others have been so kind to have presented me with over 200 resolutions, plaques, certificates and various mementoes. These include the US Senate and US House of Representatives, Resolutions from the California's State Senate and Assembly, numerous counties and cities such as Los Angeles, Sacramento, Torrance, Bakersfield, Rolling Hills Estates, Long Beach, Riverside, Ventura, Santa Ana, Palm Springs, San Diego, Harbor City, Santa Ana and Huntington Beach.

Colorful certificates and shiny plaques do not define me. The real me is humble and wise enough to know that ...*only what you do for Christ will last (1 Corinthians 15:58)*.

VISITS WITH HEADS OF STATE

In 2001, I was honored to receive a gift from the Secretary of Defense of South Korea personally presented by him in his office at that Nations Capitol in Seoul during one of my tours of duty there. The gift was a hand painted ceramic vase which he designed, crafted and painted.

I have been in the presence of the Chancellor of Germany, had lunch with the President of Mexico and introduced to US Presidents Reagan and Ford and had a personal conversation with Vice President Al Gore.

My wife Blanche and I were honored to have received an engraved invitation to attend the swearing-in ceremony of President Barak Obama for his first term in 2009. Although there were an estimated two and a half million people watching in person spread along the Mall in Washington DC, we were in a reserved and personal high security area near the Capitol steps with a close up view of the ceremony. Other personal invitees in our section included Oprah Winfrey and Reverend Jesse Jackson.

During the several days visit to Washington for the ceremony we were quartered in a 150 year old house at Fort Myers adjacent to Arlington National Cemetery reserved for senior military officers. This was convenient to return following the ceremony and dress for the Presidential Ball.

PRINCE WILLIAM AND PRINCESS KATHERINE (KATE)

In 2013, my wife Blanche and I, while serving as Secretary of the California Department of Veteran Affairs, organized and co-sponsored a jobs fair for veterans and their spouses which was attended by over 2,000 veterans and family members. More than 200 of the Fortune 500 Companies participated and several of their CEO's and their spouses were present.

At the event we, along with just nine CEO couples, joined in a private reception hosted for the Duke and Duchess of Cambridge, Prince William and Princess Katherine of England. William was second in line of succession to his father, Prince Charles, to inherit the Throne in The British Commonwealth of Nations. The reception was held at the Sony Motion Pictures Studios in Culver City, California. This culminated a series of forums whereby veterans were matched with prospective employers. William and Kate attended to gage whether a similar event could be held for veterans of the United Kingdom.

During the reception Blanche and the Princess had a one on one conversation initiated by the Princess where she remarked to Blanche that the two of them had something in common, both being married to military men. They also briefly chatted on other subjects. Prince William remarked to me that he was thoroughly impressed that America was doing so much to employ returning veterans and he would take the formula back to England.

PRINCESS HAYA HUSSEIN OF THE KINGDOM OF JORDAN

It was my honor to have had lunch with Princess Haya Hussein of Jordan. This occurred in San Diego in 1993 while attending the International Forum of Women in the

Military sponsored by the US Department of Defense. The event brought together women military personnel from numerous countries throughout the free world for a discussion of the roles of women serving in the armed forces of their respective countries.

The event was held in San Diego and I was then serving as Chief of Staff of the 40th Infantry Division and had been invited to lead several round table discussions. I was accompanied by several female soldiers from the 40th Division. Princess Haya attended representing her country as she was then a 21 year old Colonel in the Jordanian Army having been appointed and commissioned by her father King Hussein.

As one of the senior officers present I was seated at her table during one of the business luncheons, along with other members from various countries, both male and female. She and I were able to have an exchange of information and ideas regarding the roles of women in the military of Jordan and the US. I also espoused how the US methods differed from those of Jordanian women to receive military commissions.

It was coincidental that in 1999 when I accompanied my then wife Dorothy to the Mayo Clinic in Rochester, Minnesota to await a heart transplant Princess Haya's father, King Hussein, was there at the same time and he and Dorothy passed away the same week as will be discussed.

COMMISSIONING OF THE USS CALIFORNIA

Probably one of the seminal events during my tenure as Secretary of the California Department of Veteran Affairs was being given the honor to commission a US Navy Ship. The "USS California", a nuclear powered submarine, was to be launched at Newport News, Virginia by Governor Brown. He had been given this honor due to the ship's name but when his schedule did not allow him to leave the state to attend the ceremony due to critical pending legislative deadlines the honor was delegated to me as his

Secretary of Veteran Affairs. The fact that a soldier commissioned a navy ship must have been unique.

Cal Vet Secretary Gravett at Commissioning of USS California.

The launching in 2013 culminated a series of ceremonial events over several days which included receptions, dinners and touring parts of the ship by the public and California's Congressional Delegation. USS California has been the name of several Navy ships dating back to a dual mast US Navy sailing vessel in the late 1880's to a battleship in World War One. The ship's motto is "Silence is Golden" no doubt a play on lyrics of a popular recording with that name which was high on the charts in 2009. The submarine service has always been referred to as the "Silent Service." Of course the other part of the picture is that California's motto is "The Golden State."

USS IOWA

Blanche and I were invited to sail aboard the USS Iowa Battleship during the final leg of her cruise from Northern California into the Port of Los Angeles where she would

Crew of USS California.

be decommissioned and reflagged as Battleship Iowa and dedicated as a floating museum.

Standing aboard her deck as we sailed into the harbor was an experience to behold. All of the dignitaries aboard marveled at her enormity, especially its sixteen inch guns. During World War Two it had the capability to hurl a round of ammunition almost 25 miles with each round weighing almost as much as a Volkswagen Bug.

ADMIRAL SAMUEL L. GRAVELY LEADERSHIP AND SERVICE AWARD

In 2018, I was the recipient of the Annual Admiral Samuel L. Gravely Leadership and Service Award presented by the Battle Ship Iowa Awards Committee. Vice Admiral Gravely had achieved numerous firsts in naval education and appointments including once serving aboard the battle ship USS Iowa.

He was the first African-American to receive a commission upon graduating from Midshipmen School. This eventually led to him being the first black officer to command a US warship, the first black naval officer to attend the Naval War College and the first black naval officer to achieve the rank of Rear Admiral. He was the first black naval officer to achieve the three star rank of Vice Admiral and the first black Admiral to be appointed a Fleet Commander of 100 warships.

USS RENTZ

We had another honorable experience sailing aboard a US Naval vessel and that was the USS Rentz, a Guided Missile Cruiser. Several Los Angeles area guests received special invitations for the privilege of sailing from San Diego to Los Angeles's Port of San Pedro. This was a community relations event for the Navy to enlighten leaders of the community on the roles and duties of sailors aboard ship with the overall objective of them supporting the Navy's public relations program. The cruise was co-sponsored by the Employer Support for the Guard and Reserves. The key leaders invited aboard were from education, government, business, industry, commerce, non-profit and the public sector.

About 80 of us gathered at a pier in San Pedro at 4 AM where we parked our automobiles and boarded busses destined for San Diego. En route attendants served a continental breakfast. Just over three hours later we arrived at the Navy pier where the ship was docked and the Captain and crew welcomed us aboard. Once we were all assembled on deck the Captain extended a personal welcome on behalf of her crew and briefed us on the specifications, mission and capabilities of the ship. We were given a safety briefing and a talk on what to expect during the cruise, including crew drills.

We embarked from San Diego while observing all of the actions required to get the ship under way. From that point on we were on our own to tour all parts of the ship except the battle command center, which was top secret. We had been encouraged to have personal conversations with crew members, which were both male and female, to determine where they were from, why they had joined the Navy, their duty description and how long they had been in the service. It was astonishing to learn that the average age of the crew, except for the officers and the Chief Petty Officers, was 19 years old. Just to know that his billion dollar vessel was in the hands of America's finest teenagers was phenomenal.

We were very fortunate to have a calm and clear day during the voyage. I was personally impressed with the expertise and vigor of the young sailors. Mid-way during the all day voyage we were served lunch in the galley to experience a Navy meal. The galley was several steps above the typical Army mess hall food and just below that of a five star fine dining civilian restaurant. Daily the crew have a variety of dishes on the menu from which to choose each meal, all of them nutritious and healthy. Upon debarking in San Pedro we were thanked for our support of the "Greatest Navy in the World" and encouraged to share our experiences.

At this point I would like to acknowledge and make it abundantly clear that none of the aforementioned honors would have never been received without the assistance and support of family and especially the soldiers over a full career. To them I am forever grateful. An excellent leader is often judged by the competence of those led and most achievements would be difficult at best without the support of family.

CHAPTER 4 CAMP ROBERTS

During my 40 plus years serving in the United States Army, both Regular Army and the Army National Guard, I had the experience of serving at numerous military installations, both in the United States and overseas. This including several countries in Western Europe, Central Europe, Central America, The Caribbean, The Pacific and Asia. Here in the good old US of A, training scenarios, conferences, tactical exercises and military schools presented the opportunity for me to perform duty in over 30 states, the District of Columbia, United States Virgin Islands and the Commonwealth of Puerto Rico, at one time or another.

Much of my service, however, was at the numerous training facilities in California. These included not only Army posts but also Navy, Marine Corps and Air Force Bases.

The California Army National Guard operates two primary maneuver training facilities in the state, Camp San Luis Obispo on the Central Coast just north of the city bearing that name and Camp Roberts, about 50 miles north from there. The National Guard also operate air facilities, including the Joint Forces Training Base at the Los Alamitos Army Air Field. California Army and Air National Guard also have fixed and rotary winged aircraft stationed at March Air Reserve Base, Mather Air Reserve Base, Point Mugu Naval Air Station and the Fresno Regional Airport.

It is at Camp Roberts, however, where the first part of my story unfolds and sets the stage. Camp Roberts, is located in the agriculturally rich delta over the mountain and east of the Central Coast and is bifurcated into two geographical maneuver training  sections, the main post on the western portion of the installation and a training area on the eastern portion. The two are bisected by US Highway 101.

The Eastern part of the post is referred to as **East Garrison.** The Main Post, or West Garrison, has more spacious maneuver training areas as one would expect, and contains a plethora of barracks, maintenance and support facilities, a military museum and also administrative facilities. In recent years it has undergone extensive modernization.

The most historic building on the post, however, is the **Ranch House** located approximately seven miles into the post's interior from the main gate and about ten miles from East Garrison. The house itself has a very rich history.

The original ranch house was built in 1870 by the then land grant owner on the east side of the Nacimiento River on a flat piece of land some 100 feet above the River. Also constructed were stables, barn, granary, corrals, store rooms and rodeo grounds.

Due to time, deterioration, weather and lack of upkeep the ranch house had to be refurbished in 1928 replacing some of the red brick roof tiles and upgrading the electrical and plumbing systems. The house consists of a U-shaped entry facing south from the front with several bedrooms, all open towards a center courtyard, a full kitchen, living room, dining room, two bath rooms, fire places, a covered rear porch, and an office.

The rear of the house facing north features a patio over-looking the Nacimiento River, since renamed the

The Ranch House in an earlier time

Salinas River, with a covered outdoor eating area. The structure has a Spanish motif and architectural design.

Since World War Two the Ranch House has been exclusively used by senior officers, primarily Generals of every star rank, for temporary housing when their commands were undergoing training or maneuvers there. The House was also used to quarter visiting dignitaries, to include high federal government officials, to host receptions and to host other ceremonial events.

SPANISH LAND GRANT

The approximately 44,000 acres which comprise Camp Roberts today have long held the encampments of soldiers. The early Indian tribes of California hunted and lived on this land and exploration detachments of the Colonial Spanish Army mounted escorting parties throughout the area. It is located on what follows the old Mission Trail which is still referred to as "El Camino Real", which broadly translates from Spanish as "The Kings Highway" or the "Royal Road." Today it is US Highway 101.

Located nearby is the historic Mission San Miguel, which is one of the 21 Missions established in Alta California by the Franciscans and originally produced grain and livestock. The land which encompasses what is now Camp Roberts was, in fact, part of the original holdings of the mission that was founded in 1797.

In 1826 when Mexico declared its independence from Spain the Mexican government confiscated vast parcels of land and distributed the holdings to favorite "Dons" and other privileged individuals. Mission San Miguel however remained in the hands of the Franciscans. One of these

34

land grants became "El Rancho Nacimiento", or "Ranch of the Nativity" the area which now comprises the Camp. In 1850 when California was admitted to the Union the "Territory of California" came under American jurisdiction.

CAMP NACIMIENTO

In 1902 Congress authorized a study to locate and describe lands suitable for the development of new military posts. Among the many sites examined was one referred to as the "Nacimiento Rancho." The study indicated that the ranch *was "healthy as any in the State of California and suitable for one Regiment of Cavalry"* and the US Army Corps of Engineers was ordered to make a detailed survey and report their findings.

The Army met its training needs through World War One without the use and benefit of Camp Roberts but just prior to World War Two the Army acquired six adjoining ranches for training. Construction of the Main Garrison Cantonment areas began in 1940 with a few buildings. From these humble beginnings the operation grew to ultimately involving 8,000 workers in the construction of a training station capable of housing 30,000 trainees at the same time.

It was while the site was still under construction that the original name of Camp Nacimiento Replacement Training Center was changed to Camp Roberts. This was in honor of a 19 year old San Francisco, California soldier killed in World War One, Corporal Harold W. Roberts, who was posthumously awarded the Congressional Medal of Honor. Corporal Roberts was a member of Company A, 344th Tank Battalion fighting in the Montrebeau Woods, France. During a battle he sacrificed his life on October 4, 1918 to save the life of a fellow tank crewman. Camp Roberts is the only US Military Base named for an enlisted soldier.

WORLD WAR TWO

Camp Roberts officially began its mission as a replacement training center in March 1941. At that time it ranked with the world's largest military training facilities and featured the largest parade ground (the length of fourteen football fields) on any military facility. Having personally marched from end to end and ran the circumference many times during physical training I can attest to its' vastness.

According to documents in the Camp Archives over 436,000 World War Two infantry and field artillery troops passed through an intensive seventeen week training cycle and a peak population was achieved in 1945 when 45,000 troops were quartered there.

During this time in the Army's history units were segregated according to race including at Camp Roberts with White soldiers being housed on the Main or West Post and "Colored" soldiers being house at East Garrison.

ENEMY PRISONER OF WAR COMPOUND

Also contained at East Garrison were compounds for Italian and German prisoners of war housed in barracks constructed for them by Colored soldiers while they themselves were house in tents. Just as in other military communities around the country, enemy prisoners of war were extended privileges not given to American Colored troops.

For example, German and Italian prisoners of war at Camp Roberts, in some instances, did not require guards and had comfortable beds in newly built barracks while Colored troops slept on cots in tents. Some prisoners were issued passes and given permission to visit local people of Italian and German decent who took them in for dinner with wine, and other social events, such as national days, while providing transportation to and from the camp. All of this was chronicled in a 2000 Documentary called "Prisoners in Paradise" which extoled the niceties extended to German and Italian POWs housed on US military bases during the war.

Also chronicled in the documentary was that Italian Prisoners of War had clean sheets, nice blankets and in some POW camps there was a vase of flowers on each table and the YMCA sent boxes of books to them written in English and Italian.

Additionally, if a German Officer POW died in captivity they received a funeral with full military honors, given a rifle salute while some Colored soldiers guarding them did not receive such an honor. German POWs were required to move out of the way for an approaching White American soldier but not so for an approaching Colored American Officer.

During the rare opportunities Colored troops were able to secure off-post passes at Camp Roberts there was little to

Negro Troops to Be Entertained In East Garrison

Camp Roberts' most talented entertainers and musicians will present a gala variety show for Negro troops stationed in East Garrison tonight at 2000 o'clock. It was announced by Lt. A. L. Blodgett, camp entertainment officer.

At the request of Lt. Leland F. Morse, the entertainment branch has spliced an interesting 90-minute show, replete with comedy, jive and novelty acts. Pfc. George R. Batchelier, ex-Hollywood movie production executive, will direct the special revue.

The camp Special Service office has allocated considerable athletic equipment and a piano for the troops' diversion.

do as most local establishments served "Whites" only. The Post's only swimming pool in fact had separate use hours for White and Colored soldiers with just a few hours per week by the latter. On-Post USO Shows were separate with White entertainers entertaining White soldiers and Colored entertainers performing for Colored soldiers.

White and Colored Soldiers had separate Post Exchanges (PX) on some installations but if there was only one PX, it was used only by White Soldiers and Colored Soldiers were barred. However German POWs could use it.

In July 1946, with the out-processing of returning soldiers from World War Two complete, Camp Roberts went from a busy city overnight to one with a small cadre of care taker-soldiers. Its use then was relegated to just the National Guard and Army Reserve conducting two-week summer training cycles.

This all changed in June 1950 at the onset of the Korean War. The next month Camp Roberts was reactivated for troop training however, this time, with some integrated federal units following the signing of President Harry Truman's Executive Order 9981 in 1948. This Order directed that all active military services be integrated but the Order did not pertain to the National Guard.

Armor (tank) training was added to the previous Infantry and Field Artillery training. By the end of 1953, following the cessation of hostilities between North and South Korea, over 300,000 men had completed training there, most in integrated units. The next year, 1954, once again the Post was reverted to care-taker status and training continued during weekends by the Army Reserve and the Army National Guard.

In 1970, the Camp was officially closed by the Army as an active post and in 1971 the California National Guard received control of the site and established a Reserve Component Training Center there.

In decades following the Korean War the post once again became active to intensify the training of National Guard and Army Reserve units mobilized for deployments to Bosnia, Kosovo, Iraq and later Afghanistan. As of this writing it remains one of the few US Army Training Centers on the West Coast.

RANCH HOUSE RESIDENCY

California was admitted to the Union in 1850, and in that same year the State Militia was created. In 1903, all State Militias were re-designated "National Guard." Since that time California previously had only two Black Officers obtain the rank of General prior to my promotion to the One Star Rank of Brigadier General in December 1996.

One General served his duty with the District of Columbia National Guard in Washington DC, and the other, the State Adjutant General, was headquartered in Sacramento near the Capitol. Research could not determine whether either one of them, prior to my promotion to Major General in July 1999, had been quartered at the Ranch House as its' primary tenant.

Over a period of several years while performing military duty at Camp Roberts, first as an enlisted soldier and later as a commissioned officer, I had multiple occasions to visit the Ranch House. As a junior enlisted soldier performing duties as a driver for several officers I spent considerable time there waiting in the parking lot for a meeting to conclude. Later as a Non-Commissioned Officer (NCO) I had several occasions to be on the property where unit end-of-training receptions were often held.

After receiving my commission as a military officer in 1968, and in several years following, I finally had the opportunity to spend time in the Ranch House with other officers while attending briefings. These were short lived and just an hour or two each.

As a Brigadier General between 1996 and 1999 I routinely visited the Commanding General there while he was in residence but had never personally resided there. In April 2000, as the Ranch Houses' primary tenant, it is believed that I became the first African American Military Officer to reside there as its' primary resident. A Colored soldier had gone from sleeping in a tent on a cot in East Garrison to a Black General occupying the Ranch House as its' primary tenant.

The journey from Colored soldiers living in tents and sleeping on cots at East Garrison to an African American Army General taking up residence at the Ranch House was quite a trek. Although the distance from point A to point B was about 10 miles in distance it took almost 150 years in time. That was my journey and this book will allow the reader to accompany me further on that trek.

CHAPTER 5 THE FAMILY TREE

RESEARCH METHODOLOGY

The Mormon Church's Genealogical Center houses the world's most comprehensive reservoir of information on family ancestries and histories. Much of the forgoing information regarding the Gravett, Campbell and Harris Families, prior to and after the Civil War, was derived from there. Although the primary source of information came from Church Stakes in Long Beach and Rancho Palos Verdes, California however their primary center is in Salt Lake City, Utah.

Considerable addition information was derived from *The Encyclopedia of Arkansas History and Culture* but these pale to information derived from my personal research visits to Little Rock, North Little Rock and Scott, Arkansas. My research included obtaining considerable information from the Scott Historical and Cultural Center which was formally the general location of the plantation where my ancestors toiled, perhaps some in slavery. Much about Scott, Arkansas will be forthcoming.

It has been widely published and historical facts show that slaves were considered as personal property by the slave master prior to the 1860-1865 American Civil War and for that reason slaves generally did not have last names. Following their emancipation in 1865 some, generally, acquired last names from a variety of places which included taking the name of the plantation where they had been enslaved. This could account for our family name.

Another origin of former slave's last names were that they adopted the surnames of the current President or former Presidents before the emancipation. This would account for a vast number of African American families bearing the surnames of Lincoln, Washington, Adams, Jefferson, Jackson, Taylor, Tyler, Buchanan and others.

According to Henry Louis Gates writing in *In Search of Our Roots,* following the Emancipation Proclamation many former free African Americans assumed the last name of Freeman, a derivative of the word "freedmen" which was applied to the blacks who had always been free. Adopting the name "Freeman" was a significant act, a symbolic breaking of all former ties with slavery and a means of differentiating one from the many former slaves who took the names of their former masters"

Some former slaves even assumed the last names of their slave brokers, men who bought, sold and traded slaves. Research shows that some former slaves even made up last names.

The name Gravett is an English surname but of Norman French origin. It is thought to be a medieval diminutive of the occupational name Graff, a derivative of the pre 7th century word "Grafe" and meaning a quill, and hence a clerk or scribe. To this has been added the suffix "et" to give son of Graff or perhaps a Little Graff.

It is through the empirical research of historical records housed at the Genealogical Center of the Mormon Church, it was learned that the Anne Gravett and Henry Gravett arrived in Virginia from England in 1702 and were among the first European's arriving in America with the name Gravett and obviously they were Anglo Saxon. Over 300 years later the name Gravett is still not commonly found in the United States. According to the 2010 US census count there were less than 900 Gravett households nationwide with just over five percent (45+/-) being black or African American. In 2018 there were less than 20 Gravett households in my immediate and extended family.

Unlike other ethnicities and for varying reasons blacks and African American cannot easily trace their ancestry in this country partly due to slavery. As mentioned, slaves were considered property on many plantations and were bought and sold as such. This separated kin folks with no regard to biological relationships. Three hundred years later blacks are still attempting to identify relatives. More recently, in the past fifty years or so, due to the advent of better technical search methods, to include biological matching, individuals are at least able to identify ancestors and connect with relatives heretofore unknown to them. This piecemeal approach which follows provides the best available information of my ancestry.

CHAPTER 6 HERITAGE PATERNAL GREAT-GREAT GRAND PARENTS

My paternal great-great grandparents and Great Gandparents were Phillip and Rosa Mae Gravett and were born into slavery in Alabama or Mississippi, he in 1825 and she in 1830. They had one child, Isam Gravett, born in August 1854 in Alabama. In 1884 Isam married Mary Elizabeth, unknown last name, who was born in January 1867 in Alabama or Arkansas. Isam was my paternal great grandfather.

Since the birth of Isam Gravett in 1854 was prior to the Emancipation Proclamation in 1865 it is problematic that Phillip and Rosa Mae were possibly not legally married as, in most instances, slaves were forbidden to marry as they were considered as property and marriages most likely not recorded. Isam died on August 13, 1920 in Arkansas and Mary Elizabeth died in Arkansas, on an unknown date.

Paternal Grand Parents

Isom and Mary Elizabeth had seven children including, James 'Jimmie' (Driver) Gravett, my paternal grandfather, who was born on July 30, 1892 in Arkansas, as were their other children. They were Oparis born in 1881, Ada born in 1890, Mamie also born in 1890, Calip born in 1895, Clarence born in 1896, and William born in 1899.

James Gravett married Beulah A. Gilbert, my paternal grandmother, in 1915. She was born in December 1899, in South Carolina. They had one child, a son, Clarence Gravett, my father, born on November 26, 1915* in Scott, Pulaski County, Arkansas.

James Gravett was drafted into the Army during World War One in 1917 and served in the Expeditionary Force in Europe in the 369th Infantry Regiment (Colored) known as the "Harlem Hell Fighters" (also called the Hell

Fighters from Harlem).” This Regiment included Colored soldiers from throughout the country. He was discharged in 1918 and died February 16, 1921 in Arkansas. It was not determined whether or not his demise was the result of war wounds.

NOTE: Various documents list Clarence Gravett's birth year as 1914 (1920 census), 1915 (1930 census) and 1916 (military induction card written by his own hand) and 1917 (as listed on my birth certificate). The family generally celebrated his birth year as 1915.

Beulah's parents, my paternal great-grandparents, were Frank Gilbert, Sr. born in 1844 and Eliza Gilbert, born in 1867. They married in 1885 in Arkansas. Beulah's siblings were Frank Gilbert, Jr. born in 1889 and passed away in 1974. His wife was Mamie with no additional documentation.

Her other siblings were Boyd Gilbert born in 1880, Rufus Gilbert in 1881, Frederick Gilbert in 1892, Anthony Gilbert in 1899 and Ulysses (Ulie) Gilbert born on an unknown date. The dates of death for Beulah's other siblings was not available. All of the siblings were born in South Carolina except the two youngest, Anthony and Ulysses, who were born in Arkansas. All of these would have been my father's aunts and uncles and therefor my great aunts and uncles.

Paternal Grandparents Peter and Beulah Booth. Beulah is holding brother Darnell, age 6 months

In 1925, Beulah was remarried to Peter Booth, Jr. He was born on July 14, 1892 in Jefferson, Arkansas to parents Peter Booth, Sr. and mother Millie Smith. They had no children and after World War Two, probably around 1946, relocated to Wilmington, California where they resided at 1215 Banning Boulevard. This was in an apartment over the garage in the rear of the main house. The house may have been the parsonage for Wilmington's First Presbyterian Church as they were employed there as care takers. The church was just three blocks away, walking distance to their residence, located on the corner of L Street and Marine Avenue in Wilmington.

As a very young child I recall my brother Charles and I spending several days at their home while on vacation from school probably during summer months as many kids our ages at that time often visited grandparents. We accompanied them to their jobs at the church where we spent the day playing with the toys in the church's nursery while they performed their custodial duties.

In 1949, they returned to Arkansas where they passed away, she in 1955 and he preceded her in death on an unknown date.

My Parents Clarence and Alice

Clarence Gravett, my father, named for his uncle Clarence Gravett, married Alice Mae Harris, my mother, on February 1, 1934 in Pulaski County, Arkansas. She was born July 1, 1918. They had 12 children which will be discussed later. I was the seventh child, born June 2, 1941 in Scott, Pulaski County, Arkansas. My father passed away April 19, 1989 in San Pedro, California and my mother passed away October 28, 2008 in Compton, California.

Going back, I was also unable to determine where or how my great-great grandfather Phillip Gravett acquired his first or last name; perhaps associated with Gravette, Arkansas. Gravette, Arkansas, is a small city in the northwestern most portion of the state in Benton, County near the University of Arkansas at Fayetteville. Gravette is approximately 200 miles from Little Rock and its suburb Scott, Arkansas.

Upon personally visiting and touring the city I learned that although the town's name is spelled ending with the letter "e", as does the local bank, Bank of Gravette, and the local high school, Gravette High School, the hardware store and various other businesses bear the spelling same as my family. Also several of the towns' residents with the name Gravett, both black and White, spell the name without the suffix "e." Historical records also list ancestors with their name spelled as Gravitt, a third rendition of the family name.

Perhaps it was divine intervention that my grandparents and great grandparents grew up in Arkansas rather than Mississippi and specifically Tallahatchi County, Mississippi. According to Dr. Lewis Gates, writing in his book *In search of Our Roots*, *"In 1936 there were only enough funding for black children to attend school for four months out of the year, thus ensuring a workforce that was undereducated and underpaid."* This continued well into the 1960's in some areas.

MARRIAGES AND LAST NAMES PRE-CIVIL WAR

Since my preliminary genealogy research of my ancestors prior to the Civil War revealed that most, if not all, had last names, I found this peculiar in that, although there were numerous free blacks residing in the south on plantations, the majority were enslaved thus having no last names and were prohibited from legally marrying. As such they were considered personal property and usually having only a first name, after-all one piece of property could not marry another piece of property. As Oprah Winfrey framed it, *"slaves were listed on census reports prior to 1860 as property along with the chickens and cows."*

There were situations, however, whereby some marriages were consummated, though not legally. Often a black slave could claim to be a mulatto thus making it legal to marry with both being the property of the same owner and in some rare instances a White slave owner could marry one of his slaves if he portended himself to be other than White. Also prior to the Civil War some slave owners gave his last name to his slaves during census taking to ensure that his property would remain secure. Whichever of these occurred with my ancestors, will require additional empirical research and reported in another volume. However, Henry Louis Gates writing in his book *In Search of Our Roots* reports that over half of the free Negro population during slavery lived in the south.

MATERNAL GREAT-GREAT GRAND PARENTS

My paternal great-great-great grandfather was Henry Harris born about 1820 in Virginia and my great great-

great grandmother was Libbie Adalin Harris born about 1815 in Alabama. Their son, Harrison, my great-great uncle was born in 1851 and his wife Hanna was born in 1855.

My maternal great-great grandparents were Rasberry Campbell and Betsy Campbell. He was born in 1815 in Tennessee and died in Mississippi in 1894. Betsy Campbell was born in 1825 in Alabama which no information on the date or location of her death. Their son was William Campbell.

MATERNAL GREAT-GRAND PARENTS

William Campbell, my maternal great grandfather, was born in 1854 in Mississippi and passed away in 1929 in Mississippi. He married Jane Dunn, born March 1855. They were married in 1872 in Arkansas. Her parents were Mr. & Mrs. Dunn (unknown given names) and were both born in Alabama on unknown dates. William and Jane resided in Little Rock, Arkansas and had 9 children.

Their children were Gertrude, my grandmother, born in 1880; Sarah born in 1883; Annie born in 1884; Frances (Fannie) born in 1886; Robert born in 1890; Crockett (Crock) born in 1892; Lucinda (Lula) born in 1893; Ada born in 1895; and Isaiah (Izeer) born in 1897.

MATERNAL GRAND PARENTS

My maternal grandmother, Gertrude Campbell, born in 1880, married Phillip Thomas Harris, born in 1878, in Little Rock, Arkansas. My mother recollects that her father Phillip was born in Alabama to a Black Choctaw Indian father and a mother who was a member of the Muskogean Band of the Choctaw Nation Indians, both Black Indian Tribes. Additional research is required to substantiate this.

DNA shows my ethnic background as coming from Africa (77%), Europe (21%) and West Asia (2%). A very thorough review of Henry Louis Gates, Jr.' research in his book *In Search of Our Roots* offers a dynamic explanation why my Native American ancestry was not revealed in the cursory review of my DNA but may be revealed in the more intense analysis of admixture, mitochondrial or patrilineal genealogical testing.

My European DNA coincides with research that revealed almost all blacks in America whose ancestors arrived in the country prior to 1900 will show at least 12.5% European DNA. This results from births by black slave women being impregnated by White slave owners.

Following high school, according to my mother, my grandfather attended and graduated from a Colored College in Birmingham, Alabama, with a Bachelor's Degree in Business. Phillip and Gertrude had 12 children; Goldine born in 1903, McHenry (Mack) born 1904, Jane (Janie) born in 1906, Harrison (Harry) born in 1908, Maudie (Modie; Modia, Molly) born in 1909, Willa Mae (Willie Mae) born in 1911, Robert born in 1912, James born in 1914, Adell born in 1915, and twins Rosa Mae and my mother Alice Mae, (born in 1918). Rosa (Rosie) passed away two weeks after birth. Alice Mae, my mother, the younger of the two, passed away in 2008.

The 1930 census revealed that there was a younger child in the family, not previously known to my siblings and me, and his name was Jeeves born in 1926, but no further information is available. Perhaps he passed away at a young age but neither his birth nor death certificate could be located. He would have been younger to my mother by eight years. I have no recollection of my Mother ever mentioning him if she knew of him. Additional research may be required.

Gertrude Harris & children, 1960

Gertude Harris, (seated)
& children, left to right
Maudie Harris Hall
Goldine Battle
Robert Harris
Willie Mae Lewis
Geannecy Harris, (daughter-in-law)
Alice Gravett, (on floor)

Mother's Day 1963

Gertude Harris and her daughters, left to right
Geannecy Harris, (wife of son Adell)
Maudie Harris Hall
Goldine Battle
Gertrude Harris (mother)
Willie Mae Lewis
Alice Gravett

From the left: daughter-in-law Gennesse, daughters Maudie and Goldine, Grandmother Gertrude Harris, aunt Willie Mae and Alice (my mother).

Grandparents Phillip and Gertrude Harris (front).
Back row from left to right: Aunt Goldine, uncle Robert, aunt Willie Mae, uncle Adell and Alice (my mother).

CHAPTER 7

MY MOTHER'S REMEMBRANCES

My mother remembered her mother, my grandmother Gertrude, telling her the circumstances surrounding the premature death of her twin sister Rosa Mae. Her mother told her that the delivery doctor was being assisted by a family friend, a mid-wife by the name of Mary Lewis. The mid-wife was standing by the bed when the doctor began to cut the umbilical cord and she told the doctor that he was about to cut it too short.

Reenacting the event to me, and probably as her own mother had reenacted it to her, my mother extended her left index finger and cupped it with the right index and middle fingers of her right hand in a scissors-like fashion to a point mid finger. The doctor asked who she was and she identified herself as a mid-wife. The doctor then slipped the knife back some to avoid cutting it too short but apparently not far enough as her twin sister bled profusely for two weeks then passed away from loss of blood.

Another remembrance of my mother was her father taking her to visit his mother in Alabama on an Indian Reservation. For a young child it was a scary experience because, as she remembered, her grandmother, an Indian, was very dark and short, probably less than five feet tall, with "red eyes" and her hair was so long that it touched the floor. She remembered that her grandmother used her floor length hair to sweep the dirt floor of her house. With all of this going on she would often hide behind her father holding on to his leg because she was afraid of the "scary lady".

Mother's transcribed remembrances of the visit:
"Birmingham, Alabama is where my dad was from and he went back to his people. And he took me back with him and I (wanted) to leave the whole time (I) was there. I was afraid of my grandmother. I had never in my life thought nothing looked so scary. She was short like this (gesturing) and her

hair touched the ground. She had long hair. All the way to the ground which she used to sweep the dirt floor. Full Indian all the way. Grandpa was the Choctaw Indian and she was a Moskogean Indian. Muskogean is the dark Indian, that is what she was and I was afraid I haven't seen anything like that never. I didn't tell her the whole time we were there for two weeks. I was just scared of that woman. She had red eyes. When I looked and saw her coming I'd hide behind my dad who was padding me down. I have never seen an Indian before like that. Real Indians. I'm talking about all Indian. My dad was an Indian too. He was called a Choctaw Indian because he had high cheek bones and my grandmother was dark and short with long hair. She put it in a bow."

My mother's words of: *"She was full Indian all the way; All Indian. She was dark. My dad was an Indian too"* resonated within me as I researched and read of the various nations of black Indians in America. William Loren Katz captures the story in his book: *Black Indians A Hidden Heritage,* where he writes: *"Today most Black Indians do not live in the forests or on the broad plains of the United States....They have made a long march from farms, woods and ranches to skyscrapers, subways and ghettos. Most have arrived...."*

MY PARENTS CLARENCE AND ALICE

My parents, Clarence and Alice, met at Little Rock's Pleasant Grove Missionary Baptist Church (founded in 1861) when she was 13 and they attended school together at Bale (pronounced Bailey) Chaplin Elementary School, the local school for Colored children. Classes there ended in the eighth grade. She next attended North Little Rock Colored High School.

By all accounts my mother was an excellent student who participated in oral contests and won first place in a speech contest. She recalled traveling to other schools to participate in debates. She also participated in a track meet while wearing a special dress made for that purpose and once won first place in a race. Her favorite teachers were Arleia Ellison and Martha Murphy.

They were married in 1933 at Pleasant Grove Missionary Baptist Arkansas Church by the Reverend Smith and lived the first three months of their marriage with my father's parents in Scott.

According to my mother my paternal grandfather's employer, George Alexander, who owned property with houses, "gave" them their first house (address unknown but probably a tenant house for share croppers on the Alexander Plantation) and they later moved to a larger house on the opposite side of the Arkansas River in North Little Rock.

My personal thoughts were that Mr. Alexander, in a nefarious way, probably provided them the house as their residence as they were share croppers with the intent of deducting the rents from my parents' share of the cotton they were raising. It was typical for several share cropping families to occupy tenant houses on a plantation provided by the plantation owner with rents later to be deducted from proceeds from cotton harvested should there be any.

In Beth Macy's book titled "Truevine", a story about two young Albino Negro brothers and sons of sharecroppers who were kidnapped and placed in the side show of a traveling circus at the end of the 19th Century, she writes "*Share croppers only received one quarter to less than half of the money the farmer received when the crops were eventually sold rather than the standard sharecropping fifty-fifty split. But that was only if the farmer was honest about how much the crops brought. Often they received nothing the farmer claiming his expenses had consumed their share of the money.*" In my view no doubt George Alexander's expenses included charges for a house "given" to the worker.

I never discussed with my mother whether or not George Alexander was honest but she did cite a very important and particular event where he was deceptive which will be chronicled later.

Share cropping in Arkansas and other parts of the south was a disadvantage to the Negros participating but very advantages to the White land owner. Share Croppers, generally, ended each growing season deeper in debt. What with having to pay the land owner rent for "shot gun" houses, rent for the use of tools to cultivate, fees for the use of horses and mules, loans to purchase food with exorbitant interest rates and then having to provide the land owner with the lion's share of the cotton or other crop made it almost impossible to turn a profit. Additionally there were fees for transporting the crop to market, even transporting the land owner's share of the booty.

By all indications my family fared very well share cropping but no doubt due to the business acumen of my grandfather, Phillip Thomas Harris, and no thanks to Mr. Alexander.

CLARENCE AND ALICE START A FAMILY

My parents eventually had twelve children, eight born in Arkansas and four born in California. According to my mother the first four children were born at the family's then home at 1923 Pulaski Street, Ashley Township, Scott, Arkansas however this may differ from information recorded on individual birth certificates.   They are Clarence Curtis, born in 1934, Phillip Thomas, born in 1935, Leon, born in 1936 and William Earl, born in 1937.

She related that the next four children were born at the Colored Baptist Hospital in Little Rock, Arkansas. They are Alice Marie, born in 1939, Charles Edward, born in 1940 and yours truly Peter James, born in 1941. At the time of my birth our home was Route 1, Box 135, Ashley Township, Scott, Arkansas.

To some generations much is given
Of other generations much is expected
This generation . . .
Has a rendezvous with destiny

- President Franklin D. Roosevelt

Harrison was born in 1943 at the Colored Baptist Hospital in Little Rock. The youngest four children were born in California; Darnell, born in 1945 at Seaside Hospital in Long Beach, Gloria Jean, born in 1946 at Seaside Hospital in Long Beach, Melvin Eugene, born in 1947 at Harbor General Hospital in Torrance, California (since renamed Harbor UCLA Medical Center in Carson, California) and Paula Ann, born in 1955 at the San Pedro Community Hospital (since renamed Little Company of Mary Hospital). Paula passed away at birth.

For as far back as I can remember we have always been a close knit family but, as in most families, there were always exceptions. Growing up and in later life we always offered support to one another. If someone required anything others generally were there to assist.

NAMING OF CHILDREN

My mother's oldest sibling, Goldine, was like a second or surrogate mother due to the wide disparity in their ages, Goldine being the eldest and my mother being the youngest. My Aunt Goldine named all of the children in our family except my sister Gloria Jean who was named by my Paternal Grandmother, Gertrude Harris.

My father's mother, Beulah, who had a family name of "Momma Doll," wanted the name to be Beulah after her but my father insisted that was an "old" name and instead she was named Gloria Jean. My sister Alice Marie was initially named Alice Mae after my mother but her middle name was later changed to Marie.

As both told by my mother and empirical research my siblings first names were derived from the following: Clarence for my father Clarence and his uncle Clarence; Phillip from my paternal grandfather and paternal great-grandfather both named Phillip Thomas; Leon *(original name)*, William for my aunt Willa Mae, whom we called Aunt Willie Mae, who was named for her Uncle William; Alice for my mother Alice and Charles, *(original name)*.

Peter Booth, Jr. was named for his father Peter Booth, Sr. and for my mother's brother James also James. Yours truly, Peter James for my step-grandfather Peter Booth and for my paternal grandfather James and my mother's brother also James. Harrison (Harry) was named for my mothers' brother Harrison (Harry) who had been named for his uncle also Harrison (Harry) Harris. He was my paternal grandfather's brother. He had been named for his Uncle Harrison, born in 1851. Darnell, *(original name)*, and Gloria whose name was selected by my maternal grandmother. Melvin, named for my grandfather's brother, Melvin Harris who would be my brother Melvin's and my great uncle.

As young children and teens growing up one of our cousins, Minnie Bea Harris, daughter of Aunt Willie Mae and older than us all, was a surrogate big sister to us. Her twin brother Jimmy Lee passed away while in his youth.

Mother related that as a young toddler in Arkansas I was always "into things" and being where I should not have been. Most of her recollections in Arkansas were of my older siblings. I was two and a half years of age when we departed Arkansas thus have no personal recollection of my life there. The following remembrances are from both of my parents, conversations having taken place sporadically over a lifetime with them.

In Arkansas, my father worked at a number of jobs though he was primarily a sharecropper. As an entrepreneur of sorts, one side job was renting small recreational boats on the Arkansas River near our home. This was generally on the weekends during the spring and summer months. It was a small business enterprise but brought additional income to the family's meager savings. Fulltime he share cropped on the plantation owned by Mr. George Alexander.

The main crop grown was cotton and at times my older brothers would assist him in picking. Mr. Alexander had a brother, Frank, a sister, Virginia and a young daughter also named Virginia. His daughter would often drive the tractor which pulled the wagon with bales of cotton.

Records indicated that Mr. Alexander also grew alfalfa and owned the first registered dairy bull and purebred cattle in the county. He also had "registered" hogs in addition to operating a cypress mill.

My paternal grandfather, Phillip Harris, was the manager, book keeper and foreman on the plantation and oddly, according to my mother, always wore a business suit and tie. He took care of all business matters for Mr. Alexander which included traveling a lot throughout the region representing him at business meetings. I am certain this was a rarity in the south during this era.

Mr. Alexander's grandmother, Otelia, named the plantation "Illallee" after a Native American word meaning "home." It just so happens that my mother's Brother Harry, raised in the same general area, eventually married a woman from the area named "Illallee" but was called Ida Lee by the family. The connection could not be a mere coincidence.

CALIFORNIA "HERE WE COME"

My mother and father, realizing there was no future for their family working in the Jim Crow South all the while had been saving and making plans to leave the state and relocate to California where we had relatives.

My Aunt Goldine was the first relative to have relocated west then followed by Uncles' Harry and Mack. This was in the late 1930's. Mother recollects that once they were settled the three got together and decided to bring out other family members. My grandmother Gertrude and grandfather Phillip Harris followed three months later then aunts Willie Mae and Modie. Eventually by the early 1940's the entire family had relocated to California all seeking better lives.

At the onset of World War Two Uncle Robert was drafted into the Army and Uncle James decided to join the Navy.

Mr. Alexander, on the other hand, believed that he had a bright financial future for his plantation because his sharecropping Gravett family had several young boys who would be available to pick his cotton for many years to come. Obviously my parents' plans differed.

When my parents had saved sufficient funds to purchase one way train fare to California for two adults and eight children they notified Mr. Alexander of the family's intention to move west. This infuriated the plantation owner who used various deceptive tactics and nefarious ruses to persuade our family to remain "down on the farm." Upon learning that was not going to happen he relented and appeared very supportive, though at that time, it was not known that he had ulterior motives.

At the appointed time my mother departed for California by train with the eight children packing enough non-perishable food as she could while my father remained in Arkansas for an additional week or two to close out the family's affairs. The family dog, named "Bosco," also remained behind though cared for.

LEAVING ARKANSAS

On the day of my family's departure Mr. Alexander requested that my parents provide him with an address in Los Angeles so he could write them and maintain contact to ensure they were "OK". He said he knew we were not going to make it out there and believed he would have to send fare for us to return to his plantation. He was given both the address where my Aunt Goldine resided and also given the address of the house she had rented for us near the residence of Aunt Willie Mae. For some unexplained reason we never moved into that house.

Among the eventful remembrances on the train west, named the Rock Island Special, was my mother's recollection that my brother Phillip sang and shined shoes for soldiers for tips. This was in 1943 during World War Two and the passengers were limited to just families with small children and military personnel. Initially the family was seated in the Colored passengers' train car and later when the train had left the southern states and changed engines we were in a car with mixed races. The train ride took five days. Because of age I have no recollections of this.

CALIFORNIA "WE HAVE ARRIVED"

Upon arriving at Union Station, in downtown Los Angeles, my mother and the children were met by my mother's sisters Goldine, Willie Mae (wearing a red dress to be identified) and Modie. The first evening Aunt Goldine took my mother and the four younger children to her home in

Wilmington and the older four children went home with Aunt Willie Mae to her home in Los Angeles.

The decision for my parents to relocate to the San Pedro Community in the City of Los Angeles, at the Harbor, was primarily based upon future employment for my father. With eight children this was no doubt a pressing need. Although my father had begun his job search in Los Angeles he had no success.

At that time, we had several relatives residing in the Los Angeles Harbor area, including my mother's eldest sibling, Goldine Battle as mentioned. My Aunt Goldine and her husband John Battle resided in the community of Wilmington having relocated from Arkansas years earlier with friends, a couple by the name of McBride.

My mother tells the story that her sister Goldine and husband John drove to California following the McBride's car sometime in the late 1930's; the McBride's destination was to Long Beach where they had family and the Battles' destination was about 15 miles further west to San Pedro. About half way from Long Beach their car broke down in Wilmington so they remained there as other relatives were living in the area in the eastern part of Wilmington. They eventually built a home at 1414 East O Street.

During the Great Migration from the south during the 1930's and 1940's, rather than head north to Chicago or Detroit my relatives made the decision to migrated west to Southern California. Perhaps this was Devine intervention as there was an abundance of jobs a few years later during the war and the weather was nicer. During this time in our nation's history both parts of the country were highly segregated.

My uncle John later opened a hand car wash business in downtown Wilmington which he operated for many years. The McBride's became a very prominent and socially active family in Long Beach with a city park named for their patriarch, Ernest McBride, Sr. Not only did he found the local chapter of the NAACP but though his social activism he was instrumental in the city's police and fire

60

departments to be integrated and various segregated housing restrictions to be eliminated.

Two generations later a member of the Gravett family, Curt's son Jacques, would marry a member of the McBride family, Earnest McBride Jr.'s daughter Nicole. Earlier a member of both families, William Gravett and Earnest McBride Jr., were drafted into the Army and serviced together.

In 2017 this author received the Ernest McBride Sr. Award for community service presented by Long Beach's Ernest McBride Chapter of the NAACP the chapter bearing the name of its' founder.

In early December 1943, my parents initially made application to move into the Harbor Hills public housing project near what is now the corner of Western Avenue and Palos Verdes Drive North in the City of Lomita, though at that time, it was an unincorporated area. They were informed that the housing there was for Whites only even though it was a public housing project operated by the County of Los Angeles.

Uncle John and Aunt Goldine learned of a new public housing project just a few miles away in San Pedro. It was recently built by the City of Los Angeles to house shipyard workers and their families during the war and suggested that my parents move there. This was in December 1943.

This new area was called Channel Heights as it sat on the heights overlooking the San Pedro Channel of the Los Angeles Harbor. The complex was about two miles south on Western Avenue from the Harbor Hills project and also the soon to be opened Green Hills Cemetery.

As a note when the Green Hills Cemetery opened, like most cemeteries in the area, it was a segregated memorial park and was for the burial of Whites only. Blacks were not allowed to bury their dead there until many years later and had previously been directed to the area's only black cemetery, Lincoln Park in the unincorporated southern part of the City of Compton, then also a segregated White city.

My parent's application for housing at Channel Heights was accepted and in late December of that year they moved their fledging family of then eight children there. Research showed the Channel Heights Housing Project was an experiment in public housing; some would later refer to it as an experiment in communal living. We moved into a three bedroom duplex which had a full kitchen, living room and a single bathroom. Our address was 1514 Osorno Court, unit #136, San Pedro.

CHAPTER 9 CHANNEL HEIGHTS

The entire Channel Heights complex consisted of about 600 one and two story dwellings constructed on land bounded by Western Avenue on the west, the Banning Homes public housing project down the hill on the east, Summerland Avenue on the south and the US Navy's Fire Fighting School on the north.

After the war this north side property was eventually taken over by Connor's Chicken Ranch in the late 1940's and then even later, in the mid 1950's, by Lochman's Dairy Farm. When the land was vacated by Lochman's Farm in the early 1970's the US Navy constructed a vast military family housing community for Navy personnel stationed at the Long Beach Naval Station. That complex was eventually removed in the 1990's and a private developer planned a middle class complex of private homes in the early 2000's to be called Ponte Vista but was finally identified as High Point.

Channel Heights was constructed with Federal Public Housing Authority funding and designed by Richard Joseph Neutra then a world renowned designer and architect. In researching this book I located and regularly corresponded with his son, Dion Neutra, over a period of months and was later extended an invitation to attend Dion's 90th birthday party.

The event was held at his art institute, photo gallery and museum in the Silver Lake District of Los Angeles. Blanche and I learned from the large gathering of artists and architects there that Dion was also a world renowned architect and prize winning artist in his own right. Researching Channel Heights led me to the University of California at Los Angeles' School of Urban Planning where the senior Mr. Neutra had established archives for his library.

Most of the streets in the housing project, called courts, were named for Central and South American countries and cities. These included Peru, Ecuador, Aruba,

Bolivia, Bronco, Bogota, Castro, Natal, Fuego, Chaco, Pisco and more than a dozen others including Osorno, our court. Each court was a cul-de-sac.

My conversations with Dion revealed that his father had personally named all of the courts as he had traveled extensively in Central and South America as well as the Caribbean and was fond of those places.

Residing in Channel Heights was to have an everlasting very positive impact on me and our family and throughout our lives. My siblings and I would often refer to it as the "good old Channel Heights days" but we were blind to the racism that existed there due to our youth and naiveté which is later discussed.

Channel Heights Housing Project, San Pedro, Calif., 1943

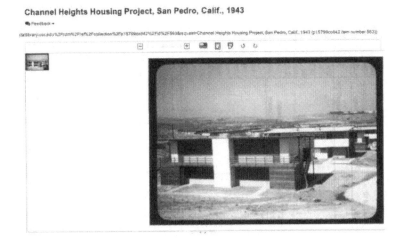

Ice was delivered weekly to our "ice box" for refrigeration. The ice box was a free standing type of appliance which resembled a modern day refrigerator though it was non-electric. The upper compartment was insulated into which an ice block was placed to be used for cooling and preserving food, beverages and some condiments used for cooking.

We had a diamond shaped four cornered yellow and black sign we placed in the kitchen window visible from the street indicating how many pounds of ice needed on a delivery day; 25, 50, 75 or 100 pounds. The ice man came into the kitchen, usually without knocking as they did to all of the houses, and placed the ice directly into the ice box. For a long time after we acquired our refrigerator we still referred to it as the ice box.

I do not recall exactly when we obtained our first refrigerator, perhaps in 1947 after the War, but it was a "Philco" brand. Our first television set was a 16" black and white "Muntz" brand purchased about 1949.

Vendors frequented the neighborhood peddling many days old "fresh" fruits and vegetables especially water melons during the season. The infamous Helms Bakery truck delivered freshly baked bread and pastries and the Good Humor, Pony Cart and Bell Anders ice cream trucks made their daily rounds.

Vendors also included door to door salesmen peddling pots and pans, insurance policies of every kind, encyclopedias, bibles and other books. Down town cleaners sent their trucks and their vans up to the neighborhood to collect clothes for cleaning to be returned a week later as there was no cleaning establishment in the area.

CHANNEL HEIGHTS MEMORIES

Community clinics were part the complex and were staffed by registered nurses who lived in an adjoining unit of the single story duplex health center. These were built for that purpose with their residence on one side and the clinic adjoining on the other. The nurses treated minor illnesses and injuries at no charge. I recall that our nurse was a Miss Clark.

Most of the units had views of the ocean, open gardens and expansive lawns in the front with a drive way in the back. My family and our neighbors planted personal vegetable gardens and there were various fruit trees throughout the neighborhood especially cumquats we called "low quats."

Each family was responsible for maintaining and cutting their own lawns and other vegetation however the large common areas were maintained by project staff. Necessary gardening tools were available from a central location and checked out and in as needed and younger kids were required to have an authorization note from their parents for this purpose. My brother Charles and I surreptitiously wrote our own notes which were somehow "signed" by a parent. It was not uncommon for us young kids to cut neighbors' lawns for a nominal charge, usually a quarter or fifty cents depending on the size of the lawn.

There was regular garbage pick-up but no trash pick-up and every court, as the streets in the complex were called, had an incinerator for trash burning. The incinerator can best be described as an enormous outdoor brick fire place with a metal door at the top where burnable trash was inserted and bottom door where the ashes and soot was removed ever so often by workers. The recycling phenomenon would arrive some 50 plus years later in most communities. The garbage truck collected the garbage and deposited it at a hog farm in Torrance on property what is now Del Amo Fashion Center.

My brother Charles and I would often scour the neighborhood to collect discarded soft drink bottles which had a redemption value of one cent each at the local market. This was in 1949 and the best place to gather them was at the construction site where new homes were being built across Western Avenue where they were discarded by workmen. Soft drink cans were yet to come.

This new development was in an unincorporated area of San Pedro which would be named Western View. Many years later the area would be incorporated as part of the new City of Rancho Palos Verdes with Western Avenue dividing that city from the City of Los Angeles. In the 1970's the buildings at Channel Heights were demolished and a few years later replaced by two middle class housing areas. One consisted of a series of two story apartment buildings and the other single story private homes.

Everyday life in Channel Heights were care free times. Memories of Channel Heights was that the younger kids on our court always looked forward to a visit by the aunt of the Dominguez family, our next door neighbors after the Gordon family had moved away. "Tia" generally came bearing bags of pan dulce (Mexican sweet pastries) from a bakery in East L.A.

Another regular treat on our court was an occasional visit by the grandfather of the young girl across the street Judy Galloway. Daddy Ben, as he was called by everyone, always bought ice cream for most of the neighborhood kids. He was an elderly Southern White gentleman and one of the kindest and most generous person I had ever met.

I recall frequently wanting to accompany my oldest brother Curt on his paper route in the neighborhood. Curt always instructed me to place each newspaper on the porch of his customers rather than throwing them in the yard. I really enjoyed him allowing me to do that. I was probably seven or eight years old then and felt so grown-up.

On one particular day as we approached one of his customers' house a dog with a menacing growl was on the sidewalk leading up to the porch and I was afraid to continue but Curt insisted that the dog didn't bite and coaxed me on. As I walked past the dog he eyed me but I continued on and

Brother Curt and his bicycle.

delivered the paper. Coming back down the sidewalk the dog lunged at me and I fell down with the dog on top biting me.

The owner, Mr. Early Harris, ran out and finally pulled the dog away. I suffered several superficial bites but still had to be taken to Nurse Clark's clinic for treatment. The only positive thing about that experience was Mr. Harris bought me a new shirt as mine had been ripped into shreds. A lesson learned.

CHANNEL HEIGHTS AMENITIES

Built within the Channel Heights complex was a large commercial building which we called the Channel Heights Market. It housed a grocery store, meat market a novelty store and it later housed a cleaners. A child care center was adjacent to the school. Recreational facilities were available at nearby Peck Park which included tennis courts, baseball diamonds (constructed later), swings and climbing bars for children. These amenities and conveniences met the vision of the complex's designer, Richard Joseph Neutra.

I recall several of us children taking an all-day hike up the Palos Verdes Hill to the three trees at what appeared to be the apex of the mountain. These geographical terrain features were visible from the base along Western avenue. During that time the Palos Verdes hillside was sparsely populated with houses but rich with agricultural farms and commercial flower gardens. The occasional family Sunday afternoon drives around the Palos Verdes Peninsula in Curt's 1937 Ford, purchased in the early 1950's, was always a treat for us kids. The area was very rural and devoid of traffic signals but bridle trails were abundant. Most of the side roads were unpaved.

I was the seventh child in the family to be enrolled in the elementary school which was situated in the center of the complex and walking distance for all of the students. Channel Heights Elementary School had a large multipurpose room for dual use by the school for assemblies and special events for the community at large. Since the nearest commercial movie theater was several miles away in downtown San Pedro the multipurpose room was used to show first run movies for a nominal charge of ten cents, generally on Friday nights. This became very popular for both young and old. The facility was often used for non-denominational church services on Sundays.

The community center was also used to host the annual Halloween Carnival. This special event included the parade of costumes, all home-made of course, and the traditional musical chairs event, a favorite. The winner of this fun event had their choice of any one of the home baked cakes donated for that purpose and other fun filled competitive events.

Annual IOWA Picnic

At the conclusion of World War Two hundreds and perhaps even several thousand residents of Iowa relocated to Long Beach, California and San Pedro's Peck Park became ground zero for their annual reunion picnic gathering. These former residents of that state gathered at Peck Park to meet, greet and socialize. There was always lots of catered food for everyone, including for the kids of Channel Heights. Sixty five years later, there were still several thousand descendants of the original sojourners still residing in Long Beach according to city officials there.

When the Naval vessel USS Iowa was decommissioned and made available by the Navy as a museum, San Pedro, along with various other seaport cities around the country, made bids to have it relocated to their city. San Pedro was eventually selected primarily due to legislation brought forth by the Iowa Legislature endorsing the move to San Pedro while also appropriating $3 million dollars of state funds for the purpose of refurbishing it; one dollar for each Iowa resident. This was done due to the close proximity of San Pedro to Long Beach, and the Iowa descendants, which lies just across the bay.

Kiwanis Easter Egg Hunt

Peck Park was also a social center of activity for the Channel Heights residents and where the Kiwanis Club annually staged an Easter egg hunt. Members of the organization spent many hours the day before Easter "planting" multi-colored Easter eggs throughout the park. The search was limited to younger children who were brought there by their parents. The grand prizes were a boys and a girls bicycle given to the lucky finders of the golden Easter eggs.

According to a 2009 story in the South Bay Daily Breeze newspaper, Peck Park was named for George Peck who was a turn of the century land baron with holdings in Los Angeles, San Pedro and surrounding South Bay communities. He also had cornered the market transporting goods from the ships in the harbor to downtown Los Angeles. He had gifted the land to the City of San Pedro prior to San Pedro being annexed by the City of Los Angeles in 1909. He also had donated

Mother on the grass at Peck Park with youngest children Left to right: peter(age 8), Gloria Jean, held by Alice Marie, Darnell,, mother, Charles, Harry

land for other parks in San Pedro and each one was named for one of his children. Leland Street and Alma Street also were so named.

Today Rena Park, Leland Park and Alma Park still adorn the landscape of the port community. He also gifted the land for Point Fermin Park in San Pedro named in honor of Father Francisco Fermin de Lasuen, a Franciscan Friar at the Carmel Mission. Quite the businessman, he helped organize the Bank of San Pedro in 1889 and in 1913 negotiated the sale of 104 acres of his holdings that would become Fort MacArthur in San Pedro.

CHRISTMAS IN CHANNEL HEIGHTS

One of the special remembrances of Channel Heights was the family Christmas'. Our parents seemed to always stretch their earnings to ensure every child received a gift. Presents, at times, consisted of roller skates, cap pistols, games (Monopoly was a favorite), and of course clothing items.

It was a treat to watch mother and other church volunteer women stuff Christmas stockings with fruit, candy and nuts in our house which would be passed out to the children at the Annual Sunday School Christmas Party at the church. They also wrapped gifts which had been purchased and secured at our house awaiting distribution at the party.

One year one of the Ministers dressed as Santa Claus for the Christmas party which startled some of the younger children, and perhaps surprised others, as they had never before seen a Black Santa. Me either. Maybe some children believed him to be a fake as most and perhaps all had never seen a Santa other than a White Santa in stores or in a magazine.

CHANNEL HEIGHTS NEIGHBORS

The Channel Heights manager was a Mrs. Patricia Colby who befriended our family and became my mother's life-long friend as did her daughter Pat with her class mates, my brothers and sister. Mrs. Colby was well liked and respected by the Channel Heights residents in general and, according to her performance record with the Los Angeles City Housing Authority leadership, received numerous managerial promotions during her more than 40 years with the agency.

In 1984 upon retiring as the third most senior executive in the city agency she was awarded Los Angeles' Service Medallion which recognized her for extensive work in public service. This is the City's highest award and the presentation was made by then Mayor Tom Bradley and his wife Ethel in their home at a reception held in her honor. Mrs. Colby passed away in her San Pedro home in 2004.

Channel Heights was truly a multi-cultural community which housed families of varying ethnicities. As an indication of this some of our neighbors' surnames on Osorno Court and neighboring Natal Court alone were Curly, Ray and Jones (black); Kittingsberg, Debanski, Bulwa and Mossberg (Jewish); Dominguez and Soto (Mexican), Pugh, Gordon, Pharr, Stacey, Vance, Aders & Hale-Galloway (White); Carpentier & Badgett (Trinidadian) and later, a few years after the war and after returning from the Internment Camp, the Itow and Emai families (Japanese).

Channel Heights alumni (left to right) Ed Fitzgerald, Peter, Blanche, brother Leon, Brian Raber & wife, John Gray & Marilyn Fitzgerald

Our first next door neighbors were the Gordon family with twins Bud and Betty and baby Ronnie. Ronnie and I were able to reconnect in 2017 over 65 years after his family having moved away and we remembered one another and reminisced as best as we could.

When they moved away our new neighbors were the Dominguez family with parents Sam and Nicky and children Adele, Sam Jr. (Butchie), Myron (Curly) and Daniel (Danny Boy).

Mr. Stacey, mentioned above, who lived down the hill from us, was always on call by any neighbor who needed to have a gofer terminated from their yard. He lived just down the embankment from us and had a collection of military rifles and was never hesitant to accommodate a request by taking careful aim and hitting the disrupting rodent on the first shot.

The Stacey's two sons were James Houston and Lee Austin (do you think the family might have been from Texas)? They both had been Army Air Corps pilots in the war and often "buzzed" the neighborhood and tipped their wings while flying small private airplanes probably having taken off from nearby Lomita Army Air Field later to be renamed Torrance Municipal Airport and finally Zamperini Field.

Channel Heights Alumni (second from left Peter, Marilyn Fitzgerald, brother William, sister Alice, Blanche. Far right Ed Fitzgerald

What is interesting is that the Stacey's oldest daughter, Hilda, got married and moved to Compton, California, then a predominantly White city. Her parents told my parents that when Hilda moved there she told them that she could not have any Negro visitors. The Stacey's younger daughter Patsy became a model of some distinction.

The Ramos family lived on the next court and was a multiracial family of Filipino, White and black. The mother, Mary, had a White parent and a Negro parent and the father, Gregg, was Filipino and mainly spoke Tagalong but in time we began to understand his broken English. His brother Sergio, "Sergie", was in the US Navy and visited often when in port. Their children were Gregg, Jr. (Tony), Robert, Julita (named for her father's home town in the Philippines), Richard (Butchie), Johnny and Billy.

I believed we all lived harmoniously.

CHANNEL HEIGHTS PASTIMES

After school and on weekends we engaged in a lot of outdoor activities. Much of my older brothers' free time was spent playing an improvised soft ball game called "over the line." The game had modified traditional soft ball rules which I do not recall, just the name. We skate boarded on homemade skate boards fashioned by separating the two ends of metal roller skates and nailing them to both ends a wooden board.

The difference from the current commercial skate board was that we sat on the skate board while going downhill. We also built our own go-carts which were similar to skate boards but larger and were guided by a foot pedal cross panel with ropes attached for steering.

We enjoyed sliding down the side of the Channel Heights Canyon on flattened card board boxes imitating snow sledding which we had only seen on television. Purchasing a new bicycle was unheard of so my older brothers and other boys in the neighborhood fashioned bicycles by collecting various bicycle parts over a period of time to make one.

During the late 1940's the Eastern slope of the Palos Verdes Hill was primarily agricultural and devoid of houses. My brothers and I, along with neighborhood boys, took advantage of the open space to go hiking there and to pick strawberries and vegetables which were grown in abundance.

On special holidays our family joined the Ramos family picnicking at White's Point, a tide pool area below the cliffs at Point Fermin. This part of the San Pedro's seashore was then replete with abalone beds. This is also where the patriarch of the Ramos family, Gregg and his brother Sergie, would free dive for abalones for all to roast and consume. My recollection was that they were very tasty.

FAMILY BASKETBALL TEAM AND WOULD BE BAND

All of boys in the family had the inclination to play sports, primarily basketball. They first joined teams at the local Boys Club while in elementary and junior high school. Later they played on sports teams in high school.

My recollection was that Curt, Phillip and William played in the forward position and Leon and Harry played in the guard position. Not all played at once but had that been the case we could have had our own basketball team.

The boys were also attracted to other sports while in high school, such as Curt and Melvin, baseball; Darnell and yours truly, football, and Harry swimming. Everyone had a place or two on the track team. The two girls in the family participated in sports with the Girls Athletic Club in junior high school and then Girls Athletic Association in high school.

Although no one in the family became a professional musician, several did take up playing musical instruments. Some even played in the high school orchestra or band. These were Curt, saxophone; Phillip, trombone; Leon, baritone; Harry, saxophone; and yours truly, the percussions.

From time to time other boys from the neighborhood with musical instruments would come to our house and express their musical talents.

THE DARK SIDE OF CHANNEL HEIGHTS

All was not well in Channel Heights according to author Henry Kraus in his 1951 published book "In the City was a Garden" which was a parity on Channel Heights. In his writing the name had been changed "to protect the innocent."

Channel Heights had been constructed in 1942 to house shipyard workers and their families during World War Two and the initial residents consisted of a conglomerate of families from throughout the country but primarily from the south and west; Arkansas (Arkies), Oklahoma (Oakies), Utah and Idaho, as well as Californians. These were Whites, blacks and Mexicans.

Henry Klaus writes that "in several instances Whites refused to live near Coloreds or Nig....'s and some even refused housing that was offered and needed. Some early White residents thought that Negroes should not be allowed to join the PTA at Channel Heights School. Other Whites wondered why Negroes would even be allowed to attend the

76

non-denominational church services arranged in the community center as they believed, at least did the several Mormon families from Idaho that Negroes could not go to heaven as it was for Whites only and they had always been taught that." Again, these excerpts were chronicled in Mr. Klaus' book as noted.

Still writing citing Henry Klaus... *"Some of these same White parents refused to allow their children to play with 'Nig....'er children' because sooner or later those children would be in their house, they would have to feed them and afterwards the plates and silverware would have to be thrown away."*

Other issues of race involved the school itself as some parents believed that the classes should be segregated between Whites and Coloreds. Condoleezza Rice, writing in her book "Democracy" argued *"As long as human beings fear those who are 'different', prejudice and suspicion will be part of the human experience-and America is no exception."*

On the social spectrum there was much disagreement amongst early members of the community group planning a "get acquainted" dance as to whether or not Negroes should be invited. They were but none attended.

Admittedly none of these issues were known to me and probably not to my siblings and as I wrote earlier, everyone got along "harmoniously." Regretfully my mother had passed away by the time I acquired Henry Klaus' publication. Undoubtedly she would have been able to substantiate or repudiate his writings.

Chapter 10 Dad goes off to the Army

My father's first job was working as a member of the Channel Heights maintenance staff as did many of the fathers in the neighborhood who had not yet been drafted or volunteered for the military. Within a year, however, he received his draft notice. This was in 1944. It was later learned that Mr. George Alexander, the plantation owner in Arkansas, had given my father's personal information to the Little Rock Draft Board advising them that my father had moved to California to avoid being drafted and suggested they contact the Draft Board in Los Angeles. He probably made no mention that my father was married and had a large family. Perhaps, Mr. Alexander was the impetus for my father being drafted. This was despite him being almost 30 years old with eight children.

He reported for induction at nearby Fort Mac Arthur located in San Pedro, California after, according to my mother, receiving his draft notice in an envelope accompanied by a five cent bus token for the 30 minute bus ride. Upon arriving there, he was processed-in with an interesting twist as he related to me. I recall him telling the story that inductees were of all ethnic groups but with Colored inductees placed in one group and Whites and all others placed in another group. This was when the US Military was segregated by race.

Even though dad had entered a segregated army, after having been living in an integrated housing project in the City of Los Angeles, he quickly adapted to those conditions as he had experienced segregation much of his life up until then in segregated Arkansas. His initial view of the army was that it was a piece of Arkansas.

After a few days, he and his fellow Colored inductees were first shipped to Camp Hood, Texas for boot camp training and then he was later shipped to Selfridge Army Air Field, Illinois where he was assigned to the Army Air

Corps all-black 99th Pursuit Squadron as a driver. According to him, he received this assignment at his own request as he was given two choices of duty, one being a driver and the other being a cook. Since he had lots of experience assisting my mother cooking for the family he did not want that job so he volunteered for the other. He was accepted, according to him, because he was the only soldier in his immediate group who possessed a driver's license.

This and other all black flying units became known as the Tuskegee Airmen as the pilots were first trained to fly at the Tuskegee Institute, Alabama now named Tuskegee University. Advanced flight training was at Selfridge and other air bases.

After the War my father and other enlisted support personnel who had been assigned to any of America's "Colored Air Force" regardless of rank or duty, received the designation as "Tuskegee Airmen." These included aircraft mechanics, petroleum handlers, supply personnel, ordnance, communications staff, drivers, gunners, navigators, base operations staff and even cooks and bakers.

At Selfridge, he was assigned to base operations ferrying pilot trainees to and from their aircraft on a Jitney. The next year he served at Camp Walterboro, South Carolina and finally Mitchell Army Air Field, New York which became the temporary home of the 477th to which the 99th was assigned. He was discharged there in 1946, the year after the war ended with "mustering out pay" totaling $256.55 which included a month's salary, allotments, leave pay and travel funds to return to California.

My earliest memory of my father was when he was home on furlough I recall seeing him in uniform standing in the kitchen of our Channel Heights apartment talking to my mother. I was probably four or five years old at the time. He removed his uniform hat and placed it on my head and I marched off into the room pretending to be a soldier.

Perhaps that became the impetus for me desiring to become a soldier myself.

Southern politicians referred to them as "Eleanor's Nigger Air force; Eleanor being the First Lady and Wife of President Roosevelt. It was she who petitioned the President to commission the unit.

It was fortunate that my father came home from the Army wearing his uniform in California because had he still been in Arkansas or some other parts of the south often times Negro soldiers were beaten and some killed for wearing "White man's hero clothes" as uniforms were called in some local towns, as author Janet Cohen writes in her book *"From Rage to Reason, My Life in Two Americas."*

THOSE WHO SIT AND WAIT ALSO SERVE

During my father's time in the Army my mother received a monetary allotment from the government of, according to her, $4.00 per month for each child and $6.00 per month for the oldest child. She was issued ration books with tear out script to purchase perishable grocery items such as eggs, bread, milk, butter and some staples and also clothing. Had she owned an automobile she would have also been issued ration books for gasoline.

Serving at the same time in the Army as my dad were my mother's brother Robert Harris and another one of her brothers' James Harris was serving in the Navy as mentioned. Uncle Robert served in the 93rd Infantry Division throughout Europe, an all Colored unit, and post-war served with the Occupation Forces in Germany.

I recall as a child while occasionally spending weekends with he and his wife Aunt Adele in their small Wilmington apartment, he reminisced that he and other American Negro soldiers serving in Germany often gave some of their rations to German civilians who, in many cases, were starving.

A related story: When Dorothy and I purchased our home on Taper Avenue in San Pedro in the mid 1960's our next door neighbors were the Robert and his wife Erica. Robert had served in the US Army and stationed in Germany immediately after the war in the late 1940's. While there he met and married Erica, a young German woman. Following his discharge he and Erica relocated to San Pedro, Robert's hometown, and started a family.

I spent many hours over the years speaking to Erica as she related her World War Two experiences. She often talked about how hungry she and her parents were and they were always out scrounging for food scraps in between bombing raids in the City of Nuremburg where they lived. After the war they survived mainly due to the food that American Negro Soldiers gave them. She recalled the chocolate bars and small tins of meat became their only substance for a while. Later the American Red Cross provided food.

When Dorothy and I selected the house to purchase on Taper Avenue it was not an easy process. The location was a former public housing project called Banning Homes which had been demolished and replaced with a middle class housing track with only two black families among the more than 500 residences. A few of the all-White families in the neighborhood were chagrin to know that the neighborhood was being integrated.

Our black realtor, working for a White realty company, alerted us that there might be issues with our prospective new neighbors so for that reason she advised us to visit the house after dark. We met her there around midnight careful to avoid lights and noises where we were introduced to the sellers, a nice Jewish family. We visited all of the rooms without turning on lights and entered the back yard in the darkness. We loved the house and the purchase was completed.

Just days prior to our wedding Dorothy and I along with her mother began moving personal belonging into the house mid-day. A neighbor two houses away came over and inquired if in fact we had purchased the home and upon learning that we had extended a warm welcome to the neighborhood. The next day another neighbor visited us bringing freshly baked cookies with a welcoming smile. All was well and for the remainder of our time there we got along just fine with everyone. Times had changed and Bob and Erika became some of our best friends.

Uncle Robert shared with me that his unit's mission in Germany after the war was to provide security of the railroads to ensure that former Nazi soldiers did not attempt to perform sabotage. One day he and two other soldiers were monitoring the rail yards when a passing train moved slowly bye. There were three German soldiers atop one of the cars each still wearing their Nazi uniforms which were forbidden to be worn post war. The three took aim with their rifles perhaps intending to shoot or just scare them but when the soldiers waived at them they lowered their rifles. Afterwards they discussed which soldier each had been aiming at and all three indicated the one in the center. He told me whatever I do never be in the center and I have always remembered that story.

My Uncle James served over 40 years in the Navy making it a career with both shore duty in Hawaii and sea duty based out of both Terminal Island at Los Angeles Harbor and at San Diego. While in Hawaii he fathered a son with a Hawaiian woman who he named after him. At a very young age James Harris Jr, Butchie as he was called by family, was sent to California to be raised by my grandmother, Gertrude Harris, James Senior's mother.

BAND OF BROTHERS

Our family can clearly be seen as a patriotic family who loved and supported the American ideals as evidenced in that members were willing to defend them by serving. In addition to my fathers' service in the Army Air Corps along with service by my Uncle James and Uncle Robert, all of this mentioned earlier, many years' later eight Gravett brothers would serve in the United States Army.

Five sons were conscripted after which two, following their honorable discharges, voluntarily continued their military service in the reserves. Three volunteered to serve in the military.

The eight Gravett sons serving were Curt, Fort Campbell, Kentucky; Phillip, Fort Leonard Wood, Missouri; William, Fort Bragg, North Carolina; Charles, Fort Bragg, North Carolina; Peter, throughout the US and international, Harry, Schofield Barracks, Hawaii; Darnell, Vietnam and Melvin, Vicenza, Italy. My two sisters experienced the military in a different way, Alice having married a former Marine and Gloria having married a soldier. My extensive military service is chronicled later in the book.

My brother Darnell passed away several years after returning from Viet Nam. In my view his premature demise was a direct result of the ravages of having served in that war torn country as had many other returning young soldiers of his time. His ravages continued even while temporarily serving in the reserves. One could argue that he gave his life for his country by belatedly succumbing to the ravages that claimed him.

While in Viet Nam Darnell happened upon several friends whom he had known at home prior to themselves being drafted. It was a bad omen that war had to bring them together.

My brother Melvin, following his discharge from serving an active duty tour in the Army, had a long and distinguished career as a military reservist and rising to the highest enlisted military rank of Command Sergeant Major while simultaneously pursuing a civilian career. At one time he was the youngest Command Sergeant Major in the 40th Infantry Division and retired with more than 30 years in uniform.

Melvin had been drafted and following his training in the US he was stationed in Vicenza, Italy at a NATO Missile Base. He tells the story that it was good duty and a nice place to serve, especially during the Viet Nam War but he was keenly aware that at that time his brother Darnell was in Viet Nam. In his off duty time he and his fellow American soldiers assisted a local farmer in building a barn. Conversations with the farmer revealed that he had a son attending Stanford University in the US. This no doubt made for a lively verbal interchange, each probably attempting to understand the others language. Upon returning to the US Melvin made a decision to continue his military career by serving and promoting in the Army National Guard.

DAD'S POST WAR EMPLOYMENT

Upon discharge from the Army Dad became employed as a custodian at Regan Forge and Engineering Company, 1301 Regan Street, San Pedro, California. My mother's brother-in-law, my uncle John Battle, had applied first for the job opening and was accepted but knowing well that my father was in dire need of a job following his discharge from the Army, requested that my father be hired instead, which he was.

Dad became ingratiated with members of the Regan family especially brothers Joe and George. For a while the company had a soft ball team and my dad played center field during a few games played at San Pedro's Daniel's Field. Our family always enjoyed the Annual Regan Employees Family picnics which were generally held at Banning Park in Wilmington but on occasion at Peck Park. There were various athletic contests, races of every caliber and games for children and teens. Catered food was always plentiful.

After the war dad almost always had two jobs. While working at Regan during the day for some time he also had a fulltime night job at the Todd Shipyard also in San Pedro; walking distance to Regan. This was a way to ensure that his family was better cared for financially. After leaving the shipyard he later acquired a part-time evening custodial job at Banning High School in Wilmington.

While at Todd Shipyard he usually arrived home close to midnight and Charles and I would make every effort to remain awake to eat the remains of his lunch in his black metal lunch pail. Conveniently he would also leave a small amount for us to eat. We were never hungry at night just competing with one another. Dad also brought home left over donuts from Regan.

CHAPTER 11

RELIGIOUS UPBRINGING

The family attended religious services at the New Testament Missionary Baptist Church in Wilmington. The church was founded in 1938 by relatives including my Aunt Goldine, who served as the Church's first Trustee, and other extended family. My parents joined there in late 1943 shortly following our California arrival.

HISTORY OF THE NEW TESTAMENT BAPTIST CHURCH

In 1937 a group of parishioners who would later become the founding and first members of the church held an organizational meeting in the home of William and Elizabeth Clark, located at 1027 East Cruces Street in Wilmington where Reverend Coleman was called as the Pastor. The Clark's were two of the seven founding members. Others were Crockett and Verna Campbell, my great uncle and great aunt, George and Rosia (Rosie) Hobbs, my mother's cousins, and Goldine Battle, who was my aunt and my mother's oldest sister.

The first service was held in a borrowed tent erected in the front yard of the Hobbs' residence at 1205 East "0" Street in Wilmington. The following year the first church building was constructed at 1327 East Mauretania Street. This location was just few blocks away on the south side of what was then US Highway 1 now US Highway 101.

Initially the whole family took the street car (Red Car) to church after taking the bus from Channel Heights down the hill to the depot at the San Pedro waterfront. Church Deacon L.D. Jackson would occasionally give a ride to some of the children. Deacon Jackson, a World War Two veteran himself, served with the "Red Ball Express" in General Patton's Third Army in Europe during World War Two. My oldest brother, Clarence (Curt), later purchased a

1937 Ford which was also used to shuttle some of the family to and from church.

Quite often we attended Sunday school early in the morning followed by morning worship service. We attended Baptist Training Union (BTU) on Sunday evenings and frequently visited other churches on special Sundays. Years later my older brothers attended a church camp in San Luis Obispo and on occasion others attended church camp in the San Bernardino Mountains. Wednesday nights were prayer meetings and choir rehearsals were held Thursday evenings. Later some of us joined a Los Angeles area youth choir called "Songs of the Cross" and gave gospel concerts throughout the city.

My siblings and I were baptized under the Pastorate of the then Reverend Robert George Washington. In the early years the family participated in all ministries of the church. We children sang in the junior choir and I served on the junior usher board along with my brother Charles. My father served as a senior usher for a few years when I was younger. My mother, as did most active women in the church, served in multiple roles. She was in the adult choir, coordinator for special programs and she arranged the Sunday School Programs for Easter, Mother's Day, Father's Day Christmas and other holidays and celebrations.

In later years mother served as the church secretary and assistant church treasurer. Her most enjoyable services to the church were serving as Chairwoman the of the Pastor's Aide Ministry and as the after-service refreshments coordinator. In addition to all of this she mentored many young Christian Women through the Serendipity Program. In 1988 she was the Chairperson for the church's 50th anniversary celebration.

In earlier years the church held an annual picnic at Lincoln Park in East Los Angeles. Deacon L.D. Jackson somehow managed to procure a church bus to borrow which transported many of the adults and children. This was long before the Harbor Freeway (CA 110) was constructed and the route taken from the harbor area was traveling north on Alameda Street through all of the cities what is now the Alameda Corridor. I suspect Lincoln Park was selected due to its' ample space, merry-go-round, motor boat lake, bicycle rentals, swimming pool and other recreational amenities.

Attending the New Testament Missionary Baptist Church during my formative years allows me to often recall the strains of old Negro spirituals sung by the older congregants such as:

'Bread of Heaven,
Bread of Heaven
Feed Me 'Till I Want No More
I am weak but Thou art mighty
Hold me with Thou powerful hand
and...
God's gettin' us ready for that 'gret day (hallelujah)
The mountains' will be movin' own that 'gret day
(hallelujah)
Sinners will be runnin' on that 'gret day (hallelujah)
who shall be able to stand?

-Old Negro Spiritual

With the passing of Pastor Washington the church was briefly under the leadership of Reverend Clyde Moss who was replaced by Pastor Felton Simpson, PhD. Dr. Simpson brought the church further into the 20th century with his academic preparation, teachings and preaching. The church progressed extensively and, during the first half of his more than 30 years in the pulpit, grew more members and numerous ministries were formed.

Over the course of several years however, as teens went off to college, young adults were drafted or joined the military or sought greener pastures, older members passed away and, this coupled with the neighborhood ethnically changing, membership dwindled. At this point the church could not sustain itself to the point where it was eventually shuttered in 2009. This was in spite of Pastor Simpson's invigorating preaching and teaching. At the final service many generations of former members returned to celebrate the 71 years of the church having served the Wilmington community.

Our parents instilled in all of us the ethics of good citizenship, honesty and a plethora of other Christian values. These included attending school every day dressed properly and arriving on time. Modest behavior in the class room was stressed with a modicum of distraction and always having excellent deportment which, as an elementary school kid, I had no idea what that meant. My parents always anticipated reviewing report cards.

My parents were enterprising and industrious and they inspired education so dropping out of school was never an option and all of my siblings graduated from high school, all attended college, some graduating from community college and then attending a four year university. We were always admonished to never tarnish the Gravett name in any way. None ever did.

CHAPTER 12

ELEMENTARY SCHOOL ACTIVITIES

I attended Channel Heights School from Kindergarten through sixth grade and, while still living in the projects, attended Dana Junior High School for one year then we moved. The Channel Heights Elementary school Principal was Irene B. Harms (who would forget) and no one wanted to be sent to her office for disciplinary reasons as she was thought to be a strict disciplinarian. I suspect she was just doing her job.

Some of my teachers, as I recall, were Miss Katterjohn, Kindergarten, Miss Jafferty, first grade, Miss Gutnick, second grade, Miss Starkovich, third grade, Mr. Layton, fourth grade, Miss Hurran, fifth grade and Miss Iva M. Gustafson, sixth grade. Miss Jolliff was the office manager and our cousin, Mrs. Altha Mae Campbell, was one of the custodians along with Mrs. Ola Mae Musgrove, my mother's good friend.

Most of these same teachers had previously taught my older siblings. I recalled that Miss Jafferty also owned a bakery in town and would sometimes bring treats to her class. Sixty years later Blanche and I often visited her in the convalescent home where she was residing as did our friends Eddie Fitzgerald and his wife Marilyn who also visited her there. Eddie was also a former Channel Heights resident and student.

Our school had no cafeteria and all students either brought a lunch or just walked home since we all lived in the same neighborhood as the school and we were within walking distance. I recall mother making lunches in the evening for the next day and lining up the brown bags on the kitchen table, unlabeled, but each one knew which was theirs. These were for elementary, junior high and high school as there were family members attended all three concurrently.

Each new semester for me started the same way with the teachers' admonition that they knew my mother and that she had taught my older brothers and sister so I had better be good. Mother was an active member of the PTA for several years and often served as a Room Mother and thus was on a personal basis with most of the teachers. While there I was very proud to have been selected to serve as a School Safety and in the 6th grade selected to assist in raising the flag every morning.

Other remembrances were that every year each class performed a May Day dance on the playground for all of the students and parents in attendance. This took weeks of rehearsals. We took trips to the Garden Center on Weymouth Avenue to tend the vegetables we had planted earlier and also to feed the small farm animals boarded there. We also took trips to various locations of educational interest including the Mansion in Banning Park, former home of General Banning, in nearby Wilmington. Phineas Banning, a Civil War General, was one of the founders of the Los Angeles Harbor. The desert city of Banning, California also bears his name as did another public housing project previously mentioned, Banning Homes, on land donated to the city by his descendants.

We always looked forward to the visit by Western Movie Star Monty Montana who came with an array of farm animals to "show and tell." His rodeo roping exhibition was always a treat. This would be the first time most children in Channel Heights had ever seen live farm animals.

On Saturdays during the season we were offered a trip to downtown Los Angeles to the Philharmonic Auditorium where we attended concerts performed by the Philharmonic Orchestra. These concerts were specifically for elementary school children and contributed to our cultural enrichment. The school district provided the buses and each student was required to pay ten cents. I never knew what the stipend was for as it obviously did not cover expenses. Perhaps it was just to teach us that nothing was free.

CLASS MATES

Throughout elementary school my best friends and class mates were Joe Jones, Ronny Itow, Richard (Butchie) Ramos and Richard Cole. Richard Cole had a younger brother, Val, who hung around us sometime and he also had a younger sister Diane. Ronny's siblings were bothers Lucky and Mickey as well as his sister Betty Jo. Joe Jones' sisters were Marjorie and Marva.

Ronny and Butchie were from the same two families on Osorno Court mentioned earlier. Having gone from kindergarten through the sixth grade with them we spent much of our non-school hours paling around, including going to the San Pedro downtown YMCA to swim on Fridays after school.

PETER VS. AUTOMOBILE

One Friday after school, my brother Charles and I went to the YMCA to swim and later watch a movie there, as we often did. During the movie someone yelled that the "Mighty MO" (the Battle Ship USS Missouri) was cruising down the main channel which was just across the street. I ran outside, darted across the street mid-block without looking and was hit by a car. Although my injuries were superficial word reached my mother that I had been struck and killed and that my body had been transported to the San Pedro Community Hospital.

She was driven there by neighbors only to find me sitting up on the treatment table in the emergency room talking to the medical staff. She became so excited to see me unhurt that she exclaimed *I'll kill you boy for scaring me like this* all the while crying and shaking and sometimes hugging me. She would tell this story to family and friends over and over for many years to come. It was embellished every time.

The driver of the car was the wife of a traffic police officer and daughter of the judge at the traffic court. Both the police station and traffic Court were located just two blocks away in the San Pedro City Hall. The final tally was automobile 1 and Peter 0. Since it became obvious that the accident was my fault having crossed the street mid-block outside the crosswalk, there was no retribution to the driver.

Joe Jones and I continued our friendship through junior high school and high school and have been lifelong friends. Years later I had the privilege of being a member of his wedding party. Joe later served in the US Naval Air prior to becoming a successful businessman, having a prominent position at a Hollywood television station and later owning a radio station in Chicago.

In addition to my best friends, my sixth grade classmates as I recall were Gloria Valarde (a lifelong friend), Eva Dinger (Post World War Two refugee from Norway), Louie Carbajal, Raymond Gipson, Barbara Born, Mary Ann Neal, Darlene Ronning, Lila Mae Armstrong, Trevor Duncan and Peter Barrett.

Others were Marie Odom, Bobby Gonzales, Arlene Zavala, Bessie Mae Reed, Barbara Ann Adders, Lamar Mitchell, Eddie Spears, Tom Guinn, Oren Crudupt, Olive Berg, Walter Lakey, Mary Rose Precely, Susan Darrell and Ronald Urea. Ronny Itow, mentioned previously, and his family had recently been released from a World War Two Internment Camp. A totally racially diverse group.

Why do I remember these names after 65 years? One can only speculate. I did however spend six years in the classroom with them, seven if you include kindergarten. I often wondered what the future held for all of them. To remember them and their names is perhaps sufficient evidence that I had a positive experience with each of them during my early education.

It became a ritual that when a member of the family graduated from one of the schools several family members attended the ceremony filling lots of seats. When I graduated from Channel Heights Elementary School on a Friday in January 1953 I started attending Dana Junior High School the very next Monday as was the custom with the Los Angeles Unified School District (LAUSD) then. In that era the LAUSD had two graduations per year for all schools, January and June. So if you started Kindergarten in January you graduated from the sixth grade in January seven years later and if you started in September you graduated in June. This was the system until the late 1970's when graduations were changed to once a year.

The school district provided bus transportation to Dana Junior High School from Channel Heights which made stops at strategic pick up points around the neighborhood on regular schedules. There were two pick up times spaced about 20 minutes apart and students could take either bus. So if a student missed the first bus there was always the later bus. Missing that bus the students had a problem.

VACATION BIBLE SCHOOL

Every summer while living in Channel Heights we attended Bible School at San Pedro's First Baptist Church downtown. The sessions lasted two weeks and this greatly contributed to my understanding of the Bible.

Transportation was provided by the church in either the church bus or sometimes a stake bed truck. The driver would make the rounds in Channel Heights then drive down the hill to Banning Homes, another public housing project, to collect other kids. This was when I first met Melvin Haynes. We were both about ten years old at the time and he eventually become my life-long best friend.

We also attended Bible School at the Channel Heights Community Center under the tutelage of two dynamic teachers, Miss Thomas and Miss Mills. They were missionaries and their fascinating stories of taking the gospel to third world countries and indigenous peoples were always fascinating and allowed us to visualize parts of the world and peoples unknown.

CHAPTER 13 RANCHO SAN PEDRO OUR SECOND CALIFORNIA HOME

In 1954 we moved from Channel Heights to a newly constructed residential apartment unit in another San Pedro public housing project called Rancho San Pedro. Our address was 216 South Beacon Street and it was just a couple of blocks from the water front and also the Red Light District.

Our new home was quite a change from the previous one as we now had five bedrooms and two bath rooms plus the standard full kitchen, living room and dining room. Additionally our quarters had lots of closets and storage space which we did not have previously.

Our building was one of two buildings with backyards adjoining, each building consuming an entire block with a parking lot on one end. The other building faced Harbor Boulevard. These two story buildings consisted of five apartments each with five bedrooms and a single story one bedroom apartment on each end. The large apartments were built to accommodate large families and the single story two bedroom apartments were for senior citizens equipped with handicap apparatus.

Each family living in the apartments had a minimum of ten children. This meant that there were over 130 residents total just in the two buildings. Our family was not the largest with 13 members as there were two families with 14 members each.

Some of the families carried sur-names such as Bursey, Madrid, Cooper, Hernandez, Blasing, Kramer, and others. The Hernandez family had two sets of twins and a set of triplets plus other children. As in Channel Heights all of the families were able to get along well. From time to time our family gave a house party for our friends from school and from the neighborhood.

Every year the Clyde Beatty Circus Train came to San Pedro and the train tracks were located just two blocks away at the waterfront alongside Front Street, which no longer exists. In those days the adjacent land was devoid of structures and the large circus tent was erected next to the train. This presented a grand opportunity for us pre-teens to find methods to surreptitiously enter the big top and see the shows without paying the fees.

Frequently my father would take me fishing with him off the piers on 22nd street. He had several poles and a tackle box with all of the elements to be successful snatching a few. I do not recall whether or not any of my brothers ever went along but I really enjoyed the experience.

NEWSPAPER SALES BOY

Shortly after moving to Rancho I acquired a job selling newspapers on the streets at the Los Angeles water front. I first sold the Los Angeles Mirror, for seven cents each, and that newspaper was eventually bought out by the Los Angeles Examiner, also selling for seven cents. I sold that newspaper until it was bought out by the Los Angeles Times, which was already the bestselling newspaper. The collective Times newspaper sold for a dime during the week and fifteen cents on Sundays.

Selling newspapers on the waterfront was quite a learning experience especially while walking up and down the 500, 600 and 700 blocks of the notorious Beacon Street. This was the infamous Red Light District to the fullest and known at seaports the world over and just a few blocks from our home. This area was frequented by sailors and merchant seamen as well as local longshoremen.

Beacon Street had its share of characters. I recall there was a heavy set Mexican American woman who was the "Madam" for Hispanic prostitutes whom my brother Charles gave the moniker "Queen of Beacon Street." I believe he, or someone, also labeled the heavy set man, an Italian, who was a bookie and loan shark, "The Hat." This was because he could always be seen wearing a wide brim over-sized black hat not unlike the white one worn by gangster Al Capone.

The very robust black Madam whom everybody called "Big Bertha" (pseudonym) ensured that black sailors and merchant seaman had their choice of prostitutes of color and her counter-part and good friend, Cynthia Ramocich (pseudonym) the White Madam, did the same for White clients, mostly Scandinavian merchant seamen. Charles gave names to numerous other unsavory characters there most whom I have forgotten.

Most of my newspaper sales customers were found in bars like the well-known Shanghai Red's (for Whites), the 409 Club (for blacks) and the El Zarape (for Mexicans). Other clubs and cocktail lounges catered to Scandinavian, Italian and Greek seamen. I also hustled papers in barber shops and in various diners, pool halls and billiard parlors where the managers kept track of bets by using their abacus. I sold lots of newspapers to the regulars; bookies, prostitutes, transvestites, gamblers, sailors and merchant seamen.

The front of the ferry building was a an excellent place to hawk papers to workers clad in white uniforms emerging from the various fish canneries on Terminal Island such as Star Kist Tuna, Bumble Bee Tuna, Pan Pacific Fish Cannery and others. This was just two blocks from Beacon Street.

In 1969 the Los Angeles City Council voted to replace the blighted Beacon Street area with new commercial and residential developments which meant wholesale leveling of the old buildings along the street. But before that came to pass, local civic leaders decided to hold one last fling to celebrate. For the occasion four Beacon Street bars that had already been closed reopened for the event (with no liquor licenses). Stage shows were held and the revelers danced in the middle of the street to live bands. Soon afterwards, the run down collection of bars, pawnshops, flop houses, tattoo parlors and houses of ill repute as well as Shanghai Reds and the Seafarers Social Club were demolished and the old Beacon Street was no more. As a youngster growing up there it remains part of my history.

I had excellent newspaper sales on the U.S. Coast Guard Base on Terminal Island, especially in the barracks on weekends when the Coast Guardsmen slept in. I entered the barracks very early in the morning and placed a paper on each bunk while most of them slept. Later I would return and collect the money. This was a good method to insure sales and garner good tips.

I also sold papers in front of Ante's Café when it was then a five stool walk-in located at 6th and Palos Verdes Streets. Ante later opened a restaurant on 5th and Palos Verdes Streets and finally one between 7th and 8th Streets on Palos Verdes Street. The Palos Verdes street name was later changed to Ante Perkov Way to honor him for his decade's long philanthropic endeavors to the community. His son, Ante Jr. (Tony) was my high school classmate and later my classmate in the Army's OCS Program. We received our commissions together.

My newspaperman boss was Mr. Bill Griffin and also the boss of several other boys my age selling newspapers around the waterfront. One day one of the boys mentioned to me that Mister Griffin had taken them to his house in Torrance to swim in his pool. When I mentioned that I was not told of the opportunity the boy told me that Mr. Griffin told all of the boys, all whom were White, not to mention it to me because I was Colored and Coloreds were not allowed in his neighborhood.

In Rancho it seemed that most children in the family had one kind of part time job or another creating their own funds to take care of their few school expenses and to buy their own clothes.

OTHER JOBS

As a young boy I always had a job. I guess that I developed the work ethic from my father, himself always having two jobs simultaneously as previously mentioned. As a nine year old I was selling oranges door to door with other boys my age that lived in Channel Heights. We were working from the back of a pickup truck owned by a man who gathered us up and took us to unfamiliar neighborhoods sometimes 30 or 40 miles distance. One area which I recall was an unincorporated community on the Los Angeles and Orange County line called Carmelita. Many years later it and other surrounding communities such as Dairy Valley formed the City of Cerritos.

In 1956 we moved to 790 (790 West Oliver Street, San Pedro), about age 14 where I acquired jobs washing dishes at two restaurants which will be discussed.

The fact that I had various jobs while in elementary, junior and high school was not unique. Both my parents had instilled in their children a sense of responsibility and accountability and the understanding that each of us should contribute towards his own school expenses. Perhaps that may have been the reasoning that all of us had a part-time job at one time or another.

RICHARD HENRY DANA JUNIOR HIGH SCHOOL

Rancho was closer to Dana than Channel Heights so I walked the two miles to and from school with my siblings, the older ones then attending San Pedro High School which was a block up the hill from Dana. By this time my older brothers were excelling in varsity sports at the high school, primarily basketball, and I was a member of the Junior High School orchestra playing the percussion instruments along with a new friend Fred Miller.

The Boy's Vice Principal at Dana was Mr. Thomas Lawson who was also serving in the California Army National Guard as a Captain having returned home from combat duty in the Korean War as a decorated veteran. I was his "office boy" for one period a day in the 8th grade running errands around campus. Fifteen years later after I had received my commission as a Second Lieutenant and he had promoted to Brigadier General he selected me to serve as his Aide De Camp. He passed away at the rank of a retired Major General and I was requested to be one of the speakers' at his memorial service. Given the honor of doing so I reminisced about our relationship at Dana. This very much pleased his family.

Peter in 9th Grade at Dana Junior High School

We had lots of friends of varying ages in Rancho and there was a house party given by someone almost every weekend. The center of gravity was the park in the center of the complex where most gatherings by the guys took place, along with the adjacent recreation center.

We spent a great deal of time attending dances at the local Community Center called Homer Toberman Settlement House, now called Toberman Community Center, located at First Street and Grand Avenue. I followed the lead of my older brothers by engaging in sports at the Boys Club just a block from Dana.

The annual Fisherman's Fiesta held at the outer harbor was always fun to attend. Each commercial fishing boat was decorated much like the Rose Parade floats and they paraded up and down the San Pedro Channel. The docks were like a carnival atmosphere with lots of food booths, rides and such.

Also the annual Navy Day allowed us to go aboard and tour the US Ships and a Japanese Naval Academy training ship. This was a four mast sailing Barque named the Nippon Maru as it made its' annual port call to San Pedro.

Leo's Malt Shop was just a few blocks away from our house in Rancho which was another place to gather and hang out. It was owned by my mother's cousin, Leo Jackson, and his mother my great aunt, Frances Johns, known by everyone as "Aunt Fannie." Aunt Fannie became somewhat of a celebrity when she reached the age of 116 thus becoming the oldest person in America for a short time. On her final two birthdays she received personal telephone greetings from the President of the United States.

MY FIRST "REAL" JOB

My newspaper sales job ended when I acquired a job at a Mexican restaurant on Pacific Avenue called La Paloma, and later at a restaurant called the Spinnaker Inn. This one was located at the Flietz Brothers Yacht basin at the outer harbor off 22nd Street and Miner Street in San Pedro. This was just as I was starting high school. I was a dish washer in both places and worked after school and on weekends. At Fleitz Brothers I was able to meet and know various T.V and movie personalities who owned yachts moored in the slips. Every now and then I was invited and enjoyed sailing with them on a day trip to Catalina Island.

On weekend nights the restaurant closed around 10 PM and we finished cleaning around 11 PM. Afterwards I walked home in the dark about five miles to our home at "790".

DEPUTY AUXILIARY POLICE

While in the seventh grade I became a member of the Deputy Auxiliary Police, or DAPs, a youth group sponsored by the Los Angeles Police Department. The DAPs were the forerunner of today's Police Explorer Program which most police and sheriff's departments have and it catered to boys and girls between the ages of 11 and 17.

This association would have a lasting influence on me and was the impetus for me later becoming a police officer. Each police station sponsored a DAP unit and mine was at the Harbor Division in San Pedro. Our coordinators were Policeman Morris B. (Gil) Gilmore and Policewoman Franchon Blake and later Police Woman Betty Bowden. Gil's wife, Policewoman Chloe Gilmore, often assisted although she was assigned to the Harbor Division Women's Jail.

The DAPs had boys and girls drill teams both outfitted in a blue khaki uniform with modified police shoulder patches. The boys wore military boots and painted helmet liners. The girls were similarly attired but with skirts and caps. We marched in local and regional parades.

Most of my free time as a teenager was associated with the DAPs. We had a police department rank structure and promotions were based upon a number of measures including a written test, attendance at functions, participating in the drill teams and volunteering in the community. During my time there, I was promoted to Sergeant, Lieutenant, Captain, Inspector and finally Staff Inspector. There was one boy and one girl Deputy Chief citywide selected by all of the police coordinators.

The DAPs had numerous activities for us and its members who lived throughout the L.A. Harbor area which included residents who then lived on Terminal Island, San Pedro, Harbor City, Wilmington and the Shoe String Strip. The Strip was a mile wide, geographical area which connected the Harbor area to the Southern part of the City of Los Angeles proper. The area has since been renamed Harbor Gateway.

One of our members and my very close friend was Ezekiel "Zeke" Encinas. Zeke was voted the top drill team member and called cadences as we marched. Years later, Zeke graduated from Long Beach State College, was commissioned as an Air Force officer and became a fighter pilot. During the Viet Nam War his aircraft was impacted by a Viet Cong surface to air missile and crashed. Several years later after the war his remains were recovered and he was given a military funeral with full honors. I was honored to be among the throngs in attendance including several former members of the DAPs.

The DAPs were a central part of my life until about the same time I graduated from Dana Junior High School in January 1956 and entered San Pedro High.

CHAPTER 14 THE INFAMOUS "790"

In 1956 my parents purchased a home at 790 West Oliver Street in San Pedro. This was a newly constructed home West of Gaffey Street in a new development of approximately 12 houses in a triangular fashion bordering on three streets; Oliver Street on the south, Cabrillo Avenue on the west and Summerland Avenue on the north and east.

Beginning from the time we moved there from Rancho to the current day the home has always been referred to as "790" not only by us but by all of our neighborhood friends as it was a gathering place.

This was a previously vacant area without paved streets so during our first winter we had heavy rains which muddied the hill of Oliver Street so it was coined "Mudville." The bottom of the hill was the terminus of the Bandini Canyon and walking along Marshall Court below the hill one caught the cold winds blowing down through the canyon so this area was coined "Deep Freeze." Both names probably coined by my brother Charles.

Our home at 790 became the center of gravity (no pun intended) for all of our friends. With so many boys in the family most of our friends congregated there coming from other parts of San Pedro. Friends like Billy Hurd, Melvin Haynes, Franklin Jones, John Gray, Jim Williams, Lionel Coulter, Gentry (Sonny) Montgomery, Hank Edney, Luther (L.C.) Whitsett and Ed Helms who lived down the street. Hollis Lee lived next door and a friend who Charles gave him the name "Blood" lived across the street. I never knew his given name. My cousin Ken Goolsby lived three blocks away.

Brothers Benny, Joe (Hobie) and Charles Jackson, Wally Johnson, James Richardson and Bobby Carter came over from Wilmington from time to time and James Frazier came over from Harbor City once in a while. Every now and then we would hold a house party with scores of friends attending.

By then we had several automobiles in the family. In addition to my father's car, a 1953 Pontiac, Curt, Phillip and William had cars, curt having purchased a new 1956 Chevrolet Bell Aire. My brother Charles and I had a choice of cars to use, sometimes "borrowing" the keys while its owner slept. All of the children in the family continued to reside at 790 until they were either married, went into the Army or acquired their own apartment.

SNAP SHOT OF SAN PEDRO

San Pedro in fact is not a city but one of the numerous named communities within the City of Los Angeles. Often the police are referred to as the San Pedro Police Department as is the "San Pedro" Fire Department. It is the southernmost community in Los Angeles but shares the title along with the Western half of Terminal Island which is also within the Los Angeles City Limits. The Eastern half of Terminal Island lies within the City Limits of Long Beach.

San Pedro, a former independent city itself, merged with Los Angeles in 1909 as did the City of Wilmington. The story goes that the old Wilmington City Council cut a deal with Los Angeles to become part of the larger city with one condition and that was there would always be a police station in Wilmington. San Pedro also cut a deal and that was the City of Los Angeles would construct a shipping harbor in San Pedro rather than Santa Monica which was being discussed at that time.

To fulfill the Wilmington commitment the Los Angeles Police Department established a store front police sub-station on the corner of B Street and Marine Avenue. This would be part of the police headquarters which worked out of the San Pedro City Hall at 7th and Beacon Streets. The station remained active until 1962 when a new Harbor Division Police Station was constructed at 2175 Wilmington-San Pedro Road, later renamed John S. Gipson Boulevard. This was to honor the 30 year City Councilman from the area. Theoretically this plot of land

105

lain within the old southwest city limits of Wilmington thus meeting the contractual requirement. This station remained in service until 2012 when it was replaced by the current and more modern police facility.

Albert "Lefty" Olguin in his book *Once a (San Pedro) Pirate Always a Pirate* cites Steve Marconi's description of a real San Pedran. Steve describes a Real San Pedran as a person whose last name ends in a vowel or the last syllable ends in "ich"; remembers the old Terminal Island Ferry; knows the difference between a Croatian and a Serbian; thinks San Pedro is a city; is a Catholic or lives next door to one; still has relatives in the old country; never thought there was anything wrong with the old Beacon Street; is a longshoreman or is related to one and finally a Real San Pedran, according to Steve, *never says San "Paydro" and get mad when people do."*

Today San Pedro is both old and new. It boasts the largest man-made harbor in the world which was constructed soon after becoming part of Los Angeles. The community of San Pedro boasts several middle and upper middle class enclaves but is generally a blue collar working class suburb.

During World War Two there was a glut of public housing projects constructed primarily to house shipyard workers and their families, including Channel Heights. For the next 25 years after the war, most were demolished and replaced by middle class communities. Also after the war San Pedro and Terminal Island had the world's largest commercial fishing fleet. Their catches kept the fish canneries in production 24/7; these were Star Kist, Pan Pacific, Bumble Bee, Chicken of the Sea and several others.

The fishing boats had crews of Yugoslavians (Slavs primarily of Croatian descent), Italians, Greeks and other Eastern European ethnicities. Most of the neighborhoods in town reflected these ethnicities. There were American Caucasians scattered throughout, and some blacks and Hispanics who were primarily of Mexican descent. Until the 1980's blacks in San Pedro had much difficulty purchasing middle class homes as housing segregation was perpetuated by local realty companies.

People growing up in San Pedro seldom moved away and for those who did most returned or at least wanted to return but we unable to due to the fact they could not afford to purchase the house they had grown up in and sold.

CHAPTER 15 SAN PEDRO HIGH SCHOOL

San Pedro High School

My high school years were enjoyable and dropping out was never an option for me or my siblings. Our parents were really focused and supportive to ensure that all of us graduated. I had great experiences during those years. I was involved in various extra-curricular activities including performing in the school orchestra where I played the percussion instruments. I attended most of the school dances and other functions both on and off campus.

I was savvy to have heeded my mother's sage advice that my high school counselors would attempt to place me in industrial art or shop classes as they had attempted with older brothers suggesting that they knew our destiny. I never took a shop class during my entire high school years and doubt my older brothers did either.

Peter in High School.

I was on the track team during my freshman year where I "practiced" the low hurdles and tried my hand (or feet) at the broad jump. My track career ended abruptly during the final practice before the first meet when I fell fracturing an arm in several places, including the elbow. What actually happened was the runner next to me, a team mate, stumbled over a hurdle and pulled me down with him as he was falling. This sidelined me from sports for more than a year. Once I recovered, I was on the football team playing at the position of blocking back.

San Pedro High Football Team was then playing the UCLA style single-wing formation. The coach was Bill Seixas, a former All American Guard on the USC Football Team years before. The Single-Wing formation differed from traditional football formations as the primary ball passer was the tail-back and not the quarter back. As blocking back I played in the quarter back position and the tail back, performing the duties of the quarter back, played in the right running back position with the line off balanced to the right side. This formation was confusing to some especially the opposing teams.

The offensive line had only one tackle but had three guards, the running guard, pulling guard and the standing guard. The blocking back was the primary blocker for the tail back rather than the traditional left tackle. Standouts on the team included my friends Franklin Jones, end, Hank Edney, running back and lineman Melvin Haynes. Jimmy Zar was the tail back and Bob Petrich played in the tight end position. The center was Don Vaughn. My contribution to the team overall was questionable but I had a lot of fun.

As a member of the school year book staff, we organized, planned and laid out the book for printing. This included taking photographs on campus and structuring the book's content. One of the staff members, Janice Ong, was planning to be a candidate for Student Body President and she asked me to work on her campaign. Previously there had never been a female elected to that office. I agreed and together

Peter's high school graduation photo.

with others we mounted signs around campus, campaigned for her and she won the election.

Her primary opponent was a very good friend of mine, James (Duck) McCutcheon and a star on the basketball team. His moniker obviously came from my brother Charles. James had entered the race after I had agreed to support Janice. He and I remained friends even though he lost the race to Janice. Years later Dr. Janice Ong became a full Professor at the University of California at Davis and Dr. James McCutcheon became an ordained Minister and Pastor in Texas.

San Pedro

HIGH SCHOOL

San Pedro, California

1957 - 58

STUDENT IDENTIFICATION CARD

Student's Signature

AUTHORIZED BY

PRINCIPAL

As previously mentioned, one of my good friends in high school was Fred Miller. Fred and I first met in the seventh grade at Dana when we both played percussions in the school orchestra. We were friends through high school and remained so when Fred returned from serving in the U.S. Coast Guard and I returned from my first tour in the U.S. Army.

In our spare time Fred played with a band named The Collegians, which played rock and roll while I played with a band named The Fascinators, which played rhythm and blues. In those days if a recording was made by a White recording artist it was called rock and roll and if performed by a Negro recording artist it was called rhythm and blues. These terms were coined by the radio disk jockeys primarily to appease the radio listening audiences in the south, where in many instances, White parents refused to allow their children to listen to "black music." Over the next few years they would merge into one, rock and roll.

Fred and I both met our high school dream of playing drums in a dance band and he and I remained friends for the remainder of his life. He was a railroad aficionado and I plied him with books on trains which were purchased at the Sacramento Train Museum where I would often visit for that purpose. I was a speaker at his memorial service in 2014.

Another activity while in high school was that I and several members of the school orchestra performed with the South Bay Community Symphony Orchestra which practiced at the high school in the evenings. This was a civic based orchestra comprised of local citizens, including high school students and alumni and part of the adult school curriculum. The conductor was my high school orchestra teacher, Mr. Milton Asher, who was also serving as a Captain in the Army National Guard. Many years later I served with him in the Army National Guard when I was a Lieutenant Colonel and he was a Warrant Officer after himself initially holding the rank as a Lieutenant Colonel. In order to remain in the service he voluntarily relinquished his commissioned officer rank to that of a warrant officer.

My exposure to a variety of music in the community orchestra led me to appreciate a myriad of music forms other than pop, rhythm and blues, jazz and rock and roll. Over the years I have become an aficionado of classical music and play it often along with show music, my favorites being South Pacific, Oklahoma, Porgy and Bess and Guys and Dolls.

One can never forget their high school prom and I attended two. In my junior year my date was a girl whom I invited and as a senior my date was a girl who invited me. Both went on to become college graduates. It was reported to me that one became a teacher and the other a registered nurse.

It was another high school co-ed whom I spent much of my social time with and she attended the local all-girls Catholic High School. I can best describe our relationship as pretty much platonic and never having become serious. I spent many evenings at her house visiting with her family which consisted of three brothers and three sisters. Most enjoyable to me were the conversations I had with her father, a former US Marine. During World War Two he had been what would later be called a Montfort Point Marine, black Marines who were stationed at Montfort Point, South Carolina in the then racially segregated Marine Corps. A Knight of Columbus, he occasionally spoke about his Montfort Point Marine Corps experiences.

CHAPTER 16 FIRST MILITARY CAREER; ARMY NATIONAL GUARD

I joined the Army National Guard 1959. San Pedro had a National Guard Armory just one block from the high school which I walked passed every day. That was the most logical place to enlist so I went there for that purpose. I met with the White Sergeant on duty and expressed my intentions to join but he advised that I could not join that unit because all of the positions were filled. He directed me to the next nearest unit which was in Torrance, CA about 12 miles distance.

A few days later I borrowed one of the family's cars and drove there. The White Sergeant in Torrance also advised they too had no open positions but he suggested I go to the Armory near downtown Los Angeles at Exposition Park, as they were certain to have openings. Eventually I drove there, inquired and introduced myself to the duty officer.

ENLISTMENT

The unit I was referred to was the 119th Military Police Battalion and there I met a Negro Chief Warrant Officer who was a World War Two and Korean War combat veteran. During the interview he asked where I lived and I responded that I resided in San Pedro (about 25 miles away). I recall that he remarked something to the extent that was quite a ways to come. I explained that the San Pedro Armory had no openings and he questioned why I went there in the first place.

Explaining that it was the closest to my home so then I related that I went to Torrance to enlist. Again he wondered why I went there. After explaining that it was second nearest to my home but they too had no opening and that the Sergeant there had referred me to him explaining that a Warrant Officer at the Exposition Park Armory was a good friend.

119th Military Police Battalion (Negro), Private Peter Gravett top row (6th from right)

The Warrant Officer then explained that I should have never gone to either place to enlist because they were White units and this was a Negro unit; "*our unit*" as I recall him saying. This was in 1959 and I had not realized that even though the US Army had integrated 11 years earlier the National Guard in California, and in most other states, was still segregated, some states barring Negro's from the National Guard altogether I leaned.

This was because the President's Executive Order Number 9980 in 1948 which required the military to integrate only applied to federal (regular) forces and not state military forces under the control of the Governor such as the National Guard in all of the states. I later I learned that the San Pedro unit had recently enlisted two or three Negro's and they were not about to enlist any more.

In 1959 without my parents' consent I was sworn-in a few days prior to my 18th birthday by the Chief Warrant Officer, James E. Harris, and issued my first military serial number. I am certain that the enlistment papers were pre-dated to reflect my eligibility at age 18 but I never knew at the time.

This would be the first of three different Army serial numbers I would have in my career. The second was an officers' serial number issued when I received my commission and the third was my social security number when all military services replaced service numbers with previously issued social security numbers. In retirement I was issued a fourth serial number as all military services eliminated the use of social security numbers due to the proliferation of stolen identities.

Off to Basic Training

When I enlisted with the 119th at the Exposition Park Armory and took and passed my physical examination where I was issued a duffle bag containing used military uniforms and boots. I recall that the boots had heels that were worn over and the uniform fatigue shirts and trousers were of World War Two or Korean War vintage with metal buttons. Although originally the same shade and color they did not match due to wear, wash and fading. These were the uniforms I would take to my basic training and wear during the first few weeks as was the custom in those days.

A short time later I received my orders to report to Fort Ord, California for Basic Training. A large envelop was provided containing my orders, a Greyhound Bus ticket and several tear-off scripts for food to be used at the various lunch counters at bus stations along the way.

This was my first trip on a Greyhound Bus and as it turned out it was a local run as opposed to an express run and seemed to stop at every coastal city's Greyhound Bus Station; some stops for 30 minutes or more. The whole trip took more than 14 hours and I recall traveling along the then, in some stretches, a two lane 101 highway prior to freeway construction.

At that time, little could I have imagined that this was a journey into the world of the military which would last more than 40 years and touch parts of six decades?

Fort Ord sat geographically on the mouth of the Monterey Bay and was a picturesque location though the weather could be very cold and windy even during summer

Private Gravett with broken nose.

months. During the first week of training I was appointed acting squad leader because of my expert marching ability learned in the DAPs. My only injuries in basic training was a broken nose and cheek bone.

During the fifth week, as I was lying in my lower bunk one evening as everyone in the barracks was "horsing around" two of my fellow soldiers began rocking the upper bunk in order to dislodge the soldier there. In the "horse play" the side slats supporting the upper bunk dislodged with the frame falling on my face breaking my nose and fracturing a cheek bone. I was taken to the hospital in a semi-conscious state where my nose bone was reset and stuffed with gauze. The pain, as I clearly remember, was extremely excruciating and I was bleeding profusely.

Due to my injury I was placed on light duty not having to perform physical training or field training but I was required to attend all classroom instruction. At the conclusion of training I was designated the Honor Graduate by the cadre after having been evaluated against many other soldiers and had the privilege of carrying the company guidon at the graduation ceremony.

When I graduated from Basic Training I received orders for Advanced Infantry Training at that same duty station though many of my Regular Army Basic Training buddies were shipped to other posts throughout the country.

Private Gravett Army Basic Training Graduation.

Since I had enlisted in an MP Battalion both my unit and I expected me to be sent to Fort Gordon, Georgia where I would undertake training at the Military Police School. Much later I learned that most of the new enlistees in the National Guard and Army Reserve performed their advanced training at one of the various schools at Fort Ord in order to save on travel funds. For this reason almost all reservists attended advanced infantry training, supply school training or administrative clerk training regardless of their duty position in their unit.

`The eight weeks of advanced infantry training included two weeks of bivouac, which is camping in the field, army style. During this period we practiced many field events previously taught in indoor class rooms and outdoor bleacher classrooms. Our meals consisted of C-Rations, the army having previously transitioned away from World War Two and Korean War era K-Rations. Each packet was a complete nutritious meal of a main dish canned entrée with condiments. A miniature can opener called a "P-38" was in every packet.

Hot coffee was available and consumed in the canteen cup while the canteen held water. The two-piece aluminum mess kit was used as a plate when hot meals were available. This was all exciting to me, as a young volunteer but not so to the many soldiers a few years older who had been drafted.

Night maneuvers included live fire exercises, negotiating the concentration course which consisted of soldiers crawling on their back through sand with their rifle barrel pointed over the helmet lip for safety and passing under concertina wire while a machine gun fired overhead.

119th Military Police Battalion (Negro), Private Peter Gravett top row (6th from right)

Field sanitation techniques were stressed for hygiene reasons, such as digging slit trenches to relieve one self. The steel pot (helmet) was used as a wash basin for multiple purposes. Long marches with a full field pack were standard. We slept in a pup tent made up of two shelter halves, every soldier had one half of the tent, which when combined became a full pup tent and was shared by two soldiers.

Both Basic Training and Advance Infantry Training accomplished what was intended; transitioning me from a civilian to a soldier. As mentioned training consisted of both class room and field instruction which included subjects such as drill and ceremony, physical training, battle field first aid, weapons training, squad tactics, code of conduct, nuclear, biological and chemical warfare, inspections, uniform requirements and a plethora of other subjects including recent military history. After eight weeks of advanced infantry training I was assigned to an on-post unit as permanent party as a clerk because I could type at least 30 words per minute. I quickly learned that the needs of the Army came first.

At the completion of this tour of duty I was released to report back to my home unit to attend monthly drill assemblies and two weeks of annual field training and I was promoted from Private E-1 to Private E-2. About a year later I was again promoted this time to the exalted rank of Private First Class.

HOME STATION TRAINING

In those days our drill assemblies were every other Tuesday evening and one Sunday per month all day. Years later most reserve units conducted "Battle Drills" once a month over a three day weekend as well as week night staff meeting once or twice a month. Back then once a year we would have a full weekend of training where we traveled in two and a half ton trucks to Camp Pendleton US Marine Corps Base for weapons qualifications with the M-1 rifle. This was long before the construction of the 405 and 5 freeways and from down town Los Angeles we traversed the length of US highway 101 passing through many of the beach cities and stopping at all of the red traffic signals.

For our summer field training we convoyed north to Camp Roberts passing through all of the Southern Coastal and Central Coast cities again observing all traffic lights and intermingling with the local traffic. This was also prior to the 101 freeway construction. We were advised not to stop in small towns as some fast food places and restaurants did not serve Negros.

SEGREGATION A REALITY EVEN IN CALIFORNIA

During my first training assembly with the 119th MP Battalion I was confronted with the true reality of a segregated National Guard. All of the officers were Negro except for a White Regular Army Captain whose position was unit advisor. The Headquarters Company enlisted soldiers were almost all Negro except for two Asians and two or three Jewish soldiers all whom, by choice, could be assigned there.

BATTALION ORGANIZATION

The Battalion Headquarters had excess field grade senior officers (Majors and above). Typically a Battalion will be commanded by a Lieutenant Colonel and having Majors as the Executive Officer and the S-3 or Operations Officer; three field grade officers total. This Battalion Headquarters had a full Colonel as the Commander, Colonel Orlando Flowers, and several field grade officers.

The Headquarters also had at least ten Captains. This was because the unit was one of the few Negro National Guard unit in Southern California placing the officers double and sometimes triple "slotted" in the same duty positions. Many of them were Korean War veterans and a few were World War Two veterans, including a Tuskegee Airman.

In his civilian employment our Commander, Colonel Flowers, had been appointed Postmaster of Los Angeles and was recognized many years later for having developed the nationwide Zip Code System. Some of the officers that I recall were Major William Armstrong and his brother Major Ollie Armstrong, Major Adams, a civilian Minister though not an Army Chaplain, Major Aaron Herrington, a former Tuskegee Pilot, Captain Lloyd Goddard School Teacher, Captain Cornelius Cooper, Police officer, Captain Lloyd Watson, Postal Mail Carrier, Chief Warrant Officer James E. Harris, Fulltime Duty Officer and Warrant Officer Lewis Rhone, Social Worker.

Non-Commissioned Officers were Sergeant Major Otis Hudson (a member of the family which founded black owned and operated Broadway Savings and Loan in Los Angeles), Sergeant First Class Henderson, Mess Sergeant, and Sergeant First Class Willie Washington, fulltime Supply Sergeant, Sergeant Clarence Stubblefield and Sergeant Charles Giles. There were also many others. Many years later I learned that Frances Stubblefield, Clarence's wife, and my wife, Blanche, were teachers in the same elementary school

INTEGRATION

In the early 1960's when Governor Edmund G. (Pat) Brown integrated the California National Guard the all-Negro units were disbanded and most of the Negro Field Grade Officers and Senior Non-Commissioned Officers (NCO's) involuntarily transferred to the In-Active Army Reserve by the National Guard leaders. I feel certain that this was not the intent of the new Governor but that was the unintended consequences.

Some of the lower ranking officers and NCO's, Captains, Lieutenants and Warrant Officers as well as Sergeants First Class and lower ranking Sergeants, were retained.

Most reserve units performed their annual field training during the summer months when school was out. All of the facilities at Camp Roberts were open for that purpose including the Post Exchange, Commissary, Snack Bar, Swimming Pool, Recreation Center, and the clubs;

Enlisted, NCO's and Officers. The White units had the use of these entities during their training periods however the Negro units did not perform their training until September, well after most local schools had resumed classes for the fall term, and all of these military facilities had closed down for the year.

According to a passage in Major General James Delk's book *The Fighting Fortieth; In War and Peace: "In 1967 there was only 1.97 percent Negroes in the National Guard nationwide."* It was also known that several states had no Negroes at all as their Guard was for Whites only.

Enlisting in the 119th I learned that it was not the only segregated National Guard unit in the state. Others were the 1401st Engineer Battalion headquartered in Northern California and the 1402nd Engineer Battalion with its' headquarters in Southern California. Both organizations had company size units in various communities which had a concentration of Negro residents. Both battalions were essentially general labor organizations and performed few, if any, engineering missions.

As mentioned, during the summer, my National Guard unit performed Annual Field Training at Camp Roberts. During several of these training periods I served as the driver for the Battalion Commander, Colonel Orlando Flowers. Periodically Colonel Flowers was required to attend Commanders meetings at the Ranch House where I drove him and parked the military vehicle in the parking lot. I sometimes visualized what the house' interior looked like. Later I would experience it.

A year after returning from my initial Army tour at age 19, I became employed at Douglas Aircraft Company in Long Beach, California while continuing my military service in the California Army National Guard serving in the headquarters of the 119th MP Battalion. A friend worked at Douglas and arranged for me to secure a position as a blue printer, a job which I had absolutely no experience but learned quickly.

With the integration of the National Guard the 119th MP Battalion was deactivated and I was reassigned to Troop F, 1st Squadron, 18th Armored Cavalry Regiment (Note: Armored Cavalry and Cavalry units are a mixture of tanks and armored infantry fighting vehicles, not horses, and Air Cavalry units consists of attack helicopters).

The Cavalry Squadron is where I received my initial training as a tank crewman. By this time, I had received two additional promotions; to Specialist Fourth Class and to Sergeant. I would later serve most of my assignments in armor or cavalry units. The 18th Armored Cavalry Squadron became an integrated unit once I and many of my fellow soldiers from the 119th were assigned there. There were no racial issues there that I remember.

The unit was located in Little Rock, California in the high desert east of the City of Lancaster and that unit drilled one full weekend every month. Since most of the former 119th unit members resided in the Central Los Angeles area we gathered at our former armory, loaded up on two and a half ton trucks with canvas tops and convoyed by highway to the high desert near Lancaster for the weekend.

There was a concentration site there which housed the fenced-in tanks and other military vehicles. The high desert location was ideal for tank units as they could conduct maneuvers with a wide swath of terrain devoid of any close by communities.

I spent many weekends there undergoing tank operations instruction and tank warfare training. We initially trained on the M-47 tank, a World War Two and Korean War relic and later to the upgraded M-48 (Patton) tank. These were the first of several tanks that I would eventually crew in my career. Others were the M-60 (Patton Main Battle) tank, M-60A1 & A3, M-1 and finally the M-1A1 (Abrams Main Battle) tank. This is where I received my final two promotions as an enlisted soldier; to Staff Sergeant and to Sergeant First Class.

CHAPTER 17 COLLEGE CAREER

In 1960 I enrolled at Los Angeles Harbor College as my first college experience after high school and I had no expectations of myself academically. Other than police science I had not even considered other courses which means I had no concept of what a police science major entailed. With no real counseling beforehand I felt my way through by asking friends attending there what classes they were taking. Upon learning that several were required of first semester students I enrolled in some.

The college had a contest to name the newly constructed Student Union facility so I submitted several names and was thoroughly surprised that one of mine was the winning entry. Today the name Sea Hawk Center is emblazoned on a plaque in the Student Union with my name affixed. I also pledged a fraternity, Theta Xi Omega, and I was inducted after much hazing. This was a party fraternity and we did that a lot, all too often skipping classes.

During the summer some fraternity members and I took a planned day trip to Catalina Island but we eventually stayed several days; this without required essentials. We slept on the golf course along with scores of other college students. On the second day I bumped into a cousin, Gertrude Gipson, who gave me a blanket and a few dollars which I used to buy a few notions. Gertrude lived on the island part-time with her then boyfriend who owned and operated the only recycle (junk) yard on the island.

For physical education at Harbor College I joined the intramural wrestling team and spent the first semester learning the intercollegiate form of wrestling, far different from what I had witnessed on television, which was staged. Later, I engaged in competitive matches with others in my weight class, winning some matches and losing some. I would chalk it up to the fact that I was just learning the sport while other were more experienced. No excuses. After two semesters, I transferred to Long Beach City College which had a more robust and comprehensive Police Science curriculum. Another reason for the transfer was to get serious about my fledging college education and to leave the party scene.

My study skills were deficient in high school and I took that deficiency to Harbor College. Joining the Theta Xi Omega fraternity only further exacerbated to my lack of academic focus. It was only during a graduation ceremony on campus where I looked out from my lofty perch washing dishes in the student union observing the flowing gowns worn by the graduates and their mortarboard tassels billowing in the wind that I came to the realization that if I wanted what I was viewing I needed to get serious about my college education. At that point I knew that I had to start anew at another college and transferred to Long Beach City College.

My classes there were part-time while I worked full time. For the first time I became a serious student with a focus to achieve the maximum grade in every class primarily with the specific required non-police science courses. Unlike Harbor College, Long Beach had a first class football team and although I had no interest nor the time to engage in on campus activities I did attend football games. During this period the football team won the Junior Rose Bowl championship several years running. The then Junior Rose Bowl was a game played between the top two Junior Colleges in the nation, the winner being crowned as the National Champion.

I graduated in 1965 with an Associate of Arts degree in Police Science with a substantial increase in grade point average by way of receiving A's in every one of my classes bar none. Following graduation I transferred to the then Long Beach State College. I declared a major in Criminology with a minor in Criminalistics.

NOT EVERYONE IN CALIFORNIA HAD CIVIL RIGHTS

The early 1960s was a ripe time for civil rights demonstrations everywhere. Blacks were overtly being discriminated against while seeking employment, in the public schools, by law enforcement, the courts and in the rental and the purchasing of homes.

During this era in our history for African Americans there were two paths to follow to correct these inequities. One was the passive disobedience route espoused by Dr. Martin Luther King and traditional civil rights organizations such as the National Association for the Advancement of Colored People (NAACP). The NAACP was demonstrating for the rights of Negros to vote, primarily in the south, and have equal access to fair housing nationwide. This was the oldest civil rights organization in the nation (founded in 1909) which abhorred violence.

The other approach, or path, was direct action espoused by activists such as fire brands Stokley Carmichael, H. Rapp Brown, LeRoi Jones, Cinque and others who often engaged in physical confrontation with authority. I had always respected Dr. King and followed his teachings and leadership.

After I had been a member of the local Chapter of the NAACP I was elected Chapter President and a White friend, a local union organizer, was elected Vice President. When we learned of a local super market refusing to accept job applications from blacks, there was a decision made by members to conduct an exercise in passive civil disobedience.

On several days spaced apart some chapter members, both black and White, young and old and male and female, would enter the market portending to be shoppers. They would leisurely walk the aisles filling shopping carts with both perishable and staple food items and then walk out of the store leaving the full baskets in the aisles.

This was done time and again many times on the same day with different "shoppers," each one never returning. The store personnel would never know who performed these acts or when it would occur therefor were not able to ward it off. After repeating this for a while one of the members telephoned the store manager to inquire when they would start accepting job applications from blacks and the manager got the word.

Another passive act of civil disobedience was picketing with signs on the sidewalk in front of a new housing construction site at a nearby city because the new housing had signage indicating that Negros need not apply. They were so bold to do this and it was overt discrimination at its worse. This was because the city had an ordinance barring blacks from residing within the city limits. This was not the 1920s but the early 1960s. This overt human rights violation made the evening T.V. news.

Our NAACP Chapter Vice President and I, along with many others, took on the challenge of picketing until the signage was removed and the local home builder pledging to sell the homes to anyone qualified. Shortly thereafter, the California Legislature passed the Rumford Fair House Initiative, Proposition 64, which barred discrimination in home sales. The Bill had been drafted by Assemblyman Byron Rumford. Even today there is still an undercurrent of realtors making it difficult for all Californians to purchase the home of their choice.

CHAPTER 18 PATH TO POLICE OFFICER

My two lifelong ambitions were to become both a police officer and a soldier and I eventually achieved both. From the first and only time I saw my father in his army uniform, when I was about five years old, I wanted to be like him and from the time I joined the DAPs I wanted to become a Policeman like Gil, Officer Morris Gilmore, the DAP Coordinator.

I took and passed the written examination for Police Officer at age 19 which I could do at the time but could not be appointed until age 21. The written examination was given at Hollywood High School where two of my friends from San Pedro and I were tested. We all passed.

The next phase of testing was a physical agility test given at the Police Academy in Elysian Park. This consisted of push-ups and sit-ups, a requisite number required during a given time. It also required a timed run. We all passed this phase also.

The most difficult part of the test for me and every candidate being tested was the strength test. This consisted of rapidly maneuvering a couple of two-foot long iron very heavy train rails from a chest high bench to the ground and back to the bench. This was extremely difficult and after the first minute and there was a number of repetitions required over a timed period. We also passed that test but at a price for me. For the next several days the muscles on my shoulders, forearms, back and stomach paid the price as they were extremely sore.

The next phase of the processing was appearing before an oral interview panel which consisted of two Police Sergeants and a civilian; a community leader. I was quizzed on a variety of situational questions of "what if" but where common sense answers were expected. The final question, of course, was *"why do you want to be a police officer?"* My answers to all of the questions apparently satisfied the panel and I was approved having been prepped by Police

Officer Gilmore, my DAP Coordinator. The next phase was the medical examination.

The medical examination was administered at the Los Angeles Central Receiving Hospital by a Police Physician. An examination of my entire body was checked including all vitals, measurement of hands, fingers and toes. That I never understood. Later I did understand why my finger were checked; to uncover any evidence of fingernail biting. It was believed that the habit of biting the fingernails could be a system of nervousness or fidgeting. Either could be a cause for medical or mental disqualification.

The personal background investigation was the final phase. That started by first meeting with the investigator to gather additional information not provided or required on the original application such as names, addresses and occupations of personal references. These could consist of previous employers, former teachers and neighbors. Personal friends, clergy and family members were not allowed as references.

I was quizzed on whether or not I had ever been arrested, detained or had appeared in juvenile or adult court. I was questioned as to whether or not I had used an illegal drugs, consumed alcohol or had been a party in any law suit. I was questioned on whether or not I had any traffic citations.

The three references I listed were all DAP Coordinators; Police Officers Morris Gilmore, Policewomen Chloe Gilmore and Betty Bowden and also Policewoman Franchon Blake. Even though the investigation spent considerable time interviewing family members, neighbors, school officials and others, as well as reviewing my high school and college records, I was approved in record time perhaps due to the identity of my references.

One of my friends also passed all of the phases but one was disqualified for unknown medical reasons.

In 1961 at age 20 after I had successfully completed all of the qualifying examinations I was appointed to the Department in August 1962 and graduated twelve weeks later in October 1962.

I reported to the academy prepared to undergo the rigors of training along with 68 other wide-eyed recruits, including Benny Martinez, one of my high school classmates. Benny and I would car pool during our entire time there. Benny had a new car which ran well and I had an older car which always had mechanical problems. By the end of the first day two recruits had been dismissed for unknown reasons. This caught the attention of the whole class wondering who would be next. This reinforced the chain which purported that only one in seven applicants passing the written test would eventually graduate from the academy.

Over the next twelve weeks we were taught a complete array of courses all designed to prepare us for a law enforcement career. These included criminal law, civil law, patrol procedures, juvenile procedures, report writing, weapons training and marksmanship, physical training and self-defense, first aid, defensive driving, field interrogation and interviewing techniques, arrest procedures, evidence processing techniques, search and seizure, accident investigation, court testimony, narcotics and alcohol recognition and much more, including emergency water rescue.

Weekly examinations were standard which required lots of homework and preparation. It seemed every week one or two classmates would disappear for a reason unknown to the class.

PEER EVALUATIONS AND TERMINATIONS

The Academy staff encouraged competition among class members and every week each of us were required to identify who we believed to be the top five cadets and the bottom five cadets with each person using their own criteria.

It is my recollection that it was about this time that the sole Negro Officer on the academy staff advised the

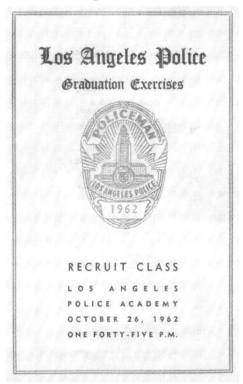

Los Angeles Police

Graduation Exercises

RECRUIT CLASS

LOS ANGELES
POLICE ACADEMY
OCTOBER 26, 1962
ONE FORTY-FIVE P.M.

LAPD Graduation Announcement

eight Negro cadets and warned us that, no matter what, of the eight only four would graduate indicating that was the way it was with the LAPD. This was regardless of standing in the class. I recall that he warned us not to worry about competing with the class as a whole but to compete against each other. True to his word only four of us eventually graduated. Though I vividly recalled the admonition given by the staff officer I learned that others did not recall such an admonition. I believe that I was never in jeopardy of failing or being terminated but one never knows.

The Los Angeles Police Department is governed under the civil service system, generally a fair system of employment, where police candidates are tested and appointed by the City Personnel Department. Termination from academy training however is the prerogative of the Police Department therefore the dismissal of a police cadet while in training lies at the hands of the academy staff with very little appeal options if any. It is not known whether or not the four Negro Officers terminated exercised any appeal or whether their termination was justified or not.

While undergoing training four of us classmates often held weekend study sessions at the home of Bill Ellis in Long Beach. Harreld Webster, Don Ferrell and I were pleased to be invited to Bill's house where his wife, Gloria, often had nice refreshments. This was pleasing because at the time Don and I were both single.

PATROL RIDE-A-LONGS

After the seventh week of training we had our first Saturday night ride-a-longs with a training officer at one of the then 16 area police stations. I was assigned to Harbor Station in San Pedro where I grew up and still lived. This was not the most practical decision because just seven weeks prior I was a young man in the neighborhood walking or driving the streets with friends and now I would be seen riding as a uniformed police officer in a police car.

At my first roll call I heard the word "Nigger" more than once when an officer was referring to a wanted suspect or a victim and I opined this was specifically for my benefit but it could have also been the norm. He was

Peter's Police Academy Graduating Class

never challenged for the remark either by the other officers or the supervisors.

At this roll call, I was introduced to my training officer for the watch. After we were seated in the police car in the station parking lot he advised me in a not so friendly manner that he had never worked with a Colored officer before and I replied that I too had never worked with a Colored officer before (truthfully I had never before worked with any officer Colored or otherwise). He then in an aggravated tone said words to the affect that I had better back him up if he needed it and I responded that I would and that I hoped that he would also back me. My non-challenging retort was to indicate to him that I was a probationary cadet and needed mentoring by him.

At this point he became antagonistic and told me to just ride and keep my mouth shut. The remainder of the evening did not go well and I felt relieved when the watch ended. His report on me back to the academy was not a pleasant one. In fact it was very negative but somehow I survived.

The remainder of the weekend ride-a-longs went better. I later learned that I was the first black police recruit in LAPD history ever assigned to Harbor Division and only the third black officer assigned there ever, the first two having been assigned there just two months earlier, one in traffic and one in patrol.

In October 1962, I graduated from the Academy and the class held a graduation party where we "roasted" some of our instructors. Some class mates reported to their first duty station the following day.

CHAPTER 19 FIRST LAPD ASSIGNMENT

As we neared our graduation date I was interviewed by two detectives who recommended that I be assigned as an undercover narcotics officer. I expressed my desire instead to be assigned to uniformed patrol but that did not happen right away. I, along with two other black officers, were assigned to undercover operations, two of us in narcotics

The Big 4 (from left) Peter Gravett, Harreld Webster, Eudon Ferrell and Bill Ellis

and the other one in vice. The final black officer, Eudon (Don) Ferrell, had been voted class president, and was assigned to uniform patrol.

The four of us would become lifelong friends and would celebrate every year with just the four of us or sometimes with our spouses. We became the "Big Four" and celebrated our reunions over the years either in Los Angeles, Las Vegas, San Diego or on a cruise. Sometimes we gathered in one of our homes.

Years later after our respective retirements from the Police Department we each had second careers. Don, after attending law school and serving as an Assistant City Attorney, was appointed to a Superior Court Judgeship. Bill, who had excelled in basketball at UCLA prior to attending the academy and being selected to the then

Big 4 with spouses (from left) Bill & Gloria Ellis, Eudon & Toni Ferrell, Harreld & Pauline Webster & Peter & Blanche Gravett.

predecessor of what is today the PAC 12 Conference, became a County Marshal in Las Vegas, Nevada. Harreld, already an ordained Deacon, attended Seminary and was ordained as a minister and served as the Assistant Pastor at a local church. I, of course after having returned to the military, was eventually promoted to the two star rank of Major General which will be discussed later. Our lives remain intertwined and also those of our wives.

UNDER COVER ASSIGNMENT

After graduation from the Academy Harreld and I was assigned to work undercover as noted. Working undercover was an interesting assignment. Thankfully I was not assigned to work back in my old neighborhood. That would not have never worked and I could never understand why it was even seriously considered.

Prior to being sent to specific locations in the city to purchase illegal drugs I was given a cursory briefing on techniques and tactics on how to engage and survive on the streets in the drug world, all of it totally useless. Having been raised in two public housing projects I already had some street smarts as drugs and crime, at times, were a way of life for many people in the neighborhood.

One of the first things I wanted to do upon academy graduation was to purchase a new car. Driving a new car was prohibited while working undercover and it was suggested that I use my then 1953 beat up Ford. Working undercover also prohibited having any police identification whatsoever. No gun, no badge and no identification card. I was instructed to never visit a police station and never be seen voluntarily conversing with any law enforcement officer. If for some reason I was stopped for a traffic citation to not identify myself as a police officer and just give the ticket to my "handler."

My handler was a seasoned narcotics detective whom I generally met with once a week to be given cash money for my operation. We always met a non-descript pre-arranged location where I was required to sign a receipt (chit) for the money and account for any previous funds given and disbursed for drug purchases.

"GOTCHA"

Of the numerous drug transactions undertaken during this time one really stood out. I had been told that a local pimp and drug dealer, Stanley Roberts (a pseudonym) in the Venice area of the City had avoided being arrested for several years and to focus on orchestrating a sale to him.

I hung around the area for some time buying drugs from many of the local dealers. Once a purchase was made I avoided them again because after their first sale to me and they were not arrested they wanted to keep selling as I became a good target for sales and also they believed I was not a police officer, a "Narc." After the first sale they were as good as "bought and paid for" with an eventual arrest. Additional purchases from the same seller would be a waste of the city's money.

Stanley was aware that I bought heroin from some of his cohorts and was familiar with me. It was my intent to not approach him to buy right away suspecting that he was still not sure if I was a cop or not. Eventually he did approach me but I made up some lame excuse and turned him down. I doubted that he even had any drugs on him then and it was probably a test.

Weeks later, knowing that no arrests had been made in the area following my drug buys he came at me again offering to sell a small balloon of heroin but I suggest that I need a "quarto", a quarter of an ounce in street jargon. He arranged it and I eventually made the buy. Sometime later he was indicted by the County Grand Jury and arrested. Since he had been selling drugs for quite some time he had no idea who the undercover officer was whom he had bought from.

When he appeared in court with his attorney and heard my initial testimony he refused to believe that I was an actual police officer and believed I was just a "snitch" off the street. He was later convicted and given a substantial prison sentence.

SLEEPING ON THE JOB

Another undercover officer, Sam Coleman (pseudonym), and I would team up once in a while to make a drug buy. On one particular transaction we were at a drug house one night in an unsavory part of the city waiting for the drugs to be delivered. Waiting in such a location for drugs was never a good situation. Normally we were quickly just in and out. Anything could go wrong.

The night prior I had been on a late date and had very little sleep prior to reporting for work the next day and was still working into the evening. Sitting on the couch in a drug house I fell asleep as it was very warm inside and the couch was very comfortable. Sam tells the story that the drug dealer was insisting that we use drugs in his presence which was sometime a ploy to ensure we were not cops. Sam insisted that I had passed out due to a drug over dose and he was not going to use drugs on the pretense that he may be stopped by the police. Apparently his ruse worked as we "escaped" from the house undetected after having completed the drug deal. Following that incident I became more cautious.

UNDER COVER PROTOCOLS

No immediate arrests were made after buying drugs from dealers but at the first opportunity I would steal away to a convenient location to record the transaction and write a full report. The drugs, either heroin, marijuana or various barbiturates, at some opportune time would be taken to the police evidence locker and booked as such.

This assignment lasted approximately three months after which I appeared before the County Grand Jury with my reports and read them aloud for the official court record. Indictments were handed down for each subject in the reports and arrest warrants issued. The arrests, or "Round Ups," were orchestrated by various detective units assigned to the geographic areas.

Once our identities were compromised by Grand Jury testimony we were reassigned to uniform patrol and the recruits from the follow-on class took our places. If the subjects plead not guilty and there was a trial I would receive a subpoena to testify in open court revealing my true identity. I also appeared in police uniform on occasion to make the point.

Some arrests were not made until months later when the suspect was finally located, some being in jail or prison on unrelated charges. These types of clandestine operations called the "Buy Program" had been in place in Los Angeles and other cities for many years.

Chapter 20 Central Division Patrol (Tour #1)

My first uniform patrol assignment was at Central Division which covered the downtown area and extended west into the Rampart and Silver Lake communities just east of Hollywood, south towards the industrial areas and the garment district, east to the Los Angeles River and north to Elysian Park and Atwater areas which included Elysian Valley.

Central Division at that time consisted of businesses, residential communities, parks and the large train yard at Union Station. I primarily worked night watch and morning watch with various partners.

Recruits are on a probationary status for nine months after graduation from the academy and generally work three months on each of the three watches before gaining regular status. The final three months is generally worked in a one officer car on the day watch in some areas of the city. Since I had worked undercover I only had six months remaining on probation and all went very smoothly.

Some of my memorable events at Central Division were that my partner, Donald Beasley, an officer a couple of years my senior, and I transported numerous shop lifting suspects to jail from the various downtown department stores after local store security had made the arrests. Several burglary suspects were arrested in the industrial areas east of down town, primarily in the early morning hours after we had staked out specific locations. There were also the routine arrests of a number of intoxicated people on the streets, mostly skid row but also in the shopping areas on Broadway and in the financial district along Flower and Figueroa Streets.

Time and again we would receive a radio call to report to Police Chief William Parker's house in the Silver Lake District where a stolen car had been abandoned.

Thieves, probably juveniles, would steal a car for the sole purpose of joy riding and then park it in front of the Chief's residence. Even though my partners and I, and other officers, often staked out the area no one was ever apprehended during my tour there.

Walking a beat by a police officer is pretty much an East Coast police tradition of law enforcement and is very limited on the West Coast and especially in Los Angeles which consists of over 460 square miles. With the responsibility of this much area it is reasonable that officers patrol in cars and other motorized vehicles.

Officers did walk beats in downtown Los Angeles especially on Main Street, Broadway and along skid row on east 5th street. I was fortunate to have actually walked a beat, stopped and met with store keepers and met other citizens face to face. What an experience.

Officer Beasley, an African American raised in Mexico, spoke fluent Spanish which made it easier to communicate with anyone having that as their primary language.

WRONG TIME, WRONG PLACE AND WRONG NAME (ONE IN A MILLION)

While assigned to Central Division often times we would receive calls to downtown business to see the store detective who had arrested a shop lifting suspect who was being detained. In most instances the arresting detective, more than likely an off-duty police officer, had the crime report and the arrest report already completed. The arrestee had been searched and handcuffed and was awaiting transportation to jail.

Arriving on one call, there was a suspect in custody in a jewelry store and the arresting officer and the proprietor having a lighthearted conversation and laughing. We asked what was going on and were informed that the suspect had attempted to purchase a piece of jewelry with a credit card. The name on the credit card was Seymour David Rosenblat (pseudonym), presumably a

Jewish name, and the person presenting the card was a young black man. Not only did the store owner believe the card did not belong to the man and knew beyond a certainly it did not because it was his own credit card which he had lost earlier in the day. When we learned of this we too started laughing.

En route to the police station I asked the arrestee if he knew why the owner and the detective were aware that the card did not belong to him he had no clue. When told of the name on the card did not match his ethnicity he still had no clue. It was only when we told him that the card actually belonged to the store owner that he confessed that he found it the next block and decided to use it. Wrong time, wrong place and wrong name.

PERHAPS I WAS THE HILLSIDE STRANGLER

On occasion uniform patrol officers are assigned in plain clothes to a Report Car. This was an unmarked police car and the officers did just that, take crime reports. Typically this was when a minor crime had been reported days earlier and the department did not waste valuable resources   sending a two man black and white patrol car to take a simple report such as a window broken by kids in the neighborhood playing ball and the like. This was just malicious mischief or accidental at best.

I was assigned such a duty one day in a one man car and was directed to take a report at a home near the Greek Theater. This was before the new Rampart Division that consumed the Western portion of Central Division.

Dressed in a nice business suit and tie I approached the house and rang the doorbell which was answered by an elderly White woman probably in her late eighties or early nineties. By protocol I identified myself as a police officer and displayed my identification card and badge. She invited me in and explained why she had called the police a few days earlier. I asked if she still wanted a report taken even though there was absolutely no chance that the culprit or culprits would be identified (she actually did have a broken window) and she replied that it was no longer necessary and that the broken window had been replaced the same day.

What came next really surprised me. She then asked if I was the "Hillside Strangler." Given her age and probable diminished mental condition I felt it important to reassure her of my identity. This was at the time that a serial killer dubbed the Hillside Strangler was roaming that part of the city and committing murders by strangling White women who lived alone.

I once again displayed my credentials and offered to have her telephone the police department to confirm my identity. When she ignored that option I explained to her that all of the television news reports and newspaper stories had reported that the Hillside Strangler was a White man and I was a black man, as if she not noticed (what I was really thinking was that if I were that criminal she would be dead by now but, again, given her age I was very understanding).

I then offered to have one of her trusted neighbors from an adjoining apartment come over but by then she was more convinced and offered me a cup of coffee. I felt that she would be more at ease if I accepted and I did. I never learned whether or not she had family or close friends and believed that given the events that had taken place she should not have been living alone. This was just one of many interesting incidents I remembered during that tour at Central Division.

CHAPTER 21 DOROTHY ARRIVES ON THE SCENE

During my second year on the Department I was introduced to the sister of a friend who resided in Long Beach. In those days most of my buddies in San Pedro and I socialized a lot in Long Beach where we would meet a host of beautiful and eligible young women. The friend, Tom Marks, lived in Long Beach but spent time with our San Pedro group.

During one conversation he casually mentioned that his sister would soon be moving to California from Mississippi to live with him. I suggested that he introduce me to her when she arrived and he did. Dorothy Marks arrived in Long Beach on January 2, 1963 and the introduction was made the very next day.

Dorothy in later years.

When I met her I was stunned and my first thoughts were what a beautiful woman. I was struck by her brown hair and green eyes; I learned early on that she abhorred the phrase "High Yellow." I later learned that her deceased father had been half White and her maternal grandmother also half White.

ENGAGEMENT AND WEDDING

Dorothy and I immediately began dating on a regular basis. Our dates took us where typical 20's something young people would go such as restaurants, museums, concerts, movies and shows and sporting events. Our favorite haunts were the Play Boy Club in Century City where I had a key, the "Whiskey A Go-Go" dance club in West Hollywood, the Cinnamon Cinder dance club in the Valley and the Light House Jazz Club in Hermosa Beach. We often double dated with my best friend Melvin Haynes who at the time was dating her cousin Marcia Perteet.

Of all of our haunts our favorite was the Cinnamon Cinder where we often participated in dance contests. The DJ was a no-name young up and coming person by the given name of Bob Eubanks. Bob Eubanks later went on to host several television dance and games shows most notably *The Newly Wed Game Show.*

Dorothy and I alternated attending each other's church, mine the New Testament Missionary Baptist Church in Wilmington and hers, by now, the New Hope Baptist Church in Long Beach. She acquired a position at Long Beach's Saint Mary's Hospital in the Cauterization Laboratory which she thoroughly enjoyed. Coincidently many years later I would serve on the Board of Ambassadors there. The hospital was conveniently located just a few blocks from the apartment she shared with her brother Tom.

The next year just prior to departing to attend a New Years' Eve party at Melvin Haynes's house on December 31, 1964 I proposed to her and she accepted. I had brought a bottle of champagne and two glasses to her apartment and suggested we have a pre-New Year's Eve toast. Unbeknown to her I placed an engagement ring in her glass and filled it. With the first sip she discovered it in astonishment while I asked if she would marry me. The rest is history.

When we arrived at the party which was in full swing she delightfully displayed her ring to the other young women and the evening became a double celebration with congratulatory comments from all.

Gravett family at
Peter & Dorothy's Wedding

We were married on September 26, 1965 at the First Assembly of God Church in the unincorporated community of Wilmington, now incorporated into the City of Carson. The ceremony was officiated by Reverend N. J. Kirkpatrick, Pastor of the New Hope Baptist Church. This was now Dorothy's Pastor as she had joined that congregation shortly after her arrival in California.

Our wedding was a beautiful one with several bridesmaids and groomsmen. The bridesmaids were my sister Gloria, my sisters-in-law Olivia, Dortha, and Marie Livingston. Others were Dorothy's cousin Marcia, her friend Thelma and another girl friend. My groomsmen were my brothers Clarence, Phillip, Leon, William, Charles, Harry and Darnell. Her Maid of Honor was her sister-in-law Betty Marks, wife of her brother Tom, and my Best Man was my best friend Melvin Haynes.

Dorothy's Wedding Party. (From left) Olivia, Thelma, Betty & Dorothy. (From right) Marcia & my sister Gloria.

I became brother-in-law to her siblings; sisters Blondell and Jimmell and brothers L.S., Jonas Jr., Marvin (Richard), Floyd and of course Tom. I also gained a mother-in-law Lilly Mae Marks, whom her children called "Miss Red." Her father, Jonas Sr., had passed away when she was age six.

We honeymooned in Monterey, Carmel and San Francisco driving my white 1960 Chevrolet Impala. We were deeply in love and had a wonderful time driving and conversing and making future plans. On the trip she introduced me to some of her relatives in San Francisco,

Vallejo and Oakland. She had previously informed me that one uncle and several of his children had blue eyes. This contrasted with their dark skin. Upon returning home she ceased her membership at New Hope Baptist Church and began attending my church which was now our church.

The Bride & Groom
Dorothy & Peter.

During our year-long engagement we had searched for a house and purchased one in San Pedro. Her mother had arrived a month prior to the wedding and together they began decorating and furnishing it. Earlier that summer I had graduated from Long Beach City College with an Associate of Arts Degree in Police Science. The ceremony was attended by Dorothy and my brother Curt.

The next year Dorothy and I became the God Parents of my niece Kimberly Gravett, daughter of my brother Phillip and sister-in-law Dortha Gravett. A few years later we became God Parents again this time to Michael Haynes, son of my best friend and wife Melvin and Margie Haynes.

CHAPTER 22 HARBOR DIVISION PATROL

My next LAPD assignment was Harbor Division patrol, the community where I grew up and where we had purchased our home. Although I had lots of friends and relatives in the area the assignment did not inhibit me from performing my duties though I probably arrested someone or issued a traffic citation to someone who knew me or knew a member of my family.

The Geographic's of Harbor Division were the Los Angeles City communities of San Pedro, Wilmington, Terminal Island, Harbor City and the Torrance Shoe String Strip but was within the Los Angeles city boundaries.

I was assigned as a training officer and had police cadets in the patrol car on a weekend ride-along just as I had done. One remarkable thing about this assignment was that I was assigned to the same police station where Policewoman Betty Bowden was assigned. Betty had been the DAP Coordinator when I was an eleven years old and was one of my police application references.

By this time her partner Policeman Morris B. Gilmore (Gil) had passed away and Gil's wife, Policewoman Chloe Gilmore, had retired. Fast forward to 2015; I presented flowers to Betty at a testimonial luncheon given for her by the Legendary Ladies organization; its members being policewomen who had served prior to the position being changed to the unisex title of police officer. This was also prior to women being allowed to serve in a patrol capacity.

The event was held at Taix's Restaurant in Los Angeles and I extended personal remarks thanking her for keeping an 11 year old youngster on the right path. At that I time had known her for over 60 years.

In most patrol divisions it was not uncommon for uniformed patrol officers to receive a 30 day loan (transfer) to perform vice operations. This time limitation served two purposes, it allowed the officer to get a taste of what vice officers experienced and it allowed the vice leadership to observe the officer in order to make a determination as to whether or not the officer should be selected for a full transfer for the standard 18 month tour of duty.

I was approached by the division leadership to determine whether or not I would be interested in the loan and I was not. I had believed that the Sergeants and the Lieutenant knew that I was raised in the area and still lived there. Either they did not know this or had little or no concern. I explained that having spent my youth growing up in the area, my teen years working in the area selling newspapers in the Red Light District, I still knew all of the unsavory characters there. Just as important they all knew me. I had to explain that having spent the better part of almost 10 recent years selling newspapers in and out of the houses of prostitution, pool halls, bars, union halls and other establishment that it would not be wise to attempt to pass myself off as a trick or mark as everyone knew me to be a cop. What were they thinking? Besides, when I was accepted to the academy many of these same individuals had offered congratulations.

WATTS RIOT

It was during this tour at Harbor Division in 1965 that a civil disturbance occurred in the South Central part of the city and was labeled the "Watts Riots" as it started in that neighborhood but quickly spread to other parts of the city. The occurrence was initiated when a California Highway Patrol Officer stopped an African American motorist suspected of driving under the influence although the motorist was later determined to not have been drinking at all. The resultant investigation determined that it was the officer's mistreatment of him as witnessed by bystanders that fueled the riot.

The riot lasted almost a week and cost the lives of scores of citizens and tens of millions of dollars in residential and commercial property loss by fire. After the first few days of the riot I was activated and mobilized with the Army National Guard and returned home and changed from my police uniform to my military uniform. When the Guard was demobilized I returned to my police duties.

More than fifty years later, much of the neighborhood still had not been rebuilt. Shells of burned out building stand as a stark reminder of what once had been various independently owned and operated stores.

A Man and His Television

Every police officer has a bazaar story to tell but some are more interesting than others. My story involves what I will refer to as "a man and his and his television."

I received a radio call to the Shoe String Strip area of the Division that a lady had reported her next door neighbor had died and left his television turned on.

The female caller reported that for a day and a half she had been knocking on his door but there was no answer. From time to time she looked through the living room window and noticed he was in the same position on the couch and looked dead as he had not moved in all of that time. I peered through the same window observed the man sprawled on the sofa.

By this time my Sergeant had arrived and with us both banging on the window and door with no response we decided this was one of those instances where we should make an emergency forced entry. By procedure the ambulance had been summoned and was en route.

We broke the window lock, slid open the window above him and the Sergeant lifted me where I climbed in being careful not to step on him. I did step on the sofa as it was directly below the window. I quickly opened the front door to let in the Sergeant and the neighbor.

The man was very jaundiced and cold to the touch. We turned off the television and stood around waiting the arrival of the ambulance crew while noticing several empty vodka bottles lying around. When the ambulance crew arrived a few minutes later they checked for a pulse or heart beat and could not detect either. Routinely they then put in a call to the Coroner's Office.

About a minute later as all of us stood around talking, the "dead" man quickly sat up in front of this now startled group of so called "dead body experts." Being totally momentarily terrified I jumped and tried to climb back out of the window; the neighbor lady passed out; the Sergeant drew his gun and the ambulance crew ran out the door which they had entered fighting each other as they ran. All of these actions occurring simultaneously.

Here was the take: the gentleman had drank himself into what we later learned to be an alcoholic stupor; consuming so much hard alcohol that he passed out into a condition which simulated death. His skin tone had turned yellowish in color, his heart and pulse rates were so faint and irregular that he had all of the trappings of being deceased as his skin was extremely cold to the touch.

A short time after awakening he was coherent and conversational. To say the least we were delighted that he was alive. Once the lady recovered and was treated by the ambulance crew the man was transported to the hospital for observation and to have his stomach pumped with whatever alcohol was remaining in his system. No doubt his favorite T.V. programs had gone off the air by then.

CHAPTER 23 CENTRAL DIVISION (TOUR #2)

After just over a year at Harbor Division I transferred back to Central Division, this time on Day Watch, in a one-man patrol car for about six months. I then transferred to night watch for a year in a two-man patrol car with partner Robert Nett.

Robert was several years senior and had patrolled Central Division for many years. Most of our patrol area consisted of the down town, skid row, the garment district and South Park near where the convention center was later built. We also patrolled in the B-Wagon (Drunk Wagon) as it was called as its' call sign was 1B1.

In 1B1 we patrolled the skid row area and arrested passed out inebriated homeless people on the sidewalks and transported them to the Parker Center Jail to "sleep it off" before being discharged the next morning. Frequently a person who had been drinking but was not intoxicated would beat on the vehicle back door and demand to be arrested so they could go to jail, have a place to sleep, have a hot shower and get a hot meal knowing full well they would be released the following morning. They were not accommodated.

Shortly thereafter, the "Sunshine Law" was passed which stated in part that habitual drunkenness associated with homelessness was not a crime but a condition. The law provided that the city was required to establish a place of refuge for citizens encountered meeting those conditions.

The law was named for a Native American man with the surname Sunshine who challenged the habitual criminal statute and the law was changed in his favor and applied to others meeting those conditions. The City then opened a facility near skid row to comply with the provisions of the new law. Though funded by the city it was operated by a non-profit community organization. This new procedure benefitted everyone.

A RIDE IN THE PARK

On a given night on patrol with Robert Nett we received a radio call that a vehicle was being driven erratically in Elysian Park. Since this was our area for the evening we quickly drove there and spotted a vehicle parked to the side of the road well within the park matching the description of the one reported. We approached and observed a male slumped over the steering wheel with blood oozing from an apparent gunshot wound to the head. A hand gun was lying nearby.

We summoned an ambulance and a detective unit had which responded took charge of the scene. A check of the license plate revealed that he lived nearby in Elysian Valley, "Frog Town," and we were dispatched to the residence to notify the family if any.

Upon answering our knock on the door a woman appeared and before we could introduce ourselves she remarked, "did he do it himself, or did he have someone else do it?" After being let inside we advised her that although the investigation was still being conducted it appeared that he had shot himself. She so much as remarked that it was expected as he had been very suicidal in the recent past and several times had threatened to shoot himself. Over several months he had received a great deal of counseling for being despondent, the nature of which she did not discuss with us. He had departed home earlier that evening telling his her that he would not be returning.

LOS ANGELES POLICE OFFICERS WIVES CLUB (LA POWS)

After I had been on the Department just a few years Dorothy was invited to become a member of the LA POWS, or the Los Angeles Police Officers Wives Club. After holding various offices for a few years she was eventually voted president. This was a social and charitable organization which provided scholarships to children of police officers. The group and their police officer-husbands socialized quite frequently and we always enjoyed our annual winter weekend trek to Big Bear Mountain where we rented an entire ski lodge.

Other officers and their wives and our friends anxiously looked forward to the LA POWS Annual Red and White Sweet Hearts Ball held at the Proud Bird Ball Room near the Los Angeles International Airport. This was usually around Valentine's Day with the room decorated to reflect the theme.

The LA POWS was formed in the 1950's as a Negro police officer's wives club because the existing LAPD wives group, WOLAPOS (Wives of Los Angeles Police Officers) was exclusively for White's only and barred Negro wives. This was at a time when the LAPD was still segregated.

LAPD SEGREGATION HISTORY

Prior to the 1960s the Los Angeles Police Department was segregated and Negro officers were assigned as patrol partners to one of three police stations in the Negro neighbors of the city, 77th Street, Newton Street and University Division, since renamed Southwest Division. The stations had both black and White officers assigned but were not permitted to patrol with one another.

Black officers generally coordinated their days off together but if one officer needed to take a sick day off his partner reluctantly had to take one of his regular days off. The department gradually began to integrate in the early 1960s but a black detective was not allowed to work with a White female detective until the 1980s.

Also during the 1960's Police Sergeant Tom Bradley, later Mayor Bradley, promoted to Lieutenant, then the highest rank which could be held by a black officer, and only one at a time. Policewomen of all ethnic groups were capped at the rank of Sergeant until the 1970s when then

Policewoman Sergeant Franchon Blake, a White Police Woman, was successful in her law suit against the city which lifted the artificial barrier. Sergeant Blake had been one of my character references when I had applied to the Department. She was an Army Veteran of World War Two who had attained the rank of Major, prior to discharge.

Until the 1960s black officers were also barred from performing in the LAPD Band. A black officer once related to me that when his application to join the band had been denied due to his race he appealed directly to Police Chief Parker. The Chief told him that he had the best police band in the nation and the reason was that he never interfered with the band rules, regulations and policies. So if the band director denied him entry that was OK by him. Often times black officers found it difficult to acquire an "inside" or administrative staff assignment which was crucial for promotional purposes.

These practices by Chief Parker were not surprising as during the sixteen years he served as Chief of police he condoned a segregated department. Following his demise while still in office a series of future Chiefs of Police rolled back Chief Parker's unofficial policies and practices of covert segregation.

CHAPTER 24 ACCIDENT INVESTIGATION DIVISION

Following Central Division I next transferred to Accident Investigation Division (A.I.D.), the white hats, which operated out of the same facility as Central Division. The facility was called Parker Center and named after the former and late Police Chief William H. Parker. He had been the Chief from 1950 to his passing in 1966. During most of that time by his own policies he led a segregated police department as mentioned.

My partner at A.I.D. was James Scott, a black officer and product of the former segregated LAPD. During the year we investigated accidents and enforced the traffic laws he imparted to me many stories of the department when it had been segregated confirming some of the foregoing and other such segregated issues of the day.

The primary function of AID was to investigate vehicle traffic accidents and enforcement of traffic laws. During that time LAPD had enforcement responsibilities on freeways within the city limits which were later delegated to the California Highway Patrol. We investigated most traffic accidents on surface streets throughout Metropolitan Los Angeles. The West Los Angeles, Los Angeles Harbor and the San Fernando Valley areas deployed their own traffic units. Our call signs varied depending upon which Division in the metropolitan area of the city we were was assigned.

Many traffic accidents occurred late at night on weekends and usually involved a driver or two who had been drinking. Most field sobriety examinations were given on a well-lit city sidewalk unless the driver in question was so obvious drunk that they were just taken to the police station where they were administered the Breathalyzer test. During those days every driver suspected of driving under the influence were given an option of taking the Breathalyzer test at the police station or having blood drawn by a medical professional. The refusal of either one could result in a suspension of the driver's license for a six month period. This would occur whether or not a conviction in court had been rendered for driving under the influence.

CHAPTER 25 TRAFFIC ENFORCEMENT DIVISION (FOUR WHEELED)

While assigned to AID an experimental police operation was initiated which placed officers in traffic cars for the primary purpose of enforcing traffic but not investigating accidents. Heretofore, this function had only been assigned to motorcycle officers. I was one of sixteen officers selected and assigned to Harbor Division Traffic Enforcement after first undergoing a two week classroom and field driving school. This was in addition to our academy traffic education and the one week traffic school when first assigned to AID. Our police cars replaced the motor cycle officers.

We did not investigate traffic accidents nor were we assigned to respond to radio calls for service though we frequently rolled on calls to provide backup to the patrol officers. We also assisted AID officers with major accident investigations. The replacement of motor cycle officers was seen a way to increase the visibility of black and white police cars on the street because we could work around the clock and not be inhibited by in climate weather as were motor cycle officers.

These were one officer cars during daylight hours and two officer cars at night. The night watch began around 3 PM with one officer cars and around 7 PM two officers teamed in a single police car. My call sign was 5E106. The call sign of my partner, Gary Boyd, was 5E103. These were permanently assigned call signs and were only used when we were on duty. Every officer in the experiment had their own individual call signs. When we were off duty our call sign not used. For my call sign the number 5 represent Harbor Division which was division number 5. The letter E represented a traffic enforcement car and the 106 represented my personal number alphabetically by last name of the sixteen officers.

Gary also attended San Pedro High School though he was one year behind me. Because I was black and Gary was White we were called the "Eye Spy" team, coined after the popular T. V. show during that time starring black actor Bill Cosby and his White actor partner Robert Culp. During this assignment it was estimated that I issued over 6,000 traffic citations in four years.

While off duty during this assignment and attending a sporting event at the Los Angeles Memorial Coliseum I aided in the rescue of a White boy being beaten by a mob of riotous black spectators. Witnesses interviewed later reported that I lifted the boy and pushed him through a one-way peristyle gate while also pulling myself through the small opening. This allowed me to run a block and a half to a nearby three story apartment building while carrying him. I recalled climbing the stairs to the roof and as I was exiting down the outside fire escape to the alley the police were arriving and rescued the two of us. In the melee I received several broken ribs and a concussion. The rescued boy received brain injuries. For my actions at the event I was later presented with the LAPD's highest award the Medal of Valor.

The presentation ceremony was held at the Hollywood Palladium organized by the Los Angeles Area Chamber of Commerce and presided over by Police Chief Tom Reddin. Ten other officers were also awarded the Medal each for risking their lives to save others.

For my actions I was selected as the South Bay Citizen of the Year by the Federation of South Bay Chambers of Commerce and presented with a watch, plaque and trophy at their annual awards luncheon. The trophy was placed in the San Pedro High School trophy case located in the hallway of the administration building at the school. Many years later, I visited the school and found that the trophy had been removed from the case and nowhere to be found. Someone not knowing the history probably removed and discarded it. Oh well, it probably should have never been there anyway.

LAPD Medal of Valor recipients. Officer Gravett second row right.

Here is one traffic incident worth mentioning: One summer day while patrolling alone and monitoring traffic on Pacific Avenue near Cabrillo Beach in San Pedro the driver of a four-seat sporty red convertible committed a violation so I made a traffic stop. The driver was a young blond girl, probably about 16 years old, and there were three other young girls her age in the car and they were all wearing bikinis. I requested the driver produce her driver license and she replied that it was in her purse and the purse was at home.

As I began taking her personal information she attempted to get out of the car and I requested her to remain inside. She exited anyway as did the other three girls. I politely but firmly ordered all of them to get back in the car but they just giggled as if it was all a lot of fun.

As I was writing the citation using the limited information provided one of the girls came up behind me and grabbed my white uniform hat. As I turned to retrieve it she tossed it to another girl and they began playing "keep away" with it. All of this was being watched from across the street by a group of young beach party going teenage boys who were clapping and urging them on. It was not funny to me; in fact downright maddening and embarrassing.

I radioed the dispatcher to send a backup unit but

Officer Gravett and his police vehicle

cautioned that I did not require any assistance as that would have generated several police cars responding with red lights and siren. When the dispatcher requested the nature of assistance required I chuckled that there were young girls playing keep away with my hat. Minutes later here came several police cars red lights and sirens blaring. Now I was totally embarrassed.

I finally retrieved my hat and wrote the driver a citation for the violation and another for driving without a license. I ordered her to lock up the car and walk as she would not be allowed to drive any further with no license.

They all protested as they were bare foot and only wearing their swim suits. I considered this pay back. As they walked away just as quickly as I could I left the area. No doubt the other officers would preferred to have given them a ride but refrained from doing so. At the end of the day there were probably four pairs of blistered feet and a lot of sun burn.

I suspect those young ladies really learned several lessons that day; always have a license when driving, take shoes when going to the beach and never play keep away with a policeman's hat. I too learned a lesson; never stop a red convertible sports car with young blond girls wearing bikinis but if so, leave your hat in the police car.

Officer Gravett and his police vehicle

LYING FREEWAY FLYER

Another traffic incident worth mentioning occurred on the freeway. A speeding car passed my traffic car at excessive speed so naturally I gave chase. The speed was in excess of 85 miles per hour and in those days we generally did not use sirens on freeways. With my red lights illuminated I followed the car for about a mile with no response even while honking the horn. I believed the driver was unaware of my presence as there was no driver side rear view mirror and the back window was obstructed. After another mile or so I activated the siren with still no response so I pulled alongside of the car and finally was able to attract the driver's attention and the car pulled to the side of the freeway. I had already called for a back-up unit but had not officially gone in pursuit.

The driver was an early 30's something woman who claimed she never saw the red lights nor had she heard the siren. The back seat was filled with boxes to the roof of the car blocking the driver's view from the rear view mirror and the side view mirror was missing. She admitted exceeding the speed limit as heard by the back-up officer who had just arrived on the scene.

She explained she was moving from one apartment to another one and had to meet someone and she was running late. She wore jeans which had seen better days, an oversized long sleeve

Officer Peter Gravett – Chamber of Commerce Plaque

mans' work shirt outside the jeans and she wore a bandana covering her hair and a hat of some sort. Her face had a smudge mark as if she had been working.

Her driver's license had expired as had the vehicle license tag. A quick check with communications revealed she had a warrant for failing to pay a parking ticket so Lucy Mae Smith (pseudonym) was arrested and booked and the vehicle impounded. All of the contents in the vehicle were required to be inventoried according to policy which was conducted by a civilian station officer who responded to the impound yard. A would be simple traffic ticket became an all-day extravaganza for several people.

About a month later, I received a subpoena for traffic court as she had pled not guilty to all charges. When I arrived at the courtroom I surveyed the audience and did not recognize any one fitting her description so I believed she had not shown up. However, a check with the Bailiff revealed she had indeed checked in. When I was called to the witness stand I testified to all of the violations. When her name was called this beautiful woman with long and flowing blond hair walked to the witness stand gathering everyone's attention. She was as stately as a fashion model and wore a powder blue business suit which matched her eyes. After being sworn-in she testified she had just entered the freeway a very short distance before she was stopped; so she could not have been speeding and denied that she had been. She testified that her current license was in her purse and was not allowed to produce it though the purse was inventoried during booking and contained no driver's license. She stated she had loaned the car to a friend who probably got the parking ticket and never informed her about it. She also testified she was unaware that the tags had expired as she had not received a renewal notice from the DMV. She had an excuse for everything. She had requested a jury trial and as it turned out it was comprised of nine women and three men all the same ethnicity as she. As the jury went to deliberate the Judge requested that I remain in the courtroom should there be any additional questions of me the jury might have. They quickly returned and found her not guilty on all violations. I was not surprised and probably neither was the Judge.

I left the courtroom and summoned the elevator. This was an older building with a single working elevator so I stood there waiting quite a while. Meanwhile the Judge had dismissed the courtroom for the lunch hour and she and a few members of the jury came out and also waited for the elevator.

As we all rode down together I asked her why she had perjured herself with all of the lies and she responded, in front of the jurors present, that she knew they would believe her and not me because she was "prettier" (exact words). At this point the jurors knew they had been had. Some incidents are never forgotten.

MEDICAL EMERGENCY?

Traffic stories never cease. As a note it seemed as if several medical doctors stopped for a traffic violation would generally admit to the violation but claim they were on an emergency call to the hospital engendering the officer to let them go. This ploy may have worked in the past but procedures were put in place whereby officers would quickly take information from the driver's license and vehicle then send the doctor's on their way and to not delay any purported emergency situation. An Application for Complaint was then requested with the Office of the City Attorney and the traffic citation was sent to them in the mail much to their chagrin.

Since the violation had been admitted the doctors generally did not protest the citation as it would have been useless and in some cases a phone call to the respective hospital would have been made to confirm whether or not an emergency had existed requiring that specific doctor.

THIS WAS NOT THE PURSUIT OF HAPPINESS

One sunny day following several days of torrential rains, I was monitoring traffic conditions in the Harbor City area of Harbor Division when a call came out of a pursuit in progress in the Western part of Wilmington just about two miles away from my location. I quickly responded to the area, as did other officers, and learned that the Wilmington unit was in pursuit of a motorcyclist for a traffic violation after he failed to stop. The motorist, although still speeding, was generally remaining in the same area of about eight square blocks.

Randomly he would drive down the side walk of a public housing complex, drive between apartment buildings and exiting on another street. I sped ahead to a point where I believed he would return to the street where I became the lead officer in the pursuit. In an attempt to avoid me he drove onto the side walk and into a large vacant lot adjacent to a field of oil wells. The field was very wet from the recent rains and the mud was thick and deep.

As he rode his motorcycle into the lot his vehicle dug deep into the mud to the point where it totally bogged down so he laid down the bike and began an attempt to escape on foot. He was repeatedly falling down in the deep mud. I had followed him into the oil field and my police car also dug deeply into the mud whereby I could go no further. I shut off the engine and had difficulty opening the door and was able to exit only after several quick attempts in pushing away the mud which was up and over the bottom of the door.

I gave chase on foot sloughing through the mud, all the while yelling for him to stop or I would shoot but he kept going. I removed my weapon and fired one round into the mud and he dove face down and appeared to be attempting to dig himself a hole. He was totally frightened and begging me not to shoot him. I placed the handcuffs on him then pulled him up.

The other officers seeing us drive into the muddy field elected to drive around to the other side. I walked the now arrestee to the waiting officers and who took him into custody after inquiring if I had shot at him because they believed they had heard a shot. I denied firing the shot as that was totally out of department policy as we never fired at fleeing suspects. An officer found guilty of that by a Board of Rights would be severely admonished or suspended for doing so if not outright fired.

The suspect never mentioned it and the officers never brought it up again. I got away with that one. I can now admit to my violating the department policy as the statute of limitations has run and I have long since retired. The station fund purchased me a new uniform and a new pair of shoes. Hours after the incident the Department's Motor Transport civilian staff were able to remove the police car and the motor cycle from the morass of mud.

DOUBLE HEADER

While patrolling was the primary function of enforcing traffic laws it was not uncommon to cite two separate drivers for violations within the close proximity to one another. In traffic officers jargon this was called a "double header."

Generally traffic officers are assigned to just two shifts, or watches, day watch or night watch. When there is a surge in accidents after midnight in a given area a modified shift is deployed called a "deuce" watch. The word was coined when the California Vehicle Code violation for a "drunk driver" was number Section 502, deuce referring to the number two. The code number was changed some years later, however, the jargon has remained over the years but the classification changed to "driving under the influence" or DUI Section 23102.

The deuce watch starts later at night and extends into the early morning hours and generally only on weekends as many inebriated drivers are on the streets after the bars close. There have been times where officers have arrested two DUI drivers in a single stop and this was called a Double Header Deuce. To my knowledge there had never been a Triple Header Deuce previously recorded until the Eye Spy Team, recorded one.

TRIPLE HEADER

My partner and I became famous around the police station because we once arrested three drunk drivers in one traffic stop. While patrolling along Anaheim Street in Wilmington, we observed a vehicle driving much slower than traffic and swerving; obvious signs of an impaired driver so we executed a traffic stop. It did not take much to determine that the driver was driving under the influence.

To be certain we removed him from his vehicle and began administering the Field Sobriety Test on the sidewalk. While doing so we observed another car approaching from the same direction swerving and moving at an extremely slow speed probably homing in on our flashing lights. As the car was slowly passing we yelled for the driver to pull over and he did just a few feet in front of us while bumping the curb in the process. We then observed the driver and the passenger switching seats and the passenger, now driving, began to very slowly pull away from the curb.

I ran after the car and banged on the trunk and the driver stopped the car. Upon removing both driver and passenger from the vehicle we determined that they were both intoxicated as determined by their failed Field Sobriety Tests and physical conditions. Both were arrested and all three drivers were booked for DUI. This is what became known as the infamous triple header deuce.

During my four year tour in Traffic Enforcement Division I probably arrested about 400 citizens for driving under the influence of either alcohol or drugs and sometimes both. Some arrests I was alone and others with partners.

The four wheel traffic enforcement experiment, although successful, lasted four years and was then discontinued. A few of the officers assigned there opined that the four wheeled traffic operation was discontinued due to the overt lobbying by motor cycle officers arguing that was their venue.

Chapter 26 Central Division Patrol (Tour 3)

With discontinuance of the four wheel traffic enforcement experiment at LAPD's Harbor Division all sixteen officers were reassigned to various patrol divisions, me returning to Central Division, though I had requested any other division to broaden my geographical knowledge of the city.

This time my primary patrol areas were China Town, "Dog Town," a public housing project just north of China Town, and "Frog Town," the area north of the Police Academy and Elysian Park wedged between the Golden State Freeway (Inter State 5) and the Los Angeles River. While in this assignment I was promoted to the rank of Policeman Three.

Dog Town received its moniker as the public housing project was adjacent to the city animal shelter which, when opened more 60 years earlier, was actually named the Dog Pound. The name animal shelter came later. Frog Town received its moniker as it bordered the Los Angeles River which many years earlier was replete with frogs.

In the Basic Car Plan I was assigned on day watch with two partners, Richard Ranck and Luis Lozano, two of us working at any given time. While patrolling with Richard we had lots of conversation regarding his US Air Force experience especially regarding his tour of duty in Spain. He had much to say about his excellent tour of duty perhaps it was because he met and married his wife there. Over the years he became fluent in Spanish which came in handy when conversing with citizens which included, criminals, victims and community leaders.

Richard's wife was an accomplished Spanish guitarist and singer who perform professionally throughout Southern California. Judging by his comments he was extremely proud of her and her talents.

Luis (Lou) was a Vietnam Veteran who joined the police department shortly returning from his Viet Nam tour with the Army. While assigned with him, he announced the pregnancy of his wife and months later he became the proud father of twins. Lou was also fluent in Spanish given his ethnicity so working with either one of them I always had an interpreter if needed.

CHAPTER 27 US ARMY OFFICER'S CANDIDATE SCHOOL (OCS)

After having served almost ten years as an enlisted soldier in the Army and Army National Guard and promoting through the ranks to Sergeant First Class I applied to become a commissioned officer. This included passing a rigorous written examination and appearing before a panel of officers. Having passed both I ventured into the unknown preparing to become a military leader. I was accepted and was granted military leave from the police department to attend OCS with the Army.

Following many months of training at Camp Luis Obispo and Fort Ord in California and later at and Fort Benning, Georgia I was commissioned a Second Lieutenant in the Army assigned to the Army National Guard.

Our training began in 1967 and concluded in 1968. The Viet Nam War was nearing its' end at this time. My class of officer candidates was the largest ever, starting with over 750 and graduating only 268. The high failure and dropout rate can be contributed to numerous factors such as involuntary dismissal for not "cutting the mustard" academically or emotionally. Some Candidates voluntarily dropped out due to the physical regimen of the training and many for other personal or family reasons. Some candidates voluntarily left the training as they did not want the responsibility for potentially having to lead soldiers in combat probably having not considered that prior to applying.

One of my TAC officers (Teach, Advise and Counsel) at Camp San Luis Obispo was Second Lieutenant Guido Portante. A TAC officer's role is similar to that of a Drill Sergeant but at a higher level and with more authority. The other candidates and I believed him to be one of the harshest military officer we had ever encountered. Some, not me, even shuddered when he came around. All of this meant that he was performing his duties as designed while training us to become military officers ourselves.

Several years later I served with Guido Portante when he was a Lieutenant Colonel and I was a Major, later promoted to Lieutenant Colonel myself and him to Colonel. We both held prominent positions in the same division. On several occasions we had disagreements on policy and practice which sometimes surfaced in public though I was always respectful of his seniority. Over time we resolved our differences and I engendered the greatest respect for him. Our careers resulted in success as we were both eventually promoted to General Officer though he attained the rank prior to myself. In retirement we remained friends and bonded closer.

Of the many Non-Commissioned Officers and Commissioned Officers I encountered during my military career I can say that probably I learned as much from him as anyone and though I never expressed this I attribute a large degree of my success to his leadership and mentoring along the way.

While both of us was in retirement Brigadier General Portante penned me a note which read in part, "I was your superior and then you became my superior, neither of us skipped a beat. I worked as your ADC (Assistant Division Commander) without question and with pride to serve you, and always the Division. I believe that is the time when we both got to know each other in a different light, and our bonding occurred. That is what soldiering is about. That is all I ever wanted to do in my career. It rankled a lot of people."

My Officer Candidate School graduation was attended by my mother and step-father. Unfortunately Dorothy was hospitalized at the time and was unable to attend and I feel certain that everyone in the class, was extremely proud to have received a commission as a United States Army officer.

The candidate class did not receive individual numerical ratings based upon achievement during training and all of the 268 graduates were considered as equals. Three years later, by Army promotional regulations, we were all promoted to First Lieutenant. This would be the only automatic promotion under these regulations. Future promotions following First Lieutenant were based upon a plethora of criteria such as proficiency in individual skill, competence, leadership, assignments, time in grade, military and civilian education requirements and many other considerations including proficiency reports and commander's recommendation. Just over a year later I was promoted to Captain, the third in my class of 268 to achieve that rank.

Thereafter over the full course of my career I was the first in my class to be promoted to each subsequent ranks; Major, Lieutenant Colonel, Colonel, Brigadier General and Major General, although many did not serve as career officers. Five in my class promoted to Brigadier General and only two of us promoted to Major General. The other was my good friend Bill Davies and, by coincidence, more than 30 years later we were serving in Germany together as two star Generals.

FIELD ARTILLERY – THE ILLUSIVE BRANCH

Just prior to my graduation from OCS all candidates appeared before a "Branching Board" to determine which branch in the Army they will be commissioned. Generally each candidate will list their top three choices in priority but it is up to the needs of the service which branch they will be assigned.

In priority, my choices were, Field Artillery, Armor and Infantry. I specifically did not want to be branched Military Police as I had served there as an enlisted soldier. Each cadet was directed to report to the office where the Branching Board was empaneled to receive their branch assignment. The Board consisted of, as I recall, a Lieutenant Colonel, a Major and a Captain. Just as I was about to enter and within hearing distance though not eavesdropping I overheard a casual remark by a Board Member, unknown which, suggesting that I not be branched Field Artillery as *"Field Artillery requires a lot of mathematics and computations and blacks generally lack that ability."* The other board members made no comment as I recall.

This was in 1968 and my minor in college was criminalistics requiring several courses of advanced mathematics and I was also very familiar with the tactical and operational employment of Artillery in support of Infantry and Armor operations. Additionally, if that person had studied military history, past and current, he would have known that black soldiers had served in Field Artillery units for almost 200 years beginning in the Revolutionary War, again in the War of 1812 and continuing through the Civil War, World Wars One and Two, Korean War and were currently serving in Viet Nam in such units.

In fact during World War Two alone no fewer than nine of the Field Artillery Battalions in VIII Corps had been composed of black soldiers, as was four of the VII Corps Artillery Battalions supporting the 106th Division. Two of them moved to Bastogne and played an important part in the defense of the perimeter and were ordered to hold Bastogne at all costs which they did. One of these was the 969th Field Artillery Battalion. These historical feats were chronicled in Lieutenant Colonel (Retired) Michael Lee Lanning's book "African – American Soldier: Chrispus Attucks to Colin Powell."

But the story of the 969th Field Artillery Battalion does not end there as there is a beginning according to authors Denise George and Robert Child in their recently published account book *"The Lost Eleven, The Forgotten Story of Black American Soldiers Brutally Massacred in World War II."* Prior to the Bastogne liberation the 333rd Artillery Battalion had been merged with the 969th due to severe battle fatalities and wounded soldiers. These included eleven of their members captured by soldiers of Germany's First SS Reconnaissance Battalion and massacred at the Baugnez Crossroads near the town of Wereth, Belgium.

The follow-on investigation revealed the "Wereth Eleven" were clubbed, skulls crushed, shot and some of their extremities cut off. The 333rd Field Artillery Battalion, with their 155 MM Howitzer Long Tom Guns, had been the first black combat unit to land in Europe coming ashore four days after D-Day at Normandy's Utah Beach. From there they fought with VIII Corps engaging the enemy for the better part of a year.

Following the War and recognizing their combat record the 333rd was awarded the Presidential Distinguished Unit Citation for their extraordinary courage and undaunted determination in the defense of Bastogne, the highest honor bestowed by the President of the United States upon an army unit. They were the first African American combat unit to receive this award during World War II. The Battalion also received the Belgian Croix de Guerre (War Cross) with Palm for their heroic actions.

At the time the remark was uttered regarding blacks lacking math ability a black officer, Lieutenant Colonel Julius W. Becton. Jr. was then commanding a Field Artillery Battalion in Viet Nam. Colonel Becton later went on to command the 1st Cavalry Division as a Major General and finally VII Corps in Germany as a Lieutenant General. No doubt he knew a thing or two about Field Artillery.

Perhaps that officer's professional reading regimen, which all officers are recommended to have, was limited to a 60 year old study that began at Carlisle Barracks in 1906 and published in 1907 which Lieutenant Colonel Michael Lee Lanning (Retired) cited in his book *African - American Soldier From Chrispus Attucks to Colin Powell* which recommended that (in 1907) *"continued exclusion of African – Americans from artillery because of the technical skills required to properly operate the guns and provide accurate safe fire."* The report went on to say that *"blacks were inferior to the White race in intellectual and mental abilities."* Did the authors of that long ago report and the officer on the Branching Board not realize that blacks had designed and built the pyramids which required hundreds of mathematical equations?

If the person who uttered the remark was a Field Artillery Officer himself perhaps he must have also only read the ... *War College Report of 1925 – 'Use of Negro Manpower in War' which read in part "Compared to the White man, he (The Negro) is admittedly of inferior mentality ...*

A gun section of the 332nd FAB in Normandy | Source

Black Soldiers in Field Artillery.

inherently weak in character ... If he makes good, he will have the opportunity eventually to fight in the war with All-Negro organizations. He (the Negro Man) has not the initiative and resourcefulness of the White Man. (He) is by nature subservient ... Most susceptible to the crowd psychology, and cannot control himself in the fear of danger ... In the process of evolution, the American Negro has not progressed as far as the sub-species of the human family ... All officers, without exception, agree that the Negro lacks initiative, displays little or no leadership, and cannot accept responsibility. The Negro does not desire combat duty under conditions of present day warfare. That if drafted into the service he was given a choice of assignment to a combat organization or to a 'Labor Battalion' the majority would chose the less dangerous service." Perhaps it was an error that White officers before him had awarded Congressional Medals of Honor to deserving Negro Field Artillery soldiers in almost every previous war.

Upon hearing the remark I was reticent though the comment was not officially part of my board discussion which had not officially convened. I was not going to possibly jeopardize my commissioning opportunity so I remained muted. I graduated and to my chagrin was commissioned in the Military Police Corps and assigned as such.

CHAPTER 28 OFFICERS COURSES

All newly commissioned officers generally must attend their Officer Basic Course prior to reporting to the first assignment. This includes those commissioned from the United States Military Academy at West Point, those commissioned via Officer Candidate School and those commissioned through the college Reserve Officer Training Corps (ROTC). This also include the very few who receive direct commissions.

While undergoing Officer Candidate training to be a leader upon graduation they have no specific specialty or branch qualification. The basic course fills that gap. The Basic Course was generally eight week to 12 weeks in length and depending upon the branch is conducted at various military bases around the country.

For example Infantry at Fort Benning Georgia; Armor at Fort Knox Kentucky; Artillery at Fort Sill, Oklahoma; Logistics at Fort Lee, Virginia; Engineer at Fort Leonard Wood, Missouri; Army Security Agency at Fort Holabird and Ordnance at Aberdeen Proving Grounds, both in Maryland; Transportation at Fort Eustis, Virginia; Intelligence at Fort Huachuca, Arizona; Administration and Finance at Fort Benjamin Harrison, Indiana; Military Police and Signal Communications at Fort Gordon, Georgia; Women's Army Corps (WACs) (before discontinued) at Fort McClellan and Aviation at Fort Rucker both in Alabama. Several other branch schools existed at the time of my commissioning each at differing locations such as Chaplain at Fort Hamilton, New York and Medical at Fort Sam Houston, Texas. Following graduation from civilian Law Schools newly commissioned JAG Officers attend their Basic Couse at the University of Virginia Law School.

In 1969 I received basic branch school orders and reported to the Military Police (MP) School for Officer

Branch Training. This was my first time in the south as an adult. Fort Gordon was situated in Augusta County just a few miles from the South Carolina border and I quickly learned that is was in a "dry" county where alcohol was not sold and soldiers routinely drove just across the state line to South Carolina to make their purchases.

Generally officers are housed in Bachelor Officer Quarters (BOQs) however, when our class reported for training there was a two week overlap with the previous class with no other facilities available. To house our class the Army contracted with a very large senior citizens retirement home where we were billeted. At one time the facility had been the private and segregated headquarters hotel for the Augusta National Golf Tournament, The Masters.

The all-White senior citizens residing there did not openly accept the African American and Puerto Rican officers residing among them especially since we sat for breakfast and dinner among them. Some refused to eat until after I and other minority officers had departed. On the other hand others were very cordial and conversational.

The fact that many of the Puerto Rican Officers spoke little or no English made the situation more caustic as the some of the staff and residents perceived them as being foreigners. One year later I was transferred to the Armor Branch which became my primary Branch throughout my career save for two follow-on assignments in the MP Corps. I served as a Military Police Company Commander as a Captain and Division Provost Marshal as a Lieutenant Colonel. Overall I commanded three separate companies. In my follow-on training I attended Armor School.

MILITARY OFFICER PROFESSIONAL TRAINING

Over the next 25 years or so, I attended a plethora of other required officer training schools and courses in addition to the primary ones such as the Officer's Basic Course, but also the Armor Advanced Course, Fort Knox, Kentucky; Command and General Staff College at both Fort Leavenworth, Kansas and the University of Nevada at Reno; Battalion and Brigade Pre-Command Courses at Fort Knox, Kentucky and the Army War College at Carlisle Barracks, Pennsylvania. At the War College my class mates and I studied the command of divisions, corps' and armies in the field. We were instructed on the organization and workings of the Department of Defense which not only included dissecting the defense budget but also national policy and war plans for the nation. Table top exercises with wartime scenarios were routine.

A few of the shorter courses were the Force Integration Course at the Presidio of San Francisco; Equal Opportunity Course, Patrick Air Force Base, Florida; General Officer's Training Course (Charm School), Fort Leavenworth, Kansas; General Officer's Legal Course, University of Virginia Law School; Division Commanders Orientation Course, Fort Robinson, Arkansas; Displaced Equipment Transition Training, Boise, Idaho; Logistical Training Course, Fort A. P. Hill, Virginia and probably a dozen or more others.

While attending one such course while off duty at Fort Knox, Kentucky as a Captain in 1974, I along with friends and class mates from California, then Captain Fred Darley and Captain David Gustafson, went touring in the Kentucky Mountains and stopped at a road house for lunch. It was named the "Doe Run Inn." This being the 1970's and since I was not certain blacks would be served there David and Fred did a quick reconnaissance and after inquiring reported back to me anxiously waiting in the car that everything was OK. At the entrance to the facility there was a cornerstone with an inscription which noted that it was laid by Abraham Lincoln's father. The roadhouse presented a great southern style lunch served by both

White and Negro staff. The very cordial hostess was also Negro.

CHAPTER 29 CALIFORNIA STATE UNIVERSITY LONG BEACH

A year following my graduation from Long Beach City College I was enrolled as a student at California State College Long Beach, the name having been officially changed from Long Beach State College. A few years later it would have its' name changed one final time to California State University Long Beach and it's mascot of an 1849'er panning for gold changed from the "49'ers" to "The Beach."

Much like my tenure at Long Beach City College I began attending college part-time and working full time which did not allow sufficient time to engage in college activities on and off campus. I was however able to attend some sporting events and listen to two of my classmates playing their music in the open air quad on Friday's at noon. They were Karen and Richard Carpenter who went on to become Grammy award winners and record many hit songs.

Karen played the drums at that time and she and I talked often because I was also a drummer, or I had been. Later after becoming famous she dropped the drumming gig and became a standup solo vocalist.

In 1969 having completed my course of study I graduated from California State University Long Beach with a Bachelor of Science Degree with the ceremony being held at the Long Beach Convention Center. My major was Criminology (the psychology of crime) having taken classes in criminal and civil law, psychology, abnormal psychology, criminal investigation, forensic sciences, constitutional criminal procedures, research methods, sociology and others. My minor was Criminalistics (today known as crime scene investigation) having taken classes in the mathematics, laboratory research techniques and procedures as well as various forensic science courses.

My good friend and neighbor as well as family friend Lionel Coulter attended Cal State Long Beach along with me and we had the undergraduate major but different minors. We graduated together and Lionel was accepted into the first graduate class of Criminology at the school and received his Master's Degree there. Afterwards he matriculated to Claremont University where he earned a Doctorate Degree. Lionel applied his higher education experience to having a full career as a probation officer and college professor teaching at various venues.

CHAPTER 30 FIRST EUROPEAN VACATION

Dorothy and I had planned for a year to take a European vacation and in 1971 we embarked on our first trip to Europe. Since we were unfamiliar with the Continent we opted to join a small tour group of about 30 individuals from various part of the US. This would be a four week excursion to visit England and several countries in Western and Southern Europe.

We landed at Gatwick Airport just outside London and were bused to our hotel where there was a reception to meet and greet the other tour members. From that initial meeting we all knew that we would enjoy the tour as everyone seemed very genuine.

The next morning we departed on the first leg of the bus tour viewing and visiting the typical tourist sites in downtown London and also touring the countryside. We visited the London Bridge, Windsor Castle, observed the changing of the Guard at Buckingham Palace and visited Piccadilly Circus which is not a circus but is reminiscent of New York's

Dorothy enjoying the Hawaiian sun

Times Square. We heard the bell "Big Ben" ring and we visited Scotland Yard.

After another day or two the bus took us onto a commercial auto ferry and we crossed the English Channel to the Continent of Europe. For the next three weeks we toured several countries including France, Belgium, Luxembourg, Netherlands (Holland), Austria, Greece and Italy. There we heard the Pope give a blessing from the balcony at Saint Peter's Basilica in Rome and we toured the Coliseum and tossed coins in Trevi Fountain where nomadic American college students quickly retrieved them.

An interesting site we visited was a former civilization at the base of Mount Vesuvius, Pompeii, which was destroyed by a cataclysmic volcano eruption in 76 AD. Some of the various ruins were still visible and contours of the village outlined.

After spending several days in Italy visiting several cities including Pisa, Venice and Naples we flew to Greece and visited several historical sites such as the Acropolis and the original Olympic Stadium in the City of Olympia.

We took a boat ride to the Isle of Capri where a flat bottom boat scurried us into the Blue Grotto, a cave with an entrance only about four feet in height at high tide. By lying flat we were able to maneuver into position and then view the crystal waters highlighted by the penetrating rays of the sun outside. We also visited the Greek Isle of Corfu.

Our next flight was to Germany which was one of our favorite countries. We toured from the south in Munich in the Bavarian Region to Hamburg in the north. Our stay in Berlin was interesting in that we visited the Berlin Wall and checked out Check Point Charlie, the entry and exit to Soviet controlled East Berlin. Our luxury bus trip also took us to Luxemburg and Belgium where we toured NATO Headquarters in Brussels.

Austria also had so many interesting places to see. We spent one night in a 400 year old Inn and slept in a 200 year old bed in Rotenberg, a walled medieval city with access to the city's underground tunnels connecting many of the buildings.

Peter & Dorothy
Vacationing in Hawaii.

We confirmed that Switzerland's reputation for its excellent cheeses is warranted as we had several opportunities to experience Fondue, a Swiss dish of breads dipped in melted cheese served in a communal pot or portable stove. The cities of Bern and Lucerne also possessed Swiss charm. Lake Lucerne was placid and reminiscent of a picture post card.

There was so much to see and do during this extended trip that we regretted having to return home. Upon departure Dorothy opted to fly directly to Chicago when we landed at Bangor, Maine for US Customs screening and to change planes. She had several relatives there which included two sisters. I returned directly to Los Angeles and returned to work the next day as scheduled.

Dorothy Cooling it in Hawaii.

We both had experienced a busy month. The following year we took the first of several vacation trips to Hawaii over many years. One vacation trip there was with several LAPD civilian employees from Records and Identification Division where I was assigned as a Watch Commander. The Division had a travel club which arranged several excursion annually. The large numbers traveling in a group allowed for discounted fares and fees. Mark went along with us on that trip, his first to the Islands and he had a wonderful time. He was water proof having spent considerable time on the beaches of Catalina Island where we visited every summer, this along with his swimming lessons at the local YMCA.

Dorothy enjoying the pool aboard the cruise ship

During the ensuing years' we also took several cruises to various destinations, one such cruise was a

Western Cruise Lines   S.S. AZURE SEAS

Gravett Family on Cruise. Dorothy (center in black dress), Peter (far right in Uniform) & Mark (second row seated second from right).

Mexico cruise with about 45 relatives which was a small portion of my immediate and extended family.

CHAPTER 31 FOLLOW-ON MILITARY ASSIGNMENTS

Upon receiving my Army Commission as a Second Lieutenant my first assignment in the Army National Guard was as a Military Police platoon leader commanding 36 soldiers in Headquarters and Headquarters Company, 40th Infantry Brigade (Separate).

As mentioned earlier, I had requested first to have a Field Artillery assignment but instead was given the Military Police assignment. In the Army's organizational structure a Separate Brigade, not organic to a division, has an independent Military Police platoon assigned that is not organic to a Military Police Company which would have several platoons. As such my reporting chain was to the Headquarters Company Commander, a Captain.

The Separate Brigade was comprised of two infantry battalions and one armor battalion along with a support battalion, a signal platoon and the independent MP Platoon which had a small Provost Marshal Section attached headed by a Major.

A year later, I transferred to Troop E, 140th Cavalry first as a platoon leader commanding 30 soldiers and later as the Troop Executive Officer where I was promoted to First Lieutenant in 1971. With the premature departure of the troop commander I was appointed acting Troop Commander where I remained until I was given command of a support company, HHC 223rd Area Support Command. This was in 1972.

TROOP E, 140TH CAVALRY

When assigned to Troop E this allowed me to have my first command, albeit acting, at the company level. The unit consisted of about 140 soldiers and five officers; company commander, company executive officer and three platoon leaders.

The Cavalry Troop was the "eyes and ears" of the Brigade and whose mission was to perform scouting and reconnaissance missions. Tactically the Troop would generally make effort to avoid decisive engagements but rather report on enemy strength, movements, composition, location and other intelligence information. This would allow the more robust Infantry and Armor Battalions to plan their operational strategy for engaging and defeating the opposition.

Each platoon in Troop E was configured with four tanks (M48's), four infantry fighting vehicles (M-113's) with an infantry squad each, a 4.2 MM mortar squad configured in an armored weapons carrier and an array of wheeled and tracked support vehicles. The unit also had a small cadre of administrative and logistical support personnel.

It was quite common for senior officers to visit subordinate units for inspection and morale purposes but not common for a General to visit a company size unit like Troop E. The Troop was assigned to the 40th Infantry Brigade (Separate) which had a Brigadier General as Commander, Brigadier General Charles Starr. After having been alerted of his pending visit we made all preparations to make a good impression both tactically and personally. This included an inspection of vehicles, equipment as well as an in-ranks inspection of the individual soldiers.

At the appointed time I had all of the soldiers in the standard formation as the General went down the ranks inspecting all of them and briefly pausing to speak with some. He stopped by one E-4 soldier, Richard Houseman (pseudonym), and inquired as to what kind of work he did and the soldier replied that he was an ice cream man. Without hesitation the General remarked something to the extent that he appreciated him serving and that it takes all occupations no matter what description to make our military great.

The soldier was factually correct in that he did sell ice cream but what he neglected to tell the General was that he was extremely well off financially and owned numerous, over a dozen, nationally franchised ice cream stores. No doubt he was financially worth more than the General.

Troop E generally performed tactical and maneuver training at Camp Roberts along with other elements of the Brigade. This included individual platoon tactics, and when proficient at that level, collective Troop tactics.

EAST GARRISON TRAINING

Over the years the East Garrison area of Camp Roberts had transitioned from a small unit Infantry tactics training area to a tank maneuver training area. This was ideal for Troop E, 140th Cavalry due to its' rolling hills separated by valleys with miles of flat terrain populated by low scrub and other indigenous greenery. The ground alternated between soft dirt and sand. Many of the armored units trained there on alternating weekends. This was also the site of the Material and Training Equipment Site (MATES).

MATES was the storage area for all armor equipment including tanks, infantry fighting vehicles, armored recover vehicles (considered a tow truck for tanks), heavy and light wheeled vehicles and a plethora of field artillery cannon. There was a large cadre of military technicians assigned there fulltime to maintain the fleet of vehicles.

CHAPTER 32 DOROTHY AND I START OUR FAMILY

While I was assigned to Troop E we anxiously awaited the arrival of our son who was born in 1972 weighing in at five pounds five ounces and 19 and a half inches long. We both had previously agreed that his first name would be Mark, Dorothy's family's surname, and the middle name Loren. Although Dorothy carried her maiden name of Marks, as did her brothers and sisters, most of their relatives did not use the last letter in the name so he was given the name Mark without the "s."

He was given the middle name Loren because Dorothy liked the name and for no other reason. Mark immediately joined the Gravett and Marks families with literally dozens of cousins and extended family in Mississippi, Louisiana, and Chicago, Illinois in addition to California. He immediately had 17 aunts and uncles from both sides of the families, two grandmothers, a grandfather and several extended members of both families including over 30 cousins.

Anticipating his arrival we had arranged for one of the bedrooms to be converted into a nursery with all of the furnishings and other accoutrements. Just two days old when we were taking him to his first address at 1719 Taper Avenue in San Pedro we stopped at my sister Alice's law office in Long Beach just for her to see her newest nephew. Her position there was legal secretary.

Over the next several weeks we received numerous visits by members of both families and friends anxious to see the new arrival. Dorothy's girl friends had previously given her a baby shower so we had ample amounts of baby clothes and other necessities. As a very proud dad I received well wishes from my police and military friends as I passed out cigars.

Dorothy and I agreed that Mark would attend the California Military Academy in the City of Signal Hill adjacent to Long Beach and we enrolled him in kindergarten there. He and the other kids in his class experienced the same educational program as public schools however the classes had much fewer students and each class had two fulltime teachers. This allowed for him to have a better initial learning opportunity. Students did not wear uniforms until first grade and then they donned a uniform of khaki shirts and pants, a cap and a tie.

Mark (age 2)

We began his education at home by reading to him daily beginning when he was just a year old and continued until he was able recognize words and began reading himself a few years later.

At the end of the third grade we transferred him to Taper Avenue Elementary School just across the street from our home. Suffice to say he was probably never late for school. From the beginning he was a pace ahead of his classmates, especially with reading ability. Dorothy and I spent considerable time conversing with Mark's teachers to track his progress and we also attended all of the school celebrations as most parents do.

Mark age 5

Most of his classmates lived in the immediate neighborhood which provided playmates after school and on weekends. While in elementary school Mark participated in community sports including T-Ball, Little

League Baseball, Biddy Basketball, football, Y-Indian Guides and swimming at the San Pedro and Peninsula YMCA.

Mark and I and his dog Scorpio routinely took several one day snow trips to the mountains. I am not certain who had the most fun Mark or his

Dorothy, Mark (age 3) & Peter

dog. A few years later we were very proud to see him graduate from elementary school while receiving an award for perfect attendance.

Mark was born the week of Halloween and for several early birthday parties we presented him a birthday cake with a Halloween theme. It was around about the fifth or sixth grade that Mark pointedly informed his parents that he was not born on Halloween and did not want any more birthday cakes decorated like Halloween. That was the end of that era and the beginning of another.

While attending Dodson Middle School he was on a local junior bowling team and competed in regional tournaments. Some of his team mates were the children of my best friend Melvin Haynes; his son Michael and daughters Mayesha and Merriam. He won several individual trophies and the team won several trophies.

Mark in Little League.

Mark in Biddy Basketball.

This was an activity which really got his attention and he enjoyed very much.

From time to time he wore dressy sports jackets with open collar dress shirts and slacks to Dodson Middle School after having us purchase them for him. He considered himself as modeling his favorite television personalities in the television show Miami Vice.

At San Pedro High School he made many new friends and most of them hung out at our home. On his 16th birthday his parents gifted him with a new car, 1988 gold Honda Prelude. His first date in the car was when he took a very nice girl to the high school prom. When he graduated in 1990 he received special awards from the school and from the Los Angeles Unified School District for having never missed a day of class and had perfect attendance record for twelve years which included his first few years in private school. This was a remarkable achievement. He was the only one in his graduating class to achieve this milestone.

Mark with His Dog Scorpio.

After attending classes at Los Angeles Harbor College he was accepted at the Western Culinary Institute at Portland State University fulfilling his dream and was on the path to becoming a professional chef. We packed him up and borrowed my Brother Melvin's customized van and the three of us made the trip there into a mini vacation after his registration.

During his almost two years in culinary school we visited him there often and enjoyed several meals prepared in their public restaurant, some prepared especially by him for us. We were elated to return to the school one final time to attend his graduation ceremony. The ceremony was impressive with all graduates wearing their white chef's smocks.

Mark Dressed for Class in Junior High School.

Mark was able to intern at several restaurants in the Portland area prior to returning to Southern California where he refined his culinary skills in restaurants in the South Bay such as Ocean Trails Golf Resort in Rancho Palos Verdes, Chez Melange in Redondo Beach and Simba's in Palm Springs.

Mark's Graduation from Culinary School.

Mark was born with an independent streak and chartered his own course. He had no inclination to follow my footsteps in the military or law enforcement and I was not disappointed that he did not. Becoming a chef was his forte', a goal he set for himself while in middle school which his mother Dorothy and I supported. He remained true to his goal.

Proud Parents at Mark's Culinary School Graduation.

CHAPTER 33 223RD AREA SUPPORT GROUP

After a year serving as Acting Troop Commander in Troop E, 140th Cavalry, I was reassigned to a newly organized unit in 1972, the 223rd Area Support Group, as the Headquarters and Headquarters Company Commander, my second company command, and promoted to Captain.

The Area Support Group's mission was to provide logistical support to various combat units which included fuel, rations, ammunition, construction materials, repair parts, maintenance support and various other logistical support services to the maneuver units in an area of operations. Most of our weekend and summer training was conducted at Fort Irwin, then a downsized reserve training facility but which years later would balloon into a massive desert training facility with the designation as the National Training Center. The new mission there was to prepare units for deployment to Iraq and later Afghanistan.

I thoroughly enjoyed this assignment more than others as it allowed me for the first time to serve alongside Melvin who was a Specialist Fourth Class in the unit. He had recently returned to the US after having served an Army tour of duty in Vicenza, Italy. This would be the only time in our military careers that we would serve together in a company size unit. He eventually retired as a Command Sergeant Major, the Army's highest Non-Commissioned Officer rank.

Captain Peter Gravett, Company Commander.

The Area Support Group assignment came shortly following the US decision to eliminate the involuntary draft which was causing so much consternation in the country.

Lieutenant Colonel Peter Gravett & First Sergeant Melvin Gravett at Fort Irwin, CA

With the draft eliminated voluntary enlistments in the active military and the reserve military plummeted. If a young man had no obligation to serve in the military other than for patriotism, financial or educational benefits, why would he join as some opined?

The preceding War in Viet Nam had divided the country between the "hawks" and the "doves"; those who supported our engagement in South Viet Nam and those opposed. Anti-War demonstrations were staged throughout the country and "sit-ins'" were commonplace on college campuses, outside military bases and at government buildings.

News outlets reported that some military personnel in uniform in the public arena were experiencing taunts and derogatory comments to the point whereby the military encouraged soldiers to wear civilian attire when off the base off duty.

With the Army National Guard enlistments plummeting to an all-time low many units were seeking innovative ways and means to encourage new enlistments and to enlist prior service soldiers as well. As the Commander I was responsible for the company's strength levels which became my primary objective, switching away from training which always had been the priority. This was prior to the National Guard having a full-time recruiting cadre. In order to recruit and entice new members we set up recruiting booths in shopping malls, set up tables with brochures at neighborhood fairs and celebrations and reached out to high schools and community colleges. With all of this energy being exerted we marginally successful if at all. Other reserve units were also employing these same measures with fierce competition.

One enterprising young soldier suggested that we go to the beach and recruit. This had never been done so we developed an operational plan to do just that. After all this was Southern California with a plethora of beaches frequented by military entry age young men.

During one weekend drill assembly I invited all of the company soldiers to meet at a local beach with their swim wear or similar attire which they did. We brought along a two and a half ton camouflaged Army truck and table and chairs along with signage. We also had an array of literature detailing opportunities for training and other benefits.

The soldiers took turns staffing the table and speaking with young men (women we not serving the National Guard at that time but were serving in the Army Reserve). The truck on the beach did attract considerable interest and some young men believed that if they joined the National Guard they would sometimes perform their duty on the beach.

Even though we never misled anyone to believe this could be possible we did not discourage their thoughts. We developed various leads and perhaps later we may have even enlisted one or two. In any event this was unique but my superiors, although supportive of what I had done, suggested that we return to more traditional recruiting measures.

CHAPTER 34 40TH MILITARY POLICE COMPANY

I discussed earlier that every Army division has a Military Police Company organic to its structure bearing the numeral of that division. I was given the command of the 40th Military Police Company organic to the 40th Infantry Division (Mechanized). This assignment was an unheard of third company command opportunity which set me apart.

The company consisted of my Executive Officer at the rank of First Lieutenant, five platoons each led by a Second Lieutenant with a cadre of 30 soldiers in each plus a Provost Marshal Section which was staffed by a Lieutenant Colonel assisted by a Major, a Captain and about seven enlisted soldiers, about 165 personnel total. I reported directly to the Provost Marshal. One of the highlights of my assignment there was meeting General of the Army Omar Bradley, the nation's last surviving military officer with five stars; Congress earlier having eliminated the five star rank in all military services.

In World War Two General Bradley, then wearing three and later four stars, had served alongside Generals Devers, Patton, Clark, Allen and British Field Marshal Montgomery, all under the Command of General Dwight Eisenhower, in the European Theater.

Already many years in retirement, he had been the recipient of an elaborate farewell ceremony hosted at the Armed Forces Training Base, Los Alamitos (as it was named then) on the occasion of his departure from Southern California to his final retirement location at Fort Hood, Texas.

He conducted his final review of military personnel by riding in President Eisenhower's former Presidential Limousine, a 1952 specially built Chrysler Imperial six door three seat stretch convertible complete with side and rear running boards for the Secret Service. I had arranged a loan of the vehicle from the City of Los Angeles which owned the car and used it for ceremonial events, such as parades. I received numerous looks on the freeway as I chauffeured it from the Los Angeles City Hall garage to Los Alamitos traversing the freeways.

The military formation for the Five Star General consisted of four platoons; one Army, one Navy, one Air Force and one Marine Corps. The acting platoon leaders were Two Star Generals and a two star Admiral. The Chief of Staff was a Three Star General and the Commander of Troops was a Four Star General. This was quite impressive and was to be the last if its kind.

The MP Company normally conducted annual training at Fort Hunter Liggett during the humid summer months. Even though the reservation is located on the Central Coast just about 10 miles inland, it is situated in a valley with minimal ocean breezes.

BOYS WILL BE BOYS

While at my headquarters at Fort Hunter Liggett I received word that soldiers from the division were disappearing from their units' mid-day and swimming in a nearby lake which was actually a large pond. I accompanied several MPs to the location and not only found several soldiers swimming nude but also several, what later were determined to be "Hippie's", both male and female, also nude. Adjacent to the lake the Hippies had established a camp complete with military tents, a canvas military lister bag used for storing drinking water and military marmite hot food containers nearby.

The soldiers had been supplying the "campers" with US Government owned equipment, including food, in return for "favors" though the ensuing investigation could not positively establish that. All of the equipment was confiscated and appropriate action taken against the soldiers involved. If I could have drained the lake I would have done so.

Several months after taking command of the MP Company the 1-18th Cavalry Squadron was alerted for mobilization and deployment to Viet Nam. The war had taken a down turn whereby Army Reserve and Army National Guard units were being called up. I made a request to immediately transfer to the 1-18th Cavalry but since it had been alerted for deployment it was "frozen" meaning no personnel could either transfer in or transfer out.

As a Captain I was informed by the Army that if I wanted to be mobilized with the unit I was required to resign my commission, which was a federal commission, and reenlist as a Specialist E-4 even though I had been an E-7 Platoon Sergeant prior to being commissioned. I was not willing to waive my hard earned rank so I declined. My various appeals were ignored, and also that of others, and with some I received no response.

The Cavalry Squadron was initially mobilized at Fort Lewis, Washington and disbanded there and each individual sent to Viet Nam to fill vacancies in units' in-country. Owning to political games-play by the Regular Army the 1-18th did not fight the war as a contiguous unit as they had been trained to do. This would not be practice in the future.

CHAPTER 35 COMMAND AND GENERAL STAFF COLLEGE

Just as I had attended my officer basic course at Fort Gordon, Georgia and the Officer's Advance Course at Fort Knox, Kentucky in my military reserve status I again took short military leave from the police department when I applied for and was selected to attend the Command and General Staff College.

Parts of the course were held at both the University of Nevada, Reno, and Fort Leavenworth, Kansas in two-week increments. Every year the University was home to several schools and in-service courses for Army personnel. The university was located uphill just a few blocks from downtown Reno and close to the casinos. In those days the casinos catered to the military who were permitted by the Army to enter the casinos in uniform.

A quick story regarding three friends and I while visiting a casino one evening after class. We had been there for several hours and were preparing to walk back to our dormitory but instead decided to have a late night meal. We sat and ordered breakfast in the casino coffee shop and I recall that the cost was about $2.95 for breakfast steak and eggs. The waitress informed us that if we waited until midnight to order the cost would only be $1.00 and it was around 11:40 PM then. She cautioned us to return before 1:00 AM as the special offer returned to the original price at that time so it was only good for the one hour.

We decided to wait the extra half hour by returning to the Black Jack tables and trying our luck which already had been bad. We were carried away with the time and when we rushed back to the coffee shop it was a few minutes past 1 o'clock so we lost the bargain meal special price. The cost in reality was the $200.00 which combined we had lost at the Black Jack table while trying to save $1.95. We were not very smart military officers – and we were expected to lead soldiers in combat?

Non-the-less this Command and General Staff College course qualified a field grade officer for assignment as a battalion or brigade staff officer and also battalion command. Completion of the course played a crucial role in my future military career.

CHAPTER 36 1ST SQUADRON, 18TH CAVALRY RETURNS

A year later when the 1-18th Cavalry was reconstituted and returned to California my request to transfer there was approved and I could retain my rank of Captain. I was first assigned as the S-4, Logistics Officer, then a year later as the S-2, Intelligence Officer. Both of these were Captain's positions on the staff. Later with the transfer of the Squadron's S-3, Operations Officer, a Major, I was transferred to that position as the Acting S-3 for a year pending the arrival of a qualified Major.

These assignments allowed me to gain valuable staff experience at the battalion level and immediately subordinate to another Lieutenant Colonel, the Squadron Commander, though I judged him to be deficient in his leadership abilities. The Squadron's organic make-up was three ground troops, A, B & C, equipped with armored vehicles, similar to that in Troop E, 140th Cavalry, and one air cavalry troop, D Troop, consisting of Cobra Attack Helicopters.

With the arrival of the Major to fill the position on a permanent basis I was transferred to the 40th Division Headquarters as Division Transportation Officer and placed on the Division Staff as a Captain which was quite an achievement. The position called for a Major but I did not have sufficient time in grade for promotion but within a few months I was promoted with just the minimum time in grade. Officers promoted to Major generally had six or seven years' time in grade, sometimes more, and I had just the minimum four years.

CHAPTER 37 DOROTHY'S ACTIVITIES

During this time Dorothy was actively engaged with her social club, the Eclygians, whose membership was almost exclusively women who had attended Long Beach Poly High School together and had been friends since childhood. Dorothy was only one of two members of the approximately 25 members who had not been lifelong friends. She considered it quite an honor to have been invited to membership. The Eclygians resembled a sorority but without the Greek paraphernalia and rituals. Their mantra was just enjoying each other's friendship.

Dorothy enjoyed her position in the cauterization Laboratory at Long Beach's Saint Mary's Hospital but was eventually offered a more senior position at a recently constructed hospital in Los Angeles, the West Adams Community Hospital, which she accepted. This would be a further commute but it was pleasant driving our recently purchased new Mercedes Benz car. One day after work she discovered that the car was missing from the guarded employee's parking lot so she telephoned me to confirm whether or not I had taken it which I explained that I had not and directed that she telephone the police which she did.

The investigation disclosed that a tow truck driver had approached the security guard on duty at the parking lot and exhibiting a clip board with official looking papers attached announced that he had orders to pick up a vehicle and described our vehicle by make, model, and color and license number. The unsuspecting guard raised the security arm and not only let the driver enter but also assisted him with attaching the vehicle. The car had been stolen right under his nose.

Many years later the vehicle body had been located when a "chop shop" had been raided. The vehicle, identified by VIN number, was minus tires, wheels, head lights, hood, trunk, wind shields, doors and front and rear bumpers. The engine and transmission were also missing. Since the insurance company had financially reimbursed us I informed the detectives that we no longer owned what was remaining of the car that it now belonged to the insurance company.

Over the years of our marriage Dorothy was always active in church activities. She sang in the adult choir, was a member of the hospitality committee and often assisted my mother with refreshments after services. We did some entertaining at our home often inviting friends and family to dinner. She spent considerable time with her girlfriends in the LA POWS and was always quick to offer to assist in the planning family gathering and providing food dishes.

Military social engagements were her favorites. This allowed her to spend time with spouses of military personnel where they would often compare notes on their husband's double lives; having a fulltime civilian job and serving part time in the military, as she told me.

CHAPTER 38 40TH DIVISION TRANSPORTATION OFFICER

My new duties and responsibilities as the Division Transportation Officer (DTO) involved planning all convoy movements for units maneuvering around the state and generally traveling to one of the various military bases. These included Fort Ord, Camp Roberts, Fort Hunter Leggett and Camp San Luis Obispo on the Central Coast and Camp Parks and the Presidio of San Francisco in the Bay area. Also Fort Irwin in the Mojave Desert North of Barstow and Camp Pendleton in the South near San Diego.

Units convoyed from starting points throughout the state including far reaches in the northern part of the state from such places as Redding and other locations near the Oregon Border to Calexico alongside the Mexican Border in the south. Timing was critical as it was important that convoys originating from various locations north and south arrived to their final destinations so as not to interfere with other convoys with the same destination.

The planning considered rest halts and expected traffic conditions based upon the latest information derived from the California Department of Transportation and the California Highway Patrol. The calculations were derived prior to the wide-spread use of computers.

My small staff, a Captain and five enlisted personnel, and I were required to coordinate movements with not only several state agencies but in some circumstances with county and city agencies as portions of convoy routes were on city streets, county roads and highways other than freeways. Additionally we coordinated internal convoy movements within the geographical boundaries of the aforementioned military installations.

Following this three year assignment, I was selected to serve as the Division Provost Marshal. This was a Lieutenant Colonel's position although I was one year short of being qualified for promotion. Again, this was a below zone transfer and there were several officers with more time in grade for promotion and many of them had aspired to the position. The next year while still serving in the position I was promoted to Lieutenant Colonel with the minimum time in grade.

The small promotion ceremony took place in the Office of the Division's Assistant Commander-Support, then Brigadier General Calvin Franklin. General Franklin himself had recently been promoted as the first African American General in the California National Guard. Within days of my promotion he was dispatched to Washington DC when he was appointed by the President of the United States as the Commanding General of the District of Columbia (DC) National Guard. The DC National Guard is the only National Guard in the United States and its territories that is headed by a Commanding General. All others are headed by a soldier with the title of Adjutant General. The DC Commanding General reports directly to the President.

Various members of my personal and special staff were in attendance at my brief Lieutenant Colonel pinning ceremony. Family members attending included my wife Dorothy, son Mark and nephew Gary Young, son of my sister Alice. At that time Gary was serving in the Army Reserve stationed at the same base having recently returned from his active duty training out of state. Gary looked "spiffy" in his military uniform, his father James Young having been a US Marine. My late father would have been so proud that

Dorothy & Brigadier General Franklin Pinning Lieutenant Colonel Gravett.

another of his sons had achieved prominent rank in the military the other being my brother Melvin having been previously been promoted to the rank of First Sergeant.

CHAPTER 39 40TH DIVISION PROVOST MARSHAL

This was my third Military Police assignment as an officer, the first one having been as a platoon leader in Headquarters and Headquarters Company, 40th Infantry Brigade while a Second Lieutenant and the second one as the Company Commander, 40th Military Police Company.

The Provost Marshal is the chief law enforcement officer in a division however, law enforcement and policing are not the MP's primary duties. Their tactical and operational duties are first, battle field circulation control, then enemy prisoner of war operations and finally division command post security. These are followed by law enforcement missions.

As mentioned earlier the Provost Marshal Section is organic to the Military Police Company which is commanded by a Captain subordinate to the Provost Marshal (PM). In this assignment I had the honor of serving with several soldiers with whom I would become personal friends throughout my military career and beyond.

These were Major Robert Berg, my OCS classmate and Costa Mesa police officer, Master Sergeant John Sack, an LAPD officer whom I had previously served with when I commanded a platoon, Sergeant (later Command Sergeant Major) Patrick Flannery and his brother, Staff Sergeant William Flannery, an LAPD officer and Sergeant First Class Lee Stewart, a Los Angeles Schools police officer. Years later I lauded Lee's military service to the nation and state while speaking at his funeral service.

During one annual training period at Fort Irwin another one of my younger brothers, Darnell, was also assigned there with his National Guard unit, the Class IX Section (repair parts) of Headquarters and Headquarters Company, 40th Division Support Command (40th DISCOM). Darnell and a close friend, Robert Williams, had recently enlisted in the National Guard shortly after them both having recently returned from Viet Nam.

When I visited Darnell in the field one day at Fort Irwin he asked if he could come to my BOQ to take a shower. Generally enlisted soldiers are not permitted in officer billets but blood is thicker than rules sometime. I told him that it would not be a problem and that I would be there that evening. Sometime after 6 PM a deuce and a half (two and a half ton truck) pulled up to my BOQ and deposited a dozen soldiers carrying cases of beer and other alcoholic beverages as well as a very large boom box. No soldiers are allowed to consume alcohol when in a field environment so Darnell had brought a party to my house to dodge the rules.

I was not about to throw them out but did suggest that they do two things, be extremely quiet and to not brag about the activity once they returned to their unit. They did not comply with either request. Several times during the evening I had to caution them to lower their voices while playing dominoes and a card game called bid whist and the talk in the field the next day was the blast of a party they had at Darnell's "brother's house." Nothing ever came of the incident but there was the potential for disciplinary action being taken on all sides.

The Provost Marshal position would be my longest assignment in the military, six years from 1980 to 1986. As one General remarked to me the extended length of time assigned there would allow my former peer officers to catch up with me in rank as some were still at the rank of Captain.

SPACE SHUTTLE LANDING

Our operations included deploying several times to Edwards Air Force Base in the high desert assisting the Air Force by performing ground perimeter security operations for several landings of the Space Shuttle. The Space Shuttle was America's answer to launching into space a reusable space vehicle which would reduce the overall cost of the country's exploration of the ionosphere

Edwards Air Force Base, 470 square miles, was home of the Air Forces' Flight Test Center and Test Pilot School. The base proper is surrounded by open desert leaving the major runways open to unwanted intrusion, save for the close up perimeter. The United States Air Force lacking the necessary vehicles to patrol the outer perimeters of the base with all-terrain wheeled and tracked vehicle called upon the Army to assist with the mission. The California Army National Guard to the rescue.

The 40th Infantry Division (Mechanized) with its' plethora of tracked armored personnel carriers and four wheel drive jeeps and other all-terrain vehicles set about designing a plan to patrol the perimeter prior to, during and for some time following the space craft landing.

The President of the United States, Ronald Reagan, was present at one of the landings along with over a half million viewers scattered throughout the open desert. The Army Military Police on the detail were stretched thinly around the base's 47 mile perimeter but were successful in maintaining security of the runways as required.

Lieutenant Colonel Gravett at Space Shuttle Landing

The ground patrols were assisted by air crews from units of the 40th Division Aviation Brigade flying UH-1 Huey and OH-58 helicopters. In directly they were also providing security for the Commander-in-Chief, the President. During one landing while serving as Chief of Ground Security, I had the opportunity and good fortune to be a member of the official greeting party as the astronaut's ascended down the stairs from the space ship. What an experience and honor.

In addition to Edwards Air Force Base the PM Section spent many weekends in the field with the MP Company overseeing operations. On several of these excursions my son Mark accompanied me as a youngster and really enjoyed eating in the field, sleeping on a cot in a tent and riding in a jeep. Other than the cold weather he enjoyed it all.

CHAPTER 40 NATIONAL GUARD ASSOCIATION OF THE UNITED STATES

As part of my military duties on numerous occasions I attended military conferences throughout the Continental US, Hawaii, the US Virgin Islands and Puerto Rico. These were the annual conferences of the National Guard Association of the United States (NGAUS). Our mission was to engage Members Congress to gain resources ranging from modernized equipment, salary increases and retirement benefits for all National Guard members regardless of rank. It is the oldest lobbing organization of its kind and is similar to the Association of the United States Army and Air Force Association. When members of all of these organization visit Congressional offices for dialogue they are off military duty and wear civilian attire. Funding is all private and no government funds expended in the effort.

Over the years I served on a several national committees. Committeemen are appointed by the National President based upon home state, army branch and unit assigned. As an Armor Branch Officer serving in a Mechanized Infantry Division it was natural that I serve on the tracked vehicle committee along with other senior officers serving in various combat units.

Attending the conferences was extremely educational to me personally as annually I would link up with friends from other states and territories and draft resolutions which addressed our needs nationwide.

At the conclusion of one of the conferences in Puerto Rico Dorothy, my brother Phillip and sister-in-law Dortha, joined me there and the four of us took a planned cruise from St. Thomas, Virgin Islands to South America visiting the countries of Columbia and Venezuela. Cruising back north we made port calls at St. Vincent and the Grenadines, St. Lucia and Grenada prior returning to St. Thomas where we debarked for the flight home. Military can also be fun.

CHAPTER 41 JAPAN ASSIGNMENT

While assigned as the Provost Marshal I deployed twice to Japan for joint operational exercises with the Japanese Ground Defense Force which by any other another name is their Army. The Allied Article of Surrender which ended their engagement in World War Two prohibited that country from having an Army per se. The Ground Self Defense Force resembles an Army in all respects though it is limited in numbers of personnel and equipment and are not permitted to deploy outside their country.

The operations which I participated in were named Yama Sakkara and Ulchi Focus Lens. Both were held on the Northern Japanese Island of Okido in the Prefecture of Sendai.

Northern Japan is extremely cold during the winter and during Yama Sakkara our division headquarters was housed in a very cold abandoned warehouse with ice on some parts of the cement floor. The exercises themselves were TEwT's (Pronounced TOOTS) Tactical Exercise without Troops. Line troops were not deployed in the field but the various headquarters' were deployed and all events were under simulated wartime conditions. The exercises were computer driven with a real time scenario. They were crucial for both countries to ensure the capabilities of each should they be confronted by a common foe.

During off-duty time we explored the area for cultural enrichment which included taking the opportunity to ride the Bullet Train and experiencing a hot bath in the Ufuru or community hot bath.

The Ufuru is a traditional phenomenon in the Japanese culture and foreign to most Americans. By description it is an intensely heated what Americans would consider a large bath tub but the size of four average back yard swimming pools but shallow all around. Everyone was nude with the male side separated from the female side by only a chest high tile wall. In their culture the bath is not about cleaning the body as it is about cleansing the soul by just soaking in the heated water while at the same time ridding the body of impurities.

Prior to entering the Ufuru everyone was required to take a soapy shower and scrub down very thoroughly and rinse while seated on a small stool. This was done in separate rooms for males and females but then everyone entered the same pool area nude and went to their side of the pool which was separated the chest high tile wall. Parents and children came as a family. Many of the adults had casual conversations at the wall much like Americans do over the back yard fence. No one seemed pretentious. Many lounged in the bath for up to an hour or more.

The Japanese restrooms on the military bases were another story. Given the physical stature of Japanese soldiers as compared to American soldiers it was challenging for us to use their latrines in comfort. Their military latrines were so small that when I used one it was so cramped that when seated on the toilet, if I could find a toilet, I had to stretch one leg out the door leaving the door open and me exposed. Other American soldiers did the same. Most restrooms in Sendai did not have seat toilets but just a porcelain lined hole in the restroom floor called a Benjo where the user squatted to use it however the flushing mechanism was similar to a toilet.

Unlike South Koreans it was my personal and biased assessment that the Japanese populous were not as accommodating to American Military and were just accepting the fact that our presence was required by Treaty for the most part. Unlike the US Navy and Marine Corps where American Sailors and Marines spend most of the shore leave at or near port cities where their presence has been accepted since the end of World War Two we were in different parts of the country where US military is seldom seen if ever.

My biased view was that the Japanese military are not well respected by their own countrymen. Perhaps this dates back to the issues of World War Two when the

Japanese populous had the war thrust upon them by the Japanese military in their attempt to convince the civilian government that Japan could win the war and eventually hold world dominance. The issues are purely political and much has been written on the subject so it is not my intent to dwell further.

CHAPTER 42 PUBLIC AFFAIRS DIVISION (TOUR ONE)

My next LAPD assignment was to another innovative program this time at Public Affairs Division. The program was called Police Role in Government (PRIG). This program had 30 officers assigned as a fulltime teachers at schools in the Los Angeles Unified School District, 15 in middle schools and 15 in high schools.

The officers were selected jointly by the Police Department, the Los Angeles Unified School District Administration and the respective school Principals. I taught at John C. Fremont High School in South Central Los Angeles. All of the officers held the rank of Policeman III.

One Lieutenant and two Sergeants supervised the program from the LAPD perspective and the various Social Studies Department Chairmen of the respective schools supervised and evaluated the program from the schools perspective.

We taught in the class room while in uniform but without the gun belt and weapon. Each officer was required to have a Bachelor's Degree and a teaching credential. By this time I had graduated from California State University Long Beach and met the degree requirement and took additional courses to satisfy the credential requirement.

Instruction covered parts and branches of the US Government as they pertained to the police, US History and Criminal Justice. Most of the officers' Bachelors' Degree majors were Government, History, Political Science or Criminology. This was a great opportunity to interact with students and serve as a liaison between them and the officers on the street. We taught from a core curriculum designed by instructors at the police academy but approved by the school district. This was an elective course.

We were not on campus to enforce the law nor were we part of the School District's Police Force. Some of us even volunteered after school to serve as assistant athletic coaches. I volunteered to coach the track team's shot putters as the track coach had been a college classmate. And although I had never participated in shot put competition the track coach provided some rudimentary instruction which served me and the team members well.

My respective PRIG class was part of the Social Studies Department and one of my friends in an adjacent class room was a woman by the name of Gloria Allred. Gloria taught American History and Government for several years at Fremont while attending law school in the evening. Upon her graduation and passing the Bar Exam she left teaching and opened her own law practice specializing in women's rights.

Over the ensuing years Gloria became extremely proficient in laws pertaining to women's rights and representing women in high profile cases and established a successful national reputation. One year while at Fremont she hosted the department's teachers and spouses at her home for a Holiday Party during the season.

CHAPTER 43 DETECTIVE HEADQUARTERS DIVISION

HOMICIDE ROLL-OUT INVESTIGATOR

In my next LAPD assignment I was promoted to Investigator 1 at Parker Center downtown at Police Headquarters. The City had contracted with the Jacobs Engineering Corporation to review the rank structure in the Department and to make recommendations for improved proficiency while at the same time improving morale. The survey recommended changing the ranks from the tradition Patrolman, Sergeant, Lieutenant, Captain, etc, along the military structure to some more clearly identified with the function performed.

In the past becoming a Detective was generally based upon who you knew as opposed to what you knew. For this reason, new recommended rank structure put in place a civil service examination process which must be passed to become a Detective. Three levels of Detective were recommended, I, II, & III. In the first exam process I passed the written part and also the interview portion and was promoted to Investigator I in the first group of officers with that title. Investigator was the original title for the new rank, but was later changed to Detective I as well as II & III. Several other titles were implemented such as two ranks of Sergeant, two for Lieutenant, three for Captain and the Inspector rank was changed to Commander. Along the way a new rank above Deputy Chief was added and that was Assistant Chief; three positions. All together the Department went from seven ranks to well over 20, many of them specialized.

My first assignment as an Investigator I was to the Homicide "Roll Out" Team with the designation as a K-Car Investigator and assigned to Detective Headquarters Division. K-Car designation was given to the night watch detectives who had initial jurisdiction over homicide investigations.

At that time, geographical Division Homicide Detectives generally worked daytime hours on their various cases. When a homicide occurred during night time or early morning hours the K-Car Investigators responded to the scene and took charge directing the uniform officers, protecting the scene, collecting evidence, interviewing witnesses and detaining potential suspects. All of this is done awaiting the arrival from home of the detectives who would be handling the case until completion. Once they arrived the cases were turned over to them.

The K-Car officers had citywide jurisdiction for this function. That being the case we were involved at the outset of numerous homicide investigations and accidental death incidents which were also under the jurisdiction of Homicide Investigators. We also did the preliminary investigation on deaths occurring outside of a medical facility, other than traffic accidents, until they determined to be natural deaths. Some of the most personal and challenging investigations I conducted were suicides, especially of young people, and Sudden Infant Death Syndrome known as SIDS. These were where young babies who died in their cribs for many unknown reasons.

GANG DETAIL INVESTIGATOR

Later I was assigned to the Gang Detail in the same division. Our mission was to monitor and track gang members citywide. In this assignment I attended several funerals of deceased (murdered) gang members to ensure the maintenance of order and to have an omnipresence should there be drive byes by rival gangs. Uniformed patrol officers were also in the area.

My partners and I became to know several gang members on a personal basis and were saddened to see one of them murdered after we had spent considerable time attempting to convince him to leave the gang scene. He had excellent grades in school and played sports but had still acquiesced to the gang culture and was killed in a shootout with another gang.

TELEVISION TALK SHOW

While assigned to the Gang Investigation Detail my partner Francois L'Toile and I were invited to a local television station to tape a Talk Show segment on gangs. We were asked to be prepared to paint a picture of the gang problem in the city and county and describe law enforcement methods that were being employed to abate the problem. The television host was Bryant Gumble who received his start in television in the Los Angeles market prior to going on to the national stage as both a sports commentator and hosting a series of news specials.

During the taping we explained to Mr. Gumble that both the Los Angeles Police Department and the Los Angeles County Sheriffs were deploying specialized task forces to track the gang activity but voiced that neither agency did not publicly discuss law enforcement methods, means, tactics and procedures in public as that would provide information to the gangs who would develop counter methods. We also explained that we never identified any gang by its name as that would embolden them and give them unwarranted publicity which would enhance their recruitment of additional gang members. We did discuss gangs in a general way.

We related that although the gang menace appeared to some as a new and emerging phenomenon, gangs had been in and around Los Angeles since the 1930's and before. We explained that gangs differed in ethnicity, type of crimes committed, locations referred to as turf, initiation rituals and preferred criminal activity.

To place the gang menace in perspective and comparison we noted that on June 25, 1950 the North Korean Army invaded South Korea which started the Korean War. They attacked with 100,000 soldiers armed primarily with small arm weaponry and a few obsolete tanks from World War Two. In Los Angeles County, we explained, there were over 125,000 identified gang members almost all possessing weapons more sophisticated that those by which the cops and deputies were so armed and many more sophisticated than those which the United States Army had in 1950. This provided him and the public with a better perspective on the immense criminal gang problem affecting the community.

CHAPTER 44 77TH STREET DIVISION PATROL

Two years later I was promoted to Sergeant 1, the equivalent to Detective II, and transferred to 77th Division Patrol working the overnight shift called the morning watch. This was my first supervisory assignment and I applied all of my previously learned law enforcement and military leadership skills in supervising the approximately 30 officers in 15 patrol cars under my supervision as well as the other three Sergeants 1 on the watch on a given night.

A Lieutenant 1 served as the Watch Commander and a Sergeant II served as the Assistant Watch Commander. One of my challenges there was to remain alert while driving alone in the wee hours of the morning when not responding to supervise and backup officers performing their duties.

77th Street Division at that time was very notorious for the presence of numerous gangs and gang activity which included murders, drive-by shootings, heavy drug activity, gun running and other heinous crimes. The primary gangs were Hipsters and Bad Boys (pseudonyms). Newer gangs such as the Hipsters identified themselves by wearing red attire of all sorts which included hats and caps, shirts, pants with a bandana or scarf hanging from the back pocket, red under shorts revealed by low hanging pants and some also wore red socks and sneakers.

The Bad Boys, also a new gang, were involved in similar gang activity and were attired in blue clothing and accessories much like the Hipsters. Each gang had various factions with their geographical territory, usually a street or neighborhood name, preceding the gang name whether Hipster or Bad Boy.

Many were the same gangs which I encountered during my former assignment at the Gang Detail at Detective Headquarters Division.   Much had changed including the number, which had increased exponentially, of young African American and Hispanic American boys, young men and adults identifying themselves as gang members. As noted earlier the gang activity was certainly not limited to 77th Street Division and was wide-spread throughout South Central Los Angeles and other parts of the city and county.

In other parts of the city there were other gangs such as Hispanic gangs on the east side and White motor cycle gangs in the San Fernando Valley.

As a Patrol Sergeant I was able to observe first-hand the remarkable job the patrol officers were performing in the division's area suppressing crime while at the same time assisting law abiding citizens. The gang activity was so extensive that the rapport between the police and community was enhanced because gangs had for the most part held some small enclaves of the division "captive" and citizens were eager to now report on gang individuals which had not always been the situation.

Patrol Sergeants responsibilities also included writing performance reviews on individual officers on the watch. For this reason it was important to make notes and information on individual officers as incidents occurred whether positive or negative. Generally there was collaboration among the supervisors regarding individual officers if there were questions or there issues regarding an officer's work performance. Most officers were dedicated in performing their duties judiciously.

An interesting note regarding my assignment to 77th Street Division. This coincided with the assignment of two neighborhood friends whom I had grown up with in the neighborhood in San Pedro. They were Hollis Lee and Billie Jean Prince Taylor. Hollis was the supervising Detective III of the Juvenile Unit and Billie, also a Detective, served as his subordinate partner.

It was previously mentioned that Hollis had been my next door neighbor when I resided at "790" and Billie grew up just two blocks away. I had known both just about my entire life. After all three of us retired from the department we remained friends.

CHAPTER 45 PUBLIC AFFAIRS DIVISION (TOUR #2)

After my six month Sergeant 1 probationary period was concluded, which I passed with flying colors, I had a return assignment to Public Affairs Division where I was promoted to Sergeant II. There I was given responsibility for supervising 15 of the 30 officers in the Police Role in Government Program where I had previously been assigned to teach. This supervisory assignment lasted approximately 18 months. Sergeant II was a rank just below Detective III but higher than Detective II.

Once a month all 30 officers attended a special roll call at Parker Center where the supervisors passed our subpoenas if the officers had court cases and training was conducted. New department policies and procedures were discussed and the officers compared notes on the in-class activities at their respective schools. We also used that time to refine curriculum and to receive updates on criminal activity around our respective schools for our own situational awareness.

This assignment allowed me to routinely make supervisory visits to the schools of the officers under my supervision and observe them in their classroom situations. Most were prearranged as I had notified each school and made appropriate appointments to visit with both the school principal and department chairpersons. This was done for several reasons; to receive reviews from the school leadership on both the practicality of the program and to garner results from opinions of the students and other teachers expressed to the leadership, if any. Another was to show visibility of the Department's supervision.

CHAPTER 46 EMPLOYEE OPPORTUNITY AND DEVELOPMENT DIVISION (EODD)

Over the years the Los Angeles Police Department had been cited by the federal government for not having sufficient measures in place to recruit minorities and women to the point where the department would reflect the makeup of the city's ethnic populations. Additionally the supervisory, management and senior leadership of the Department possessed some of the same discrepancies. A Federal Court Consent Decree was agreed upon and put in place whereby the Department would begin to make necessary corrections.

It was for this reason that a specialized division was created to focus on improving upon these conditions. I was part of the initial cadre at Employee Opportunity and Development Division (EODD) and served as a Supervising Sergeant II having

MG Gravett and L.A. Police Chief Bernard Parks

been requested to be assigned there by the newly appointed Commanding Officer, Captain Joe Rouzan. He had selected as his Assistant Commanding Officer a sharp, and up and coming protégé, Lieutenant II Bernard Parks, who eventually rose to become the Los Angeles Chief of Police. Over a period of time his appointed Adjutant, Sergeant II Ronald Banks, rose to become the Chief of Police in nearby Inglewood and another Lieutenant II, in the division, Julius I. Davis, was later appointed Assistant Los Angeles Police Chief. Some served consecutively and not simultaneously. Perhaps had I not been in the active military reserves and taking military leave several times a year I may joined that prestigious group.

One of EODD's mission was to canvass the city, county and state for potentially qualified minority and women recruits and to assist in ushering them through the application process. This included a local physical training (PT) program for women to develop better upper body strength, that part of the entry-level physical fitness test having a high failure rate for women. The volunteer PT class was conducted after hours and on weekends at the police academy with qualified physical fitness instructors.

Another part of its mission was to develop mentoring programs for patrol officers seeking to promote to Detective or Sergeant. These included staging off-duty volunteer study groups and one-on-one mentoring. In my two year assignment there, I and other staff, were able to put in place programs and practices which would enhance mission accomplishment. We commenced on recruiting trips to military bases throughout California after first coordinating with Base Commanders and Employment Counselors. Special focus was given to military policemen in the Army and Security Police personnel in the Air Force. Women of all military skills and occupations were sought.

A lesson learned during our recruiting excursions was that corporate America also had recruiting programs in place to recruit some of the same qualified ethnic minorities and women. It takes a special mindset for a person to seek a career in law enforcement and convincing citizens to adopt to that mindset was not easy and often not successful.

EODD was the only assignment within the LAPD where I believe the work performed by our staff was not overly appreciated by many in the Department especially some of those in the supervisory, management and command positions. The specific recruitment of minorities and women did not sit well with the non-minority rank and file officers even though several were included in the EODD staff and were selected based upon their sensitivity to the division's mission. It was my experience however that most officers at all ranks throughout the department were reticent to express these personal views on the practicability of EODD.

Over time minorities and women were beginning to attain rank in greater numbers when the playing field was leveled in terms of the oral interview portion of the promotional process. This accounted for half of the over-all promotional score. Some minorities and women, again from my biased and lofty height, were finally beginning to be seen as equals to non-minorities and had a role to play in keeping the city safe from crime.

On the social front since the division was small in number, totaling about 25 sworn police officers and civilian support staff, Dorothy and I hosted the entire division cadre and their spouses at our home for a costume Halloween party. Interesting enough we had one hundred percent participation rate with all wearing costumes. This event served two purposes, it let us gather in a less formal social gathering and it tended to build morale. It met its intent.

Another internal program instituted to enhance morale was that the division formed soft ball and basketball teams and played in the LAPD athletic leagues. Since we were such a small division in numbers and therefor light on talent we did not do so well but there was a lot of camaraderie. The non-players, both sworn and civilian, attended the games to cheer us on. I played on both teams and performed my best and the end result was that it was questionable as to whether or not my presence made a difference.

CHAPTER 47 UNIVERSITY OF SOUTHERN CALIFORNIA (USC)

It was about this time in 1977 that I graduated from the University of Southern California with a Masters' Degree in Public Administration having enrolled two years earlier. I had selected USC for my graduate studies for its national reputation and also it had been my high school ambition to always attend there at some point and become a life-long Trojan.

Just as important USC had recently been funded with a grant by the U.S. Department of Justice *"to create greater professionalism in criminal justice through higher education."* This was tuition assistance, books and materials costs as well as travel costs to qualified law enforcement personnel with demonstrated potential for higher responsibility.

Curriculum and scheduling allowed me to attend fulltime while still working fulltime. With this I managed to cram a three year part-time program into two years. This was partly accomplished by using accumulated overtime and vacation time to attend some "intensive" classes.

An intensive class was a regular course taught over eight consecutive days; eight hours per day. The course was preceded by a requirement to write a subject matter scholarly paper due at the beginning of each course and another at the end of the course. I would not have advised any student to follow this path as the title "intensive" was properly titled.

Graduate level courses at any university far exceed classes taken at the Bachelor level in terms of program requirements, The University of Southern California being no exception. Most of my classes required strategic level thinking and presentation. My class mates possessed differing experiences both in and out of government and whose prior college preparation had been from institutions from throughout the country. This provided an interchange of ideas and of concepts learned in other regions. Some instructors were visiting professors from other universities, especially those leading the intensive forums.

USC being a research university has a plethora of libraries and learning centers for which to garner information and I seemed to utilize most of them. My School, the School of Public Administration, Center for Training and Development, provided me the requisite background, training and experience which would greatly assist me in the higher levels of government which at that time I had not imagined.

Upon completing my coursework and the submission and approval of my Master's Thesis my petition for graduation was approved. The graduation ceremony was held at the Shrine Auditorium adjacent to the University and was attended by Dorothy, our son Mark and my brother Leon. My academic focus then was on the potential of studying for a doctorate degree but that did not occur as shall be reported.

.

CHAPTER 48 POLICE ANTICS

GOBBLE GOBBLE

Police officers are notorious for playing pranks on one another and also on their bosses. Some are funny but others could lead to serious consequences. Here are some of those stories.

At a police station where I was assigned as a Patrol Sergeant a prank was played on its Commanding Officer. Whether the officers loved and respected him or otherwise was not known but over a four day holiday period when he was away some officers placed a live turkey in his office along with enough feed for a week; guess what holiday? They went a step further by opening the file cabinet and desk drawers. Turkeys were known to eat everything in sight even when full and expelled their food expeditiously. When the Commanding Officer returned after the four day holiday period he encountered much of a surprise and Internal Affairs was called in to conduct an investigation.

His entire office had turkey excrement throughout including his desk top, in file drawers and on his chair. The station custodian was called in but refused to clean up the droppings claiming, probably rightfully so, that cleaning up the mess was not in his civil service job description. The city had to contract with a commercial cleaning service for the cleanup and many of the official files had to be cleaned or destroyed. It was not known if the culprit(s) were ever identified but if so they stood to have been given a lengthy suspension if not outright terminated.

THE INFAMOUS CODE 7 RUN

LAPD officers have always been involved in other non-threatening antics of every sort. One antic was to see which officers could drive round trip on their Code 7 lunch break the greatest distance, in a black and white police car, without being detected by a supervisor. To document the experience the officers were required to have a cash register receipt or photograph noting the date and time. A lunch break, or Code 7, was 45 minutes so the distance ordinarily could not be too great. This story had been around the Department a long time and some of the old timers claim its authenticity.

Two ingenious officers set the record traveling round trip from down town Los Angeles to Las Vegas and return without being detected. This has long been part of LAPD lore for quite some time and I have no personal knowledge of the event.

The story goes that this was accomplished with the assistance of several officers covering the daring police officers' patrol area and answering their radio calls for service. This also required coordinating with the California Highway Patrol (no CHP supervisors obviously) and the Nevada Highway Patrol (again no supervisors). This was to seek their assistance to ignore a speeding LAPD black and white police car with red lights flashing all the way through L.A. County and San Bernardino County and into to Nevada. Scheduled stops for gas were built in to this masquerade.

These enterprising (or dumb) officers probably also had coordinated with other law enforcement agencies to ignore the speeding car which would explain they were not in hot pursuit of any motorist.

A quick stop on Las Vegas Boulevard in front of Caesar's Palace for a date and time stamped documented Polaroid photograph produced the evidence needed and they were off back to down town L.A. reversing their route with the same assistance given. They made history with this probably five hour plus excursion and I seriously doubt that trip was ever attempted or accomplished again and never will for good reason. All police cars now are equipped with digital mobile tracking devices where their locations are monitored 24/7 from a command center at police headquarters.

I can now confess since the statute of limitation has long passed that while working at Central Division a partner, Abel Gomez (pseudonym), and I did once make a round trip run to the City of Ventura from down town. No record there.

MAGAZINES FOR SALE?

As stated earlier for years Police Officers have been known to pull pranks on their Supervisors or even Commanding Officers. At one unnamed Police Division for one reason or another the Commanding Officer was not well respected by a plurality of officers assigned there.

Some enterprising cops decided to "take the law into their own hands" by taking out over 25 or so magazine subscriptions in the Captain's name using his home address. He was not amused when his wife observed that he was receiving the Play Boy and other risqué magazines, including those directed towards gay men, began arriving at their home.

Certainly when the payment invoices began arriving he spent part of his time trying to convince the companies that he had received them in error. The follow-on Internal Affairs investigation to determine who was responsible was inconclusive.

Chapter 49 FBI National Academy

The Federal Bureau of Investigation National Academy (FBINA) is housed at the FBI Academy at Quantico, Virginia about 30 miles south of Washington DC. The National Academy is a twelve week intensive course whereby selected federal, state and local law enforcement commanders, managers and supervisors attend executive level training. The selection process is extremely competitive and the LAPD generally is allowed to nominate one or two candidates in each of the four classes every year.

In 1977 I was selected to attend the March class and decided to drive our new Mercedes Benz car there having just received it as a replacement for our other car which had been stolen. I would have my own car during the three month duration of the class. Also I could transport more personal items than would be possible to carry on the airplane. I bade Dorothy and Mark farewell and departed on my expected four or five day trip.

On the morning of the third day while driving on Good Friday near Springfield, Missouri I encountered black ice and skidded off the road, hit a road sign which shattered a rear window. The car hydroplaned and landed on a snow bank. I was not injured. A passing highway snow plow vehicle attached a cable and pulled my car back onto the road. With a rear side window gone I drove to the Mercedes Benz dealership in Springfield only to find the business closed for the holiday. Luckily some technicians were on duty who sealed the window space with plastic material which was sufficient enough for me to continue on my journey. The glass was later replaced in Arlington, Virginia after I had reported in to FBI Academy.

I graduated in June and Dorothy and Mark were able to travel to Virginia for a week to attend the graduation ceremony and we made the time a family vacation. They really enjoyed the historical sites of Washington DC and surrounding areas.

During my training there I relished the opportunity to meet and establish friendships with classmates from throughout the country and with several international classmates. This additional managerial training greatly assisted me in follow-on assignment with the LAPD though it was the opinion of many that I would have eventually achieved even greater responsibility than actually achieved had a not been an active military reservist though a few other reservists were able to promote.

Concurrent with my studies at the FBINA I earned a diploma from the University of Virginia in Executive Law Enforcement through their partnership program with the FBI. Several of our instructors were from the University of Virginia Law School. FBI Agents, generally and after receiving their Bachelors or Masters degrees, possess either a law degree or are a Certified Public Accountant.

The FBI National Academy is somewhat comparable to the regular FBI Academy in that much of the same instruction is given but lack the basics of law enforcement as all of the attendees are seasoned in their respective law enforcement fields. Most have been practicing their profession for several years and had become supervisors, managers or command staff in their respective agencies.

One of my FBINA classmates was Helena Ashby, a Lieutenant from the Los Angeles County Sheriff's Department. I had met her once before at a law enforcement conclave and knew of her stellar reputation as a superb law enforcement professional. She and I quickly became colleagues when we learned that we were born in the same year, same month, same day and same hour. With that we considered ourselves as twins and for a few years thereafter exchanges birthday cards. Helena eventually retired at the high rank of Chief which was only subordinate to Assistant Sheriffs, Under Sheriff and the Sheriff. An extraordinary achievement.

CHAPTER 50 INTERNAL AFFAIRS DIVISION

Few Investigators are selected for assignment to Internal Affairs Division (I. A. D.) and it generally has an eighteen month tour limit. The mission of I. A.D., referred to as I. A., is to instill confidence in the local citizenry that the department is transparent in enforcing the law with every complaint. No matter how superfluous a complaint against an officer appeared on the surface it at least received a cursory review. This is often referred to as Constitutional Law Enforcement. If the complaint appeared to have any merit whatsoever it then received a more thorough investigation.

Eighteen months was the assignment limit to ensure that the investigators, all Sergeants II, would not develop the mindset that viewed all other officers with suspicion or guilt.

First allow me two discuss the Internal Affairs assignment protocol. Investigators are assigned in pairs, generally based upon where they reside geographically. Los Angeles County is 454 square miles and quite often investigators are called out after hours for an immediate investigation. It is reasonable that when investigators reside within the general proximity of one another they can link up within a respectable amount of time to initiate the investigation together.

On occasion officers can request to be assigned together based upon just knowing one another and knowing the others' investigative capabilities. After having been assigned to I. A. for a few months my friend Lawrence Donaldson (pseudonym) and I requested to be assigned together and we were.

When I. A. Investigators travel to one of the geographical police stations for the purpose of investigating an officer or an incident the standard protocol is that the

Team first pays a courtesy visit on the Division Commanding Officer, usually a Captain III, and advise him or her of their presence at that station. The Commander is then required to make available to the investigators any and all records requested and generally without question. The Commander is also required to make any officer to be interviewed available for that purpose. Most Captains themselves have had a stint as an I. A. Investigator and will not inquire as to the nature, scope or purpose of the investigation.

One day Lawrence and I responded to a geographical station to conduct an investigation and made the requisite courtesy call at the Captain's office. The Captain, somewhat taken aback when seeing us, remarked something to the extent that he doubted we were from Internal Affairs and questioned our right to be in "his" station. He remarked that he was going to telephone I. A. to confirm that in fact we were I .A. investigators even though we had shown him our credentials. Surprisingly he in fact did telephone our office.

Here is the rub, Lawrence and I were both black and the White Captain opined that I. A. would be vane to assign two black Investigators as partners reasoning that two blacks working together would undoubtedly give black officers under investigation a break or smooth over an investigation. In the history of the LAPD Lawrence and I were the first two black investigators to be assigned as partners at Internal Affairs Division.

I. A. D. Case #1 (AKA The one that slid away)

Internal Affairs received a report that a suspect, possibly an off-duty police officer, was making purchases at various Sears & Roebuck Stores around the county buying various high end lighting fixtures. He would pay for the merchandise in cash, take the boxes home, carefully open the bottom of the box and remove the lighting. He then would place junk items in the box weighing about the same as the lighting and carefully reseal the box as if it had not been tampered with and leaving no fingerprints.

A day later, he would return to the store claiming that he no longer wanted the lighting and requested a cash refund which he would always receive. The box would be carefully inspected at the top and sides which never showed signs of being opened. This occurred many times and in those days there was very little communication between the stores. The ploy only came to light by reports of an unsuspecting legitimate customer who took home a box of junk when the box he believed contained lighting had been resold to them. The thief probably then resold the fixtures at swap meets and the money pocketed.

Swap meets, then and now, are notorious for peddling stolen merchandise (once while on patrol I received a call to a local swap meet where a vendor was selling used water hoses. He had a stack of approximately 30 or 40 hoses no doubt stolen from residents' front lawns).

When interviewing one of the store restocking clerks he stated that he believed the suspect was a police officer based upon a brief conversation with the purchaser at the time. He described the suspect as a man whom he had seen in the store several weeks earlier when he had returned some actual merchandise and gave a description. The investigation disclosed that this person also matched the description from other Sears' stores.

After several weeks of dead ends we received a call that the suspect had made a legitimate purchase of building supplies at a store using his personal credit card and was recognized by an employee. A thorough check revealed that he was in fact a Los Angeles Police Officer. Since we did not have sufficient proof that he had been involved in the crime, we decided to visit his residence just to ask a few routine questions which we were allowed to do.

When we arrived he invited us into his home and right away we observed a lighting fixture in the entry way identical to one to which we had a photograph as having been stolen. Now we had reasonable cause to believe that he had possibly committed a crime so we asked him where he received the light. Right away he ordered us out of his residence and we complied departing immediately.

Knowing that we now needed a warrant to search for the evidence, I remained at a neighborhood park across the street while Lawrence quickly drove to the nearest court house to seek a warrant. The local Judge was on a nearby golf course but Lawrence arranged transportation for him back to his chambers where he issued the warrant.

Upon Lawrence's return we approached the house, displayed the warrant, and upon entering noticed that the light fixture was now missing with an empty faded space visible where we had observed it. We asked where the light had been removed to and the officer replied that there had never been a light there although the discoloration of the "popcorn" ceiling indicated otherwise.

We then served the warrant and began a thorough search of the home which was a single story multi-bedroom house with a six foot wooden back and side yard fence. The property abutted against a cemented dry riverbed which was also had a six foot chain link fence.

Lawrence and I searched every crevice in the house but could not locate the missing light fixture. This included searching the attic crawl space, the foundation crawl space and the attached garage and car. We searched all bedrooms, bathrooms, kitchen, his yard and his neighbor's yards on both sides and even the roof tops. We spent considerable time searching the dry river bed after removing our coats and climbing the fences.

The item was never found and we were stymied because the officer had never left his house. Our only theory was that he somehow broke it up into small pieces and flushed it down the toilet, but this was only a theory. In any event if he actually did that he later had a major plumbing problem.

There was insufficient evidence to charge the officer with a crime nor was he charged by the Department and he invoked his police officer rights and refused to take a Polygraph Test. Much later he was eventually terminated by the Police Department for violating unrelated Department policies. The chickens had come home to roost.

I.A.D. CASE #2 (A FREE SWIMMING LESSON)

Under certain conditions police officers are permitted to work off-duty security jobs a few hours per week if there is no conflict with their regular duties. All such positions must be approved in advance and except for movie shoots and sporting events, all are generally worked in civilian attire. Officers cannot use accumulated sick time for this purpose and they must have an excellent performance history. All job requests must be pre-approved by the Commanding Officer. While working off-duty jobs the officers are held to the same high standards of conduct as if they were on duty.

We were assigned a case whereby a citizen complained that a police officer working off-duty security at an apartment complex, for no reason, "threw" him into the apartment swimming pool while he was fully clothed and that he almost drowned because he could not swim. Purportedly the officer then stood by laughing.

The circumstances were that late one evening while the officer was performing his security duties at the complex the resident was playing music very loudly which was disturbing his neighbors. His apartment was on the ground floor with a glass sliding door opening onto the pool deck and was open without a screen. Several neighbors had complained to him by knocking on his door and requesting him to lower the sound.

The officer under investigation first decided to allow the neighbors to settle their issues but eventually, with no response from the resident, decided to approach him by knocking on this glass door without entering. A heated conversation ensued which led to the resident yelling at the officer and flailing his arms while following the officer outside near the pool. At a certain point the resident ended up in the swimming pool and screaming for help as he could not swim. The resident alleged that the officer threw him into the pool then laughed at him when he called for help but finally extending a pole which he used to extract himself.

The office's version was that when the resident was flailing his arms he lost his balance and fell into the pool. Seeing him in distress he extended a pole and assisted him out. There were no witness to the incident and obviously their accounts differed.

The result was that the complaint was unsubstantiated (not proven) but "in the interest of justice" the officers' permit to work off-duty there was canceled. He probably got away with one. The complainant refused to take a voluntary polygraph test so by Department policy the officer was not requested to take one and doubted that he would have even if the citizen's test results had shone him as being truthful as was the Department's policy.

CHAPTER 51 RECORDS AND IDENTIFICATION DIVISION (R&I)

After my tour in Internal Affairs Division I was assigned to a Watch Commander's position at Records and Identification (R&I) Division. In staffing numbers R&I was then the largest Division in the Department and was staffed by over 400 civilian personnel on three watches around the clock. The only sworn staff were the Commanding Officer, a Police Captain, a Police Lieutenant as Assistant Commanding Officer and six Sergeants II as Watch Commanders.

R&I was the repository for all reports filed by the Department and citizens including arrest reports, criminal records (called rap sheets), booking records, jail reports, medical records, evidence reports, traffic accident reports, a repository for all fingerprints, photographs, warrants, computer files and backup systems and other technical equipment. This was basically a paper operation as computers were just making their way into the Department in more substantial numbers.

California State Law required that all of these files and functions be overseen by a sworn Police Officer and the sworn Watch Commanders on each shift met that requirement with generally only one on duty at a time but the six of us providing 24/7/365 coverage.

The day to day supervision of the civilian staff in the Division however, was performed by a Chief Clerk on each Watch. This was a senior managerial ranking civil service civilian with many years' experience. I recall that when I transferred to the Division one of the Chief Clerks pulled me aside and in a very nice and cordial way told me that Chief Clerks were in charge of that Division and any and all coordination with staff should be (would be) channeled through them. In other words, just stay in the Watch

Commander's office and let the Chief Clerks do their job. I learned very quickly.

The R&I Watch Commander position was in itself very important and demanding. During each watch my responsibilities ranged from accepting warrants from the courts to be placed in the system to maintaining the fledging computer systems which connected, at that time, to the over twenty large refrigerator size free standing main frame hard drives to the more than one hundred desk top terminals.

Additionally, when arrests were made throughout the city and arrestees without identification refused to identify themselves, they were transported to R&I Division where I would authorize their fingerprinting. In almost all cases most were immediately identified by one of our superb fingerprint technicians. Often times most arrestees had previous arrest records and most had other outstanding warrants for various offenses, both misdemeanor and felony, and I would authorize their booking.

With over 125 personnel on each watch, almost all women, on every shift there was always some kind of celebration. Just about every week there was a reception or a celebration of sorts with lots of cakes, pies and home baked cookies. They celebrated birthdays, weddings, anniversaries, sport team wins, promotions, transfers, graduations, announced pregnancies, births, adoptions and all holidays and, of course, retirements. Watch Commanders were invited to partake in every event. With all of that going on work was still accomplished.

CHAPTER 52 OLYMPIC SUPPORT COORDINATING COMMITTEE

In 1982 I was still serving in the California Army National Guard when I was given two year orders placing me on active duty for the purpose of joining the military support staff planning for its' role in the upcoming Olympic Games two years hence. I then departed from the Department on a military leave of absence.

That would be my last year physically on the Los Angeles Police Department as I joined the Military Task Force. The unit was located just a few blocks away from the LAPD Headquarters at Parker Center to the more expansive Piper Technical Building which housed the city archives with the police department's ASTRO Division, as it was called, on the roof top. ASTRO stood for Air Support to Regular Operations, the police department's helicopter fleet.

The Military Task Force, official named the Olympic Support Coordinating Center (OSCC), was actually a Fusion Center. It housed representatives from more than 300 federal, state and local organizations, agencies and departments. These included civilian federal, state and municipal law enforcement agencies, both domestic and international, state and local fire departments, intelligence apparatus both military and civilian, government first responders of every nature and civilian agencies such as the Red Cross, the Salvation Army and representatives from major medical centers.

Non-Profit organizations also had a seat at the warehouse size table. Public and private colleges and universities were represented as their campuses were the site of some events and some of their dormitories were used for athlete housing especially UCLA whose expansive Westwood campus became the Olympic Village. All branches of the military had a strong presence there. Direct coordination was simplified by having all coordinators in close proximity where they could coordinate face to face rather than by telephone or computer. One of the greatest activities there was the trading of Olympic pins representing their respective organizations.

Though I was one of the military liaison officers in military uniform I was on official leave from the LAPD and still had status there. The Olympic Games closing date was my last official day as a member of the Los Angeles Police Department as my military leave terminated then. The date was August 22, 1984.

Retirement is not complete until all of the "paper work is done." The next week I returned to the LAPD Personnel Division to out-process and return all of my LAPD issued equipment. I visited R&I Division for the last time and while there was informed that they were planning a retirement dinner for me. This was unexpected as I had been gone for about two years and even though I visited there on several occasions.

Chapter 53 LAPD Retirement & Second Career

A few weeks after the close of the Olympics R & I Division held a nice farewell dinner in my honor at the Police Academy in the very room where I studied as a cadet which was now a banquet hall. The event was attended by a large grouping such as R&I staff, fellow police officers, military personnel, and a host of family, friends and neighbors.

I was humbled when presented with several certificates, plaques and mementoes. The best presentation of course was my retired badge and retired identification card. Then I was officially retired. During the program it was noted that I had one seventeen year stretch without taking a day of sick leave but which did not include "injury on duty" absences.

Fulltime Military Operations

Now that I was officially retired from the Police Department I began my new fulltime military duties. Since 1982, two years prior to the Olympic Games, I had been assigned as Provost Marshal of the 40th Infantry Division at the rank of Lieutenant Colonel and I retained that assignment and rank. The PM position was a reserve position so I was posted in a concurrent assignment with a fulltime position at Division Headquarters as Special Projects Officer (SPO). This worked out very well as both positions were at the Los Alamitos Joint Forces Training Base.

Between 1982 and 1986 while assigned at the PM and SPO the Division participated in numerous domestic and international training operations and field exercises which tested the capabilities of various units and their commanders.

Operation Gallant Eagle was conducted in 1982 at the US Army's National Training Center at Fort Irwin in the Mojave Desert north of Barstow and near Death Valley. Other military facilities in the scenario included Nellis Air Force Base in North Las Vegas, Nevada from where air sorties were flown and Twenty Nine Palms Marine Corps Base where the Marine Corps participants were based. Navy aircraft carriers were stationed off shore.

This was a force-on-force exercise, meaning it pitted the 40th Infantry Division (Mechanized) against elements of the US Army's elite 82nd Airborne Division and this was one of America's largest military field exercises in over 25 years. It held a desert warfare scenario (preview of wars to come) and involved numerous military units and thousands of personnel from all of the services.

A Mechanized Division is composed of tanks, armored personnel carriers, self-propelled artillery and numerous other armored and wheeled vehicles of varying heavy tonnage. When at full strength the Division would have over 18,000 soldiers and over 8,000 heavy and light vehicles. An Airborne Infantry Division, however, is generally only equipped with light vehicles and equipment that is air transportable and when at full strength has a compliment of between 10,000 and 12,000 soldiers.

This operation deployed about half of the 40th Division's capability with units convoying in from various parts of California, some as far as 600 miles. Other Division elements deployed from the neighboring states of Nevada, Arizona and Idaho.

In 1982, I had been assigned as the Division Provost Marshal with command and control responsibility of the Division's single Military Police Company. For Operation Gallant Eagle the Division received the attachment of two additional Military Police Companies so a Provisional Military Police Battalion was organized with me serving as the Provisional Battalion Commander. This task organization was created earlier and remained throughout the duration of the exercise.

In this operation the MP Companies were able to exercise their primary and secondary missions as described previously; traffic circulation control, security of the Division's Main Command Post and Tactical Command Post (TAC CP) and enemy prisoner of war operations. The individual soldiers were combat ready in full tactical gear.

As scripted, the 82nd Airborne Division deployed just a single brigade of about 3,000 soldiers all flown in from their home base at Fort Bragg, North Carolina and air dropped in the desert. This was in the spring of the year, usually mild weather for the desert but in this case the weather was not cooperative and the airborne soldiers parachuted into a freak snow storm for which they were not prepared. The winds were extremely high, so much so that at one point there was consideration given for canceling the air drop though it did go forward.

The weather caused havoc with the exercise as there were several casualties amongst the airborne troops including some with broken extremities and numerous soldiers suffering frost bite. There were also four deaths associated with the exercise and although unfortunate as it was it mimicked realism of what could occur under wartime conditions where the weather cannot be precisely predicted or controlled.

Once the exercise got under way however, it accomplished what was intended and that was to validate the capability of each Division, the 82nd Airborne as the Rapid Deployment Joint Task Force and the 40th Divisions' capability as a lethal desert fighting force. Many lessons were learned. Some were actually put to use about 15 years later when elements of the 40th Division mobilized and deployed to Iraq and Afghanistan.

In wartime, intelligence information is crucial and if timely received, analyzed, processed and acted upon can make the difference between the success and failure of an operation. An example of this was during World War Two when the US Intelligence apparatus intercepted and broke the Japanese code and learned the path and time of Admiral Yamamoto's flight. Navy fighters interdicted his aircraft at the proper time and place and destroyed his aircraft. His loss left a void in the Japanese leadership for the remainder of the war.

During Operation Gallant Eagle both the 40th Division and 82nd Airborne Division elements took extreme caution to protect their internal and external communications but also used methods to deceive one another with deceptive intelligence.

The 40th Division's Commanding General, Major General Anthony Palombo, used the call sign "Sunburst Six" and the six suffix is usually used to identify unit commanders at all levels of command. Since the 40th has the nickname as the Sunburst Division it was obviously to most that the call sign Sunburst six was the Commanding General.

While flying around the "battle field" of Fort Irwin a 40th Division helicopter pilot reported in the clear that his aircraft was experiencing mechanical difficulties and he was having to land immediately and gave his map coordinates. He also reported that he was over enemy territory and that he had Sunburst Six aboard. This was intercepted by the 82nd Airborne Division Intelligence elements who were monitoring the transmission. They immediately scrambled ground units to the area and "captured" Major General Palumbo. This was a coop by any means. To capture or eliminate the enemy commander has intense political and media ramifications.

Major General Palumbo was transported to the 82nd Division field headquarters where he was detained and questioned. His photograph had been posted in that location so that their soldiers knew the face of the leader of the opposing forces. Word was quickly relayed back to their headquarters at Fort Bragg, North Carolina where stay-behind units were intensely monitoring the battle. They quickly drafted a news release of the capture and printed it on the front page of their daily on-post newspaper and probably just as quick printed a special addition.

When the '"actual" 40th Division, Commander Major General Anthony Palumbo, learned of the celebration at Fort Bragg he held a news conference at Fort Irwin announcing that his deception plan had worked and that the person captured was in fact an imposter who resembled him in all respects and was wearing the General's shirt uniform with name tag. This incident became an embarrassment for the 82nd Division's Commanding General and a political nightmare because it demonstrated that 40th Division comprised of part-time soldiers could deceive America's greatest quick reaction force.

At the conclusion of the exercise, I returned to my SPO duties which included drafting operation orders for various full time state active duty missions that the National Guard was tasked to perform. Many of these missions were counter-drug related as we had numerous soldiers deployed around the state assisting state and local law enforcement officers abating drug cultivating, drug smuggling and transporting. Two high profile missions at that time were "Operation Green Sweep" in the North and "Operation Border Ranger" in the South.

DRUG ENFORCEMENT OPERATIONS

The Northwestern part of California, especially along the Northern Coast, was known for the extensive illegal growing of marijuana plants, mostly on federal lands in the national forests. In many such areas marijuana growing was the largest cash crop and was cultivated by the tons. Many communities, small towns and hamlets based there day to day financial existence on these products as some of their law abiding and God fearing residents were "employed" in the growing and harvesting.

For example there was the incident whereby a pickup truck loaded with so many bales of marijuana that the tires were somewhat deflated, obviously too heavy of a load for that vehicle and thus a vehicle code violation. A local police officer observing this stopped the vehicle and issued the driver a citation for an unsafe load while ignoring the marijuana which was strapped down uncovered and in plain sight.

In the Southern part of the state along the International Border with Mexico drug smuggling across the border takes many forms. These range from individuals on foot crossing the border with duffle bags filled with the contraband, cars and trucks attempting to enter via the established check points, small water craft and submersible water craft entering the various ports and inlets and private aircraft entering US Air Space with contraband intending to land at isolated landing strips.

Due to the magnitude of the problem federal law enforcement was unable to provide enforcement as required and some local law enforcement agencies had decided long before not to engage in its enforcement. For these reasons, the National Guard was called in to assist. This would be only in a support role due the Posse Comitatus Federal Law which forbade military from enforcing civilian laws.

Operation Green Sweep

Once we received the "Warning Order" of the upcoming mission to provide logistical support for law enforcement all staff sections went to work on preparing their portion of the order but entirely working in concert with one another which was essential. Within time the Operation Order was completed, reviewed, approved then published.

Every operation is given a name, or "moniker" which in some way connects with the operation. This particular operational event was dubbed Operation Green Sweep for obvious reasons. The reason were that marijuana was a "green" agricultural plant grown illegally and the mission was to "sweep" or cut it down and destroy the plants.

The first phase of the Northwestern California operation lasted about two weeks and involved approximately two hundred soldiers. Observation helicopters flew numerous missions over the area to identify marijuana growing farms. From low flying aircraft marijuana fields are rather easy to locate as the crop clearly stands out from other plant life and are much darker than surrounding greenery.

Once the illegal crop was located convoys of ground troops with an enormous logistical package moved in, set up a base camp with a command center and field housing facilities and began removing the plants by cutting them down and moving them out by ground and air.

The plants were stacked and secured in bales, tied and sling loaded out by large heavy lift helicopters and deposited onto trucks where they were driven from the area and destroyed. Several tons were removed during this operation which was repeated over time.

For several years I employed these same operational concepts that were used for numerous state missions for wild fires, floods, civil disorder, searches for contraband on state prison grounds and preparing for major community sporting events.

Operation Green Sweep was not overly supported by the community and in some instances employed covert road blocks to inhibit success. Some of these included local post office employees nefariously not forwarding mail to soldiers from their families although this could not be proven and mom and pop stores refusing to sell merchandise to soldiers.

FIVE PARAGRAPH FIELD ORDERS

All military operations and missions require a plan of action and the written document to execute the plan is called a Five Paragraph Field Order. Most Field Orders are very voluminous and can contain anywhere from a few pages to more than 50 or more depending on the mission. The reference to "paragraph" should not be confused with a book paragraph. It is much more.

Field Orders are a compilation of information generated by staff at any given headquarters once the commander has provided the mission requirement. These staff sections are the G-1 (Personnel and Administration), G-2 (Intelligence), G-3 (Operations and Training), G-4 (Logistics) and G-5 (Civil-Military Operations, also called Civil Affairs). At the Division level the head of each of these staff sections holds the rank of Lieutenant Colonel and all report to the Division Chief of Staff, a Colonel.

The five paragraphs are the same whether in war time or peace time and contain information as follows:

- **Paragraph 1: Situation.** This paragraph, in lay terms, specifically describes what is confronting the military unit, i.e. the illegal growing of marijuana for example.

- **Paragraph 2: Mission.** The entire operation centers on the Mission. In this case the Mission was to provide logistical support to civilian law enforcement in eradicating the marijuana plants and dislodging the marijuana growers from federal lands.

- **Paragraph 3: Execution**. This is the "how" of the operation. This paragraph describes the date and time for commencing the operation, bench marks and time lines to be met, which units to participate and the overall plan for successfully accomplishing the mission. This paragraph would ordinarily be five to ten pages in length.

- **Paragraph 4: Service and Support.** In simple terms logistics are the "things" required to accomplish the mission without which the mission would not be successful. These include a laundry list of military hardware and software; trucks, jeeps, helicopters, weapons (if required), rations, radios, fuel, repair parts, slings ropes, sleeping tents, generators, lighting systems, field kitchens, portable latrines, satellite hook ups and scores of other items, some large and some small. Housekeeping equipment is also required: command tents, cots, heaters, refrigeration, and concertina wire for security and much more.

- **Paragraph 5**: Command and Signal. This paragraph describes "who" will be in command, where the command post will be locate and identifies how the soldiers will communicate and which satellite, digital and redundant systems will be deployed.

Since marijuana abatement is not the garden variety of missions normally assigned to the military, the Chief of Staff and the Assistant Chiefs of Staff still had the requirement of focusing on normal assigned missions so as the SPO I was assigned the responsibility of coordinating the work of the staff sections to ensure that the Order was published which required coordinating, planning and publishing the Five Paragraph Field Order. The G-3, under the supervision of the Chief of Staff, was responsible for the execution.

OPERATION BORDER RANGER

This operation involved surveillance missions in and around the numerous mountain passes overlooking our Southern International Border with Mexico. These were frequently used by drug smugglers driving cars, trucks and all-terrain vehicles, illegally crossing the border to link up with larger vehicles in the area which would continue further into the interior of the US by use of the interstate highways systems.

These were 24/7 operations which required deployed soldiers to be equipped with all necessary equipment to sustain them in the field for up to five days at a time, unseen, in an observation post before rotating out. No weapons were employed by each contingent of soldiers but they were equipped with cold weather gear, sleeping bags, high tech sophisticated camera devices, upgraded communications equipment and police radio equipment to communicate with civilian law enforcement which had the mission of interdicting the smugglers. Rations and sanitation requirements for five days were part of the logistical package.

One of the many ruses used by smugglers was to have a panel truck slowly cross over the border into the US and perform a reconnaissance of the area for the purpose of intentionally being detected by the border patrol. After circling the area for several minutes to ensure they were detected the truck would return to Mexico using the same entry point.

Sometime later that same truck would reenter the US at a high rate of speed followed by up to three or four other vehicles, usually vans. This caused the law enforcement Task Force to react by pursuing and stopping the convoy of vehicles a mile or two beyond the border fully engaging the US authorities deployed in the area. When this occurred a second convoy of vehicles would enter the US at a high rate of speed and proceed in the opposite direction toward another interstate highway. When the first convoy was stopped, in most cases, all of the vehicles were empty except for the single driver.

The follow-on convoy contained all of the "real" drug contraband. Since the only violation of the apprehended drivers was entering the US illegally they were merely escorted back to the border where they returned to Mexico as they expected. In almost all cases, the drivers had no identification and were just hired off the street for a few dollars by the smugglers to drive the vehicle knowing they would not be detained. No doubt the driver went home with a pocket full of cash; prized United States currency.

OPERATIONAL EXERCISES

Throughout my career in addition to those previously mentioned I participated in numerous operations and exercises both in the US and abroad. Some of them and their locations included Gallant Eagle (Fort

Irwin, California); LOGEX (Fort A.P. Hill, Virginia); Team Spirit (Republic of South Korea); Wounded Warrior (Camp Roberts, California); War Fighter (Fort Leavenworth, Kansas); ARTBASS (San Bernardino, California); Yama Sakkara (Japan); REFORGER (Germany); Partnership for Peace, (Ukraine); Counter Drug (Honduras); Desert Strike (California Desert Areas); Corps Defender (Fort Lewis, Washington) Golden Bear (Camp Roberts, California), Operation Cold Steel, (San Diego), Sunburst (Camp Roberts) and many others.

OPERATION SEOUL MAN

Another special duty was having served as the honor guard commander at the Los Angeles International Airport welcoming the President of South Korea in what we comically named, Operation "Seoul Man" with a play on that nation's capital city of Seoul and also on rhythm and blues singer James Brown affectionately known as Soul Man.

The President made a brief stopover at the airport to meet and greet some of his local countrymen and women and ex-patriots while en route to meet with the President of the United States at the White House. Los Angeles hosts the second largest Korean population of any city in the world outside of Seoul.

The military police formed a two-column honor guard in Class A uniforms adorned with white web belts and gloves and wearing chromed helmets. The soldiers were equipped with M-16 Rifles. Upon first arriving at the airport, all weapons were checked and double checked for ammunition by the US Secret Service and again by their Korean counterpart. Additionally, all soldiers were personally checked for ammunition. I walked alongside the President as he inspected the troops and at the proper time they and I made the traditional ceremonial salute.

CHAPTER 54 BATTALION COMMAND

Lieutenant Colonel Gravett Commanding 1st Battalion, 185th Armor Regiment.

During the winter of 1986, the Command Board, which consisted of one and two star General Officers, met to consider various field grade officers for assignment to Battalion Command positions. I was selected to command the 1st Battalion of the 185th Armor Regiment headquartered at San Bernardino, California.

In this assignment I was following in the legacy of the famed 761st Tank Battalion of World War Two, the unit in which Kareem Abdul-Jabbar's family friend served as chronicled in Kareem's book with Anthony Walton, *"Brothers in Arms."* The 761st was the first Colored armor unit to fight on foreign soil and one of the first Colored combat units to fight side by side with a White unit. The difference being this was now generations later and the battalion was totally integrated.

I held the rank of Lieutenant Colonel at the time and the change of command ceremony was staged at the National Training Center, Fort Irwin, California with many of the battalion's 50 tanks on line. I was fortunate to have my wife Dorothy and son Mark in attendance. They had arrived earlier and was quartered on post for the weekend in visiting family housing. Mark was very excited about being around the military equipment and soldiers again.

Lieutenant Colonel Gravett M-60A3 Tank Commander.

This assignment coincided with the time the Division Command was transitioning from Major General William Jefferds to Major General James Delk. In civilian life General Jefferds, PhD, was the Superintendent of the Alum Rock School District in San Jose. General Delk had a stellar reputation as a well-respected leader of soldiers who was a great tactician with superb organizational skills coupled with his leadership acumen. He was a published author and was seen by most as an intellectual, his Eagle Scout achievement as a young man having served him throughout his civilian and military careers. He was an excellent mentor and role model to me.

General Delk was completing a tour of duty at National Guard Bureau in Washington DC where he had been assigned earlier from California. His duties their included serving in a senior leadership position in making operational, administrative, logistical and planning decisions which affected the National Guard in the various states and territories. His wealth of experience, information gathering and knowledge there would now be put to great use in California and specifically in the 40th Division. The battalion change of command ceremony went well as expected and I felt extremely proud to be receiving the colors of the battalion especially with having my family there.

The Armor branch is considered the *Combat Arm of Decision* and the Armor Battalion colors, flag, consist of a bright yellow field, the color for armor, with a brown bald eagle centered. The eagle is seen holding 13 arrows in the left talon and a leaf clutched in the right talon and together symbolizing that the U.S. has a strong penchant for peace but will always be ready for war. The 185th Armor Regiment's motto was "Fulmen Jacio" translated from Latin reads "I Hurl the Thunderbolt."

BATTALION DYNAMICS

The Battalion Headquarters was located in San Bernardino with A Company in Palmdale, B Company in Apple Valley, C Company in Hemet and D Company located in the community of Indio. The Headquarters and Headquarters Company, of course, was co-located with the Battalion Headquarters. All of these locations were in desert communities. A & B Companies were located in the high desert and C & D Companies located in the low desert areas of Southern California.

The Battalion was equipped with 50 M-60A3 Main Battle Tanks, 12 assigned to each of the line companies and two at the Battalion Headquarters. In the field the Battalion Commander commands from either a tank, as does the Battalion S-3 (Operations Officer) thus two tanks assigned there. The commander may also command from a M577 armored tracked command vehicle which follows his tank while in convoy or when dispersed.

This vehicle is equipped with ample maps of the terrain of operation and additional communications equipment permitting redundant interfacing capability with several layers of upper and adjacent commands. When the Commander is positioned in the command vehicle his gunner replaces him as the tank commander and the vehicle may then be operated with a diminished crew level of three or a tank qualified soldier from the M577 may serve as a crew member.

Each Line Company had two tanks positioned at the local armories for non-maneuver training purposes while the remainder were housed at the Mobilization and Training Equipment Site (MATES) at Fort Irwin where the full units trained during weekends and other times of the year. The Camp Roberts MATES also had a full battalion set of tanks.

Each tank had a crew of four; tank commander, gunner, loader and driver and each with specific duties which are constantly drilled. The tank commander sits in the cupola and is the senior soldier in the tank whether it be an officer, senior NCO or mid-level NCO. His seat is adjustable; lowered when the tank is buttoned up and using vision blocks to see the battlefield and a higher seat with his head and shoulders protruding from the top while viewing the battlefield with binoculars. He is the decision maker when the main gun is to be fired and also mans a machine gun.

The Gunner sits just below the tank commander and is number two in-charge. Both he and the tank commander are able to spot targets. He too mans a machine gun.

The loader has the important responsibility of selecting and placing the main gun ammunition in the gun breach based upon the nature of the target as identified by the commander or gunner. The tank is equipped with several type of main gun ammunition with each fired based upon the nature of the target.

Internally this is the most dangerous assignment for a crew member as they may be exposed to the recoil of the tanks' cannon thus the main gun is only fired after the loader has given the command "up" which indicates he is in a safe place away from the recoil area. The loader also doubles as a machine gunner.

The fourth and lowest ranking of the crew is the driver but obviously an important position requiring substantial training. The driver has the ability to maneuver the vehicle while buttoned up and inside the tank or using vision blocks for sight or may have his head exposed above the hatch while his shoulders, arms and hands are inside the tank. All crew members wear a combat vehicle communications (CVC) helmet.

The overall mobile equipment count in the Battalion was over 200 consisting of wheeled and other tracked armored vehicles. The Battalion head count was about 700 soldiers, all male at the time.

TANK TRANSITION

The aforementioned the M-60A3 Main Battle Tank had a 90 Millimeter (MM) main gun and was equipped with one 240 and one .50 caliber machine gun. These tanks, though very lethal, were of the early Viet Nam variety and we immediately began planning for New Equipment Tank Training (NETT) and transitioning to the more modern M1 (Abrams) Main Battle Tank. This newer combat vehicle also still had a crew of four but was upgraded with 105 MM main gun, two 240 machine guns and a .50 caliber machine gun.

A few years later the Battalion had an equipment upgrade to the Desert Storm era M1A1 Main Battle Tank which boasted a 110 MM Main Gun; a smooth bore cannon with a stabilization (stab) system which allowed the cannon to remain locked on the target even though the vehicle was in rough and hilly terrain. It was also equipped with a laser range finder which is used to acquire the target.

It had a top speed of over 40 miles per hour and a range of over 260 miles without refueling. The NETT training took place at Gowen Field, Idaho at the Western US Tank Training Center. Every tank crewman was required to undergo the two-week tank transition course, including the Battalion Commander.

Gunnery included firing at moving and stationery targets and engaging the laser range finder which fires a laser beam directly to a target and records the exact distance from the tank and allows for an extremely accurate first round hit. The tank also had smoke screening capability, chemical detection and exposure apparatus, dispersal grenades, thermal sights allowing crew to see through weather obscuration and an on-board Position-Navigation System whereby unit commanders could track location and progress of subordinate tank crews by satellite.

Tank transition training also included assembly and disassembly of each of the machine guns, identifying engine and track failures and a plethora of other tested actions including "switchology," memorizing and understanding all of the gauges and switches in the tank.

It seemed all eyes were on me as I was expected to know all features of the tank's operation, weapon systems and maintenance requirements in detail. In addition some expected the Battalion Commander to achieve the highest score in gunnery.

I fared well and my crew and I achieved the second highest record in the Battalion of the 50 crews that went down range. At the conclusion of the training I publically recognized and decorated the number one crew.

WHAT'S IN A NAME?

Much like fighter pilots who name their aircraft and have it emblazoned on the exterior as a code of honor tankers also sometimes follow this practice and early on I had decided to follow this regimen.

Being the seventh child born in my family I was considered to have been lucky but to my recollection that never occurred. By using the family name as a play on the scientific word gravitation I thought that to be cool.

When I was in college I pledged a fraternity and one of the requirements of new pledges was to adopt a name which had some connection to themselves. Whatever name chosen was be their name for as long as they had a connection or relationship to the fraternity. Also that name went on the individual beer stein which all members had and were required to bring to all fraternity events (parties). I chose the name "Gravettation VII."

To continue with the fraternity name as Battalion Commander I had Gravettation VII chalked on my command tank, most or probably no one knowing the origin though no one inquired as I recall. After almost sixty years later, I still have my Gravettation VII stein.

Battalion Convoy Operations

Most of our field training maneuvers were conducted at the National Training Center, Fort Irwin as this was ideal terrain for tanks as it consisted of dirt plains and sand that were inter-dispersed with low hills and mountains with gaps and scrub brush. Summer daytime temperatures could often range above 120 degrees during the summer which was still uncomfortable in air conditioned tanks.

The Battalion also trained at Camp Roberts which had a battalion set of tanks for use there and for use at Fort Hunter Leggett, some 50 miles north via a tank trail. The convoy march to Fort Hunter Leggett was tedious at best and the very dusty tank trail ran alongside two lakes and several small mobile home parks just a few hundred yards off the trail.

On one convoy operation I decided to march the entire Battalion up the trail and was smart enough to have my tank in the lead though generally the Commander would be somewhere within the convoy where he could best affect command and control. This decision was made because I knew that the dust would be thick and it was. All tankers wear eye protection and bandanas covering them nose and mouth.

Being the lead tank, I avoided the dust during the maneuver which took more than four hours, including periods of rest for both the men and the equipment. During the convoy operation en route there were few mechanical breakdowns this owing to the superb training of the maintenance crews. After many years of "eating dust" in convoy formations I looked forward for the first time in leading the charge. The narrowness of the trail only allowed the formation to be in a single column which stretched on for several miles. Trail dust could also be seen for several miles and from satellites.

Food for Thought

My Brigade Commander was Colonel William Stewart, in civilian life an attorney but serving in a high executive position with the Los Angeles County Government. Our command relationship was generally very positive but there was one incident where we differed.

I had my battalion in the field at Fort Hunter Liggett performing tank gunnery training and on a given day our food rations had not been delivered from the Brigade Logistical Operations Center at Camp Roberts. Previously noted this was about 40 miles south down the tank trail or about 30 miles by country road. Soldiers need to eat on a regular time schedule to perform at their best.

I directed my S-4 (Logistics Officer) to drive to Camp Roberts and determine the problem. Several hours later he contact me through the radios system and informed me that that food would not be delivered until the next day as there was miscommunication in the ordering process. I then dispatched my Executive Officer there to impress upon the Brigade Logisticians the need for the rations immediately as the soldiers had already been without two meals and were about to be without a third.

With no resolution to the situation by the Executive Officer I personally responded to Camp Roberts that evening and arranged for the logisticians to take partial food stuffs from units that had already been fed and quickly delivery them to Fort Hunter Liggett to my troops which they did, finally enjoying a late evening meal.

During the absence from my command location my headquarters was visited by Colonel Stewart and he was briefed on the reason for my absence. Upon reporting to him late that night as directed, he pointed out that my place should have been on the tank ranges orchestrating tank gunnery as that was the priority. I disagreed with him and voiced that even though in the army mission comes first there are always circumstances which changes the scenario. In this scenario I had left the battalion and indeed tank gunnery in the capable hand of my S-3 (Operations Officer) and training was ongoing and uninhibited. I would ensure that my soldiers would not go over 30 hours without a meal through no fault of their own or the unit but at the fault of his very own logistical staff.

I held my ground and he directed me to always be with my soldiers during training which I agreed I would do but reminded him that it was his own logistics personnel who caused me to go to Camp Roberts to ensure that all of the units in his brigade receive rations timely. He took this as an affront though I was always respectful and courteous in my comments to him and the matter was discussed no further.

Following two years of successful battalion command in 1988 I relinquished command to an in-coming new commander with the traditional change of command ceremony held in the desert. My mother went along to experience what soldiers do in a field environment and test the weather conditions which she had always heard about. That day the temperature was very mild as I recall and around 100 degrees. The highlight of her trip was when she was given the opportunity to drive a tank.

She was hoisted up to the cupola by four soldiers and lowered into the hatch of the tank. One of the crew members maneuvered her into the driver's seat where she popped her head out of the driver's hatch and took control of the steering mechanisms, the Cadillac's as they are called. Firmly in control she was shown how to start the engine and release the braking mechanism. With the tank commander sitting behind her off she went at a slow speed across the desert. She was elated and would often times brag that she drove a tank.

CHAPTER 55 DIVISION CIVIL AFFAIRS OFFICER (G-5)

In my next assignment I was transferred to Division Headquarters at the Joint Forces Training Base as the G-5 Civil Affairs Officer. Many of my duties there would consist of serving as the interface between the military and the civilian community. The Division Commander Major General Delk assigned me to be the Division point of contact with a Korean War Veterans Group called the Chosin Few. This was a collection of US Marine and US Army veterans who fought the battle at the Chosin Reservoir in North Korea in 1950. This was often referred to as the "Forgotten War."

The battle was chronicled in numerous books written about the event and mainly focused on the below zero temperature and the lack of food and heating apparatus by the U.S. servicemen. The veterans group consisted of members from Orange County's Colonel William Barber Chapter of the Chosin Few; with the then Captain Barber, Commander of Fox Company, 2nd Battalion, 7th Marine Regiment, being one of the most decorated Marines during the battle.

The Colonel Barber Chapter was making preparations to erect a monument commemorating the gallantry of the soldiers and Marines from the 22 United Nations countries who served in the War as part of the allied force. Twenty one nations provided combat troops and Norway provided medical personnel only.

The Chosin Few had selected a small atoll on the Upper Reservation of Fort McArthur in San Pedro, California for their monument which was to face west towards South Korea. This was my grand opportunity to meet heroes of that War, some whom would become long-time friends, especially Jack Stites, a retired Marine Captain.

Jack was a Marine Corps Mustang (former enlisted Marine) who received his direct commission following many years of Marine Corps service. Though he had retired from the Corps, he and about fifty of his fellow former Marines and one soldier worked tirelessly over a period of several years in effort to erect the memorial but finally without success.

For a number of reasons the memorial never came to fruition, some causes of which were lack of sufficient funding and the bureaucratic malaise and anti-military attitudes by the Los Angeles City Department of Cultural Affairs which held sway on the approval process. The Department of Recreation and Parks and City Council Committees were always eager to lend a listening ear to a very small but vocal group of left-leaning anti-war activists from the Point Fermin neighborhood in San Pedro which adjoined the military property.

A few years later when the 40th Infantry Division moved ahead to erect a monument at Vandenberg Air Force Base to recognize its participation in the Korean War, Captain Stites was tapped to design it. As a hobbyist, Jack had been an award winning designer of Christmas and other holiday greeting cards. He also drew battle scenes of the Korean War as he lived it. To recognize his voluntary contribution in designing the monument and for his previous efforts in planning for a monument at Fort McArthur he was awarded the Order of California by direction of the Governor.

The Order of California is the highest state award and may only be presented by the Governor or by the Adjutant General on behalf of the Governor. The award has three components, a two inch wide medallion affixed to a blue and yellow lanyard worn around the neck, a military ribbon in the same color scheme which is affixed to the military uniform ribbon bar and a miniature of the medallion in the form of a lapel pin.

At the dedication ceremony Captain Stites was officially recognized as the inspiration for the endeavor; a Marine paying homage to the Army at an Air Force Base was truly joint service. Vandenberg Air Force Base was selected as the site as it was the debarkation point for the 40th Division when it was mobilized and deployed to the War in Korea in 1950. It was then named Camp Cook, a US Army Post.

Jack and his wife Pat remained friends with Blanche and me for many years and he was the inspiration to have us inducted into his Chosin Few Chapter has honorary members. Over the years Blanche and I made regular visits to their home where we socialized with our now Marine Corps friends and we continued our visits when they relocated to a nearby retirement community prior to them both passing away.

In my various conversation with Captain Stites he had confirmed the heroism of then Captain Barber at the Chosin Reservoir which was later chronicled by author Jeff Shaara in his book *The Frozen Hours*. Captain Barber was depicted, and rightfully so according to Captain Stites, as the most superb combat leader during their units' withdrawal from the Reservoir. It was for this reason that the Orange County (California) Chapter was named for him.

During my tenure as the Civil Affairs Officer for the Division I had numerous opportunities to interface with local community groups and the cities surrounding the Los Alamitos military installation. These included the Orange County Regional Military Affairs Committee (RMAC). The RMAC support was always instrumental in being out front to ensure the base did not meet closure as some small but vocal activists insisted. Los Alamitos was a financial engine which drove a good portion of the local economy as well as civilian employment.

CHAPTER 56 THE MENTORING PROCESS

Mentoring is the process whereby an experienced person provides that experience and advice to a less experienced person with the ultimate objective to make the mentee successful. Often the mentor is disinterested and detached which allows for an objective view point. The mentoring process can be formal or informal and can be overt or covert. Mentoring occurs in all walks of life not only in the military. However in the military it is more than often encouraged.

During my early years in the military both as an enlisted soldier and as a junior officer I received minimal if any overt mentoring. I suggest however that every time I was corrected or received positive criticism for whatever reason that in itself could have been overt or covert mentoring.

It was during the time I became a field grade officer that I made gradual attempts to speak with more senior officers regarding my military career. At that time I was seriously considering requesting a transfer from the Army National Guard to the Army Reserve. I was aware that the Army Reserve was not structured with combat units and that their structure consisted of combat support and combat service units only. My basic branch was armor, a combat branch, and a transfer would necessitate beginning anew in establishing a career in one of the branches in the Army Reserve structure.

I made it a point to discuss my dilemma with several more senior officers as well as some of my peers as they can also serve as mentors. The consensus was that I had established a commendable record in the Army National Guard and in particularly the armor corps and that I should remain which I did.

That decision making process perhaps was my impetus for actively reaching out to younger soldiers, both officer and enlisted, and providing sage unsolicited advice on their careers. I also took the covert mentoring process a step further by conducting "mentoring forums" for anyone electing to attend with the focus of discussing the mentoring process and identifying the methodology for selecting a mentor. These sessions were short term and were not conducted on government time. In my view mentoring is leadership at its best.

> *"Leadership is planting trees under whose shade you will never sit."*
> **Old Chinese Proverb**

My tour of duty as the G-5 was abbreviated as just ten months later I was transferred to the 2nd Armor Brigade as the Executive Officer continuing at the rank of Lieutenant Colonel. This new assignment was indicative that my decision to remain in the Army National Guard was a wise one. Assignment as a Brigade Executive Officer, in general, could be seen as a part of the building block to a future assignment as Brigade Commander.

CHAPTER 57 ARMOR BRIGADE
EXECUTIVE OFFICER

The Second Armor Brigade was headquartered in the Kearney Mesa Area of San Diego where I commuted to one or sometimes twice a week. In between I took up residence at the Miramar Naval Air Station. Organically the Brigade consisted of two Armor Battalions; 2-185th Armor Battalion in San Diego, 3-185th Armor Battalion in Chula Vista and 4-160th Infantry Battalion in Santa Ana. Supporting elements were 2-144th Field Artillery Battalion located in Burbank, 132nd Engineer Battalion located in Manhattan Beach and the 240th Forward Support Battalion located in Long Beach. Smaller slice units of Military Police, Intelligence, Signal and Medical were stationed in other parts of Southern California.

The Brigade Commander, Colonel Richard Metcalf, and I got along swimmingly well as he focused on the subordinate Battalion Commanders and I focused on the Brigade Staff and the Headquarters and Headquarters Company. This arrangement was consisted with Army protocol. In civilian life Colonel Metcalf was a very successful senior executive in a fortune 500 company. Previously he also had commanded an Armor Battalion and also had served as a Brigade Executive Officer.

The various Companies within the Brigade were dispersed throughout Southern California ranging from the San Fernando Valley, to Barstow, to Imperial County to the Mexican Border. This wide swath of area was challenging for command and control but all commanders, staff and soldiers did their part to ensure success.

One tank company was located in Calexico just a few yards from the International border with Mexico and several unit members, all US citizens, actually resided in Mexico with their families but were employed in the US. This was not uncommon as the US had military reservists residing in other foreign countries such as Germany, South

Korea, Philippines, and Canada and probably others which was permitted by regulations though the US and Mexico did not have a Status of Forces (SOFA) Agreement as did aforementioned countries.

SOFA is an agreement between a host country and a foreign nation stationing military forces in that country. SOFAs are often included with other types of military agreements as part of a comprehensive security agreement.

Prior to my arriving at the brigade, however, an investigation revealed that one soldier, a Mexican National, who had been in the unit for many years had fraudulently enlisted citing prior military service by using the identification of a former US Army soldier. He apparently received on the job training over time and was considered to be a superb tank crewman. He had one name while in his native Mexico and another in the US. As expected his enlistment was voided Ex Post Facto.

CHAPTER 58 SOUTH KOREA

Every January or February the South Korean and US Military hold a joint military field exercise called Team Spirit where they square off against each other in a realistic wartime like scripted battle. Even though the US have about 40,000 military personnel stationed there it deploys several thousand additional personnel from all services as well as large amounts of equipment to participate in the exercise. This drill was designed anticipating another invasion into South Korea by North Koreans just as they did on June 25, 1950.

The exercises are very realistic and the South Korean military is heavily armed with live ammunition. In 1986 and again in 1988, both while assigned as Battalion Commander, and in 1989 while assigned as the G-5, I deployed there on short duration tours to participate, twice as an on the ground unit participant and once as an Observer/Controller.

In winter on the Korean Peninsula the weather is very cold, below freezing, and the rice patties are frozen over allowing some traffic ability over them by light weight wheel vehicles but obviously not heavier armored tracked vehicles.

Most of my duty locations were either in Pyeongtaek, Anjoeng-ri, and Osan in the center of the country and at US Army posts at Camp Casey or Camp Hovey in the north. There was often quick trip up to Demilitarized Zone above Dongducheon where the North and South Koreans, still at war, faced each other with the neutral zone, often called "No Man's Land", separating them at the 38th parallel.

As an Observer/Controller I had a team of about 20 American soldiers, an Australian Solder and five KATUSA arrayed in several wheel vehicles with white bands visibly displayed on our helmets to identify us from opposing participants in the exercise.

KATUSA, or Korean Augmentation to the United States Army, consist of Korean enlisted personnel who are augmented to the Eighth United States Army who are dispatched throughout the US Army in Korea filling in vacant positions of enlisted soldiers and junior non-commissioned officers. They also serve as translators between the local populace and US Army and guide the US Army units maneuvering in unfamiliar areas of the country. All are volunteers and serve in lieu of drafted service into their own Army. Proficiency in English is a must and they are selected from a pool of applicants, most of which are college graduates and hail from a family with influence and means.

My KATUSA soldiers served the team well as we maneuvered throughout the exercise area passing through villages, towns, hamlets and the outskirts of a few small cities. They wore the US Army uniform with KATUSA insignia and required minimal direction and supervision. With any dereliction of duty they would be sent to the Korean Army and perform their undesirable duty there.

Our mission and that of all Observers/Controllers was to monitor both opposing forces to ensure rules of engagements were being followed. This required the team to constantly be on the move following the maneuvering units being controlled as the "battle" progressed. Our follow-on logistics vehicle carried most of our equipment such as tents, cots, rations, water, fuel, porta potties and other essentials.

Every day we would bivouac in a different location and set up camp. Young South Korean boys, known as "Slicky Boys," followed most of the Observer/Controller teams with the intent to confiscate any equipment they could carry away. For this reason, we always had two soldiers remain at the camp to safe guard everything while the team's other members trailed behind the maneuvering units.

When the maneuvering unit bivouacked for the evening or a prolonged cessation of the battle was called to readjust forces the Team would return to the base camp and temporarily stand down. One day as we returned to our camp, I discovered that all of mine and that of a few other soldier's personal equipment and sleeping bags had been confiscated no doubt by the Slicky Boys. The two soldiers who been on guard duty to prevent this very occurrence had no explanation how that could have occurred. Truth of the matter was that they had remained in the heating tent to keep warm instead of rotating outside and being on guard in the well below freezing weather. Their punishment was the embarrassment they suffered and the judgment discussion on their future evaluation report.

With all of my personal gear and sleeping bag stolen, and that of several other soldiers, it was evident we could not sleep in the elements without a fleece lined sleeping bag, even in a heated tent. The few of us then drove to a roadside inn in the vicinity where we rented several rooms for the night.

The rooms were outfitted for Koreans and had no beds but had straw mattresses on the floor. The toilet was a porcelain lined hole in the bathroom floor, as in the typical rural Korean homes, but with water flushing capability much like the Benjo's in Japan as described earlier. We made do. The next morning I dispatched a two man team to the rear logistics area to requisition and obtain replacement equipment.

In my view Sticky Boys was the appropriate name for these young slick thieves who probably sold the confiscated "booty" on the thriving black market which was always in existence there.

In 1994 I returned to South Korea on a confidential investigation I was conducting at the behest of the US Army's Inspector General. Several of the soldiers I had identified to be interviewed were stationed there at two of the military posts. During the week of temporary duty in and around Seoul I took up residence at a first class civilian hotel and used a KATUSA driver to transport me from place to place.

Major General Gravett Greeted by Four Star
General and South Korean Army Chief of Staff

Hotels in South Korea are equipped with protective gas masks in the rooms always anticipating another attack from North Korea. Another note is that freeways around the country are designed to be used as secondary war time runways for military aircraft with attendant aviation refueling stations sporadically disbursed.

In general I have always noted that the American military stationed in South Korea share a very warm bond with the older Korean people.

CHAPTER 59 DIVISION CHIEF OF STAFF

Typically every two or three years the senior leadership in an Army Division changes for one reason or another. Senior officers retire and others transfer. This allows for a "shuffling of the decks chairs on the Titanic" allowing other qualified officers to assume positions of increased responsibility.

After serving just over one year as Brigade Executive Officer I was appointed Division Chief of Staff in 1990 still at the rank of Lieutenant Colonel. This was my fourth assignment in less than two years after having been assigned as the Provost, Battalion Commander and Brigade Executive Officer. Each of my previous assignments served as building blocks for my elevation to the position of Division Chief of Staff. Dorothy was delighted that I no longer had the tedious commute to San Diego.

The Chief of Staff is a Colonel's position which was extremely coveted, and I was very elated to have been selected by the board of General officers. This was especially so since there were several officers, both Lieutenant Colonels and Colonels, more senior but in my biased perspective lacked the experience I had gained in my assignments.

The assignment came with a promotion to Colonel and is often the final step in a long career to becoming a General Officer though Army-wide generally only one tenth of one percent of all officers ever attain the rank of Brigadier General. Cumulative this includes the Regular Army, Army Reserve and Army National Guard. I made a point to focus on my new important duties rather than focusing on a potential promotion to General Officer. I honestly believed this had the potential to be my terminal assignment however it was about this time that I was "invited" to make application to attend the War College. An invitation to attend rather than a personal decision to apply, in some instances, could set an officer on a path for much higher responsibility and leadership.

The Adjutant General flew in from Sacramento to make my pinning ceremony a media event so the ceremony took place at the Bob Hope Patriotic Hall, the Veterans Building in downtown Los Angeles. His staff had invited several dignitaries and elected officials. This was not the typical ceremonial promotion for a Colonel so, in a particular way, I felt that I was being patronized as the California National Guard had promoted so few officers to Colonel and wanted to demonstrate a commitment to equality though I was imminently qualified. I invited some veteran friends and just my immediate family to the event.

CHIEF OF STAFF DUTIES

The Chief of Staff in any organization, military, civilian or political, is essentially the point person for the Commander or the official. Since a US Army Mechanized Infantry Division, such as the 40th Division, consists of approximately 18,000 male and female soldiers, the Chief of Staff is the principal advisor to the Commanding General and is responsible for day to day operation of the Division.

As "Chief" I directed and coordinated the activities of the Division's General Staff (G-1 through G-5) which distilled huge amounts of information and made it manageable for the Commanding General. Once the Commanding General made his decision based upon that information I took appropriate action and communicated that decision throughout the command.

I was usually the sounding board for the Brigade Commanders prior to them interacting with the Division Commander, but not always as they always had direct access whenever needed. As the Commander's direct representative to the staff, it was important that I had a very close relationship with the commander and a clear understanding of the commander's vision which I made a point to always have. This worked well with both Major

General Hawkins and Major General Hernandez, the two Commanders with whom I served.

Both had differing command styles and personalities but both top notch leaders from my perspective. Major General Hawkins, from a rural farming community in the Central Valley of California, was viewed by some as possessing the General George Patton persona and was very clear in his directives, orders and commands which left no doubt of his vision for the Division. These were derived from his career long infantry background. Once he gave his clear guidance for any mission he stepped back and allowed me and his Brigade Commanders to use our own methods to achieve it based upon sound Army doctrine, tactics, principles and practices. But also employing our individual leadership styles, background, experience and training. He always made and maintained eye to eye contact when addressing a soldier of any rank.

I was allowed to suggest and recommend specific officers for the Division Staff following my interview with them and reviewing their body of work as a soldier and leader and often the appointments were based upon my professional judgment and recommendation. General Hawkins always had the total respect of his Brigade Commanders.

Major General Hernandez hailed from an inner city East Los Angeles background. He had joined the military at age 15 the same age when he deployed as a Private to South Korea during that War when his National Guard unit was mobilized though had his age had been documented he would not have been deployed. He had volunteered and was enlisted without his parents' permission or knowledge.

He spent several years as an enlisted soldier prior to being commissioned. He was more hands on, not only with me as his Chief but also with his subordinate Brigade Commanders. He more routinely performed his own follow-up and suggested corrective action mid-stream while the staff was carrying out his directive. This would be prior to the staff providing him his initial briefing. He personally interviewed officers for the staff and personally affected transfers of others, a typical duty of the Chief.

All in all few officers of any rank or position were more respected by the enlisted soldiers than was General Hernandez. He had commanded at all levels in the military support community which culminated with his assignment as Assistant Division Commander-Support prior to assuming division command. This said, his operational and strategic tactics were sound. Commissioned Officers of all branches in the army attend the same senior schools to prepare them for high leadership positions and General Hernandez had excelled at all levels.

Combat Veterans (left to right) Sergeants Verdell Samuel, Donna Lopez, Brenda Minor & Melissa Billups.

One of the high points during my tour as Chief of Staff was working with a clerical and administrative inner office staff of high performing and extremely competent soldiers, all women. They were Sergeant First Class Brenda Minor (originally from New York), Sergeant Frieda Payne (Chicago), Sergeant Verdell Samuel (US Virgin Islands), Sergeant Melissa Billups (California) and Specialist Donna Lopez (New Mexico).

All of the soldiers, except Specialist Lopez, had matriculated in the division and had proven themselves with superior efficiency rating which positioned them for eventual transfers to the Division staff.

I had met Specialist Lopez in New Mexico while attending a Counter-Drug Conference in her then hometown of Albuquerque where she was part of the host

282

state administrative staff. She boldly introduced herself and made an unusual direct request of me to transfer to California and specifically to 40th Division Headquarters at Los Alamitos.

As a fully qualified intelligence and counter-drug analyst her transfer between states' was approved by all of the leaders in the decision cycle and she and her family were in California within a week. She filled an open fulltime position on the staff reserved for a qualified and trained counter drug analyst and met all qualifications. This time line was unusually fast but according to policy and procedures.

My wife Dorothy and Sergeant First Class Minor whom I had known for many years became well acquainted with one another while working on mutual military family support projects at the Division. This became somewhat of a family affair as she often acted as a surrogate big sister to our son Mark. I respected the Army's doctrine to avoid fraternizations but Dorothy always reminded me that it was me who was in the military and not her.

Brenda's final assignment was at the Pentagon where she was promoted to Sergeant Major and I had the honor of traveling there assisting a Three Star General pinning on her new rank. Her Washington duties included serving as an Executive Assistant in the Office of the Secretary of Defense. During the Gulf War or Afghanistan War many of these women soldiers deployed to the war zone.

I had become aware of Sergeant Melissa Billups operational talents during several of my brief interactions with the Counter-Drug staff. Her eventual transfer to the Chief's Office allowed her to better display her administrative skills. Sergeants Payne and Samuel rounded out the extremely competent inner office staff.

In addition to the Division Primary Staff mention, G-1 through G-5 (to which G-6 Information Operations & G-7 Command, Control & Computers have been added), there was also Division Headquarters Special Staff Officers and

Personal Staff. These were the subject matter experts on specific topics. Some of the Special Staff included, but were not limited to the Division Engineer, Signal Officer, Air Defense Officer, Fire Support Coordinator, Aviation Officer, Resource Management, Adjutant General Staff Officer, Tactical Air Control (US Air Force) Officer, Provost Marshal, Psychological Operations, Finance, Chemical, Surgeon, US Air Force Weather Officer, and others.

Personal Staff included the Headquarters Commandant, Secretary to the General Staff, Inspector General, Chaplain, Staff Judge Advocate (commonly known as the JAG), Public Affairs, Aide de Camp, and Command Sergeant Major. My personal security team from the Military Police Company and driver from Headquarters Company were always nearby.

THE PASSING OF MY FATHER

Many of my duties as Chief of Staff required attending to administrative requirements in the office initially upon arrival each morning. During this time my father was in failing health and had required several hospital stays and procedures. My morning routine was that upon departing from home to the office I diverted to my father's house to say hello as he was bedridden but conversational. He never complained about his cancerous condition.

My visits were brief but always special. He was also visited regularly by all of his children and many of his grandchildren. On the morning of his passing in 1989 like clockwork I visited him that morning and we had a brief conversation but I could surmise this was not going to be one of his better days so I lingered a while longer before taking the 30 minute drive to the office.

When I arrived staff informed me that a family member had telephoned reporting that my father had passed away. This was prior to our wide-spread use of cell phones and pagers. I immediately returned to his home where some family members had already gathered.

Cancer is unlike a cowardly thief who lurks in the darkness of back streets and alleys while stalking an unsuspecting victim. It then leaps and attacks its prey with wanton abandon and robbing them of their dignity and ability to care for their personal needs and finally their life.

The victim's family also falls prey to the coward by involuntarily falling into the deep abyss mourning the anticipated loss of not only their loved one but their own precious personal time while still providing loving care to the victim. With a myriad of continuing research endeavors the criminal has yet to be apprehended.

Our father's funeral service was monumental in terms of numbers in attendance; some surmising that the procession from the church to the cemetery was the longest San Pedro had ever seen. We heard later that some residents believed that a VIP must have passed away because the traffic was blocked for such a long time.

In fact the procession was for a VIP, Clarence Gravett Sr., our dad. He was that well known and respected and loved by

Peter & dad; Clarence Gravett, Sr.

many. I was disappointed that he was not provided cemetery military honors he so richly deserved and was available to veterans, especially World War Two Veterans, but this was the wishes of some of the family even though several of his sons were themselves veterans. That decision I could never understand and I remain disappointed to this day. That said and done I can report that his service was still first class.

He was interred at Green Hills Memorial Park in Rancho Palos Verdes and a legend had left us and ever since there has been a void in my life and the lives of all of us.

As noted earlier my father was sage to always support his family generally working two jobs which ensured the family would never depend on any other source of public or private assistance and we never did. Between his two jobs and my mother working they earned sufficient income to support their family prior to the children coming of age and going off on their own.

DESERT STORM

In 1991, during my tour of duty as Chief of Staff to Major General Averill Hawkins, elements of the Division were alerted for possible mobilization and deployment for the war in Iraq, as we had deployed soldiers to the conflicts in Bosnia and Kosovo the year prior. Since it was unknown what role the Division was destined to play we maneuvered onto a wartime footing and increased our training regimen.

During the first few months of that war several Army National Guard organizations around the country were mobilized, sent to active military bases for additional training and deployed to the war zone. The 40th Division was directed to "plus up" (add soldiers and equipment) some of our units and some were eventually deployed.

The Division Headquarters itself was not alerted as most mobilizations were company and battalion size units; the thoughts being that they could more easily be meshed with active units with minimal consternation. For the duration of my assignment we continued to train the remaining units for any contingency.

LOS ANGELES RIOTS

While serving as Chief of Staff under Major General Hernandez in 1992 rioting broke out in Los Angeles and several surrounding communities. This occurred due to the televised brutal beating of an unarmed black motorist by what news outlets considered to be rogue members of the Los Angeles Police Department.

This was similar to the 1965 L.A. riots instigated by a law enforcement officer stopping an unarmed black motorist suspected of driving under the influence who was later found not guilty by jury. The difference however, was that in the 1965 incident, the officer was a member of the California Highway Patrol.

In this incident a motorist by the name of Rodney King was stopped and mercifully beaten by police officers Sergeant Stacey Koon, Officer Laurence Powell, Officer Theodore Briseno and Probationary Officer Timothy Wind who had less than six months on the Department. Their actions appeared to be racially motivated, why else would four White police officers beat an unarmed black man offering no resistance while lying face down helpless on the pavement? The case has been closed and will not be retried here.

They were all indicted by the Los Angeles County Grand Jury and because of the perception they would not receive a fair trial in Los Angeles the trial was moved to Ventura County in the City of Simi Valley, an all-White suburb. When the all-White jury found the officers not guilty as expected rioting broke out in Los Angeles and throughout other parts Southern California.

While in the Division Command Center at the Joint Forces Training Base at Los Alamitos watching the riot unfold on live television I realized that it was quickly getting out of hand. There was no doubt that it was unable to be controlled by law enforcement, so I advised the Commander that this incident no doubt was going to require our assistance and recommended he alert some local National Guard units, which he did.

We immediately notified the Office of the Adjutant General in Sacramento of our actions and cautioned that we were not mobilizing any units as that was the prerogative of the Adjutant General. Mid-level staff in his office, typical of micro-managing subordinate units throughout the state, upon learning that Division units had been alerted for possible state active duty, quickly denounced the action and suggested that only that Headquarters possessed that option.

This was at the same time that the Mayor of Los Angeles and the Sheriff of Los Angeles County were on the telephone in a conference call urgently requesting the Governor to provide National Guard units be sent to assist with quelling the riot as it was quickly expanding beyond their control.

In other words, while the Governor was speaking to the Adjutant General ordering the Guard to be deployed, his staff was admonishing Division Staff for acting without authority rather than praising our initiative. Silently I applauded General Hernandez for holding his ground and standing by his decision.

Not only were most units in the Division eventually mobilized but the Governor called upon the President of the United States (POTUS) to send Federal Military Forces to Los Angeles to supplement the State Military Forces. When this request was approved the Division units were federalized and were no longer under the control of the superb Adjutant General and his micro-managing mid-level staff. National Guard units then reverted from Title 32 US Code, state control, to Title 10 US Code, federal control.

The Adjutant General in Sacramento dispatched Major General James Delk, a former Division Commander, to Los Alamitos as the Senior California National Guard Military Representative on the scene working strategy and policy issues. I had great respect for General Delk as I had served as his G-5 when he commanded the Division.

A Brigade of the 7th Infantry Division of the US Army stationed at Fort Ord some 350 miles to the north was ordered to Los Angeles under command of their Division Artillery Commander, a Colonel. Other units of the 7th Division included Military Police, Aviation and Logistics.

Since the 40th Division had been federalized and was on federal duty, the Brigade of that Division was attached to the 40th Division and under the Command of its' Commanding General, Major General Daniel Hernandez. As Chief of Staff for the entire operation I exercised staff responsibility over the 7th Division Brigade for the duration of the mobilization.

While in the Division Command Center at Los Alamitos much of my duties included monitoring the situation as it unfolded throughout the county and having situational awareness of when and in what numbers the military units should be deployed. This required maneuvering units to various geographical locations while responding to civilian law enforcement requests for support, assisting with required logistics whether it be at the Los Angeles Coliseum, Whittier Narrows Recreation Center, armories, schools, regional command centers, government facilities or other key locations.

KOREAN AMERICAN COMMUNITY

Years earlier while serving as the Civil Military Officer, G-5, I had spent considerable time with members of the Korean community in Los Angeles. One individual with whom I had established a strong bond was Dr. In Ha Cho, a member of the Korea-America Society and an officer in the Korean Veterans Association. These were veterans of the Republic of Korea Army now residing in the United States. During quieter times Dr. Cho served as the unofficial liaison between the Korean American Community and the Division. He was often instrumental in coordinating the annual trips by Division leaders to Gapyong High School in South Korea which ensured the ongoing relationship.

Gapyong High School was originally named Kenneth Kaiser High School in honor of the first 40th Division soldier who lost his life in the Korean War. Men of the Division had reached in their pockets and made large contributions to purchase building materials for the school which Division Engineers designed and built. Division soldiers also wrote home to families and friends for used clothing for the destitute students and their families.

During the riot I received a telephone call from Dr. Cho's daughter which was patched in to me in the Division Command Post. She frantically informed me that her father, Dr. Cho, had been shot and wounded by gang members and had been evacuated to a local hospital. She was pleading with me to go to the hospital to see him which obviously I could not do at the time.

She related that when gang members and Korean businessmen in Korea Town had exchanged automatic gun fire during a confrontation a bullet had struck her father though, according to her, he did not have a weapon and was unarmed. A report by the LAPD after the incident, revealed that both the gang members and the businessmen had had semi-automatic weapons during one of the shootouts. None were ever located and I believe that the police never knew that such weapons were in possession of either group. Days later I visited Dr. Cho in the hospital who was recovering from his wound and he thanked me for the visit. Later he fully recovered.

Quite often when Republic of Korea senior military officer retire from the military in their native country many relocate to Los Angeles with their families. Most affiliate with the Korean Veterans Association of the Western United States which has its offices in Los Angeles. Several years earlier I had been made an Honorary Member and even golfed a time or two in their tournaments. Los Angeles had the largest concentration of Koreans of any city in the world outside of South Korea's Capital, Seoul.

LOS ANGELES POLICE RIOT LIAISON

Few of the senior leaders in the Los Angeles Police Department during the riots had previous military experience and those who did had served in the lower enlisted ranks before beginning their law enforcement careers many years earlier. With the need to understand military missions, capabilities, weapons, command and control system, federal versus state control, Posse Commitatus and a plethora of other issues the Los Angeles Chief of Police wisely appointed Police Captain Keith Bushey as the Police Department's liaison to the 40th Division at the Joint Forces Training Base in Los Alamitos.

Captain Bushey was a natural selection as he was currently serving in the United States Marine Corps Reserve as a Lieutenant Colonel, later a Colonel, and was well known to the division's leadership and I knew him personally. Keith was a decorated combat veteran from the Gulf War and clearly understood what actions needed to be taken to remedy what was occurring. This worked out well as he had direct access to the Division Commander, Chief of Staff and the Division Staff and more importantly to Major General Delk, the most senior officer.

Captain Bushey provided sage advice, suggestions and recommendation with respect to the deployment of military forces while explaining the organizational structure of the Police department. For example, police cars are generally staffed with two uniformed officers who respond to calls for service within their geographical patrol division. During civil disturbances however, it was not uncommon to have patrol cars staffed with four officers to provide a more robust appearance when arriving at the scene of a call. Also on occasion several patrol cars together with four officers each would be dispatched if a more robust presence was required. This was called a "Brush Fire Team."

The US Army trains as a team in preparation for possible deployments at civil disturbances. After mobilization of a large force the smallest element dispatched to a location is generally a platoon led by a commissioned officer which can range from 30 to 40 soldiers. They can easily be spread out in the area in squads of about 10 to 12 soldiers each led by a senior non-commissioned officer. Should a police leader request the assistance of, say three or four soldiers, a Police Liaison Officer would have the ability to quickly analyze the request to identify what exactly the mission would be and recommend the size of military element to be disbursed.

Following three years as Chief of Staff, I was appointed as Commander of the Second Armor Brigade. The Division office staff honored my service at Division Headquarters with a farewell cruise around the Long Beach Harbor. Most of the active duty staff found it invigorating to take a day of personal leave to honor me in that fashion but also perhaps just to see a part of Long Beach from the water side. Several of my brothers were serving in positions at the water front and came to the pier to see us embark.

CHAPTER 60 BRIGADE COMMAND

In 1993 the Command Board of General Officers selected me to command the 2nd Brigade, 40th Infantry Division (Mechanized) organized as previously described and where I had a previous posting as Executive Officer.

The Battalions in the Armor Brigade were equipped with M-60A3 main battle tanks so a National Guard Bureau decision was made to reorganize the Brigade because other battalions were scheduled to undergo NETT to the M-1 main battle tank at Gowen Field, Idaho just as the 1-185th Armor Battalion had done previously.

To systemize training and for more efficient command and control all Division Armor Battalions, in addition to the already 2-185th and 3-185th, were attached to the 2nd Brigade. These included the 1-149th Armor Battalion based in Salinas, CA, 1-18th Cavalry Squadron based in Ontario, CA, the 8-40th Armor Battalion based in Arizona, the 1-221st Armor Battalion based in Nevada and a battalion of the 81st Armor Brigade based in Washington State. Having previously undergone the training the 1-185th was also attached to be used as trainers.

With this temporary configuration of attachments the Brigade possessed more tanks in its arsenal, over 500, than did German Field Marshal Erwin Rommel had in his Africa Corps during World War Two. In fact at that time the 40th Division was the largest reserve division in the Free World.

With the Army reorganizing based upon the Wars being fought in the Iraq and Afghanistan by 2015 all tank battalions had been eliminated from the division structure and some replaced by striker battalions, the striker being an eight rubber-wheeled light armored vehicle deemed more suitable for urban warfare. Some would say that this reconfiguration lived up to the saying that *"we are always fighting the previous war."*

The Tank that Got Away (AKA High 'O Silver)

It was during my command tour at Second Brigade that a very unfortunate incident occurred involving the theft of one of the tanks. The home station tank had been housed in the tank park at the vast complex of the San Diego's Kearney Mesa Armory. This enormous facility not only housed the Brigade Headquarters but also housed the Headquarters of 2-185 Armor Battalion and two of its' line tank companies.

There were approximately twelve tanks at the complex which were used for limited tank training (such as switchology) on fenced acreage with its array of dirt tank trails and small mounds. When not in use, all tanks and other vehicles, both armored and wheeled, were securely looked in conformance with US Army security regulations and standards. For the tanks this included having high security pad locks on hatches, the driver's hatch being on the tanks lower structure and the commander's hatch higher up on the cupola.

A distraught former Regular Army tank crewman recently discharged from Germany where he had served in an armor unit and who had been trained, as all armor crewmen were, to affect a "combat entry" into the tank under emergency conditions. This entry can also be affected with the hatches locked. This is only to be used when an attack was imminent and the tanks were parked and locked with the pad lock keys not readily available. It was designed for use primarily in Western Europe where an invasion by the Soviets from the east through the Fulda Gap was probable.   .

Without going into great detail of the entry method the soldier entered the tank, drove it from the yard and throughout the local neighborhood destroying vehicles, drive ways, fences and other residential property and was finally impaled on a freeway divider.

Other than the death of the criminal who stole the vehicle at the hands of San Diego Police Officers there were no civilian deaths or injuries. The officer involved shooting came as a last resort following the drivers' refusal to halt the vehicle and with his attempt to crash into on-coming freeway traffic.

There were several ensuing investigations that followed the incident. They were conducted by the US Army, National Guard Bureau in Washington DC, Office of the Adjutant General in Sacramento and Division Headquarters. These were complimented by various civilian governmental agencies seeking their own answers. The final outcome was they all concluded that all required security measures had been in place and all safety and security regulations had been followed. There were no recriminations against any military personnel, however, a few years later all tanks were voluntarily relocated from the neighborhood to an active Army installation.

Following a three year tour of duty in Brigade Command I was selected by the General Officer Selection Panel as Assistant Division Commander – Support, a Brigadier General position. My change of command ceremony from the Brigade was scheduled with invitations extended to many of the residents in the local community. This is one of the very few armories that was situated in a residential area and therefore the soldiers had over the years established a strong bond with the residents of the neighborhood.

The San Diego National Guard Armory is located in the Mesa College District which was immediately adjacent to Mesa Community College and Mesa High School, both on either side of the armory and was just a few miles north of downtown.

Residents from the community attended the change of command ceremony in large numbers as did several of my family members and friends who convoyed to San Diego for the day to witness the ceremony.

CHAPTER 61 SELECTION AND APPOINTMENT PROCESS: AKA THE ACCIDENTAL GENERAL

While serving as Brigade Commander in 1994, I was directed to attend a strategic planning meeting at Travis Air Force Base in Northern California. At the meeting there were three Army Generals and two Air Force Generals, as I recall. Noticeably I was the only Colonel.

I thought this peculiar in that a strategic planning meeting would normally have had several Colonels in attendance. The most senior General present was Air Force Major General Tandy Bozeman, then The Adjutant General (TAG). TAG is appointed by the Governor and must be confirmed by the State Senate. In all states and territories he or she commands both the Army and Air National Guard and serve in the Governor's Cabinet at the state level just as the Chairman of the Joint Chiefs of Staff serves in the President's Cabinet at the federal level.

Right away General Bozeman began by announcing the purpose of the meeting was to announce that I had been selected for the rank of Brigadier General. I was totally unaware this announcement was forthcoming. One always has aspirations of attaining the highest positions of responsibility possible but this was not expected. Obviously the Generals had contemplated and discussed this decision while weighing the capabilities of several other imminently qualified colonels.

General Bozeman extended his hand and offered congratulations on my selection as did all of the other Generals. We had a brief conversation then General Bozeman asked me if I intended to telephone my wife and what was I waiting for?

I telephoned Dorothy with the much surprised but good news and then the Generals and I departed to a pre-planned luncheon at the Officer's Club to celebrate. This had been the strategic planning meeting.

Once a Colonel is selected for General Officer the process begins to confirm that the individual is fully qualified over and above what had already been reviewed. The process takes from 12 to 18 months of intensive review of the officer's background and credentials. All efficiency reports from the time of commissioning are checked and double checked. Every order containing the officer's name is reviewed for accuracy. Inspector General files are reviewed to determine whether or not the officer has complaints or charges filed against them during the entire career and determine whether any charges were substantiated.

All civilian educational records and degrees are checked to determine authenticity with every educational institution attended requested to provide to the government authenticated and sealed true copies of all degrees and certificates and any and all other records or reports bearing the officer's name.

Military medical records are reviewed to determine evidence of illnesses or injuries which would prohibit the officer from performing the duties of a General Officer or contain any evidence or history of conditions which, according to regulations, would be grounds for elimination.

Every official military photograph taken of the officer in dress or field uniform are carefully scrutinized to ensure all awards and decorations worn are authorized and documented by official orders in the officer's personnel file. Even minor discrepancies can be basis for disqualification. Civilian letters of commendation are traced back to the issuing agency or individual to document realism.

Once most of these administrative checks and balances are under way, the officer is subjected to another thorough medical examination performed at specific active military medical centers around the country conducted by specialists to determine medical fitness. Typically every medical examination known to man-kind is performed on the individual (this was a good thing). Once my medical examination was completed I was found fit.

Once the officer has been cleared from processing by the US Army the name of the officer is submitted for promotion to the Secretary of the Army who convenes a selection board chaired by a four star General and comprised of three and two star Generals. This could be as many as 10 or more Generals.

Generally several Colonel Candidates from various states and territories are submitted along with Regular Army Colonels and Army Reserve Colonels. Territories having National Guard units are the Commonwealth of Puerto Rico, United States Virgin Islands, United States Trust Territory of Guam, The Northern Marianas (Saipan) and the District of Columbia.

Once the Board makes the selection the Secretary of the Army refers the actions to the President who officially nominates the officer to the US Senate. The Senate Armed Services Committee takes up the review of all actions performed. Once this is done the nomination then goes to the full Senate for confirmation. If the officer is confirmed his or her nomination is placed on a Senate Bill for voting.

Typically the nomination is placed on the next Senate Bill going through the process. This could be a Water Bill, Farm Bill, Highway Construction Bill etc. When the Bill is approved (voted) then the officer's name is placed on the General Officer eligibility list awaiting a General Officer position opening.

There is a legal limit on the number of Army General Officers serving at any given time. Typically fifty one percent of all Generals must be one star Generals (Brigadier General) and forty nine percent are Generals above one star, i.e. Major General (2 star), Lieutenant General (3 star) and General (four star). This metric can be adjusted based upon the needs of the nation. In 1981 following the passing of General of the Army Omar Bradley, the last surviving five star military officer, Congress eliminated the rank in all services.

CHAPTER 62 CRITERIA FOR BRIGADIER GENERAL

Based upon the forgoing it is obviously that the elevation of a Colonel to a General Officer in the United States Army is extremely complicated, rigid, protocol laced and involves several components of the Legislative and Executive Branches of the federal Government, and with the National Guard, the Executive Branch of the State Government.

In the Army National Guard of the various states and territories the process begins with the officer at the rank of colonel themselves. The individual must have a totally unblemished record of achievement and having had recognition as a top notch soldier and leader going back to the time of commissioning as a Second Lieutenant, which in many instances could be 25 years or more.

At every turn they must have been clearly identified having superb potential at the operational and later strategic level. This must be documented in annual Officer Efficiency Reports and having been assigned to key staff positions and command positions at all levels.

These include having had successful company command, battalion command and brigade or equivalent level command. Key staff positions would include battalion and brigade experience as an Executive Officer (X.O.), Operations Officer (S-3), Intelligence Officer (S-2), Personnel Officer (S-1) or Logistics Officer (S-4). A multiple of these positions would be a plus. Having served on the staff at a Division, Brigade or other senior level headquarters is extremely beneficial.

MILITARY AND CIVILIAN EDUCATION REQUIREMENTS

A requirement of military education would include the Officer Basic Course, Officers Advance Course, Combined Arms and Services Course (CAS3), now called the Captain's Course, Command and General Staff College (C&GSC) and numerous technical, administrative and leadership courses taken throughout ones career would be a necessity. Cumulative these would consume several years of study at various military locations. The C&GSC alone could be at least six months in duration at Fort Leavenworth, Kansas.

The Army War College is the top level and premier educational plateau in the Army, the other services having similar colleges. It is based at Carlisle Barracks, Pennsylvania, just outside Washington DC .This school is almost a full one year course of study if in resident status or two years if in a combination of resident-nonresident status and is mandatory for promotion to General Officer. Typically less than one percent of officers are selected to attend this school.

All Generals are graduates of the War College but not all graduates of the War College are promoted to General Officer. The larger than needed pool of officers allows for a more scrutinized selection. I was fortunate to have been selected and attended the US Army War College.

Following my commissioning at Officer Candidate School over the years my military education had included Officer Basic Course at Fort Gordon Georgia, Officer Advanced Course at Fort Knox, Kentucky, Command and General Staff College at Fort Leavenworth, Kansas and the Army War College at Carlisle Barracks, Pennsylvania.

Colonels may also be selected to attend any one of the various War Colleges and all have similar curricula. These are the national War College, National Naval College and Air War College. There is also a program whereby a Colonel may be selected to study for a year at a prestigious university and receive War College equivalency. These included several of the Ivy League Schools, Tufts University, Stanford University, University of Pennsylvania, the University of Texas and others.

In Addition to the War College I attended over a dozen other courses of medium and short duration. Most of this information was presented earlier but is outlined again to place the military educational requirement for General Officer in perspective.

My civilian education included an Associate Degree from Long Beach City College, Bachelors' Degree from California State University at Long Beach, Masters' Degree from the University of Southern California and Executive Diploma's from the University of Virginia and, later, from the JFK School of Government at Harvard University. Additionally I had graduated from the Federal Bureau of Investigation National Academy, Quantico, Virginia. All of my War College classmates possessed similar military and civilian academic credentials, some possessing Doctorates, Law and Medical or Allied Medical Degrees.

At the conclusion of my studies at the Army War College Dorothy and Mark arrived at Carlisle and attended my graduation ceremony along with my secretary now Master Sergeant (later Sergeant Major) Brenda Minor. Following the ceremony the family then spent several days visiting the sites in Washington DC.

CHARM SCHOOL

Once a Colonel has been confirmed for promotion to Brigadier General but prior to promotion he or she is scheduled to attend the "Charm School" the name frequently given for the General Officers Training Course (the course has nothing to do with charm). This strategic level course is held at Fort Leavenworth, Kansas on the campus of the Command and General Staff College and is the final hurdle prior to being promoted.

It focuses on specific constitutional duties and responsibilities of a General. The senior instructor is the Chief of Staff of the Army, a four star General, who is by position the Army's most senior General.

Each of his Department of the Army Assistant Chiefs of Staff, three stars each, participate by providing strategic briefings on their offices; such as Personnel, Intelligence, Plans and Operations and Army Logistics. Other senior staff officers also visit the course and engage with the class.

These often include the Chief of Engineers, The Judge Advocate General, Chief of Aviation, Chief Medical Officer, Chief of Infantry, Chief of Armor, Chief of Artillery, Chief of Chaplains, and many others including the Chief Communications and Cyber Security Officer and the Provost Marshal General.

The course curricula also focused on the strategic issues which affect the nation's security. Table top exercises are part of the course whereby class members play the roles of Generals in the field of operations with strategic decision making scenarios. These are similar to the ones I participated in with War Fighter exercises but at a much higher level.

Since Generals are not only responsible for the welfare of soldiers in the command but, in some instances, especially active duty Generals, are also responsible for the welfare of family members. For this reason wives and husbands of class members also attend this course and sit side by side with their spouses during non-classified briefing periods.

One of the most interesting comments made by the Army Chief of Staff to my class was when he encouraged all of to learn to *Lie, Cheat* and *Steal.* This unusual comment quickly garnered everyone's attention. He went on to say that as a General we will be working a minimum of 18 hours a day for the remainder of our careers and it was important that we always be at our best to make strategic life or death decisions should the situation arise.

First he encouraged us to find time in mid-afternoon to *Lie* down for a few minutes in a comfortable place away from noise and distractions with our eyes closed to rest our minds and bodies. Doing this would energize us for the remainder of the day and evening.

Next he encouraged us to *Cheat* the onset of premature physical disabilities by having a personal and dynamic physical fitness routine to keep our bodies fit for the rigors of command.

Finally he encouraged us to *Steal* away from the military whenever we had time for annual leave or just a weekend. We were advised to steal away from the Post with our families and take a well needed vacation and rest which would allow us to reconnect with our families 24/7.

The Chief's comments reminded me of comments by Cartoonist Bill Keane which I have always treasured: *"Yesterday is history. Tomorrow is a mystery. Today is a gift. That's why it's called the present."* The point the Chief made was that lying, cheating and stealing can be positive attributes if understood and applied effectively.

Dorothy's visit to Fort Leavenworth allowed her to receive a real good taste of Army life with 14-16 hour days which began at five AM with structured physical fitness training for the class members given by an NCO who was a Master Physical Fitness Trainer. He relished at the opportunity to give orders to the soon to be Generals and he possessed the smirk and smile to prove it.

CHAPTER 63 FEDERAL REPUBLIC OF GERMANY

During the late 1990's and early 2000's I had several short duration deployments to the Federal Republic of Germany to both coordinate with their Army and to complete the official partnership agreement which would match the US 40th Infantry Division (Mechanized) with the Federal Republic of Germany's First Mountain Division. Although their Division had no tanks or armored vehicles the two units had many other similarities, including both being Reserve Divisions.

These visits were made both in springtime and winter. I was able to see firsthand how German soldiers adapted based upon the weather conditions. They trained just as hard in the winter months as in other times of the year, notwithstanding snow and icy conditions.

Most of my time there was spent in the Bavarian area of Southern Germany where their Division was headquartered. My Kerserne (military housing), was in Munich but I traveled throughout the area visiting units in Augsburg, Stuttgart, Berchtesgaden, Wurzburg, Schweinfurt, Nuremburg, and visiting Dachau.

Dauchau was infamous for the concentration camp during World War Two where many of the millions of Jews and other minorities were exterminated by the Nazis. The camp was actually located a short distance outside the city. There I was able to see firsthand the ovens used by the Nazis in this one of the most horrific events of human existence.

One of the most pleasant experiences of one of my trips was visiting with my God son, Michael Haynes, son of my best friend Melvin. Michael had deployed there where

German Army Reserve Chief of Staff COL Reischal (left) and First German Mountain Division Commanding General (right).

he was assigned to the 40th Division's Long Range Reconnaissance Detachment (Airborne) and was training with elements of the First Mountain Division in mountain warfare operations. Michael was somewhat embarrassed when his God father extended a personal greeting to him in the mess hall while the contingent of American and German soldiers coming to rigid attention upon my entry. It became obvious that he had not shared that his God Father was also the Commanding General of the Division to which his unit was assigned.

The 1st German Mountain Division Commanding General took me along in his Command Helicopter where we flew to the German Alps to monitor the progress of a contingent of Mountain Warfare Soldiers on their annual march. This three day trek over mountains and through passes was part of their continuing training and were accompanied by a large contingent of Italian Mountain Soldiers.

Another trip with him coincided with Oktober Fest. The celebration of this beer festival is primarily celebrated in the Bavarian part of Southern Germany with Munich being the center of gravity. My personal staff member and assistant, Lieutenant Colonel Bernd Willand,

and I were able to experience this traditional German celebration first hand, which is actually held beginning in September with parties spilling over to the end of Oktober, as the month is spelled in German.

Later in November we visited the area what had been Adolf Hitler's Mountain Retreat: Kehlsteinhaus or "Eagle Nest" in the Bavarian Alps. The Eagles Nest building still sits on a mountain peak high above Berchtesgaden. It was a birthday gift from Martin Bormann, his Administrative Secretary, after being confiscated from their own people as war spoils.

I would have liked to have toured the facility, now a cozy restaurant with 360 degree view of the Alps, but it was closed for the winter beginning in November as the heavy mountain snows prevented access by visitors. It was open only during the late spring and summer months, the same months Hitler was in residence.

Lieutenant Colonel Willand, US Army, was born and raised in Germany where his mother still resided. My German points of contact believed that Bernd, when in civilian clothes, was German as his command of the Southern Germany dialect was so perfect. They did not realize that he had a life time to perfect it most of it in southern Germany.

While in Germany in 2001 I witnessed the total eclipse of the sun. Over the years I had been witness to many eclipses but never a total eclipse which is a rare phenomenon. On the particular day around noon the eclipse began and continued for over an hour placing everything in total darkness as the moon completely blocked the sun. This caused the street lights to automatically turn on and birds to fly to their night time nesting places while drivers turned on their vehicle headlights. I later learned that Southern Germany had been the best place in the world to make witness of that event.

MG Gravett with German Army Officers in the Black Forrest.

During all of my deployments to Germany my local host officer was Oberstleutnant (Lieutenant Colonel) Roald Rummel, himself a reserve military officer and a fulltime elementary school teacher. I would learn that his wife, Brigitte, was also an elementary school teacher. They taught at different schools however.

Their son, Matias was a manager in a telecommunications company, and Masters' Degree recipient from Wayne State University in the US. He was also a Captain in the German Army Reserve. Their daughter, Christina, was a medical doctor, a psychiatrist, and was married to a medical doctor. All had widely traveled throughout the US. Over the next several years I became very close to this family with my expansive trips to Germany and Roald and Brigitte's numerous trips to the US as will be discussed later.

CHAPTER 64 PROMOTION, TRAINING AND DEPLOYMENTS

About a year after I had been submitted for promotion to Brigadier General, in 1996, my name appeared on a Bill that was voted on and confirmed by the US Senate so I became eligible for promotion. There were seven Generals on that particular list and I was number one. At that point actions were taken to plan the promotion ceremony.

When a military officer is promoted to Flag Rank (General or Admiral) there are certain protocols, traditions and ceremonials which are followed as one would expect. On December 7, 1996 a public ceremony was held at the Joint Force Training Base, Los Alamitos, California presided over by Major General Robert Brandt, Commanding General of the California Army National Guard. General Brandt was an Army General who reported to the Adjutant General, Major General Tandy Bozeman, US Air Force. My wife Dorothy, and son Mark and various other family members and friends were in attendance as was several hundred community leaders and citizens and, of course, soldiers of the command. My brother, Command Sergeant Major Melvin Gravett, was a member of the official party.

Dorothy and Mark were so proud that day and would always remember it in conversation and I agreed that it was probably the third proudest moment of my life following our wedding day and Mark's birth.

Flag officers repeat their military oath when promoted and I repeated the one I had taken many years earlier as a teenage Private. Dorothy and Mark pinned the stars on the shoulders of my Class A Dress Uniform. Later my remarks were short and pointed giving thanks to my parents, siblings and mentors along the way. The ceremony concluded with the several mementoes' presented as protocol to a new General.

These include two Generals Flags, red with a single white star, one for indoor made of silk with dangling gold bunting and one for outdoor made of all-weather material. I was also presented with a leather pistol belt with brass embossed US Army insignia buckle, accompanying ammunition pouch and holster. I was presented with a nine millimeter Beretta automatic pistol to wear in the field and, upon retirement, keep as a personal weapon. The pistol is presented on behalf of Congress and has a specialized serial number.

Dorothy & Peter at Army Ball with Orders of Saint George.

One of my first actions as a newly minted General Officer was to appoint an Aide-De-Camp. I had pre-elected a Second Lieutenant whom I had previously interviewed after he had been recommended by Melvin. This Lieutenant had been assigned to the Division Support Command as was Melvin who had personal knowledge of his competence and leadership skills. His first duty as Aide-de-Camp was to raise my one star Generals flag during the ceremony.

DOROTHY GETS A STAR

Dorothy was also pinned but with the two stars of a Major General. In the Army there is a tradition and unofficial custom of when a Colonel is promoted to Brigadier General and receives a star representing his new rank his wife (or husband) is also promoted (honorably) and has two stars pinned on. Theory is that this will always remind the

General who is in charge of the household and from whom he, in my case, will be taking orders from at home. This also occurs should the General be promoted above the rank of one star.

CELEBRATING THE PROMOTION

About a month later my promotion party was held at Hollywood's Roosevelt Hotel hosted by Hollywood's Honorary Mayor Johnny Grant, a personal friend of many years. Not only were many family members and soldiers present, both officers and enlisted, but so were many friends. The evening celebration lasted until the last guest departed, the bartender, around 3 AM.

I learned later that there was an uninvited guest, the bartender himself. He had sort of waltzed in and started tending bar earlier in the evening and drinking as much as he served. I never knew his identity but he had a good time.

When a Colonel is promoted to Brigadier General he or she then join a very exclusive club very few soldiers belong. They receive congratulatory letters on General Officer Stationery from almost every General in the Army. The notes generally extend a warm welcome to the General Officer Corps each knowing full well the experiences and challenges the new General had overcome during a full career.

ASSISTANT DIVISION COMMANDER — SUPPORT

In addition to the Commanding General a US Army Division has two Assistant Division Commanders; Assistant Commander-Maneuver and Assistant Commander-Support, both Brigadier Generals. I was assigned as the Assistant Division Commander-Support and given command responsibility for all of the support elements in the Division.

These were the Aviation Brigade, Engineer Brigade, Division Artillery (Brigade) and the Division Support

Command (DISCOM), also a brigade size organization. Battalions included the Intelligence Battalion, Signal Battalion, Air Defense Artillery Battalion, Military Police Company, Long Range Surveillance Detachment (Airborne) and the Division Band.

An Army Division Band plays a crucial role in tactical operations. In the field it is heavily armed with automatic weapons and various other small arms. The Band's secondary mission is performing musically for the morale of the troops and at special ceremonies. Their primary mission however is providing physical security for the Division's Main Command Post during deployed field operations. Each Band member is fully trained on an array of small arms and automatic weapons.

The Assistant Division Commander-Maneuver has command of the combat elements of the Division which consists of all of the three Maneuver Brigades along with all of the Armor and Infantry Battalions, generally nine in total, as well as the Cavalry Squadron. During operations the combat and support elements are meshed to form task forces

During the next three years I became busy inspecting units, being briefed on a plethora of operational and national security issues, attending ceremonies, overseeing field training and maneuvers and pinning rank insignia on newly minted Officers, Non Commissioned Officers and soldiers. Some of my most important duties, however, was participating in War Fight Exercises and overseas deployments.

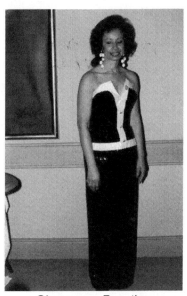

Glamorous Dorothy.

Another priority was overseeing the preparation of support annexes for Division Operation Orders. I officiated at Change of Command Ceremonies at Battalions and brigades, gave community speeches and performed various other duties associated with the position.

Dorothy really enjoyed the social aspect of my new duties as she reveled at attending military social events where she was able to look her best in formal ball gowns. Everyone in the military seemed to love her and her personality. I was fortunate to be able to share her with others and she took her responsibility of mentoring junior officer wives very seriously.

Army Ball attire.

Dorothy also saw the field side of my position often venturing out into the training areas wearing her military boots and field attire. She believed the interior of tanks were too confining and wondered why anyone wanted to be there.

HARVARD UNIVERSITY

After a year in the position I was selected by the Army to attend the International Security Course at the JFK School of Government at Harvard University. The course focused on security issues relating to Central and Eastern European Countries which were former members of the Soviet Bloc and some now Members of the North American Treaty Organization (NATO).

Several of my classmates were Generals from the Countries of Ukraine and Moldova, both former Russian led Communist countries. Ukraine, formerly referred to as "The Ukraine" and Moldova, like other former Soviet Bloc countries, became independent once again following the collapse of the Berlin Wall and the dismantling of the Soviet Union. The Harvard course prepared me for my eventual role in NATO's Partnership for Peace Program when I later served several tours in Ukraine.

GENERAL'S AND ADMIRAL'S LEGAL COURSE

I attended the Flag Officer's Legal Course at the Army's Judge Advocate General's (JAG) School located on the campus of the University of Virginia, Charlottesville, Virginia Law School. This course is mandatory for all new Generals and Admirals and the focus is the legal aspects and some restrictions placed on them by federal law. Courts Marshal Procedures were briefed as well relationships with the Legislative and the Judicial Branches of the federal government. The course also included a series of other subjects.

Since the instruction is common core this is where JAG Officers from all of the military services receive their Basic and Advance JAG Officer training once they have graduated from law school and are commissioned as military lawyers.

UKRAINE ASSIGNMENT (PARTNERSHIP FOR PEACE)

My first of several deployments to Ukraine was in 1997 while serving as Assistant Division Commander-Support. Later I made three additional deployments there and one more visit following retirement.

California had been designated as the partnership country with Ukraine in the North Atlantic Treaty Organization's (NATO) Partnership for Peace Program. Several states were aligned with former Soviet Bloc countries for military training, exercises and operations. This was an effort to bolster those countries image as transitioning to a Non-Communist form of Government and identifying with the West as a merging democracy.

A U.S. initiative, the Partnership for Peace Program had been launched at the 1994 NATO Summit to establish strong links between NATO, its new democratic partners in the former Soviet Bloc, and some of Europe's traditional neutral partners. The primary purpose was to engage European security. It provided a framework for enhanced political-military cooperation for joint-multilateral crisis engagement activities, such as humanitarian assistance and peacekeeping. Another purpose was to enable PfP members to consult with NATO when faced with a direct threat to its security but did not extend NATO guarantees.

We observed an example of this when Russian Military Forces invaded and occupied the Crimea Region of Ukraine beginning on the closing day of the 2012 Olympic

Games while the world was distracted. This had been one of the very areas where I had served. This illegal incursion on the sovereign territory of a free country probably would not have occurred had Ukraine become a full-fledged member of NATO when they and other former Soviet Bloc countries had the opportunity extended to them. The doctrine specified that an attack or incursion against a NATO country is an attack against all of its members.

Germany was the primary opposition to Ukraine's entry into NATO as it noted at the time that the populous of Crimea region of Ukraine was predominately ethnic Russian. The German government and it' people as well still held strong remembrances of the two countries, Germany and the Soviet Union, pitting one another in World War Two to which Ukraine was a member of the Communist Bloc at that time.

Other shared objectives of PfP were to assist the countries in establishing democratic control over their military forces, develop transparency in defense planning and budgeting processes, develop inter-operability with NATO forces and to formally develop a construct to meet the objectives.

Our deploying task forces were small by design, about 70 Officers, NCO's and soldiers. All possessed varied military and civilian backgrounds and were exploited to train with counterparts of the Ukraine Army. We were joined with a like number of soldiers from a half dozen other NATO countries in table-top exercises and field maneuvers without weapons.

A side benefit of PfP was that these deployments provided us the opportunity to study Soviet Military tactics up close and personal. It was there I gathered my first-hand look at Soviet military hardware, both armored vehicles and fixed and rotary winged aircraft. These implements of war had been postured facing the US Forces in Germany as well as other Western European Countries and had been a threat in the Fulda Gap Region on the Czechoslovakian border with West Germany. These covert threats existed all during the Cold War.

In my view not only was the Soviet equipment far inferior to ours but most had not been well maintained and were debilitating. They also lacked spare repair parts which are essential for continued and prolonged operations in a conflict. It was my estimation that had the Soviet Army crossed the Czechoslovakian border into West Germany the deployed US military and NATO partners would have overwhelmed the invaders while destroying them and taking much fewer casualties though any amount of casualties are too many.

PfP also became a cultural exchange as soldier to soldier each exchanged gifts and uniform accruements. Cossack military hats were a popular item for US soldiers to acquire as well as Nesting Doll sets and Faberge Eggs and Ukraine soldiers were eager to get any items of US Army issue including canteens, pistol belts, back packs, name tags and other items which our soldiers were eventually held accountable but nonetheless voluntarily gave to their counterparts.

Many Ukraine soldiers lacked field boots and many actually wore old civilian shoes. Since our soldiers each had two pair of boots several soldiers gave their extra pair to their new Ukraine soldier-friend.

Every evening there seemed to be a banquet for the senior officers celebrating a Ukraine military historical event. This could have been a skirmish, a battle, a war or a number of other events. Some won and some lost. The dinners were replete with a full away of international foods and an unlimited supply of vodka. Ukrainians, as with their Russian cousins, learn to drink vodka at an early age, usually around 12 years old. For this reason it is understandable why so many become somewhat immune to intoxication unless they consume excessive quantities.

Each banquet had several ceremonial toasts back to back with each of our hosts drinking a full shot glass of vodka each time. Most of our officers, me included, learned to toast with water while not offending our hosts by not drinking alcohol. The US Army Regulation prohibiting the consumption of alcoholic beverages while on duty extend internationally.

During off duty hours I allowed our troops to experience the Ukrainian culture by shopping and visiting coffee shops and stores. Electricity is very limited in that country and Kiev, the Capitol City, was greatly affected by this. During the night time hours most stores down town had only a single dangling light bulb turned on. When a potential customer entered they turned on few others to display their merchandize and returned to the single light when they departed.

Each Ukraine Army Division was deployed and responsible for a specific geographical region. Under some circumstances they were responsible to grow their own vegetables, raise cattle, sheep and poultry. Soldiers also operated their own bakery. This of course was very foreign to what the US Army experienced as most logistical requirements are contracted to civilian vendors.

There were few if any safety measures employed for weapon qualifications. An example of this was a tank firing range situated between rows of civilian houses located less than a hundred yards away.

MG Gravett with Ukrainian Military Officers.

Pay for the soldiers were not always consistent nor on any recognized schedule which perpetuated their ongoing problem of soldiers deserting. Not all AWOL soldiers were pursued as some officers in the Ukraine Army viewed this as just one less mouth to mouth to feed and body to cloth.

All in all the exchanges between US Army soldiers and our hosts was very cordial and their soldiers often joked with sincerity on how they plan to immigrate to New York or Hollywood.

Sadly, as I discussed earlier, several years later the Crimea, the very part of the country where I devoted much of my service, was invaded by Russian soldiers and confiscated as part of Russia. During my duty there it was noted that the vast majority of citizens of Crimea were ethnic Russian and spoke that language even more so than the Ukrainian language. Many of their relatives lived across the border in Russia proper. History shows that Crimea over the years had been annexed as part of the Ottoman Empire and Russia as well as having been independent.

Condoleezza Rice argues in her book "Democracy" Stories from the Long Road to Freedom: *"What most of the world saw as an outright violation of international law-countries don't annex the territory of their neighbor in the twenty-first century --- Russians saw as returning the territory to its rightful home. In their version of events, Catherine the Great conquered Crimea in 1783 and Nikita Khrushchev gave it to Ukraine as a gift for three hundred years of Russian-Ukrainian friendship in 1954; when Ukraine became independent in 1991, Kiev didn't give it back. Vladimir Putin set all of that right. Crimea was once Russian, and it was Russian again."*

HONDURAS ASSIGNMENT

For many years the US and the Central American country of Honduras have had joint counter-drug operations to stem the flow of cocaine and other illegal drugs passing through that country from South America to the US. Some of the refining operations were taking place in the jungle just ten to fifteen miles from that nations' capitol of Tegucigalpa. The US military had a base of operations nearby monitoring those activities.

Perhaps it was due to my civilian law enforcement background with the LAPD, which included a narcotics assignment, the FBI National Academy background and my field operations experience with Operations Green

Sweep and Border Ranger, mentioned earlier, that I was detailed to Honduras for a short tour as a senior military officer to receive briefings and to suggest operational enhancements

I flew from Miami to the Nation's Capital of Tegucigalpa and was met at the airport by a US soldier in tropical civilian clothing and wearing a beard and driving a 20 year old topless civilian jeep. We drove out to the operating base passing through a few small villages all of which had the look of the third world country we were in. I recall passing a dead horse on the main unpaved street of a village, a dirt road actually, which had obviously been there for several days. We also passed three bare foot small children riding bare back on a horse probably en route to school. The horse appeared to be extremely emaciated.

My pre-arranged visit included briefings on the current operations and I met with local law enforcement representatives. I was quick to applaud their efforts and careful not to suggest any significant operational changes but did offer some pointed suggestions to include a better process of vetting local indigents, including civilian officials contracted to assist in the operation. Though my interactions with local law enforcement officials were brief they did not instill confidence in me with their desire to enforce drug trafficking through their domain.

I was keenly aware that a nearby city, Sulu San Pedro, had been judged by Interpol, the International Police Organization, to be the world's deadliest city per capita with three murders per day for its' small population. The violence there stems from the city's role as a major hub for illegal drugs as well as arms trafficking.

The US Government had several agencies represented in the operation there in addition to the military which clearly only played a logistical support role. These included the Drug Enforcement Administration, the lead agency, and various others.

In 1998 Dorothy and I traveled to the University of New Hampshire to attend the college graduation ceremony of the daughter of a long-time friend, Sergeant Major Richard Wall. He and wife Patricia shared longtime friendships with Dorothy and me. I had known his daughter Yvette since she was a child and had watched her mature.

Dorothy at church event.

While in New England we took the opportunity to tour the other New England States of Maine and Vermont. Though it was too early in the year for the leaves to turn nonetheless the landscapes were beautiful with magnificent vistas. Although we could not conceive it at the time but this would be her last trip.

CHAPTER 65 A WORD ABOUT DOROTHY

My lovely wife Dorothy passed away in 1999 just a few days before I was promoted to Major General and was to assume command of the 40th Division. One year later to the day of her passing I wrote a story about her which I titled *"A Word about Dorothy."* Here I am including the story in its entirety as it captures the essence of her life and our life together and paints a vivid picture of my remarkable late wife. Much of what lies in the story has been mentioned earlier but I wanted to present the story as originally written with the understanding I was very much still in a mourning state

"A WORD ABOUT DOROTHY"

One year ago on July 12th Dorothy passed away and journeyed to heaven as one of the Lord's gatekeepers. During her mortal life, in my view she had been one of God's Angels on earth, her headstone reflects this. Our beloved Dorothy, yours and mine, will never be forgotten by those who knew her and by those who benefited from her kind and generous service to mankind. She left a profound legacy of love and charitable giving to her husband, son, family, friends, church and community.

The purpose of this correspondence is to pay final tribute to my dear Dorothy and provide her the recognition she so richly deserves. This adds to her eulogy read at the services.

Who would have expected that this great person who selflessly tended to the physical heart medical needs of hundreds of patients for over 35 years would herself succumb to the pales of a weakened heart following just a few short weeks of illness. What we know of Dorothy's passing is that it was ordained by the almighty and was an integral part of the Lord's master plan for his kingdom. As an Elder remarked to me recently, the Lord took Dorothy unto his own to provide balance to his Kingdom; she was the good balance.

As remarked at her services last year, Dorothy lived a full and rich Christian experience. No one ever reaches all goals set in life but we can probably say that she reached all of hers, though she would have disagreed. God knew that her work on earth was done and rewarded her.

She was kind, to say the least. We knew of her commitment to those in need, whether physical, emotional or material. But she also had another side - her favorites. Allow me to share some of them.

Dorothy loved the Los Angeles Lakers and favored individual players such as Kareem and A.C. Green. Her all-time favorite, however, was Michael Cooper, the sixth man off the bench with his knee-high socks and long thin legs. Whenever he entered the game her cheering would drown out any remarks made by announcer Chick Hearn.

She was also a regular rooter for the Los Angeles Dodger teams of the past but lost interest in recent years as their performance declined. After many years of attempting to understand football, she gave up on the sport. She could never understand why a team would voluntarily give up the ball though it would be fourth down and thirty. Also, why would a great player like Reggie White play only half the game? It became easier for her to dutifully sit and watch the game with me and cheer when I cheered.

Looking back over Dorothy's life I recall that she also had favorite entertainers such as Jackie Wilson, Smokey Robinson, Lou Rawls, The Temptations, Sam Cooke, and others from the "hey day" of the 50's, 60's and 70's. Though she seldom *watched television, she did have a favorite show; "In The Heat of the Night". Her other favorite pastimes included shopping at Mikasa for crystal; furnishing our Palm Springs home; having lunch with former club members; vacationing on Catalina Island; international travel, ocean cruises, and taking elderly and infirm relatives and friends shopping or just a weekend drive, as well as endless telephone conversations with Mark. That our son Mark was the center of her life is an understatement. They shared a bond few Mother's and son's enjoyed. There was always much to talk about and they spent literally hours conversing.*

She enjoyed her work at Harbor-UCLA Medical Center and especially her immediate RN and Technician co-workers Jim Gibson, Janice Ramlogan, and Terry. She delighted in working with all of the medical doctors including Chiefs, Attendings, (a medical term); Fellows, Residents, and Interns; far too numerous to mention, except William French and Michael Criley. Her favorite staff member, (she had many) was Cathy Dowty. Few if any of us enjoy or enjoyed their work as did Dorothy.

It is important that we remember Dorothy this way to give her life substance and meaning. Her life became structured as it was being lived.

Throughout our marriage she often spoke of her Father, Jonas, Sr., who was accidentally killed when she was six years old. Though young, she harbored the fondest memories of him. Though her Mother, Lillie Mae, has been widowed for over 50 years, she never remarried and Dorothy (and her siblings) became very protective of her though they were geographically separated at times.

Let me recall how I came to know Dorothy Lee Marks (Doris). In the early 60's, while residing in

San Pedro, my older brothers and I had many friends in Long Beach and we frequently visited the Recreation Center ("The Rec Center") on California Avenue. Another regular visitor there was Tom Marks. Tom had only been in California a year or two and had joined his older brother, Jonas Jr., here. Jonas lived in Los Angeles with his wife and family but Tom, a bachelor, lived in Long Beach just a few blocks from The Rec Center. Shortly after I graduated from the Los Angeles Police Academy, Tom mentioned that his younger sister "Doris" would be joining him in Long Beach. I told him that I would like to meet her and show her the sites; he agreed, and from day one, our lives were touched.

I met Dorothy on January 3, 1963, the day following her arrival in California and from the beginning we became friends. I fell in love at first sight and knew right away that I wanted to marry her, though at that point in my life I had no concept of what marriage was or to what responsibilities it catered. When she passed away in 1999, I had known her for 37 years. She later confided in me that she had suffered an attraction to me also at that first meeting. Indeed, the Lord does work in mysterious ways.

An early incident occurred, however, that almost placed the relationship on the wrong track and in fact came very close to derailing our friendship. Just a few days following our first meeting Dorothy invited me to a Saturday evening dinner at Tom's apartment. I later learned that she had spent much of the week planning the menu and all day Saturday shopping for the right ingredients which would include an avocado based Chef's Salad, later to become our favorite meal. At the agreed upon time, I did not show up. In fact, I had totally forgotten about the date. She had dressed *for the occasion, prepared a nice table and excused Tom from the house. It was days later when Tom asked me if everything was o.k. that I remembered. At our next meeting she was cold and distant, and justifiably so. It took a lot of effort for me to get back in good graces.*

During our courtship the next two years we became closer friends, got to know each other, and our love for each other grew. We dated weekly and frequently went to the movies. Other places for dates included the L.A. Natural History Museum, L.A. County Museum of Art (we went there a half a dozen times) and the Museum of Science & Industry. We also did the traditional Disneyland, Knotts Berry Farm, the old Long Beach Pike, Pacific Ocean Park, Marine Land and concerts at the Greek Theater. We often doubled dated with my best friend, Melvin Haynes and her cousin, Marcia Perteet, who were also dating regularly. The four of us visited Tijuana, San Diego and traveled throughout Southern California to track meets and football games. We all enjoyed each other's company.

Melvin planned a New Year's Eve Party in 1964 for all of our friends. I dressed up in my best suit (I only had two) and went to the apartment to collect Dorothy, taking with me a bottle of champagne and two crystal glasses. She met me at the door and never looked more beautiful. She had to put on the finishing touches and I went about preparing the glasses for a pre-midnight toast. I poured the champagne when she rejoined me and we toasted each other. After sipping her drink she discovered an engagement ring in the bottom of the glass. At the same time she was startled, shocked, happy, crying and elated. She had no clue. I slipped the ring on her finger and asked her to marry me and she accepted. Then we drove to the party at Melvin's house. Sometime prior to midnight someone announced that we were engaged and suddenly it became a double celebration. We were married nine months later on September 26, 1965.

In the ensuing months following the engagement she set about busily planning for the wedding with her girlfriends which were members of her social club, the Eclygians (meaning "The Best", in Greek). All of the club members had been high school classmates and friends for years but they invited Dorothy, a new comer, to join. She was that kind of person. Today, I still remain close to a few of the Eclygians, such as Erma Seals, Ruby Lee, Gwen Morris, Olivia Augustine and others.

Our wedding was one of a kind in terms of ushers and bridesmaids. I had eight ushers, all brothers; Clarence, Phillip, Leon, William, Charles, Harry, Darnell and Melvin Gravett. Her bridesmaids consisted of my sisters Alice and Gloria, sisters-in-law (all friends of hers), Olivia, Dortha and Marie Livingston, her girlfriends, Thelma and Marcia. Her Maiden of Honor was her sister in law Betty Marks, wife of her brother Tom, who gave her away. The flower girl was Dorothy's niece, Patricia, and the ring bearer was my nephew, Gary. Dorothy had Olivia's daughters Candace and Prettice light the candles. It was a very exciting day. The ceremony was held at the First Assembly of God church in Wilmington, performed by Dorothy's pastor, Dr. N.J. Kirkpatrick of the New Hope Baptist Church, Long Beach. We honeymooned in Carmel and San Francisco driving my "white 1960 Chevrolet Impala".

Since this is "A Word About Dorothy", I want to return to my remembrances about her and less about us as a couple.

Within days of arriving in Long Beach, Dorothy secured a position at St. Mary's Hospital, just walking distance from her apartment. Her first job was as a Cath Lab Assistant, then later was as a Cath Lab Technician. What follows next is one of the many stories she related to me while at St. Mary's.

On her first day on the job, part of the orientation included being instructed where the cafeteria was located. During the lunch hour that day she followed the directions given but could not locate the lunchroom. According to her, she walked the hallway back and forth, but never found that cafeteria. The next day, reluctantly, she asked where the cafeteria was located and was again given the same directions, and there she went. After again not being able to find the place to eat her lunch, she coaxed one of the friendly coworkers to have lunch with her, believing that this was an excellent way to not show her ignorance in following directions. The coworker took her directly to the cafeteria which Dorothy had walked passed on both previous occasions. Here was the problem. Dorothy had observed staff members eating lunch each time she had passed but they were all "white". She had been looking for the cafeteria for "black" staff members. You see, being from "Mississippi", she had never been permitted to eat with "whites". From time to time she would remember the incident and laugh at herself.

At the time of our marriage we were fortunate to be able to move into a home which Dorothy had selected from the 15 or 20 that we visited. Her Mother had arrived from the South a week or two prior to the wedding and she and Dorothy began furnishing the house. Dorothy was elated. Though not an experienced decorator, she later did a great job of displaying our wedding gifts accompanied by a few newly purchased accruements. We didn't have a lot of furniture in those early days of our marriage, but we managed.

During the remaining years of the early 1970's, Dorothy, like most of us in that age group adopted the look and style of the period, bell bottoms and Afro's. Wearing a very large Afro, Doris never looked better. Family photos show her frequently outfitted in extra wide bell-bottoms with matching "combed-out" and "blown-out" hairstyle. Her favorite store for the bell bottom ensembles was a place called "Funky's" located in the Garment District of Downtown Los Angeles. The tight fitting pants really emphasized her then 26 inch (approximately) 1960's and waistline. During the transition period from bell-bottoms to "Hot pants" Doris was right out front, with a closet full. No party was given in those days without a fashion show of hot pants. For the males, I'm not certain which came first, the Nehru jacket or the Turtleneck with accompanying medallions. In any event, I had both, outfitted by Doris.

When our son Mark was born in 1972, you would have thought she invented motherhood. From the beginning she was an excellent mother. Having previously prepared a full home nursery, Mark had all the bells and whistles available. She was very happy and proud to be a mother. Her connection and bonding with our son lasted a lifetime. She shared so much of her life with him. One quick but interesting story regarding mother and son.

When Mark was just a few months old, Dorothy drove with him to visit me at a military base, Fort Irwin, California near Death Valley.

The car was air-conditioned and Mark was firmly nestled in his bassinet in the rear seat. The drive was at least a three-hour journey and the weather was extremely hot. I was on military maneuvers at the time and can attest to the high temperature. Upon arrival midday, the temperature had soared to about 120 degrees, common for Death Valley. I was in an air-conditioned building awaiting her arrival and met her in the parking lot as she drove up. At the time Doris was wearing a sleeveless summer dress.

When she opened the car door the heat consumed her like an oven blast and her skin began to sunburn immediately. I quickly carried Mark into the building with Doris right on my heels. Once inside both she and I noticed that her arms and shoulders had reddened. She was astonished that it was so hot and asked me why anyone would come to that hot and desolated place. The final 35 miles from Barstow was just sand and rock; no trees and no bushes.

After drinking water and caring for Mark, she made it clear that this was no place for her. She gathered up Mark and headed for the car. Within minutes she was departing for home on the 150-mile drive. During the remainder of my military career with duty at Fort Irwin, she only returned once, in the fall when the weather was decent. Following that episode whenever I mentioned Fort Irwin, she would shake her head in bewilderment.

From the time I met Dorothy I was in the Army National Guard performing reserve duty in addition to my fulltime employment. After I received my commission to Second Lieutenant and my commitments increased, she made it very clear that I was in the military, not her, and not to expect her to commit to anything involuntarily. Though I respected her wishes and never imposed my military commitments upon her, over the years she became my greatest supporter and assisted me in all of my military duties. I dare say that I would have never achieved whatever I did without her support and love. Not only did she push me, a time or two she pulled me. When not pushing or pulling, she was always at my side.

Dorothy's death was also a great loss to our extended military family. Over the years she had mentored many of the younger officers' wives in military social graces. What she actually taught them was that formal and informal military social events were no different than civilian affairs and to just be themselves. She was always admired and easy to be with. Not only were the military wives in awe of Dorothy but female military personnel, both officer and enlisted, were counted among her friends. Again, she was that kind of person.

On the "home front", she knew every neighbor on the block and visited frequently. Many times she would spend an hour in our driveway chatting with a neighbor after having just arrived from work, and still in her scrubs. Once her car appeared on the street, the neighbors would head her off at the driveway. Up until just a few days before she became ill, Dorothy was still engaged with our neighbors. She always had time for them and their families.

It was at the hospital where she gave her best however. During her 18 plus years at Harbor-UCLA Medical Center, she was on call every other week including the weekend. Not once did I ever hear her utter resentment for being called in to work during *her off-duty time. This included even when we were out for dinner, socializing with friends, at church or shopping. She would never venture far from home while on call lest she receive a call. Dorothy took her duties as a Heart Cauterization Laboratory Assistant very seriously, for she knew that if the call came, that someone was in need. Her heart team consisted of two cardiologists, a registered nurse and a heart technician. They performed as a team, each with specific duties. When she was called in, I would occasionally visit the cath lab to observe the procedures. It always amazed me to watch Dorothy assisting a medical doctor by inserting a wire in the groin of a newborn infant, and maneuver it up to the heart. Of course the medical doctor was always in charge and oversaw the activity. Many times the newborns were just hours old.*

Though most of her cases were successful, for a number of reasons many were not. Sometimes patients were lost even after heroic efforts by the team. When this occurred Dorothy always remained professional with the satisfaction of knowing that all that could be done to save the patient was done. Numerous times recovered patients would later return to the hospital for the specific purpose of thanking her. Somehow many would find her address or telephone number and contact her that way. She possessed the knack of reassuring patients before, after, and sometimes during the procedure that they would be just fine. She had a collection of cards and letters, some from as far away as China.

As an indication of Doris' dedication to her job and duties, in 1988 she was selected as employee of the month at the hospital. I felt very proud to have attended the ceremony where the hospital administrator honored her with a plaque and kind words of praise. Her entire department attended and showed their support. The significance of this honor is that the facility has over 3,000 staff members. What an honor! To place this in better perspective she was later selected as employee of the year.

In the community Dorothy made her mark working tirelessly with the San Pedro-Wilmington Chapter of the NAACP, which she and her best friend, Elnora Coulter toiled together. Obviously, she devoted most of her volunteer efforts there after having been raised in a very segregated Mississippi where some blacks experienced the indignity of having to step off the sidewalk to let a white person pass and having to drink from a drinking fountain labeled as "Colored". Though she had experienced some of this, those incidents had no lasting affects on her relationships. Over the years she held a myriad of elected and appointed offices and often hosted NAACP meetings in our home. Other volunteer efforts also caught her interest and she assisted where there was a perception of need. What a better community we would have if all had a giving heart such as Dorothy.

An active member of the LA POWS (Los Angeles Police Officers Wives Club), she had numerous friends there including Velma Green, Vera Ford, Charlene Toles, Judith Willis, Inez Wiggs, Eva Alexander, and many others. Her favorite, however, was her mentor, Ella Scranton.

Edna Woodward was her inspiration to join the National Council of Negro Women where they both strived to ensure a prominent place in society for women of color.

Although Dorothy did not always attend church on a regular basis, this due primarily to her job commitments on weekends, she was always there when needed, especially on special days and for special programs. There she would be, working diligently behind the scene but avoiding the spotlight or credit for things being done. That was she. Although not a gifted vocalist, she sang in the choir a number of years and even coached Mark into joining her for a while. She also served on the Usher Board, Hospitality Committee, Health Committee and Pastor's Aide Society. Many times, in my view alone however, she spread herself thin. She loved all of her church family, but especially Ozie Simpson, wife of the Pastor, Dr. Felton Simpson.

A great joy for her was to make candied long stem roses for the Mothers Board on the fifth Sunday of a month. She also made candy for the children's Sunday School Class and for her nieces and young neighborhood girls as well. Halloween was also a fun time when she gallantly passed out treats to the goblins and ghouls appearing at the door. Each year she could be counted upon to have hot chocolate brewed for her expected nieces and nephews who always came by the house accompanied by their parents.

The time eventually came when Mark asked to be permitted to go "trick or treating" alone with his young friends. Having only gone with his mother in the past, like most mothers, Dorothy did not want to face the reality that her son was growing up and didn't always want his mom around. During his first Halloween out without her, the night was tenuous until his safe return. Prior to departing however, she made sure he had a flashlight, a light Colored costume (homemade), and specific instructions to remain in the immediate area and return at a specific time. It all worked out fine.

Dorothy personally met several times each semester with every teacher Mark had in elementary school. Together they would design his program of instruction and she always monitored his classroom *work. Homework was always a must when Mark was in Junior High School and she ensured, actually insisted that Mark's school clothes met or exceeded her standard. Most parents probably did this too, but Dorothy was very particular. She taught Mark so much.*

In the late 1980's when Mark entered high school she continued involvement with his studies, always ensuring that he had the proper mix of classes. After all, wasn't he going to be President? It was Dorothy who later sat down with Mark and plotted his entry into culinary school but when he eventually moved out of state to begin his training, she felt a great loss, then the hour long telephone conversations began, originated by both.

This continued on for over two years and did not end after he had graduated, received his clef's hat and medallion and started his first job as a professional chef. She so much looked forward to the infrequent weekend visits with Mark and even sat in his culinary classes a few times.

Probably during most of Mark's life Dorothy had been planning her wardrobe for his wedding and at the ceremony she looked radiant. She looked like a bride again, only this time wearing powder blue rather than white. She wore a pastel blue two-piece ensemble with floor length skirt, with an accompanying white silk blouse. She definitely caught the attention of those in attendance. She already had mine.

Over the next two years she enjoyed Mark's visits to San Pedro and we would spend a few days relaxing in Palm Springs. Though not really a hot weather person, she adored Palm Springs, especially during the fall, winter and spring months. Her favorite restaurant there was

"Simbas", an upscale fine dining soul food establishment (can you believe it?).

In January 1999, Dorothy was well into her work at the hospital and was stepping up her pace in her afternoon power walks. This continued in early February. Not feeling well from time to time, her doctors originally diagnosed her illness as a common malady, but she knew better. Without going into details, Dorothy diagnosed herself as going into heart failure and discussed her personal findings with the Cardiologists which whom she worked. This, of course, started a series of tests, which confirmed her condition and from the beginning they were stymied as to the cause of the onset.

Most family members and close friends are aware of the actions, which occurred in the ensuing weeks. The initial days of sick leave and doctor visits followed by her hospitalization, initially at Kaiser - Harbor City and later to Kaiser - Sunset in their very fine Cardiac Center. At this point, time became a factor in attempting to identify the most effective treatment of her now diagnosed condition called Amalydosis; a very rare heart condition (affecting two or three people out of a million). From the beginning her very professionally competent doctors had informed both Dorothy and me that her condition would be fatal and there was no known cure. Common accepted procedures such as a heart transplant were not in the offing at the UCLA Medical Center in Westwood where she had been referred to by her physicians. By this time her treating physicians and those with whom she worked had teamed in a collaborative effort to assist her.

UCLA Medical Center had performed more heart transplants than any medical facility in the world, over 1,200 and with a 90% success rate, but, as they finally declared, "we don't do Amyloid patients (much like they don't do windows)". This revelation took many days to obtain consuming valuable time for treatment elsewhere. They were in no hurry. From there we quickly corresponded with other Medical Centers around the world in an effort to assist Dorothy. The London (England) School of Medicine had performed a "few" transplants on Amyloid patients but with no successes. The Cleveland (Ohio) Clinic also had no successes. Boston University was willing to review Dorothy's case but offered no encouragement. They had in fact, refused all other referrals in the past citing the same argument as had UCLA. However, The Mayo Clinic in Rochester, Minnesota was very encouraging.

From the beginning the Medical Staff there agreed to immediately review her records and previous test results with the expectation of placing her on the waiting list of new heart recipients, though they warned that her case was a "long shot". Typically the Mayo Clinic required patients to undergo extensive in-house medical testing prior to being certified as a probable heart recipient but, upon quick review of her medical testing results at three hospitals, reduced her wait from 30 to 40 days to just a week.

The very next morning we flew to Minnesota where her treatment began just minutes after checking into the clinic. The Mayo Clinic should not be confused with the local community health care facility down on the corner; in fact it is the largest medical facility in the world. It employs over 42,000 people working in seven major hospitals and numerous other allied facilities. It is indeed a medical city with something for everyone; a Catholic Hospital, a Jewish Hospital, a Baptist

Hospital, a Muslim Hospital, regular hospitals, and etc. This international facility accepts patients from the world over. The reader might recall that King Hussein from Jordan had been treated there just weeks prior to Dorothy. So, indeed, Dorothy was where she needed to be, but by the fifth day we both realized that the hill was steeper than imagined. It was at this point that she asked that Mark join us from his home in Portland, Oregon. He arrived that very evening. During times of crises when families draw together you never know what to expect. Our small family, just the three of us with the Lord as our umbrella, was together once more, and for the last time.

What a beautiful ending. Mark and I reminisced while Dorothy, in her now extremely weakened condition, smiled and winked at us. We prayed together as she laid her now listless hand on her bible. From my bible I read her favorite scriptures. This sounds very sad, but in fact we were having a joyous time given the circumstances. The next evening after tasking me to look after Mark, she passed away. No doubt the smile on her face appeared because I told her that I would not have to look after Mark. She had done a complete and wonderful job of raising him to be the man that he had become and there was no need for me to do anything more. There was no physical pain nor any suffering, just a peaceful ending, to an almost perfect life.

So this is Dorothy's Story told from my perspective and as accurately as I recall. There obviously is much more to be told about her life, but I will allow the reader to fill in their chapters about her; their relationship with her.

There was never any question where Doris' earthly final resting-place would be, Green Hills Memorial Park in Rancho Palos Verdes, California. The cemetery is just a five-minute drive from her home. Those present at the services know that she is at rest beneath a large shady tree which overlooks the Los Angeles harbor, just as the second story family-room window does from her home.

We made every attempt to conduct the services, as she would have directed. There was no continuous line of never ending speakers, though many remarked that they would have cherished the opportunity to say a few words. In their place, there were just three, one speaking about her life as a Christian, one making remarks about her volunteer work and the final one, a medical doctor, relating her work as a hospital staff member.

Believing that the expected attendance at her services would fully engage our small but beautiful church sanctuary; The New Testament Baptist Church in Wilmington, her services were held at the Rolling Hills Covenant Church, adjacent to the cemetery. The more than one thousand or so who attended were able to pay respects to their departed friend. Dr. Felton Simpson was magnificent in his eulogy and her friend Judith Willis who delivered the eulogy also spoke of her as a friend. Very fitting, indeed. Much more can be written and/or said about this beautiful lady but each should be left alone with their own personal recollections. No doubt she will never be forgotten in death just as she never forgot people during her life.

This Word about Dorothy will serve to bring peace to the author as well as to the reader. Perhaps in another time and in the future, the

grandchildren, whom she never knew, will be able to look upon this document and know that Dorothy (Doris) Marks Gravett was a quality person.

Doris, we love you.

Peter Gravett, July 2000

VISIT TO DOROTHY'S HOME TOWN

I had always planned to visit Dorothy's home town of Sandy Hook, Mississippi but never found time nor took the time to do so although she had taken Mark there several times. It was only following her death that I went there to spend an Easter weekend with her mother, Miss Redd, as all of her children addressed her. I addressed her as Mrs. Marks.

There I was able to see her home town as she had always described it only now it was more beautiful than I had imagined. I pictured her there; the house, her church, the school and especially the trees and other greenery. The green fields were magnificent; cotton fields decades before and even dating back to slavery. Regretfully I had never experienced them with her.

Her family home was one of several in a swath of land comprising several acres. The other houses, all spaced about 100 yards apart, were the homes of relatives; uncles, aunts and cousins. Some had the surname Mark and others used Marks. The family lineage, both White and black, traced back to slavery. Once Mark traces his genealogy through DNA or a more sophisticated analysis no doubt the results will show that he is equally European and black.

Sandy Hook was not a city or even a town but just a rural suburb of a town, the nearest sizable city being Hattiesburg. The family carry their name from Marks, Mississippi.

According to the local weather report the rain that Easter Day of my visit was the heaviest in several years, almost flood stage, so her mother and I stayed in her home and not chancing the trek to her church. The upside was that we spent the entire day talking about Dorothy and I learned so much of her which I did not know previously, especially about her childhood.

I had met her five brothers and two sisters but then I was able to place the entire family in perspective during our conversation. I had known that her father had passed away when she was a young girl.

Chapter 66 Promotion to Major General

In 1998 following two years in grade as a Brigadier General my records were submitted to the Pentagon to the Major General selection Board. All of the procedures for selection to Brigadier General were repeated with a full General chairing the panel as before and assisted by other Generals.

The administrative process consumes the better part of a year prior to the board session which lasts just a few days. Once selected my name was again placed into nomination by the President and then entered on a Congressional Bill awaiting confirmation. I was confirmed in late 1998 and promoted in 1999 as noted.

Division Commander

During the process for confirmation a separate General Officer Command Board had met and selected me to command the 40th Infantry Division (Mechanized). Even though I had been serving there as an Assistant Division any number of other Brigadiers General could have been selected. Preparation and plans were made for the traditional Change of Command Ceremony installing me as the incoming commander and planning the farewell event for the out-going commander.

The Division G-1 had the overall responsibility for planning the ceremony and the G-3 had responsibility for executing the ceremony; both under the auspices of the Division Chief of Staff.

CHANGE OF COMMAND CEREMONY

The US Army and other military services have a long standing tradition for staging a ceremonial event when there is a change of commanding officers. The tradition for the US Army dates back over 200 years. The ceremony honors both the outgoing commander and welcomes the incoming commander. Since a Division change of command ceremony honors two Generals, as one would imagine, it is more complex. It involves more troops and has more pomp and circumstance than units with lower ranking officers.

HAIL

Brigadier General
PETER J. GRAVET
Commanding Gener
July 1999

FAREWELL

Major General
EDMUND C. ZYSK
Commanding General
May 1996
to
July 1999

Change of Command Program.

The Division G-1 and her staff reviewed the change of command operations order and made substantial changes and updated various steps in the ceremony to include numerous appendices and annexes. This in turn was submitted to me for review and approval. Following critical review the plan was approved as it was superbly crafted. An operation can only be successfully executed if there is a superb plan to begin with and the G-1 was praised by many for her detailed planning by her and her staff. Yours truly was among the many who offered accolades.

The saddened part of the ceremony where I was to assume command of a Division consisting of approximately 18,000 soldiers was that it was taking place just three days following Dorothy's passing and two days before her funeral service.

Much consideration was given to rescheduling the ceremony but that would have affected the over 500 soldiers that had been rehearsing. Additionally

Major General Gravett at Change of Command.

hundreds of invited civilians from the community, elected officials, family, friends and senior military officers from the Pentagon in Washington DC and Sacramento, so the decision was made to proceed. I dedicated the ceremony to Dorothy. I had so much looked forward to her standing by my side as I reviewed the troops and though she was not there physically all of my thoughts were of her as the soldiers' paraded bye. Her mother, Mrs. Lilly Mae Marks, received the honor of having three stars pinned on her. Given the circumstances the follow-on reception in the back yard of my quarters on the base was upbeat and nice.

Qualified for the Command Position?

Major General Gravett at Change of Command.

It was my belief that some officers and NCOs in the headquarters were under the mistaken belief that I was given command of the division due to my ethnicity. That method of thinking has always been in the minds of the few whenever an ethnic minority reaches the pinnacle of success.

During my career I experienced much evidence of this line of thinking and unfortunately it was always to be expected. This was never verbalized but no doubt was the obvious undercurrent of hushed conversations at the "water cooler." In order to alleviate this notion I directed my Chief of Staff to gather the headquarters staff in the conference room for the purpose of laying out my Bona Fides. I very succinctly tracked my full career from date of commissioning.

This included the fact that I was an Officer Candidate School Graduate, had commanded three

MG Gravett receiving the Division Colors at Change of Command.

different platoons, had Commanded three companies, a rare number, commanded two battalions and commanded two brigades; the Division Chief of Staff assignment having command responsibility of brigade size elements. Along the way I had held key primary staff positions at the battalion, brigade and division levels. My civilian education included an Associate degree, a Bachelor's Degree and a Master's degree. Additionally I held executive diplomas from two of the most prestigious universities in the nation.

I voiced to them that militarily I had graduated from all of the requisite courses at each level of staff and command; the Officer's Basic Course, Officer's Advance Course, Command and General Staff College and the US Army War College.

Additionally, I cited a dozen or so lesser schools,

Friends posed at MG Gravett's Change of Command celebration. Left to right Charles Jackson, Lionel Coulter, Benny Jackson, Charles Gravette, Melvin Haynes, Billy Hurd, John Gray, Hollis Lee, Ed Helms, Wally Johnson & Jim Williams.

seminars, forums and refresher courses I had attended but all very important in the scheme of things. Lastly I related that over the course of my career my officer efficiency reports had routinely placed me in the upper ten percent of the total number of officers of my rank and responsibility at every level.

During my presentation I at no time made reference anyone believed that my race had played a role in my selection. I was not going to go there. At the conclusion of my remarks unexpectedly I was given an applause. My quick thoughts were that it was as if a jury had given applause to dynamic closing arguments.

40TH INFANTRY DIVISION (MECHANIZED) CONFIGURATION

At differing times the US Army has a multiple array of division's from which to deploy based on the situation which includes the configuration of enemy, the geographic, climes, terrain, logistical requirements and many other considerations. Historically these have been Armor Divisions, Infantry Divisions, Mechanized Infantry Divisions, Light Infantry Divisions, Mountain Infantry Divisions, Airborne Divisions, Air Mobile Divisions, Air Assault Divisions, Air Cavalry Divisions and Cavalry Divisions. Training Divisions and Exercise Divisions, as would be expected, are not deployable.

Not all of the divisions are operational at any one time and in actuality only a few are at any given time given the reduced size of the Army. Most can be reconfigured to meet current or future operational requirements.

The 40th was a Mechanized Infantry Division when I assumed command. As described earlier it was configured with three Maneuver Brigade Headquarters: two Infantry and one Armor, as well brigade size formations consisting of Artillery, Engineer, Aviation, Air Defense Artillery and Logistics, all with subordinate Battalions. All totaled these consisted of approximately 45 battalions and separate company size units.

The Commander cannot do it all and the great part about being in command was that I was very fortunate to have inherited a very professional primary and special staff and two of the very proficient Brigadier Generals as Deputy Commanders. Both had extensive command and leadership experience and I would use their talents and techniques for the betterment of the Division. I supplemented them with a personal staff which I selected; Chief of Staff, Secretary to the General Staff, Aide-de-Camp and Command Sergeant Major. The 40th MP Company provided my on-call four man security detail.

Theoretically I could have appointed my brother Melvin as my Division Command Sergeant Major (after all President Kennedy appointed his brother Robert Kennedy as his Attorney General) but he suggested that would be viewed as a conflict of interest though he was imminently qualified. Instead I appointed Command Sergeant Major Stuart Fuller, a top notch NCO. Stuart had served as a Battalion Command Sergeant Major and had vast experience as an Operations Sergeant Major among his other talents. He and I became a team.

CHAPTER 67 RANCH HOUSE RESIDENCY

Much of the lead-in to this book and indeed the title itself had to do with the Ranch House and its' geographical setting on the footprint of Camp Roberts. Just to recap: the Ranch House, long in early California history, in its modern day use was exclusively occupied by General Officers when visiting or stationed at the Post.

In August 1999, one month after taking command of the Division I deployed to Camp Roberts for the scheduled field training of several division units. My personal staff had previously arranged and reserved the Rancho House as my principal place of residence while there. This was done perhaps not knowing that they would be part of making history.

My Aide-de-Camp and I were flown to Camp Roberts from the Joint Forces Training Base at Los Alamitos in my command Black Hawk Helicopter and met at the airfield by my driver and enlisted aide who had driven there the day prior. They were positioned in my assigned command vehicle, a specially outfitted HUMMWV (High Mobility Multipurpose Wheeled Vehicle) or Humvee in military slang and Hummer in civilian jargon. We then drove directly to the Ranch House.

The refrigerator had been stocked with an assortment of soft drinks, and abundance of fresh fruit in various locations around the kitchen, dining room and living room, as well as other staple food items. I was now officially the first African American Division Commander to occupy the Ranch House as its official resident.

It was pre-arranged that my first visitor would be my brother Command Sergeant Major Melvin Gravett whose unit, the 540th Main Support Battalion of the 40th Division Support Command (DISCOM), was in training there.

During the next days and weeks of my initial stay I held a number of command and staff meetings at the Ranch House rather than in my command center in the cantonment area. Additionally, I held a few non-alcoholic Bar-B-Q back yard receptions and other off-duty social gatherings for enlisted soldiers selected to attend by their First Sergeants. These were coordinated by Melvin. He and I also took the liberty of spending quiet time and reflection on where we were and how far each of us had come. Residing in the house with me were my Aide-de-Camp, my driver and two members of my four-man security detail each having their own bedroom and sharing two bathrooms. My master bedroom had its own private bathroom. My enlisted Aide-de-Camp was housed on Post with other members of the unit.

The Ranch House had a pad for landing the helicopter and ample graveled parking spaces for official visitors expected in a plethora of military vehicles. There was a commercial telephone for use but my signal communications staff had emplaced a field telephone system which placed me in direct contact with my major commands on Post as well as Post Headquarters and the Office of the Post Commander, a Colonel.

Whenever I was physically at the house, by protocol, my two star Major General flag was raised on the front yard flag pole and same for my command center on the main Post.

CHAPTER 68 COMMANDING THE DIVISION

In the military, training is continuous. An aspect of every day is devoted to training, some formal and some not so formal but both important. This ranges from individual training, to section and squad level training, platoon and company level training to major maneuver field type of training for the battalion and the brigade.

At the division level training is more dynamic and frequently involves computer generated or training scenarios. One of these is the War Fighter Exercise. This exercise is designed to train the Division Commander and the Division Staff in real time but under simulated combat conditions.

Every Army Division generally undergoes an annual War Fighter Exercise. During the time I was in command, my staff and I participated in three War Fighter exercises, one at Fort Lewis, Washington as part of the First (US) Corps War Fighter, one at Fort Leavenworth, Kansas at the Army National Guard's War Fighting Center and one at our Division Headquarters at the Joint Forces Training Base at Los Alamitos.

The train up for this major event requires substantial personnel and logistical resources and generally takes several months. This consumes the greater portion of a two or three training assembly week ends in addition to numerous staff work nights during the week.

The War Fighter is a scripted around the clock computer driven exercise and is based upon a mythical strategic war engagement, however the opposing forces, their tactics, weapons and equipment do replicate some of our well known adversaries. It involves over 1,000 actual soldiers and civilian technicians on the ground clustered in a series of command modules with hundreds of computer terminals. The exercise runs continuously around the clock for approximately seven to ten days.

The facilitating civilian companies are contracted by the Department of Defense and all of their staff are experts in US Army organization, terminology, battle tactics and techniques. The purpose of the exercise is to stress the Division Commander, his Deputy Commanders and the senior staff, especially the Primary Staff. Each of the subordinate Brigades has a complete command center established and fully participates. The exercises are generally held in a field environment.

Since this event is continuous the controllers, civilian staff and the numerous personnel who monitor and evaluate all "players" and their decision making processes have subject matter experts on duty around the clock. The Senior Controllers themselves are generally retired Army Generals and Colonels.

One of my roles as Division Commander was to be prepared to answer any questions the Senior Controller had of me, often a retired General Officer more senior than me. Their role was to query me on selected operational or strategic decisions I was making or had made. They were not there to evaluate whether it was the right or wrong decision but to learn what mental, analytical and strategic processes I used to make the decision.

There were never any right or wrong decisions but there must have been a timely decision made. Quite frequently, I was required to justify in great detail to them and to myself why a particular decision was made. The evaluation of me also focused on what decisions I delegated compared to which ones I made. What was really critical was the evaluation of me as the Commander on how I paced myself; was I obtaining proper rest; eating properly and timely; was I taking the essential short naps around the clock; was I drinking sufficient amounts of water to be in a proper physical and mental place to make mythical life or death decisions. The stressors were effective and every Division Commander would experience these in actual combat. During the event the words of the Army Chief of Staff came flowing back at me; words such as *Lie, Cheat and Steal.*

By having a more senior General Officer looking over my shoulder inquiring how I derived at a certain decision gave me a real appreciation of how my Brigade Commanders and Battalion Commanders felt when I looked over their shoulders asking similar questions.

The final analysis of each exercise was that no one wins and no one loses the mythical but realistic war; that was never the intent. The intent was for everyone to become more proficient in their job through training. In that sense, I was successful as my learning curve dramatically increased each time.

NATIONAL TRAINING CENTER

Just as I had done as a Battalion Commander and Brigade Commander, as the Division Commander I spent considerable time at the National Training Center at Fort Irwin, California observing division units. In additional to being an ideal place to train in tank maneuvers, as well as the previously mentioned Gallant Eagle Exercise, in later years it became the location for active US Army Combat Battalions and Brigades to undergo an annual actual field exercise referred to as a "rotation." This was where each of the units would spend a month rehearsing and undergoing a tactical exercise in preparation for a deployment to Iraq or Afghanistan. Most rotations had a National Guard unit attached where I was able to monitor their participation.

To simulate realism entire Iraqi-like villages and towns were constructed far into the desert numerous miles away from the built up area of the post. All of the structures simulated those in the Iraqi desert and with all of the amenities normally found there. These included mosques, small stores, cafes, municipal buildings, small houses, apartments, vehicles and gas stations, a functioning post office and other life sustaining realities.

The villages were populated by Iraqi Americans who actually lived there and had ample supplies of water, electricity, a sewer system and sanitation. They were US citizens of Iraqi decent who were contracted by the US Government and rotated in and out from their Southern California homes for a month at a time. Most were residents from El Cajon, California, an upper middle-class city in San Diego County about 250 miles to the south. El Cajon had the largest population of Iraqi Americans than any city in the United States.

As the soldiers maneuvered through the towns they found them fully functional. They had a Mayor and city leaders, the cafés were open for business and soldiers could sit on the open patio and order coffee and snacks which they paid for just as any other food establishment. The post office was operated by the US Postal Service and letters and post cards could be mailed from there and taken to the post for processing. The gas stations operated from above ground storage tanks.

At any given moment, and without warning, an explosion could occur simulating an Improvised Explosive Device (IED) detonation whereby the soldiers would go into action as they had been trained to do. Safety precautions were in place to ensure that no real injuries were suffered but there were simulated casualties of both soldiers and civilians. When simulated injuries were realized medical evacuations were called in and "casualties" flown to field medical units for triage. This provided realistic training for everyone.

This greatly prepared the soldiers for what they could possibly experience once they deployed to the desert in the Middle East.

MILITARY AND THE COMMUNITY

An important aspect of a General's responsibility is connecting the military to the community, or better said, community relations. During my tenure as Division Commander I was quite frequently in demand to deliver speeches at community activities, participate in patriotic holiday events such as Memorial Day, Armed Forces Day, Viet Nam Veterans Day, Flag Day, Independence Day, Labor Day and of course Veterans Day.

I generally wrote most of my own speeches although some initial drafts were provided by a staff member after providing them points to cover. I acquired others from the Department of Defense. Each speech was tailored to fit the various communities and the occasions.

On the Army's Birthday June 14, 2001 I was invited to San Diego for the honor of throwing out the first pitch at a Padres baseball game. What an opportunity. Actor Cuba

Former Professional Baseball Players from the Old Negro League.

Gooding Junior threw out the second pitch. These were part of a celebration to recognize several surviving players of the old Negro Baseball League.

That league had been disbanded following Jackie Robinson's well known entry into the major leagues breaking the color barrier. During the next few years following Jackie's League entry several other Negro baseball players were accepted to play in the Majors including Dodger Pitcher Don Newcomb who pitched in the 1950's and early 1960's. Don had received his earlier experience as a professional baseball player in the Negro Leagues.

Prior to Jackie's playing with the then Brooklyn Dodgers no matter how talented, Negro's were not allow in the National and American professional baseball leagues.

Actor Cuba Gooding, Jr. at San Diego Padres Stadium.

The Negro league had teams in several eastern, mid-western and southern cities

BOSS LIFT

As part of the Army's outreach to the community several Boss Lifts are scheduled and planned each year whereby civilian leadership (Boss's) are invited to observe military training at various bases around the country. This program gave them a firsthand view of the duties and responsibilities of their employees while on weekend military duty and extended duty at other times.

On occasion this includes flying on military aircraft to observe training activities in and out of state. These are in concert with the Employer Support to the Guard and Reserve (ESGR), a federal volunteer agency which will be discussed later.

One particular training event took place at Camp Roberts on the Central Coast and a dozen civilian Boss's participated by traveling there including my brother Leon and MS Stacey Lee, daughter of my good friend Hollis Lee, previously mentioned. Both Leon and Stacey met the qualifications for the trip.

The Boss Lift began at the Joint Forces Training Base at Los Alamitos where the group received a flight safety briefing then boarded an Air National Guard C-130 Hercules four engine cargo airplane for a flight to the Paso Robles, California Airport near Camp Roberts. There they transferred to a UH-60 Black Hawk Helicopter for the short flight to the Camp Roberts Helipad.

After a briefing on the planned training scenario which the group would be observing they boarded a UH-1 Huey Helicopter and were air lifted out to the field training area where they observed Infantry tactics and Artillery firing. At the conclusion they were flown back to the Camp Roberts Helipad in both UH-1 and OH-58 Helicopters and transferred back to the Paso Robles Airport in UH-60 Black Hawk Helicopter. For the return flight to Los Alamitos they boarded a US Army Twin Engine Sherpa Cargo C-23 Airplane.

The purpose of them being transported on various military aircraft was to familiarize them with the various type aircraft in the Army and Air National Guard inventory and to observe air crew flight preparation procedures as part of their orientation.

The entire trip was about fourteen hours in duration and Leon, Stacey and the others had flown on five different military aircraft in a single day. Not only were they able to observe soldiers in field training but also witnessed air crews performing in-flight and landing operations. The consensus of the group was that the nation was in excellent hands with a competent military.

On a later Boss Lift a group of Clergy, including my Pastor Dr. Felton Simpson, accompanied me and the Division Chaplain on a Boss Lift helicopter flight from Los Alamitos to Camp San Luis Obispo (CSLO) on the Central

Coast to observe training there. The flight took place on a UH-60 Black Hawk Helicopter. All agreed this was their first flight on a helicopter and they thoroughly enjoyed the experience though I suspect that many prayers were offered up both en route to CSLO and on the return flight.

On occasion as part of Boss Lifts civilians are allowed to board a Navy passenger aircraft for a flight out to sea and experience landing on an aircraft carrier. Typically about 12 Bosses at a time experience this. This is an overnight trip where there are billeted on the ship and spend a day and a half observing take offs and landing of fighter jets and all of the essential tasks required by a plethora of sailors performing a myriad of jobs as part of the flight team.

NATIONAL RESPONSIBILITIES

As a Division Commander I had an indirect reporting chain to the Chief of Staff of the Army as did all Combat Division Commanders both Regular Army and Army National Guard. The Army Reserve has no such reporting

General Colin Powell

chain as their Divisions are Exercise and Training Divisions and are non-deployable though individual soldiers in those units are. Combat Divisions are the primary organizations for fighting the nation's wars and the Office of the Army Chief of Staff establishes doctrine for such and carried out by the Pentagon staff.

My duties required regular trips to the Pentagon and to National Guard Bureau for routine Top Secret Briefings and to Fort Leavenworth for conferences. Additionally frequent trips to the Pentagon were required where I served as a member of promotion panels. These I thoroughly enjoyed as I was able to review personnel files of the best and brightest that the military had to offer.

THE NATIONAL GUARD ASSOCIATION OF THE UNITED STATES (NGAUS)

NGAUS is a military professional organization whose membership consists of Army and Air National Guard Officers throughout the country. Founded almost 140 years ago it is a congressional lobbying organization for National Guard issues. It lobbies on behalf of National Guard Officers who comprise the membership. NGAUS also lobby on behalf of enlisted personnel as benefits for one are benefits for all. I had been an active participant for many years and served a term a two year term as President of California's Chapter. Almost all benefits gained over the years were a result of the active liaison and interaction by lobbyists from NGAUS with members of Congress.

An annual NGAUS conference is held which rotates among the states and territories. Attendance at these conferences are optional but is generally expected of General Officers. All members attend on their own time without compensation however one military person per state, by regulation, is permitted to attend while on duty. The California delegation numbered about 30 to 40 generally.

I really enjoyed these conferences as I was able to glean information from leaders of other states which has been beneficial to me specifically and to California's units generally. We were able to observe new and emerging military hardware as displayed by civilian vendors.

I theorize that during the many years as a commissioned officer attending various conferences, NGAUS included, I visited over 35 states and the territories of the United States Virgin Islands, the Commonwealth of Puerto Rico and the District of Columbia.

A similar organization exists for Non-Commissioned Officers, the Enlisted National Guard Association of the United States (ENGAUS), and that organization has a similar mission. Both organization work in concert with respect to benefit acquisition.

EVALUATIONS, AWARDS, COMMENDATIONS AND DECORATIONS

In 2002, as I neared my change of command and my retirement I identified a list of administrative and personal functions that needed to be accomplished. These included, but not limited to, completing numerous officer evaluation reports (OER's) and writing a series of commendations which could result in the awarding of a ribbon on the dress uniform and a medal on the formal mess uniform for deserving soldiers. I also had a list of local elected civilians and civic leaders which I intended to thank for their support of the Division.

The OER's are the annual metric whereby each officer is judged for performance over a specified period of time with comments regarding potential for higher level responsibility. They may also have remarks regarding whether the officer should continue in the service, a recommendation for promotion or involuntary retirement and in extremely rare cases dismissal. This is the same for NCOER's for enlisted personnel.

Since this is one of the most crucial documents in an soldier's personnel file I took great care to record notes on various soldiers throughout the year to be able to be accurate in my assessments. Likewise, I routinely reviewed the "report cards" on each unit in order to assess the efficiency of the local commanders.

The report card included training evaluation reports, unit strength, inspection results, vehicle and equipment maintenance record keeping and a sundry of other measures of the unit's war fighting capability. The primary criteria, however, is demonstrated leadership ability.

The more senior the officer the greater the emphasis is placed on operational and strategic capabilities, success at maneuvering soldiers, units and large formations to accomplish the mission.

Many times throughout my military career I was called upon to make crucial administrative decisions which could affect an officer's career. One time I received a request from one of my senior Commanders to discuss his upcoming OER appraisal. The officer was just about to complete his first full year in command and inquired whether or not I intended to rate him in the "upper ten percent" in my overall rating scheme.

At that time, there were 10 Colonels in the command (and 42 Lieutenant Colonels) and in following the appraisal rules only 49% or less (i.e. 4 of 10) could be rated in the upper ten percent and the remainder were required to be rated lower based upon performance; upper 25%, middle 50%, lower 25% or lower 10%.

These systems were put in to place to avoid "bloating" the ratings. The 10 Colonels included Commanders of the Infantry Brigades (2), Armor and Artillery Brigades; Aviation, Engineer and Support Brigades; Division Surgeon, Staff Judge Advocate and Chief of Staff. This metric allowed me to only rate four in the upper ten percent with the other six rated in the upper 25% or lower. This indeed was a challenge because in my view all 10 Colonels were upper ten caliber.

Ratings are never based upon seniority but all of the other senior Commanders had been in command much longer than the officer and thus had more time to prove themselves. My thoughts were that four of the above mentioned Colonels were therefore more deserving of the upper ten percent than this officer, who in time, would accomplish much more success.

With this criteria I informed the officer that he had more time to prove himself as an effective Brigade Commander without actually informing him where I would rate him. The officer very professionally challenged me and pled his case but to no avail. He believed that his career was going to end without the higher rating and I pointed out that perhaps that might be the case but he should focus on performing the best he could over the next few years to be in position to receive the higher rating if, in fact, he did not receive the higher rating this time. I noted to him that the most important job was the one he was currently performing.

When a soldier has exceeded all expectations of their duties given their rank and position of assignment coupled with frequently going above and beyond Army requirements they may be postured to receive an award, commendation or decoration.

Commanders at all levels may issue such awards each based upon the size and level of the unit in the organization. As Division Commander my focus generally remained on Battalion and Brigade Commanders and my staff at Division Headquarters. So during these final months I consulted my personal notes and gleaned suggestions and recommendations from subordinate commanders in presenting these final awards.

During my command tour I was fortunate to have received a number of presentations from the civilian community. My list included names of individuals and organizations with whom I correspond with a note or letter of thanks if not previously sent.

It was important to coordinate with my Chief of Staff as he and the staff began planning the change of command ceremony and farewell dinner. It was not unusual to have immediate family to be included in the planning process so my sister Alice and brother Command Sergeant Major Melvin joined the planning team.

As a two star Major General, I was selected to be a member of a Brigadier General Selection Board at the Pentagon. The Board President was a Four Star General with Board members comprised of Three Star and Two Star Generals. This was the one and only time I had the honor of serving on such board and it was indeed a horror to be able to participate in selecting Generals for America's Army.

Major General Gravett

The Board session lasted about four days and we had stacks of Colonel's personnel files to review. These were the crème of the crop Colonels who had excelled during their entire career and were now being considered to become a General Officer of the Line, those that command soldiers in the field. We were not considering Colonels from the professional branches as their boards were separate. These were Medical Corps, Medical Service Corps, Dental Corps, Nurse Corps, Chaplain Corps, Judge Advocate General Corps (military lawyers) and Veterinary Corps.

The Army has a very large veterinary corps. They are officers who are spread around the nation inspecting farm animals and facilities where they are processed. They also inspect orchards and farms where vegetables are grown by the various vendors contracted by the military.

Major General Gravett Greeted by Four Star General and South Korean Army Chief of Staff

In late 2001 I made my final visit to South Korea. This would be my final overseas deployment and it was memorable as Commanding General of the 40th Division I was invited to meet the Secretary of Defense in his office at the Capitol. I am almost certain that this visit had never before been extended to a 40th Division Commander since the Korean War so I was humbled.

The Secretary presented me with a ceramic vase which he had personally fashioned and painted. His hobby was developing such table and floor ornaments for special presentations. I gifted him a coffee table pictorial volume of the State of California which he much appreciated. He also presented the Division a plaque for displayed at Division Headquarters.

Major General Gravett's Office visit with South Korean Secretary of Defense who presented him with the green vase on the floor behind the table.

The 40th Division's participation was well documented during the Korean War, 1950-1953, and most senior South Koreans clearly recognize the Division shoulder patch, a bursting sun on a blue background, and the division's name as the Sunburst Division. The 40th Division was a participant in the liberation Seoul. In California the Division was known as "The Patch."

During the War, Division soldiers had constructed a school from the rubble in the town of Gapyong where intense fighting had occurred. Story has it that following the fighting in and around the town an elderly Korean man in tattered clothing was observed sitting on an upside down bucket with a book teaching a few orphaned children who sat around him.

Their school house had been destroyed as had many of the huts and other structures in the town. Seeing the spectacle of the impromptu elementary school class the 40th Division soldiers passed the hat and took up a collection to purchase construction material and Division Engineers designed and built a school house. They later added additional buildings and utilities. The Secretary wanted to recognize the Division for its assistance during the War and to recognize it for constructing the school.

Fifty years later, Gapyong Regional High School was one of the top academically rated schools in the country and was known for producing superb South Korean cyclists for the Olympic Games. Every year several of its teachers are sent to UCLA to attend advanced educational classes. Annually the Division sends a small delegation to the school and make a financial donation and present English language books for their library. All students at the school are taught English.

Black Beret Ceremony South Korea.

During this trip we were accompanied by approximately 80 Division soldiers. By coincidence this trip coincided with the US Army changing from the camouflaged field patrol cap to the black beret. To prepare for the head gear changeover we held rehearsals the day before with the soldiers in formation and upon command they removed their patrol cap and donned the new black beret.

The next morning at reveille, the first official day for the new head gear, the 40th Division contingent were part of a composite formation of US soldiers from various parts of South Korea arrayed on-line with me as the commanding officer of the 40th Division element. I was paced 5 steps forward of the first rank of our soldiers. When the command was given to don the beret all of the soldiers did so in unison just as had been practiced.

Being senior and out front of our contingent on the extreme left due to time differential from the United States I may have been considered the very first US soldier to wear the new black beret. This was never recorded as such but I will stake claim the honor anyway.

SOUTH KOREAN CULTURE

During my many trips to that country I became to understand its people and some of its culture. For example, burials are conducted with the deceased in a sitting position above ground and covered with a frame which is then covered over by a large mound of dirt. Cemeteries have rows upon rows aligned with dirt mounds. I was not able to understand why this was the standard burial method.

Other cultural phenomenon that differ from the US are that in night clubs men routinely dance with men and women with women, even on slow dances. Koreans view this as a manner of friendship and nothing more.

Perhaps for sanitary reasons all seats in taxis are covered with white sheets and the drivers wear white gloves and a white mask covering their nose and mouth. Both the interior and exterior of taxis are very clean and the drivers are well groomed and attired.

On golf courses the caddies are women wearing long white dresses made of material resembling bed sheets. They wear large bonnets which resemble the headwear worn by a particular Order of Catholic Nuns as portrayed by the "Flying Nun" in a previous television series.

Since South Korea is the only Christian country in Asia one can look around the city from a high point at night and see red Christian crosses that adorn churches and are illuminated against the night sky all night long.

South Korean public schools have a daily procedure whereby at the beginning of the school day students line up outside in a military style formation at full attention while the Principal delivers a rousing and energetic speech challenging them to do their best that day. This can last up to an hour or more with the teachers also in formation and at attention.

Academic competition is fierce as students must compete for college entrance. Subjects taught in junior high and middle school in the US are taught to elementary school children in South Korea. As mentioned English is the standard foreign language taught. All shoes are removed prior to entering the classroom as well as their homes. This ritual is pretty much standard in most Asian cultures.

What is very much the same in the cultures of the US and South Korea is that generally citizens in the two respective countries support their military with Korean supporting the US military as well as their own. Older Koreans have never forgotten the aid and assistance America brought to them when their country was invaded by North Koreans beginning on June 25, 1950. For this reason they are forever grateful.

CHAPTER 69 RETIREMENT CEREMONY AND FAREWELL DINNER

In 2002, I was closing out my 43 years of military service to the nation, state and community having gone from Private to Major General and it all seemed to have passed so quickly. The Division staff had initiated preparations for the change of command ceremony which would be

Mural painted by friend Eugene Klakovich

similar if not identical as the one described earlier when I took command but with one major exception.

Just as before the Change of Command Ceremony would be on the tarmac of the airfield at Los Alamitos Joint Forces Training Base but the dinner would be at Long Beach's Hyatt Hotel. Since a number of presentation were to be made which would lengthen both the ceremony and dinner, staff arranged for scheduled presentations to be made in my office both the day before and morning of the ceremony.

The plethora of presentations came from subordinate units, governmental agencies at all levels; federal, state and local. Family and friends were also kind to recognize me with mementos for

MG Gravett presenting friend Eugene Klakovich with his personal tank.

which I extremely appreciative. I was personally humbled by a personal gift from my brother Harry and his wife Elizabeth as well as best wishes from everyone else in the family attending. These were such a kind gestures. I knew that my transition to civilian life would be easy because for the first part of my military career had been balanced with a full time civilian career.

The dinner, taking place the evening prior to the ceremony, was a gala affair and I was appreciative of the planning that had gone into it by staff and family. I was delighted that so many friends were in attendance including junior high and high school class mates Eugene Klakovich and Michelle Lufkin Brajcich both whom I had met in the 7th grade and we had been friends continuously.

Eugene, a master mariner, school teacher and accomplished artist, was well as an in-demand custom cabinet maker, presented me with a portrait of myself in full military uniform. This five foot by five foot mural had taken him three years to complete and it was a masterpiece. Though oversized I found a prominent place to display it in my home.

Eugene had been Dorothy's mentor while she transitioned from being a healthy woman to one with a terminal condition. Eugene himself was a heart transplant recipient and at that time and now as I write this is the longest surviving heart transplant recipient from the UCLA Medical Center; over 30 years and counting.

Neighbors and former military personnel with whom I had served with for many years earlier were there including John Sack and Robert Berg. Also in attendance was Mr. Johnny Grant, the Honorary Mayor of Hollywood and long-time friend, who presented me with a replica of a Hollywood Walk of Fame Star. What a surprise. Johnny had received the first invitation to Blanche and my wedding.

True to fashion my LAPD class mates and friends, Don Ferrell, Bill Ellis and Harreld Webster were there to offer congratulations. The Big Four were riding as a Posse once again. At that point we had been friends for over 40 years.

The next morning at the Change of Command Ceremony as my two star flag was cased for the final time I had no apprehension of transferring the Division Colors which represented the change of authority and responsibility to the in-coming commander, my Deputy Commanding General-Maneuver, Brigadier General Jeff Gidley.

Though not involved in the decision to select him he had been my personal choice to succeed me as he had been my very loyal and extremely competent hired gun and close colleague and friend.

At that very moment of passing the Division Colors I then relinquished all accoutrements provided to a Division Commander which included my staff car, military HUMMMV (hummer), lap top computer, desk top computer, OH 58 and UH 60 command helicopters, access to the US Army C-12 twin engine air plane, cell phone, government credit card, e-mail address, top secret clearance access to classified documents and a few lesser important items which included "keys to the executive wash room." But most important of all I relinquished command of the soldiers.

Another important loss was the day to day interaction with my personal staff. These were my Aide-De-Camp, Executive Assistant Sergeant Linda Jones, Administrative Office Staff and my Command Sergeant Major. I would continue the relationship with most.

The Big 4 (from left) Peter Gravett, Harreld Webster, Eudon Ferrell and Bill Ellis.

Sergeant Jones served me well and also the Division Headquarters. As my gate-keeper her position was critical in that she expertly routed personal visitors and routine correspondence to subordinates which allowed me to remain focused on strategic requirements. Her personal comforting upon learning of Dorothy's passing would never be forgotten. Following my retirement Sergeant Jones deployed to the war zone in the desert and distinguished herself and her unit.

I clearly understood that my time had come, both as commander and as a soldier. I had completed over 43 three years of service since I had been sworn in to the 119th MP Battalion as a mere teenager. At the moment that I passed the Division Colors

Gravett's at family event. Left to right Darnell, Harry, Peter, Phillip, Alice, Curt, Leon, Charles and Melvin

to the new commander I relinquished all.

Following the ceremony, I hosted a luncheon in the backyard of my quarters on Post with a large gathering of invited guests and many uninvited guests which was fine as long as they were not soldiers in uniform who, by protocol, should have been attending the reception for their new commander and offering him their loyal support.

I used the opportunity to thank all who were present for the role they individually played in my career. My mother played soldier by donning and wearing my uniform

Big 4 with spouses (from left) Bill & Gloria Ellis, Eudon & Toni Ferrell, Harreld & Pauline Webster & Peter & Blanche Gravett.

beret with two stars affixed. This would probably be the last time it would be worn unofficially.

It was well into the evening hours that things began to quiet down as guests drifted away. I spent the night alone in the large house deep into my thoughts and mentally reminiscing what my experiences had been during my military career. I had few regrets as I had been so fortunate and blessed. My father would have been so proud.

During my career I had been presented with over 20 awards and

The Big 4. Left Eudon Ferrell, MG Gravett, Harreld Webster & Bill Ellis.

decorations including the Order of California, the highest state award, the Distinguished Service Medal, the nations' fourth highest award and the Legion of Merit another prestigious award. I had also received other federal awards including four awards of the Meritorious Service Medal, and three awards of the Army Commendation Medal.

Most branches in the Army present their coveted service medallion for a full career of exemplary service to that branch. Upon retiring I was the recipient of both the Silver and Bronze Order of Saint George, the Patron Saint of Armor and Cavalry; the Order of Saint Maurice, Patron Saint of Infantry; the Order of Saint Barbara, Patron Saint of Artillery and the Order of Saint Martin, Patron Saint of Quartermaster and Logistics.

Civilian medallions presented included one from the Korean Veterans in the USA Christian Council; the Bong Keon Kim Korean War Veterans Commemorative Medallion; the Founders Medal from the Association of the United States Army and the U.S. Vets America's Hero medallion though I am not.

My evolving life as a true civilian was evident as I gathered my personal belongings and cleared out of the quarters. My plans for that day and the next few days was to quickly write the several notes to individuals and military units thanking each for the support given me, and there were many, and for the gifts and mementoes associated with retirement. I had begun this process weeks earlier as mentioned but had not imagined that the list would be so exhaustive but I had culled it.

At this point, I would like to acknowledge make it abundantly clear that none of the aforementioned recognitions, awards, decorations, presentations, special honors, certificates, proclamations , successful work and achievements, mission accomplishments and other honors would have ever been achieved without the assistance and support of family and soldiers over a full career and to them I am forever grateful.

FAMILY GATHERINGS OVER THE YEARS

The after ceremony backyard event described was just one

The Big 4. Bill Ellis, Eudon Ferrell, Peter Gravett & Harreld Webster.

more opportunity for my family to gather in a picnic style event. For many years, the extended family came together on special occasions and during holidays to celebrate and enforce the bonding of members; several generations.

Some of these included attending the Campbell Family picnic which was held sporadically throughout Southern California and included various wings of that family. Campbell was the maiden name of my maternal grandmother Gertrude Campbell Harris as highlighted earlier in the book.

During some of these gatherings the Gravett wing of the Campbell Clan would identify themselves by wearing silk screened tee shirts which identified us as belonging to Grandmother Gertrude. On various years some tee shirts read "Gert's Gang", or a shirt displaying a Campbell Soup Can spilling out the names of Gertrude and her siblings.

On Thanksgiving Day it was a tradition that the Gravett family and friends to gather at the home of Harry and Elizabeth Gravett in La Palma, California for visiting and the family dinner. Not everyone attended every year as some had other in-law family obligations but the house was always full. Mother came every year bearing her freshly made sweet potato pies for each of her children with a second pie for my brother Charles.

Charles, you see, as expected every year, would whisk away a pie very early on pretending Mother had made one pie short. After he performed his ritual she would bring out the extra pie and he would end the day with two pies. This was always comical.

Brother Charles Gravette "whisking" away one of his mother's pies.

Each Labor Day Phillip and Dortha hosted the family at their home in Rancho Palos Verdes for a back yard pool party, the pool generally only used by the young children. This event was always looked forward to and was repeated for ten years or more. Later, Blanche and I hosted the same event at our home in Rolling Hills Estates for a couple of years.

It would have been ongoing but when you invite friends and they bring their friends who invite a third set friends soon you have a back yard of people whom you do not know and they do not know you as the host. A house and backyard of strangers did not make for an ideal family gathering.

Major General Gravett Advancing to Retirement

CHAPTER 70 BEYOND THE RANCH HOUSE AND LIFE AFTER

During the lion's share of my adult life I considered it important to give back to the community and I did so by volunteering as a board member with a number of community organizations.

These included not-for profit organizations, hospital boards and community based organizations, federal state and local commissions, scouting groups (Girl Scout Corporate Board – I have no daughters), YMCA, educational foundations, museum boards, civil rights groups, three college foundations, numerous veteran support organizations and veteran service organizations. I had also served on the Board of Trustee at my church for over 30 years.

EUROPEAN TRACE

A few months prior to my retirement, I had made plans to travel to Europe and visit friends and places which I had known. This time I would be a civilian. I departed within a few weeks and packing very little though I would be gone perhaps a month or more.

The first part of the trip I joined a group of military history enthusiasts for a two week trek to retrace the World War Two Allied invasion of Europe which began on June 6, 1944. The trip was titled *"Normandy to the Rhine."* Being an amateur World War Two historian for years I had studied the war through books and movies and very much looked forward to visiting locations which I had become familiar.

We began our trip in England where much of the waterborne forces had embarked. We crossed the English Channel and landed on the European Continent at Normandy, France and made preparations to follow the route which the Allied Forces had taken following their debarkation on the beaches of the Normandy Coast; Gold, Juno, Omaha and Sword Beaches.

We walked the beaches and observed remnants of the water barriers which the Germans had erected in a futile attempt to squash the beach invasion of what the German's referred to as the impregnable "Atlantic Wall." Some obstacles were still visible protruding from the waters, such as the Mulberries (portable docks), though well rusted. I stood on Point du Hawk, the high promontory which the US Rangers scaled in their mission to take the high ground overlooking the beaches.

Over the next several days we moved inland and followed the Allied route through various cities, towns and villages now well known to World War Two historians. These included Le Havre, Caen Evreux, and Saint Lo and of course the French Town of Sainte-Mere-Eglise. The town of Sainte-Mere-Eglise was where during the war an American paratrooper landed on the roof top of a church and his parachute became snagged on the church steeple leaving him dangling. This left him exposed to the Germans small arms fire as portrayed by actor Red Buttons in the movie "The Longest Day." To honor the soldier after the war the people of the town hung a mannequin in full American replica uniform and parachute on the steeple where it remains hanging to this day.

The Allied invasion force liberated town after town on their march to eventually liberate Paris. We spent several days in Paris and mostly visited sites associated with the war but we also did the tourist thing visiting the Eiffel Tower and the Louvre and once again, as before on a previous trip, marveled at the painting of Mona Lisa. This was my second trip to Paris and this time I viewed the city from a military history perspective. We then moved on through Northern France heading for the Rhine River which separated France from Germany.

CHAPTER 71 MY INVASION OF GERMANY

Since this was a historical battlefield tour we focused on German lines of resistance in its attempt to thwart the Allied advance. These included bunkers, tank ditches, dragon teeth and other impediments. Along the way to capturing Berlin the Allies captured a series of German cities such as Kassel, Dusseldorf, Wesel, Giessen and Marburg. We stopped in those locations and viewed the enemy's failed defensive positions. My vision of being in those places was unfolding before my eyes.

Germany then and now is a picturesque country replete with ancient castles and estates hundreds of years old. Many of these were confiscated by the German Army and used a regional headquarters. For this reason, several were damaged during the war as targeted by the Allies.

After almost two weeks of traveling stopping to spend time at various venues of war significance, towns, villages, fields where barriers for allied tanks and other vehicles, we arrived in Berlin. Having been to Berlin more than 30 years prior, I now was going to have a different perspective, and that was viewing it as the strong hold of the German Army sixty years earlier. Then and now most of the bombed ruins as the result of war had been rebuilt or replaced and there was little evidence that this had been Hitler's lair.

Our tour had been titled "Normandy to the Rhine" and since we had crossed the Rhine our tour had ended. Prior to the group disbanding we joined together for one final dinner where we discussed the tour and everyone reminisced regarding their most favorable experience. The next morning I then set out on my own.

VISITING GERMAN FAMILIES AND FRIENDS

While still in Germany I visited my good friends Roald and Brigitte Rummel at their home in Augsburg, their son Matias and their daughter Christina and her husband.

During my weeklong visit with them by preference I stayed at a nearby bed and breakfast inn though their home was exquisite and beautiful. During my stay I played a round of golf at their club's course, a former US Army base. I had taken them gifts of monogrammed polo golf shirts emblazoned with the 40th Division blue and yellow sunburst patch. They became my personal tour guides and we visited several points of interest and of historical significance relating to the War World Two albeit, from the German perspective. Many buildings in down town Augsburg were pock marked with numerous bullet holes from the war. They were intentionally not repaired as a reminder.

Roald and Brigitte with Blanche

I also learned from them the modern history of the Federal Republic of German Army, the Bundeswehr. Following Germany's defeat in 1945, at the end of World War Two the Allies consisting of the US, UK, Soviet Union and France, disbanded the German military, the Wehrmacht as it was called then. As directed by Allied Regulations, there would be no military for ten years.

In 1955, a new military was established named the Bundeswehr and its' founding principals were based on developing a completely new military for the defense of West Germany. It consisted of the Heer (Army), Marine (Navy), Luftwaffe (Air Force) and Streitkraftebasis (Joint Support Service). The same year the Federal Republic of Germany was admitted as a member of the North Atlantic Treaty Organization (NAT0).

Roald and Brigitte had been my friends for many years by this time having first met him during my first duty tour there. This was mentioned earlier. As a Lieutenant Colonel, in the German Army Reserve, he was very familiar with the US National Guard military system having spent time at National Guard Headquarters in Washington DC as an Exchange Officer. His capture of the English language was next to perfection.

On his first visit to California he was assigned as my Liaison Officer when I was Chief of Staff of the 40th Infantry Division. We quickly bonded as soldiers and friends which allowed us to establish a life-long friendship both in and out of the military. When they visited the US I would sometimes meet them in Los Angeles, San Diego, Palm Springs or Las Vegas.

Brigitte was also completely fluent in English as all German elementary school teachers are and the language is taught to their students. The elementary school teachers are trained swimming instructors as well and they teach their students to swim.

In addition to their command of the English language the couple were also keen on US history and they were very familiar with the geography of our country having motored cross country east to west and west to east several times stopping to enjoy Las Vegas on each trip.

Their daughter Christina was a medical doctor, a psychiatrist, who had undergone study in the US and her husband was also a medical doctor. Their son, Matias, a Captain in the German Army Reserve, had earned his Masters' Degree at Wayne State University in Detroit. Matias was a German Airborne Soldier and reservist like his father. On one of his visits to California I arranged for him to complete three parachute jumps with the 40th Division's Long Range Surveillance Detachment (Airborne), pre-approved by Department of the Army Headquarters, which qualified him to receive his US Army Parachute Wings which I pinned on him.

As I prepared to depart from Germany, Roald and Brigitte arranged a going away party for me at their home inviting several friends and neighbors most of which I had met during my current stay and on previous visits. Their friend and neighbor two houses down had a sister residing in Stanton, California and just a stone's throw from my previous headquarters at Los Alamitos. I took a photo with him and pledged to deliver it to his sister when I returned home which I did. My friendship with them lasted until Roald's death in 2014. The next year Blanche and I vacationed with Brigitte in Las Vegas.

Departing Augsburg, I traveled to Stuttgart-Vaihingen to US Army Garrison Patch Barracks. Patch Barracks was the home of the US European Command (EUCOM) with responsibility for US national security interests in 51 countries and territories including all of Europe. I was there to visit my Officer Candidate School classmate and good friend Major General William (Bill) Davies. General Davies, a California Army National Guard Officer, was stationed there as the Reserve Component Liaison Officer to the EUCOM Commander, a four star General.

Bill provided a guided tour of the installation while we reminisced and relived our days as Cadets and Second Lieutenants. A few years later, Blanche and I would visit him and his wife Dolores at their retirement residence in the countryside of Carlisle, Pennsylvania. They had made a decision to retire there when Bill attended the Army War College at Carlisle Barracks years earlier.

Next, I traveled to Munich and spent time with another German Army officer, Captain Josef Reinhold, who had arranged for my quarters during a tour of duty there years earlier. He served as the Inspector General of the Karserne (barracks) which had served as my duty station.

He and his family were very kind to host me for a few days, much longer than I had planned, with them insisting that I remain even longer. He had a very nice family. He too was a reserve military officer whose full-time employment was as a long-haul truck driver trucking back and forth from Munich and Italy. His beautiful wife was a professional model. Their three children had many questions about America and each expressed their desire to visit Hollywood and Disneyland.

My next visit was with another good friend, Colonel Reinhold Reischel, who eventually retired as the Chief of Staff of the German Army Reserve. From 1990 to 1993, while serving as the 40th Division Chief of Staff, my duties included fostering a relationship between our Division and the 1st German Mountain Division and Colonel Reischel had been one of the conduits.

Their Chief of Staff at the time, Colonel Reischel and I spent considerable time together during my trips there and his trips to California scripting out the parameters of the partnership. On one such trip I arranged a military helicopter tour along the Southern California Coastline for him and his small entourage of German officers. I had also arranged a VIP tour of the Getty Museum where they were given a personal tour by the Museum Director at no charge.

While in Germany he had often invited me to his estate on the outskirts of the City of Dachau, where his family operated a riding school for young girls; elementary and middle school age. This was a summer boarding school with dormitories and a full staff and school type atmosphere on the campus comprising hundreds of acres and over 100 horses with stables, tack rooms and riding rings.

I declined his kind offer to teach me the proper way to ride a horse. However I did once mount one for a short ride which was reminiscent of my rides with Vision Quest as will be discussed later. My visit there this time as a retiree matched his retirement from his military about the same time though just a coincidence.

CHAPTER 72 RETURNING TO UKRAINE

In the Partnership for Peace Program during my deployments to Ukraine I was assigned an interpreter by the US State Department as were all senior military officers. My interpreter, MS Svetlana Lazarenko, had an excellent command of the English language having studied it throughout her formal education years in both her native country and in England.

I flew to Ukraine to visit her and her family whom I had met during several deployments. Interpreters play a vital role in international affairs as they become the center piece in any conversation between individuals unable to speak the others' language. Svetlana was a civilian who had mastered the American and Ukrainian military technical terms and jargon. This was essential so there were no misunderstandings. Interpreters are vetted and assigned by the US Department of State and usually have a Top Secret Security Clearance which she had.

Ukraine was a former Soviet Republic which had gained its' independence from Russia when the Berlin Wall fell dismantling the Soviet Union. The Ukraine language is very similar to Russian as one could imagine. Some consider the two languages as "cousins."

Upon departing Germany for Ukraine I traded my German Marks for Ukrainian currency (Hryvnia) and was very careful not to bring more than a thousand dollars (US) into the country as it would be a federal offense, as described by Svetlana, when I coordinated with her in planning my visit.

Svetlana lived in a small three bedroom one bath room apartment with her fiancé, parents and a younger brother and sister. Most of the family spoke some English having watched a lot of English speaking television shows piped in from the US and the UK. The family had arranged for me to rent an apartment in Kiev for a week near their home suggesting to me that it would be more economical than a hotel.

When I arrived there, it was apparent that a family was living in the apartment, as it was complete with personal belongings and food stuffs in the kitchen. The cost was $60.00 (US) to be paid only in US currency; denominations smaller than a $20 bill. Obviously, a family had moved out just to make a few dollars on the Black Market.

I spent little time in the apartment as I was on the go all day and into the evenings sometimes with her and her fiance and sometimes her parents serving as my personal tour guides. We did a lot of walking but also took a taxi once in a while which for them was a luxury. There was no standard taxi fare and the fare was negotiated with the driver on each trip.

Two places stood out during my visit. I attended a performance at an Opera House where an Italian cast gave a performance in German to a Ukrainian audience with an American present. Since Operatic performances are language neutral we all seemed to enjoy it. Another interesting part of my visit was visiting a cave where Monks resided. The Monk culture had evolved over the years as the caves had tile and linoleum floors and were equipped with all modern conveniences such as plumbing, electricity, computers and televisions.

There were several cubicles in the cave I visited where souvenirs were for sale to tourists like me. Some of it made in Japan and China. When Monks were outside their caves they wore the traditional brown waist length robe but with jeans and sneakers and some were riding bicycles while wearing American baseball caps. They were playing ball in a new era.

CHAPTER 73 BLANCHE McCLURE

**On the road of life its' not where you go
But who you're with that makes the difference.
(Gift card from Blanche)**

TM DCI Studios

Although Blanche also served in the Army National Guard I originally met her on a volleyball court where we played on different teams at a city recreation center. During a game where our teams opposed each other we rotated up to the net at about the same time and we introduced ourselves and shook hands under the net just as others had done.

Bride & Groom Wedding at Wayfarers Chapel (AKA The Glass Church).

Later during the volleyball season we would go for coffee following a game. This led to dinners after the games which led to a formal dating ritual. We had a lot in common and we truly enjoyed each other's company. I proposed to her and we were married in 2004 at Wayfarer's Chapel (the Glass Church) in Rancho Palos Verdes. At the ceremony Mark served as my Best Man and her long time girl friend from high school, Caroline Hanna, served as her Matron of Honor.

She was beautiful and her wedding gown was magnificent as she walked down the aisle unescorted by her personal choice. I wore my US Army General's white Mess Dress Uniform complete white gloves and my cavalry saber. The rituals were performed by Dr. Felton Simpson, my Pastor.

Blanche & Peter's Family at Wedding. (Front row Left to right) Alice, Gloria, Wedding Couple, Mother Alice, Step Father Willie, and Charles. (Back row left to right) Melvin, Son Mark, Harry, Phillip, William & Leon.

As part of the rituals Doctor Simpson drew parallels to a marriage. He cited that there are four rivers that flow through the City of Pittsburgh, the Monongahela River, the Allegheny River and the Ohio River. The fourth river he noted, flows underground and is therefore not seen but it is there. Just like a marriage, he cautioned, there will be barriers not seen but they are there and to be mindful of them.

Following the ceremony and the taking of bridal party and family photographs Blanche and I were whisked away in a totally restored 1939 Packard touring car. The reception was held at Ocean

Blanche on Morning of Wedding.

Trails Golf Club just a mile down the coast where Mark had the position as a Souse Chef having been a culinary school graduate. We dined and danced to the lively pop music of Marilyn Andrews and her quintet with her playing the harp. Go figure.

I have been blessed in life in that I been loved unconditionally, lost, and found loved again. "God is great and God is good" my son Mark always remarks.

Having no family remaining of her own she inherited a full family of my over 100 relatives including a mother-in-law, step father-in-law and a host of in-laws, nieces, nephews and cousins; firsts, seconds and thirds. My friends became hers and her friends became mine including her three God children; Jasmin, Jacklin and Brandin Chow. They call me Uncle Peter just as my two adult God children Michael Haynes and Kimberly King.

BLANCHE AND COLLEGE BOUND KIDS

Blanche had been an educator for over 37 years and had taught all grades kindergarten through adult school. She even taught English as a second language with her ability to converse in several languages as she

Peter & Blanche Honeymooning in Hawaii.

had traveled and studied in China, Japan and Mexico. When she retired her teaching position her interaction with young students did not stop there. She became a long term substitute for a third grade teacher on leave at her former school.

While still teaching, at a grade level meeting it was brought to the teachers' attention that nearby Occidental College was offering a one week program during the summer for local 3rd and 6th grade students to introduce them to college life and to expose them to what might be available to them after high school.

Believing this would be a great opportunity for her third grade students, she approached the Vice Principal and was politely informed that this program was not possible for the students attending her school. The Principal voiced that the students were low income therefore would not benefit or be able to afford the $2,000 for the week for each student to attend.

When Blanche discussed the possibility with me of her raising the funds herself I was doubtful that she could raise that kind of money in the three short weeks she would have to do it.

Determined to make it happen she consulted with the 6th grade teacher and asked if she would like to join her in sending three of her 6th grade students, along with three of her own students, to the summer program at the College which was one quarter mile from the school campus. The total cost would be $12,000. The two of them then took on the challenge as a team.

It began with them embarking on an intense fund raising effort by selling donuts at recess, conducting car washes and requesting a donation from the PTA. At first they refused, but she would not take no for an answer so pressure was applied. She told them she would go to the press and tell them a City Councilman, who supposedly supported community activities, and his representative for the community and PTA President, refused to donate funds earmarked for the community. The two teachers asked friends for donations, arranged a 50-50 agreement with the local McDonalds whereby during a certain time period of the day they would share half of their profits for the cause. Blanche walked door to door to various small business in the area seeking donations.

The results was impressive to say the least. The two teachers raised $14,000 in less than two weeks and used the remaining funds to purchase needed summer supplies for the students. This project demonstrated and reinforced my view of her as a renaissance woman.

Blanche's ancestors migrated from Ireland to Canada in the early 1800's settling in that country prior to migrating south into various parts of Michigan. Blanche was born in Detroit and came to California with her parents as a very young girl. She attended elementary, junior high and high school in the Wilshire District and resided in Los Angeles until moving to Ventura County for a few years then finally settling in Rolling Hills Estates when we married.

Over a period of time Blanche had several honors bestowed upon her with two being very significant. In 2004 she was presented with the Order of California. This is the highest award presented to military personnel or civilians and is given on behalf of the people of California at the direction of the Governor and may only be presented by the Governor or the Adjutant General of the state.

As described, this award, in the form of a medallion with a neck ribbon, was placed around her neck while in a military formation at the Joint Forces Training Base in Los Alamitos with many of her friends looking on. A reception in her honor followed.

The year 2010 was the second significant honor bestowed upon her when she was named the Woman Veteran of the Year at UCLA. The award was presented at half time of the Bruins women's basketball game with another Pacific 12 Athletic Conference women's college team, the

Blanche exhibiting the Woman veteran of the Year award at UCLA with Bruin's

University of Arizona "Wildcats." She was introduced via the public address system and was called down to center court where the President of the University made the presentation at the televised game.

Annually for several years she had presented $5,000. in scholarships on behalf of the Association of the United States Army to deserving cadets in the school's ROTC program at their annual awards ceremony.

Militarily Blanche, a Colonel, had command assignment at all levels during her illustrious career including company, battalion and brigade equivalent. In her final assignment she held the position of Commanding Officer of the United States Property and Fiscal Office at Camp San Luis Obispo. This office had the mission of receiving and disbursing all federal military funding for both the California Army and Air National Guard and amounted to well over two billion dollars annually. She and her competent staff received many accolades for their efficiency and professionalism.

Her military education included graduation from the United States Army Command and General Staff College and the United States Air Force War College and was a graduate of numerous lesser military schools of study. When she was promoted to the rank of Colonel she became the first female officer in the California Army National Guard to attain that rank other than those in the various medical fields. Quite an achievement.

Peter & Blanche

She, reminiscent of my mother, was indeed a renaissance woman. She was multifaceted being a military officer, educator, somewhat of a linguist as she had visited Japan, China and Mexico, where she was became fluent in

Spanish. Athletically she was a swimmer, tennis player and marathoner. Additionally she was an excellent dancer. Blanche was familiar with accounting principles and she was well educated having a Bachelors' Degree, Masters' Degree and several teaching and administrative credentials.

Always a Protestant, she had been baptized as Presbyterian but in 2010 she joined of my church, the New Testament Baptist Church. She had been attending services there with me since our marriage and was the last parishioner to become a member prior to its doors being shuttered that year.

MY NEW PETS

When Blanche and I married she brought into the marriage her cat named "Scampi." It had been her mother's cat and upon her mother's passing Blanche took the cat as her own which we both loved until Scampi passed away. About a year or so later a Calico cat came into our lives, literally, who we named "Come Here." Prior to Scampi I had never owned or lived with a cat during my lifetime and really had very little use for them. But Scampi, and later Come Here, changed that.

The Calico cat had negotiated our six foot high backyard fence and begged for food on the back patio. After feeding it for several days we learned that he, finally determined to be male, had been discarded by several previous owners. After locating the most recent owner we (or I as Blanche remembers) decided to keep it and gave it the name Come Here because it responded to Blanche when she called it, much like a dog would respond. I had never envisioned a cat becoming a member of my family.

CHAPTER 74 RETIREMENT A MYTH

Following my return from the sojourn to England, Western and Central Europe, I began the next chapter in my life. After having traveled and visited various parts of the state I identified several places I considered it would be an ideal location for retirement.

I came to the realization, however that relocating to another area of the state or even to another state was not a good option for me as I did not want to distance myself from Mark. Also most of my relatives and friends were still in the area.

A couple of years after our marriage I began training Blanche to participate in the Los Angeles Marathon. For many years she and her girlfriends had volunteered at the Marathon by staffing water station number three and her intent was to participate once she had retired from her teaching career.

She developed a rigorous training routine which lasted about a year running several miles each day of between five and ten miles with longer runs on weekends. In the final weeks before the race she ran a couple of practice marathons of over 26 miles sketched out on a neighborhood course. I accompanied her in the car prepositioning myself at intervals whereby I anticipated providing her nourishments during the course which I also did during the practice runs.

This training served her well as she completed the race with a very respectable time for a novice of 7 hours and 47 minutes (AKA 747). I met her at the finish line where she was presented the participants traditional medallion. She would now always be tagged as a marathoner.

Our friends Roald and Brigitte had come over from Germany to encourage Blanche on and we cheered her from three different locations leap frogging by car over the 26.2 mile course. We had started by the three of us passing out water at water station #3 just as Blanche had done. At the finish line we greeted her with cheers and hugs.

GRAVETT AND ASSOCIATES

Over time, I periodically had performed several physical security inspections and emergency preparedness evaluations for private industry and had served on city and county emergency management panels where I had met professionals in the field. Since most were trained subject matter experts, through them, I had gained a wealth of additional knowledge to compliment what I already had.

Blanche too had experience in emergency preparedness as she had served as the emergency services coordinator at her school which required her to draft emergency plans and conduct emergency drills. We decided that the time was appropriate for us to reach out and create a company which would allow us to perform this work as a business opportunity. We would be a team. Shortly thereafter Gravett & Associates was born.

In addition to business lines in the US, a few years later, we were fully sponsored on a trip to China to join a team of entrepreneurs from various countries to partake in a business forum on entrepreneurship in Shanghai. This provided us the opportunity to gage, on the international stage, whether it would be beneficial and profitable to expand the company globally. With this in mind we created a small staff of experienced individuals to assist with the required research.

The following year we were sponsored and again, invited back to China, this time to Beijing. We met with and developed potential business partners who were interested in expanding into a myriad of entrepreneurships' into the U.S. and with the required available financial wherewithal. The focus was expanding upon the travel industry and developing small neighborhood stores in rural communities.

These were all first class VIP trips which also included five star hotel and private car with chauffeur. As part of the business excursions we visited small towns and villages in rural areas where we discussed with other invited American entrepreneurs the concept of creating 7-11 type convenience stores from the small village markets then housed in private homes. The concepts were sound and sorely needed as the existing village shopping facilities were unable to stock fresh meats and vegetables and dairy products because they lacked proper utilities such as electricity and plumbing and therefore no refrigeration so they mostly just sold staples.

After teaming with representatives of a U.S. Fortune 100 Company we both eventually had to abandon the project as this was just at the time the U.S. economy was taking a major downturn which prohibited continuing with the proposed expansion as it would not have been financially sound for anyone, them or us.

One very positive experience was while in Beijing we were able to witness the celebration of the Chinese New Year. Twenty four continuous hours of fireworks was a lot to withstand.

When we arrived back in the U.S. we later merged with another company with similar business lines in security and emergency management called Traiden Global Solutions. Our first contract provided funding to establish an emergency response center at the Ames NASA Research Park in Silicon Valley near Stanford University.

I was elected as Chief Executive Officer but shortly thereafter, I resigned my position to accept the Governor's offer to join his Cabinet. Also, I was consumed with carrying out my responsibilities as State Chairman of the Employer Support of the Guard and Reserve.

In 2006, I was contacted by the Office of the Assistant Secretary of Defense inquiring if I would be interested in a federal government appointment as the California State Chairman of the Employer Support for the Guard and Reserve (ESGR) a Department of Defense Agency.

ESGRs mission was to serve as an advocate for both businesses and their military reserve employees who were being mobilized and deployed. After serious hesitation and some prodding by friends and associates, which included my good friend of many years, Johnny Grant, Honorary Mayor of Hollywood. Johnny had been the first State Chairman when the agency was created years earlier.

I accepted the position and over the next several years I met with corporate CEO's and their Human Relations Directors with respect to insuring they were in compliance with the federal law which mandated job security for reserve military personnel that had been mobilized. The law was the United States Employment and Reemployment Rights Act (USERRA).

Every state and territory had an appointed State Chairman but California, being so large, was divided in two states across the Fresno-San Luis Obispo Line and had Northern and Southern Chairmen, each having four fulltime staff with about 300 volunteers statewide. I traveled throughout Southern California while making periodic trips to the ESGR National Offices in Washington DC.

The ESGR had a merit system which awarded employers and companies for going above and beyond Federal USERRA requirements. These were graduated awards based upon their programs in place to care for their military reserve employees, the highest award being the Freedom Award.

This prestigious award was presented annually to only twelve companies nationwide; four to large companies, four to medium sized companies and four to small companies. Governmental agencies at the federal, state, county and city were also eligible.

During my tenure, Southern California received at least one such award every year and sometimes multiple of these awards annually. Part of this can be attributed to a remarkable fulltime staff but primarily due to the exhaustive work by two highly dedicated volunteers, Dennis and Cheryl DeNoi. Dennis was a retired Marine and Cheryl was a retired public school Principal.

Representatives of the winning companies and organizations were invited to the White House where they were presented the award by the President in the Oval Office. This ceremonial event was followed by a black tie dinner. Needless to say Blanche and I made the trip to Washington every year while serving as State Chairman.

UNITED STATES MILITARY ACADEMY AT WEST POINT

For several years I had served on the advisory board of the Reserve Officer Training Corps (ROTC) at my alma mater, the University of Southern California. During this time I worked very closely with the Professor of Military Science, a Lieutenant Colonel, and I occasionally served as a guest lecturer to the cadets. This would be his final Army assignment prior to retirement and he had made preparations to remain at the university in a civilian capacity because his daughter was a student at a local high school.

She was a junior and he did not want to relocate which would cause her to change schools during her senior year. The year prior and being the dependent of a military officer, a West Point graduate, she had applied directly to West Point for admission, not having access to a Congressional appointment.

By the following spring, during her senior year, when she not received any correspondence at a time when most applicants were being accepted or denied admission, her father made a request of me, as a General Officer, to query the admission officer at West Point and to see if I could gain information on her prospects.

I knew that the Commandant of Cadets at the Academy was a West Point classmate of a senior officer who had served with me in the 40th Division so I requested that he make contact with his friend at the academy and request that he receive my call.

I made the call and he and I had a very cordial and encouraging conversation, General to General, regarding acceptance procedures. I made no specific request but only for information. To close out the conversation we talked about "news, weather and sports," purportedly the reason primary reason for the call but I did drop her name a time or two (perhaps three). Without going into detail, I advised her father that she would be receiving an acceptance letter within a few days, which she did. Whether or not I had any influence on her acceptance was never known.

In 2005 she was a West Point senior and preparing to graduate and receive her commission. Blanche and I were delighted to receive her invitation for us to attend the ceremony. We traveled to West Point in Up State New York spending a week touring the campus and attending several of the graduation week activities.

One memorable activity was witnessing the cadets enter the academy mess hall for a meal. We had learned beforehand that it was something worth witnessing. At the appointed time all 4,500 cadets marched into the dining hall coming from three entrances simultaneously and each cadet quickly standing at attention behind their assigned chairs. When told to take their seats they all did so in one swift movement and all were quickly served by a corps of civilian servers.

Just 20 minutes later, all of the cadets had departed the dining hall having consumed their meal. This was precision at its best and just knowing that this ritual occurred three times a day for four years was remarkable.

The soon to be commissioned officer, held an elective office in the senior class and was voted to serve on the graduation week activities committee where she was appointed chairperson. One of the honors of this position was to identify military invitees to serve as reviewing officers and persons to be seated in the VIP reviewing stand for the final parade the day prior to graduation.

A highly respected Four Star General and combat veteran was invited as the Reviewing Officer for the Corps of Cadets while Blanche and I had the honor of being seated behind him in the VIP reviewing stand. Just observing the precision of the cadets on the Plain with all of the pomp, I felt as if I was graduating. The next day, we attended the graduation ceremony in the West Point Stadium after which we witnessed the traditional tossing of their white hats in the air. What a sight.

Having received my commission from Officer's Candidate School and not having attended West Point I always wondered what happened to those hats when tossed and could each cadet identify his or hers later? The answer is just prior to the hat tossing protocol dozens of young children line the parade field prepared to run to get the hats. The local kids come each year to gather the hats and others are family members of the Cadets and also the staff. When the hats are tossed the kids scurry and gather them up. Some are even given to the kids to keep.

The now graduated cadet guided her father, Blanche and I and her other guests to the Eisenhower Statue where her father pinned on the gold bars of a Second Lieutenant. Blanche and I and the others looked on as proud witnesses. Her father then presented her with an historical US Army sabre which had been in her family for several generations, as several members had graduated from West Point. This memento had been passed down through the many years but she was the first female to receive it.

CHAPTER 75 MY MOTHER'S FINAL YEAR

The year 2008, began as a fun-filled year for my mother as she approached her 90th Birthday. On Easter Day after attending church services she dined with Blanche and me at our home in Rolling Hills Estates along with my step-father Willie, my sister Marie and our International College Student and house guest from China, Peng Fei (pronounced Pong Fay) Huang (pronounced Wong). Peng Fei's father was my business partner and sponsor in Beijing.

On my mother's 90th Birthday July 1st, Blanche and I held a luncheon in her honor at the Ocean Trails Golf Club in Rancho Palos Verdes. This was attended by her husband Willie, Pastor Felton Simpson and his wife, Ozie and my

Mother's 90th Birthday Party at Ocean Trails Golf Club. My mother Alice Gravett Garrison (seated), left to right Pastor (Dr.) Felton Simpson, Step father Willie Garrison, Ozie Simpson, Blanche, Peter & Clarissa Taft.

mother's best friend Clarissa Taft. We presented her with a bouquet of flowers adorned by her favorite lavender colors along with a nice birthday card and she posed for photographs.

She spent the afternoon with us "holding court" so to speak. She did this by reminiscing about her siblings, her family and the church. All the while she was enjoying the magnificent view of the ocean and Catalina Island beyond. Mother related that she was the sole survivor and youngest of the 12 children in her family.

In August the New Testament Baptist Church held a special service in her honor where Blanche read a riveting tribute which captured all of her church volunteerism. Having devoted most of her adult life to giving her talents to the church there was considerable.

Later that year, on Labor Day, her entire family held a belated celebration for her 90th Birthday party at the home of my brother Charles and his wife Martha in Moreno Valley. She enjoyed the celebration as she was surrounded by her children, grand-children, and great-grandchildren. She enjoyed the party and had a good time and she thoroughly enjoyed the decorations, including the colored lavender balloons.

MOTHER'S FINAL JOURNEY

Sadly for all of us she passed away in her sleep during the early morning hours of October 26th. Always independent she transitioned under her own terms; in her own home, in her own bed with no lengthy hospital stays with multiple surgical procedures. Her work had been done and she was called home to be with her Lord as her reward. Her reward and our great loss.

Mother's services were held at Rolling Hills Covenant Church in Rolling Hills Estates. The Going Away Service was truly memorable with all of her children and her husband Willie participated in its planning. She was interred at Green Hills Memorial Park adjacent to the church. Dr. Simpson, her Pastor, delivered a eulogy which captured her life as a Church Mother and church worker.

Mother had always been a renaissance woman; a woman of myriad of talents, a woman of her time. Always concerned with the education of her children she actively engaged with teachers and staff at Channel Heights Elementary School when her children attended there. On several occasions she volunteered as a Room Mother, many times for several class rooms at once.

She was forever active in the Parent Teachers Association and occasionally holding an elective office.

Critical in the dress of her children when we were young she insured that each child was properly attired going to school even when they were in high school.

In the later years of her life, she became a somewhat of a "stay at home" environmental activist with a keen concern for the plight of Polar Bears. She intensely followed reports of their diminishing arctic habitat being eroded away with the melting of ice floes and ice caps caused, as a result of global warming. She even made a very small contribution to a nonprofit organization organized for the preservation of Polar Bears. This was an avocation of hers known but to very few. Always as young as her children, even while in her 80's, she could be seen zipping up and down the freeways in her pin stripped customized van.

It was destined that she would take to her grave her personally concocted recipe for what has been described as the best tasting dessert dish ever developed by womankind, her infamous butter roll dish. She prepared this dessert so infrequent that when she did it was in high demand and quickly consumed.

Mother respected and valued all of her children and gave each one of us 100 percent of her love and affection. This amounts to over one thousand percent dispensed and I am probably very conservative on that figure.

Hillary Clinton, wife of former President Bill Clinton and former Presidential nominee herself, authored a book entitled *"It Takes a Village (to raise a child)."* Our family was a village, and we learned from one another, with mother orchestrating, the older children assisting with raising the younger ones. If our family were a corporation dad would have been the CEO but mother would definitely have been the Chairwoman of the Board, the hands on leader orchestrating family matters.

Even as far back as Channel Heights, mother was viewed as an excellent organizer, manager and leader of the household. Everyone was given household assignments and we all pitched in. In fact various neighbors would often remark that our house was the "cleanest" ever seen. This was no thanks to mother and her mild threats of discipline which were sometimes carried at the end of the sunbeam coffee pot rubber cord.

When the family moved to the Rancho public housing project in San Pedro it was mother who orchestrated the move and made bedroom assignments to the newly constructed five bedroom apartment. She had the respect of all of our friends who visited frequently and considered her as a second mother. The same for 790 when we moved there after she and my father purchased their first California home.

Although she did not live to see the first black US President, having passed away just days prior to Barack Obama's election, she participated in his election by casting her absentee ballot and voting for him. Given her segregated southern upbringing she would have been exhilarated on election night.

CHAPTER 76 SHARE CROPPER TO GOVERNORS CABINET

Retirement is what you make it. Some are successful at remaining retired and others are not. I failed at retirement several times becoming engaged in a number of activities following full law enforcement and military retirement as mentioned earlier. My federal government and business ventures included.

Very late on a Wednesday evening in April 2011 I received a telephone call from the Office of California's Governor Jerry Brown. The caller inquired if I would be interested in serving in the Governor's Cabinet. This was a surprise and perhaps unusual in that I had not applied for such a prestigious position, had not campaigned for the election of the Governor, though I did vote for him, nor had I made any financial contribution to his campaign prior to him taking office just weeks earlier.

Being somewhat surprised, I responded to the caller that perhaps I might be interested depending on the position offered and only if I felt that I was qualified. I was informed that the Governor was interested in appointing me as his Secretary of Veteran Affairs, a Cabinet level position.

Since military retirement, I had been very active in veteran support activities and had performed considerable volunteer work assisting veterans and their families. Serving as ESGR State Chairman placed me high in the business and government eye on behalf of veterans statewide and was seen as a prominent advocate for their issues; this I learned later. I opined that perhaps I had been recommended due to this work.

Following a conversation my retort to the staff member was that I indeed would be interested and believed it a special honor to be considered. The conversation was very brief. The caller, whom I later learned was the Governor's Appointment Secretary, advised me that the

Governor would like to have a meeting with me the next day, Thursday, and provided the address of a law office in West Los Angeles where we were to meet. The time was suggested at 10 PM.

That evening Blanche and I arrived at the location where I met with the Governor and his wife. He immediately began a conversation which focused on current events and governmental affairs.

In the previous 24 hours since the initial telephone call, I had thoroughly researched the agency to learn about its mission, goals, objectives and staffing. I pulled up the most recent annual report, current budget projections and other information found on the internet. This was done to be prepared to answer questions concerning the agency.

Having volunteered in the veteran arena I was current on veteran statistics in the state especially the plight of homeless veterans. During the course of the 30 minute meeting he asked few if any questions regarding the agency. Since I knew that he had a reputation as a fiscal conservative I had the opportunity to mention that I had conducted an empirical review of the agency's budget and identified several areas where expenditures could be reduced and specifically mentioned reducing the number of state vehicles and cell phones in the agency which numbered in the hundreds.

On the drive home I suggested to Blanche that I believed I would not be receiving an appointment as the conversation was not on point and thought perhaps he had decided otherwise on the appointment after meeting me.

When we arrived home very late that same evening, at almost midnight, I received another telephone call from the Appointment Secretary advising me that Governor had made a decision to appoint me and would I accept? When I replied in the affirmative I was told that I would be starting the next morning, Friday, in about eight hours.

She advised there was a Cal Vet Secretary's Conference Friday morning at the Los Angeles Police Academy and I was to attend and be introduced as the new Secretary. Further information provided to me was that the current, and now out-going Secretary had just been informed that he would not be reappointed and had been requested to introduce me as his replacement at the conference.

I arrived early with the intent of introducing myself to him and probably to request that perhaps he might be available for questions should I had any going forward. He refused to introduce me and departed just prior to the convening of the conference and I was introduced by one of the Deputy Secretaries who stepped in as the facilitator.

The attendees were leaders of the various veteran organizations around the state, not-for-profit veteran service organizations, county veteran service officers, veteran facility managers and some staff from Cal Vet, about 150 total. I took to the podium and introduced myself again and reported how proud I was to have been appointed and looked forward to working with all of them and their organizations. I requested their support and pledged to affectively serve veterans as I had been doing for years, letting them know full well, that I was not new to the game.

SACRAMENTO HERE WE COME

The next morning, Saturday, Blanche and I packed small bags, took care of personal business and on Sunday we drove to Sacramento where we checked into a hotel. Monday morning at the appointed time I appeared at the Governor's office in the Capitol where I was sworn in by a senior staff Member. This would be an interim swearing-in with the official one to be performed by the Governor once I was confirmed by the State Senate.

Blanche held my Bible during the brief ceremony and at that time I became the 17th California official in line to become Governor should the others become incapacitated. These included the statewide elected officers such as the Lieutenant Governor, President Pro Tem of the Senate, Assembly Speaker, Secretary of State, Attorney General, Treasurer, Controller, Insurance Commissioner and Secretary of Education. Others in line would be senior members of the Governors Cabinet.

What an honor to have been sworn-in as a member of the Cabinet. Going from a Share Cropper's son in the south, from a nappy-haired, snotty nosed young boy from Channel Heights, to the Governor's Cabinet was a fairy tale at best. The next four years would be some of the most transformative and exhilarating in my life, as I would now, and forever be addressed as The Honorable Peter Gravett, Secretary or Mr. Secretary. This was just as impressive as General Gravett.

Upon departing from the Governor's Office I drove Blanche back to the hotel and then made my first appearance at the office to introduce myself to the staff. Following staff self-introductions, I returned to pick up Blanche where we made the rounds reviewing available apartments in the area which she had been inquiring. The next morning she took a return flight back to Los Angeles and I began my first full day in the office The Cal Vet office building was just one block from the Capitol. My personal office suite was bare save for the office furniture, the former Secretary having removed his personal artifacts and belongings over the weekend. Later that afternoon I convened my first staff meeting which was intentionally brief and I provided them my initial guidance and vision.

I invited my executive secretary to be present for historical note taking. Unlike previous holders of the Office I had her attend all of my senior staff meetings for note taking, historical record keeping and documentation of my decision making.

CAL VET ORGANIZATION AND MISSION

The mission of the California Department of Veteran Affairs was to "Serve Veterans and Their Families" and was configured to do so.

"To care for him who shall have borne the battle and for his widow and children"

My initial in-briefing by the staff allowed me to know that the entire Agency consisted of approximately 2,300 personnel with about 375 at the Sacramento Headquarters and about 25 situated in various regional home loan offices throughout the state. The remaining 1,800 plus personnel were staffed at the then six veteran homes.

The veteran homes then, were located in Yountville in the wine country and recently opened homes in West Los Angeles, Ventura and Lancaster. The other veteran homes were in Barstow and Chula Vista. Yountville, the oldest and largest veterans' home in the nation alone had a staff of about 1,200 serving over 1,000 veterans in residence.

During my tenure at Cal Vet there would be two additional homes opened one in Redding and the other in Fresno. Construction of these homes had been completed the year prior but had not opened due to budget constraints. Neither one had been in the budget proposal of the Governor or the Legislature. This issue would eventually be extremely contentious during my first two years in office.

SWEARING-IN AND CONFIRMATION

My initial swearing-in was temporary. All Cabinet members are allowed to serve up to eleven months and 29 days without confirmation after which, if not confirmed, must be replaced.

During the next several months as I delved into my new position and duties the Governor's appointment staff met with me on several occasions to prep me for my Senate Rules Committee public and televised Confirmation Hearing. This was a consistent procedure with all Cabinet appointees. Once confirmed the Governor conducts the final swearing-in.

Over the next months, I conducted several "meet and greet" office visits with every member of the Senate Rules Committee where I presented my credentials, discussed my plan for the agency and sat for their questions.

As a note, in the California government system agencies are the senior organizations in the state with their heads carrying the title of Secretary. Departments are subordinate to agencies and their head carry the title of Director. Although Cal Vet carried the department title it had agency status and the head carried the title Secretary thus Secretary of Veteran Affairs.

All Agency Secretaries are members of the Governor's Cabinet along with three department heads; Department of Finance, Department of Human Resources and State Military Department; that head carrying the title of Adjutant General.

For the meet and greets I was accompanied by my Deputy Secretary for Legislation and Government Relations who arranged the appointments. This staff member would play a vital role during my tenure and to whom I give the lion's share of the credit for my eventual confirmation. Prior to each visit he prepared a briefing document identifying all pertinent information on each Senator including information on their Senatorial District, their political party affiliation, length of time in office, whether they had served in the military, what service, officer or enlisted, the veteran picture and military facilities in their district and other essential information.

At his recommendation, I also visited the downtown Sacramento offices of a key Lobbyist who was an ardent advocate for veterans. This individual, I was informed, traditionally played a key role in the Senate confirmation process. He was well respected by Legislators on both sides of the aisle and was the titular spokesperson for most veteran organization. The final draft of most veteran Bills crossed his desk prior to be submitted for Committee vote.

I already carried membership in the American Legion and Military Officers of World Wars (MOWW) Veterans organization, but the Lobbyist suggested that I seriously consider becoming a member of the all other major veteran organizations for which I was qualified, which I did. These were AMVETS, Military Officers Association of America (MOAA), Veterans of Foreign Wars (VFW) (this due to my service in South Korea), American G. I. Forum, Jewish War Veterans (open to all veterans) and others such as the Military Order of the Purple Heart Support Group.

I already held long-term memberships in allied veteran organizations such as the Tuskegee Airmen's Association as an associate member and the 9th and 10th (Horse) Cavalry Association Buffalo Soldiers where I was also was an associate member.

I learned that the Jewish War Veterans organization was the oldest veteran organization in the United States being founded one year after the Civil War which ended in 1865. During my tenure, I attended all of their state conventions.

A few months later my confirmation hearing was placed on the Senate Rules Committee calendar and I appeared before them. The Rules Committee consists of approximately nine State Senators, generally the majority made up of members of the existing majority political party.

In the past seldom were appointees confirmed without contentious debate which, in most cases, centered round politics and not veteran issues. An affirmative majority vote would send the recommendation to the full Senate to its' 40 members for final vote which mine was. During my Senate Rules Committee hearing the headquarters staff watched intently from our department offices on closed circuit television one block away as I made my opening remarks and answered their questions.

A few days following the Rules Committee hearing the full Senate voted to confirm me 38-0; two members being absent. I was told that it had been 22 years since the last unanimous confirmation vote for any Cabinet Member of either party for the position of Secretary of Veterans Affairs. This pleased me immensely.

A few days after the vote three of my brothers flew to Sacramento on a day trip to visit the Capitol and my Cal

Vet Offices. Phillip, Leon and William also accompanied me to the Senate Chambers where the Senate Veteran Affairs Committee was in session on additional veteran matters where I introduced them to the empaneled body. The Committee paused their proceedings and the Committee Chairman asked of me *"who were the impressive looking gentlemen accompanying me"* whereby I made the introductions. My brothers had been to Sacramento on numerous occasions in the past both on personal business and for sporting events but the visit to the seat of California's Government while in session may have been a first for them.

I then escorted them to my agency headquarters and introduced them to several of the Cal Vet staff members whom I had convened in the conference room. There were many questions posed from both sides.

Numerous times over the years these three brothers, as well as other family members, had attended several major events in my professional career and I was always pleased that they did so. For example, they enjoyed the UCLA Football games at the Rose Bowl, where annually, I was invited to present the Veteran of the Year at half time on the 50 yard line during the nationally televised game nearest to Veterans Day.

They also made the trek to Santa Clarita for the ground breaking that took place for the veteran's village housing complex of 83 single family homes which were to be constructed under my auspices. Time and again they appeared along parade routes where I was passing by as the Grand Marshal. This demonstration of personal support made my duties more pleasant and I was very comfortable knowing full well that I had their support.

This family support for myself and also for my brother Melvin during our respective military careers was not unique. Some members of our family were always present no matter the ceremony.

FORMAL SWEARING-IN CEREMONY

My formal swearing-in date was scheduled by the Office of the Governor and I chose the West Los Angeles Veterans Home as the venue. This was a natural location for the ceremony as I could invite friends and family from the area to attend. The staff there was capable of preparing required logistics to accommodate the more than 300 members from community, veterans and members of veteran service organization as well as family and friends who would be attending.

Again, Blanche held my Bible as I repeated the swearing-in oath. As a gesture I invited a veteran from each of the military services to stand with me as I took the oath. I was very pleased that the Governor offered kind words about my career as a military officer and my service to veterans after my military retirement. My remarks focused on thanking those who had played major roles in my life; parents, family, friends and soldiers who had shared part of my life. I then shared a brief part of my vision for the agency.

When my appointment was published in newspapers and on the internet I received scores of well-wishes from friends old and new. I was sent a congratulatory message from a childhood friend living in Idaho whom I had not seen since elementary school. I received a message from a senior military officer serving in Georgia who had been a junior subordinate of mine many years previous. I was visited there by a former Sergeant with whom I had served with in the 119th MP Battalion and we reminisced about the days we were both privates in 1959. My barber was also present.

Local and state elected officials sent representatives to the ceremony or sent nice congratulatory messages.

DUAL RESIDENCES

Blanche and I had decided early on to not make a wholesale move of our Southern California residence to Sacramento as this appointment would not be a long term position. The Governor was elected for a four year term with no expectation of reelection.

We maintained our official resident in Rolling Hills Estates and acquired an apartment just two blocks from my office. This would prove to be very convenient as I could walk to and from work saving precious commute time via the congested Sacramento area freeway system. In addition, this would be less expensive while maintaining the two residences with all of the attendant costs as the state offered no compensation for dual residences or commuting expenses.

Our plan, which worked very well, called for me to commute home to Rolling Hills Estates on weekends when I had Cal Vet business in the area otherwise Blanche would commute to Sacramento via commuter flights. We did both. It was expected that much of my time would be in Southern California as five of the eventual eight veteran homes would be located south of the Tehachapi's, two thirds of the state veterans and two thirds of the units of the California National Guard were in Southern California. This, coupled with the fact that almost two thirds of the state's population resided in the five most southern of the 58 counties in the state.

CHAPTER 77 VETERAN PICTURE IN CALIFORNIA

My role as Secretary was to be out and amongst the veteran population and visiting the veteran homes while my Undersecretary provided leadership to the headquarters staff. The California Department of Veteran Affairs had three programmatic areas: Veteran Services, Veteran Home Loans and Veteran Homes providing long term care for disabled and retired veterans with disabilities.

The Veteran Services Division focused on outreach to veterans who were in need of assistance due to an injury, illness or disabling condition caused while in the service. Their honorable discharge allowed them to claim this benefit. The Division then connected them to the US Department of Veterans Administration to receive those benefits. Local Inter-Agency Network Coordinators (LINCs) were assigned to this division and served as facilitators. They we spread throughout the state.

Most veterans qualify to purchase a home by nature of their honorable military service and Cal Vet Veteran Home Loan Division financed some of the purchases and the Federal VA financed others. It was the choice of the veteran as to which agency to use.

The Cal Vet Veteran Homes served as permanent places to reside for those veterans requiring medical care which in some instances, included homeless veterans. It too served as a retirement home for some veterans who had service connected disabilities but who were ambulatory. There are stark differences between Cal Vet and the USDVA in that the federal government administers VA Hospitals and fund disability payments while Cal Vet operates long term medical care in residential veteran homes in a home life atmosphere.

Many veterans who qualified for benefits offered by both Cal Vet and the USDVA did not access those benefit for a number of reason thus the reason for the Veterans

Services outreach programs. Special attention was paid to women and minority veterans who did not access their benefits at the numbers and frequency of non-minorities.

Native American Veterans had a very low access rate for benefits as many in their culture leaned toward not depending on the US Government, even though they were deserving and often in need. California is home to the largest Native American population in the country with over 100 federally recognized tribes. This stands to reason that California would have the largest number of Native American Veterans and it did. Special outreach programs were also targeted to them.

Women veterans were the fastest growing segment of the veteran community. As the active military continued its downsizing trend, the commensurate action was an increase in the number of veterans, especially women veterans who tended to serve a single enlistment. Many being combat veterans, they brought home many of the same issues from the war zone as their male counterpart in addition to women related issues.

It was my intent to learn as much more about the veteran picture in California than I already knew. This I wanted to do early on to be able develop my long range personal operational plan, set goals, objectives and to chart a new course forward for the department.

My staff and I conducted an analysis of who, what, how and where were the veterans. What were their needs, what was being done to address those needs, where were they and very importantly, how were they being served. I used the adaptive approach for establishing strategy to ensure our work would be long lasting with benchmark modifications.

With over two million veterans, or about ten percent of all veterans in the country, the needs for some veterans was great. Most were not in need of any services at all, but for those few who were, which could be thousands out of two million, the need could be substantial.

With the understanding that perhaps 90 percent of veterans required no assistance from either Cal Vet or the

US Department of Veteran Affairs, we began reviewing what was being done to assist those in the ten percentile; those requiring some assistance from the state or federal government with some of them being homeless. The assistance areas included **h**ousing, **e**mployment, **h**ealth care and **e**ducational assistance. This became the *"HEHE"* parlance and would later be the clarion call used by veteran support organizations statewide.

In defining "homeless" we learned that the homeless veteran definition in some counts included a simple definition as those veterans without a permanent place to stay. This included veterans residing with friends or relatives, the hundreds living in community care facilities operated by non-profit organizations and others. Not all homeless veterans were living on the street as media would have the populous believe.

Where were all the veterans in California? It was determined that of the 58 counties in the state about 65% resided in just five southern counties; Los Angeles, Orange, Riverside, San Bernardino and San Diego Counties. These counties had numerous community based programs to serve veterans both public and private. The veterans residing in the central and northern parts of the state, especially in small rural counties, were being under-served. We also learned that ethnic veterans and women veterans of all ethnicities were not accessing their well-earned benefits at the rate of others. This was especially true with women veterans because the VA had few programmatics designed specifically for them.

Veteran suicides were a concern for the entire nation, especially Californians. Some surveys had recorded there being over 20 per day nationwide. When drilling down on the data, it was determined that a veteran suicide was listed as such when anyone committing suicide had served in the military at any time during their entire lifetime was included in the count; some having served fifty or sixty years earlier and had been suffering from a non-military related terminal illness or a despondency over the death of a loved one.

Some suicides, listed as veteran suicides, were changed after a determination was made that the person in fact, had never served in the military as thought by a friend or distant family. One suicide, however, was one too many. One staggering revelation was that of younger veterans who took their lives, many had never deployed to a war zone, had never served outside the US and some had been in the military for less than a year prior to being discharged for mental or other reasons. A resulting factor in some cases was that they could not adapt to the regimen of the military life or that they brought ongoing civilian issues with them unchecked when enlisting in the military.

The "how" to serve veterans was the pillar which much focus was to be given. Collective governments each had a role to play in serving veterans albeit, primarily the federal government, as it was the only level of government which produced veterans. Additionally, veteran health care, benefits and pensions are paid by the federal government via the United States Department of Veteran Affairs.

The state, Cal Vet, as do all states, offer additional benefits to veterans as do some counties and cities. Cal Vet worked closely with local communities in its efforts to serve the veterans in the state. To ensure veterans received the assistance, benefits and services they needed, Cal Vet divided the state into eight regions and staffed each region with an outreach staff member; a LINC as noted.

These LINCS (Local Interagency Network Coordinators) played a dynamic role within counties and local communities serving as both informational conduits to the communities on veteran issues and concerns and served as a feedback resource for Cal Vet while serving as facilitators.

LINCs bridged the gap between Cal Vet and the federal, state, county and non-governmental agencies that provided services to many of our two million veterans. The LINCs served as advocates for veterans and military service members and their families in their respective regions. In addition, they supplemented and supported the County

Veteran Service Offices and regional partners in the development of improved and expanded services and support of their local veteran populations and also assisted veterans with employment and educational opportunities.

Veterans' health care in California is provided at the nine VA Regional Medical Centers and 65 community based out-patient clinics stretching from the Oregon border to the southern international border and also west to east. LINCs ensured that veterans possessed access information to these facilities.

On the federal level only the San Diego VA Medical Center provided domiciliary or residential facilities for selected veterans. This was based upon need as the VA and Housing and Urban Development (HUD) and several other federal agencies provided funding to community based non-profit organizations to house homeless veterans in the various communities requiring residential care.

Some of the community based organizations included Swords to Plow Shares in San Francisco; Pathway Home in Yountville; U.S. Vets Initiative in Los Angeles, Inglewood, Long Beach and Riverside; New Directions in West Los Angeles; Volunteers of America at various sites in Northern California, and Haven (Salvation Army) in Los Angeles County and Veterans Village in San Diego. This is just a partial listing.

Troops 'N Transition, a recently created not-for profit community based organization, was designed to provide living facilities for veterans attending community colleges who were in need of local housing. This was a need frequently overlooked by service providers. This successful organization had been established by Mark and Nancy Montgomery focusing initially on Southern Los Angeles County and Orange County. Mark had extensive experience as a major hotel chain executive and Nancy, a graduate level registered nurse, served as nurse and veterans coordinator at a community college providing her with first-hand knowledge of the needs.

Additionally, at that time the six Cal Vet veteran homes offered limited veteran outreach services and housing for some homeless veterans. Their mission was to provide residential and long-term care deferring to the community based organizations to house homeless veterans as they were the ones funded by several agencies of the federal government to do so.

The Cal Vet homes ranged from a 1,000 bed facility to a 60 bed facility. The levels of care included skilled nursing care, intermediate medical care, residential care for the elderly and memory care for those veterans with symptoms of Dementia or Alzheimer's disease. Expenses were shared among the state, the federal VA and the veterans themselves through pensions.

During my term of office we opened two additional California Veteran Homes one in Fresno and one in Redding. Both had been previously constructed but were not operational. In previous years, funding had been provided to construct the homes but not for personnel staffing and the admission of residents.

The homeless veteran question required a solution not readily available to anyone. All of the community based facilities just mentioned, as well as several others, had empty beds, while staff conducted targeted outreach to take in veterans meeting with minimal success. Truth be told and for some to understand what was revealed was that a sizable number, some would say most, homeless veterans chose to be homeless by choice.

One prime example of this was the mile long stretch of the Santa Ana River bed that had a circuitous route through central Orange County and where hundreds of homeless were encamped. When the camp was cleared out by a Federal Court Order all of the homeless there were offered secured and wholesome housing in hotels, motels, residential care facilities and other treatment enclaves. Less than half of the camp members would accept the generous offers instead preferring to continue being homeless.

Much of this perhaps was due to their mental or psychological state and others just wanted to avoid enclosure and the rules, regulations, restrictions and discipline required of facilities. This included but certainly not limited to restrictions on illegal drug use, alcohol consumption, curfews for their own safety and security and the daily personal hygiene requirement.

We learned that in some rural and mountainous regions in Northern California large veteran encampments existed, some with a similar hierarchical structure as a governmental agency. Assistance offered by Cal Vet and various non-profit organizations was routinely resisted. Unfortunately these were reminiscent of the Hobo camps during the depression era. The 1930's revisited.

Non-the-less since the City of Los Angeles had more homeless veterans than any city in the nation, in 2012 Los Angeles' Mayor Eric Garcetti and I teamed our resources and embarked on a three year dynamic plan to reduce homelessness in the city by half. This goal was realistic. The thought being since L.A. led the nation in numbers of homeless veterans they should lead the nation in eradicating it.

The results were that, although we did not achieve our goal of a 50 percent reduction, we did drastically reduce their numbers by instituting several evidenced based initiatives, which drew upon the assistance of all veteran care providers listed. The reduction of homeless veterans in Los Angeles reduced that population nationally due to the large numbers per capita.

CANVASSING THE STATE

California is an enormous state, larger than many others combined. Overlaid on a map with the eastern seaboard, California would stretch from Maine to South Carolina. During my tenure, Blanche and I traveled its' width and breath from Oregon to the Mexican border and from Los Angeles east to the High Sierra's. Veterans were scattered throughout. We were on a mission, me as Secretary and she as the supporting cast member.

San Diegans and Angelinos view Sacramento as Northern California but those residing in the Bay Area and

Sacramento view Northern California as Redding and points further north towards the Oregon border. It is all a matter of geographical perspective.

CHAPTER 78 INTERESTING PEOPLE

As Agency Secretary, my travels allowed me to meet movers and shakers in the state on behalf of veterans. I appeared before City Council's and County Boards of Supervisor's to discuss veterans issues and provided them a snapshot of the veteran picture in their political sub-division; information readily available but usually not generally known by them.

Civilians play a significant role in the various communities around the state who support veterans and I met many. One interesting person I met and who befriended me was Craig Newmark, founder of Craig's List, the internet search engine bearing his name. I was referred to Craig by his local Assembly Member in San Francisco and I arranged to personally meet him after introducing myself on a telephone call.

I drove to his office in downtown San Francisco and he was waiting for me at the appointed time standing in front of the multi-story office building in the financial district where he had his national corporate office (not offices). Right away, I knew he would be unpretentious as he was very casually attired; in a tee shirt and flip flops as I remembered. He showed me to his non-descript office and introduced me to his national corporate staff, all of about ten people, and all working in cubicles and all similarly attired. Their heads were buried in the mass of computer screen in each cubicle.

Craig had been an ardent supporter of veterans throughout the country and had appeared on 60 minutes and other syndicated television shows lamenting the cause of veterans. He had self-funded many veteran events and was interested in what my challenges were as Secretary.

He remarked to me that the chair which I was sitting in, was occupied by Dr. Jill Biden, Vice President Joe Biden's wife just the day before. She had flown there from her home in Delaware to discuss the program she co-chaired with President Obama's wife Michele, "Joining

Forces America." We discussed a wide range of proposals for him to support while I sat in the chair.

A few weeks, later Craig invited me to lunch at a small coffee and sandwich shop down the block from his apartment in a non-descript neighborhood which began a long term relationship both business and personal. We remain friends and his support for veterans is ongoing. He had invited me to his upcoming wedding which was later canceled.

Craig was the third billionaire I had met in the line of this duty but this one presented a stark difference to the other two. One was Mr. Antonio Dubonella, a well-known media mogul, Wall Street entrepreneur and the other was real estate mogul Mr. Ed Roski, a well-known benefactor of USC.

Vice President Al Gore.

I had been invited to a reception at Mr. Dubonella's expansive estate and was able to meet with a number of citizens concerned about the homeless veteran's picture. Although this was a political gathering my pitch to some of the group outlined suggestions on how they could support veterans by supporting legitimate organizations that provided direct support to veterans and veteran advocates.

Mr. Roski is a real estate investor who at one time was considering constructing a new football stadium in Southern California to entice an NFL team to relocate here. In his younger years he had served in Viet Nam as a Marine Corps officer. Dr. Nikias, USC's President, had arranged a breakfast meeting with Mr. Roski and me at the California Club in downtown Los Angeles. The purpose was to engage

Mr. Roski in a veterans' event which I was planning. The three of us had a great dialogue on a wide range of veteran issues especially student veterans. The event I was planning was held in San Diego and was a tremendous success thanks in part to Mr. Roski's support.

Dr. Nikias had been an acquaintance since I was appointed a USC Ambassador as well as serving on the USC Price School of Public Policy's Advisory Board and guest speaker at the Bedrosian Center's "Lunch with a Leader" speakers series. I was also Chairman Emeritus of the USC Army ROTC Advisory Board. In all of this I was able to unofficially interface with General (Retired) David Petraues, former Director of the Central Intelligence Agency who was then posted at USC filling an endowed Chair position.

Television Talk Show Host Larry King.

Members of the Cabinet are often invited to special events sponsored by the Governor. One such event which all Cabinet Members were invited was a luncheon he hosted for the newly elected President of Mexico, whom he had invited to Sacramento. This was even prior to that President's first trip to Washington to meet with President Obama. The event was an elegant affair replete with enormous Secret Service presence from both governments.

Celebrity Chef Wolfgang Puck.

Many of the 150 or so invitees consisting of elected officials, business leaders and leaders from the Mexican communities throughout the state had the opportunity to personally meet Mexico's

President and pose for photographs. About a week later, all Cabinet members received an individual billing invoice for $143.00 each to cover their meal cost and other incidentals. There is no "free lunch."

For a while, I had breakfast now and then with television personality Larry King at his favorite eatery in Beverly Hills. I was initially invited there by a mutual friend and I quickly began to enjoy his company. Larry and some of his friends met there on a regular basis and Larry routinely walked there from his nearby home. My meeting with him had to do solely with engaging him to use his public platform and celebrity status on behalf of homeless veterans.

Actor Ernest Borgnine.

Former Los Angeles Mayor Richard Reardon became a good friend and we golfed on occasion, him borrowing my golf shoes one day at a tournament when he forgot his. That day I golfed in my street shoes. This was before I gave up the sport. Blanche and I were often invited to his home for receptions where Who's Who in Los Angeles were in attendance.

Reverend Jesse Jackson.

We also attended several dinner parties at the posh Beverly Hills home of a very good friend and renowned Hollywood Producer Arthur Kassel. One was the birthday party for Arthur's wife, Tichi, the owner and publisher of the Hollywood Variety tabloid newspaper. Tichi passed away shortly thereafter. A few years later, Blanche and I were invited and attended the wedding ceremony when he remarried. His wedding was held at his new Ventura County hillside estate officiated by former Governor Gray Davis. We were seated with the husband and wife co-owners of a Los Angeles major league sports team. The two had been in the recent news reports regarding the future ownership of the team each making claims to their stake. Attending weddings must have a sense of solving marital issues as their behavior with one another was reminiscent of newlyweds themselves.

CHAPTER 79 FREE TIME

A WEDDING ANNIVERSARY IN SACRAMENTO

While in Sacramento we took time to celebrate one of our wedding anniversaries at the Kitchen Restaurant which, according Restaurant Writers, is considered to be the most posh eatery in all of California and we can attest to that.

The restaurant is housed in a non-descript brick building with no exterior signage whatsoever. Reservations are required months in advance and each night it hosts just 20 couples and all arrive at the parking lot at the same time and form a line and are greeted. Upon entering each person is presented with a glass of premier champagne by a staff person in formal attire including white gloves. All diners have assigned seating.

The stainless steel kitchen is the center piece of the facility where diners are encouraged stroll through while the professional culinary staff prepare the meal. All ingredients are locally grown and picked or harvested that very day. Seafood is flown in daily fresh from various seaports in the state.

At the start of the dinner all couples are requested to introduce themselves and announce whether their attendance there is to celebrate a birthday, anniversary or other milestone. The cost is prohibited for most and some may have to seek a bank loan just to dine there but the experience was for us, a grand opportunity. At the end of the dinner which included scrumptious dessert and after dinner cordials all patrons exit at the same time.

MILESTONE BIRTHDAY PARTY

During my first six months in Sacramento, Blanche was busily planning a party to celebrate my 70th Birthday in June although this was not to be a surprise party. I was unable to assist her in any appreciable way as I was busily focusing on the needs of veterans around the state. The back yard of our residence in Rolling Hills Estates would be large enough to accommodate the well over 100 invitees that would include immediate family and other relatives, many friends from the past as well as newer friends and acquaintances and past business associates.

Blanche had arranged for several 10 person large circular tables with umbrellas which later would prove to be insufficient to accommodate the 150 who attended. She also had arranged for additional pool chairs to accommodate those electing to take a dip, though none did.

She had prepared a 2 foot by 2 foot framed photo of me and invited the guests to sign the matted edges and offer a congratulatory message. I quickly became very fond of the inscriptions and it has found a prominent display place in our home. From time to time I reread some of the messages and greetings and remind myself how kind people can be. Still photographs were taken for posterity of the guests enjoying themselves.

As detailed as she was Blanche had provided each guest with a pamphlet describing food prices and other items such as automobiles and houses and the cost of each in 1941, my birth year. She provided each guest with several items first made in 1941 such as Abba Zabba candy bars, M & M's and a bottle of Dads Old Fashion Root Beer. These were presented in goodie bags which she singly prepared.

The disc jockey at the event had an array of 1950' and 1960's Oldies but Goodies hits which brought nostalgia to not only me but to probably all of the guests as they were from the era. This may have been my party but it turned out to be a reunion of sort for many of the guests as several had not seen each other for many years and the conversations around the yard focused on the past. I was very fortunate to have such nice friends.

ROANWOOD ENTERTAINING

My 70th Birthday bash was not the first such entertainment event staged in our back yard. For a couple of years Blanche and I hosted the Gravett Family's Annual Labor Day Picnic after my brother Phillip and his wife Dortha had done so for many years. Also we had hosted several groups of business partners, church members, friends and club members. These included back yard barbeques, dinners and other such gatherings small and large.

Some of these were staff members of Gravett & Associates, staff of Traiden Global Solutions, members of a social club which Blanche and I belong, the British United Services Club (BUSC), whose members are former and retired American military members and former military members from the various countries in the British Commonwealth of Nations. Later I would serve as President of the club becoming only the second American president since the club's founding in 1935.

The BUSC event had a red, white and blue theme and we had banners of those colors flowing from the trellis coverings of the red wood decking in the backyard. Blanche and I were in the mood attired in our Uncle Sam and Betsy Ross red, white and blue costumes. But that's not all.

What we really enjoyed was hosting National Foot Ball League playoff parties and Super Bowl parties. This we did for several years and our guests really looked forward to Blanche's table of treats.

One year over the Christmas holidays Blanche and I decided to have a few couples over dinner. This particular evening the table was set, the couples had arrived, and the prime rib was in the oven. When we were all settled and beginning to have a great conversation, the power in the neighborhood went out. Since we had an electric stove, this meant that the prime rib, and other dishes were not going to be cooked. Putting that aside for the moment we managed to dig out our cell phone flash lights and candles so we could see how to proceed. It was decided to finish cooking the roast and side dishes outside on the BBQ and the guests were real troopers and helped in taking the food outside and also lighting the dining room candles so we could see to eat. This was not the best solution but somehow we were able to have a meal with a very rare entrée.

The candles and cell phone lighting gave a nice soft romantic feel for the dinner for the couples. Rabbi Bob Schriebman was asked to give the blessing of the food. Just as he was concluding the Grace the lights turned on. All at the table, Catholic, Protestant and Jew alike thought it was Devine intervention. We also thought about keeping the lights off since the atmosphere was so nice. What could have been a disaster for all turned out to be entertaining for everyone and a story to tell months and years to come.

CHRISTMAS AT THE AHWAHNI HOTEL IN YOSEMITE

Another grand event was spending a snowy Christmas weekend at the Ahwahni Hotel in the Yosemite National Park and experiencing the infamous Brace Bridge Dinner. This is a 16 course meal served over a six hour period. Each course is introduced by actors clad in Renaissance costume and singing. A tuba player leads the wait staff into the room carrying each entrée while the actors recite verse and rhyme and act out parts of a play.

Hotel reservations for Christmas are required two years in advance with a three night minimum paid a year in advance. The Brace Bridge Dinner full fare, which is separate, is also required to be paid a year in advance.

While there in the Yosemite we experienced a light snow fall but found it invigorating taking walks and seeing our breath in the cold air. Our room was spacious and replete with all expected modern amenities. The hotel itself is world famous and once hosted Queen Elizabeth for a stay.

CHAPTER 80 GOVERNMENT OPERATIONS

During my tenure Blanche and I traveled throughout the state visited each Veteran Home on multiple occasions. We had decided early on that if I accepted the position and travel was required that she would accompany me most places and she did though at no expense to the state.

Her visits to the Veteran Homes were so frequent in some cases the residents believed she was part of headquarters staff paying a visit. Along the way she met hundreds of veterans, both men and women, striking up lengthy friendships. Many looked forward to her return.

A side benefit to traveling throughout the state was that we both had the opportunity to admire California for the beauty it has. On a few occasions we traveled to the North Coast attending Veteran Service Organization meetings, conferences and conventions. On one special trip we traveled north along US Highway 101 to the Northwestern most Counties of Humboldt and Del Norte, which bordered on the State of Oregon.

We drove through the Redwood Forests and even drove our car through the infamous cutout of a large Redwood tree. In the southeast we traveled to Calexico in Imperial Valley, the southeastern most part of the state, almost a thousand miles from Del Norte County by car. In Calexico we experienced a 120 degree temperature day in the city which is several feet below sea level. We visited veteran organizations everywhere in between. Most travel was by automobile with some air travel.

During many of our trips Blanche was able to interface with women veterans to discuss specific issues pertaining to them. She was able to do this effectively as she was a veteran herself. With Blanche, the State received the services of a surrogate employee at no compensation.

The USDVA had recently established programs for women veterans as they not only had some of the same medical and psychological issues as males but their specific medical and psychological issues were not being addressed. It was only after my counter-parts and I, as members of the National Association of Veteran Affairs Officers, petitioned the USDVA to affect corrective oversights that they did so. I credit my Deputy Secretary for Women Veterans, Lindsey Sin, for bringing to light these issues which we were able to take to Washington for resolution.

It was my intent to visit every VA Medical Center in the state during my first year in office and this was accomplished. Blanche and I visited hospitals in San Diego, West Los Angeles, San Francisco, Livermore, Long Beach, Loma Linda, Mather, Menlo Park, Fresno and Palo Alto. Additionally we probably visited at least 20 of the more than 60 VA Community Based Out-Patient Clinics each one a comprehensive care center of its' own.

At the medical centers I collaborated with the directors and staff and discussed ways in which Cal Vet could better partner with them in serving the needs of veterans and their families. All of the medical centers have extensions in the form of medical clinics, as mentioned above, dispersed throughout the state making VA resources accessible within reasonable commuting distance for everyone.

I visited Washington DC a number of times and met with Congressional Members of the House Veterans Affairs Sub-Committee to discuss veteran issues. California having the largest Members of the House of Representatives, 53 in all, had a majority of Members on that Sub-Committee. They played a vital role in ensuring that our state received its fair share of the veteran budget.

With all of the travel I made it a point not to miss Mark's wedding as he had requested that I be his Best Man just as I had chosen him as my Best Man when Blanche and I were married. In 2014, he married Rosalina Barro in a lavish ceremony at her family's church, St. Pius X, in Santa Fe Springs, California. This was replete with a combined Bridesmaids and Groomsmen of over 35 individuals which also included her Matron of Honor, flower girls, ring bearers and those who lit candle. By tradition in African American weddings they made the ceremony official by jumping the broom.

We danced the night away at the wedding reception and a good time was had by all. Mark was delighted to see that he had the support of his many aunts, uncles and especially his cousins. Social media works wonders.

CABINET MEETINGS

The eighteen Members of the Governor's Cabinet met monthly with the Governor's Senior Staff where each of us provided a briefing on the status of our respective agencies. Coordination was affected across agency lines to provide mutual support. This is where I requested that the Secretaries consult me regarding any issues arising with their employees who were veterans or military reservists.

Cabinet meeting, were also used as the forum for all of us to engage in the discussion of the state budget. Also once a month, we met for an informal breakfast at agency facilities which had a cafeteria. This gave us the opportunity to meet informally without the Governor or his staff present.

Even though most of us had been appointed within a month or two of each other, at the beginning of his first term, all seemed to have known each other for quite some time. I suspect that they had worked with the Governor previously and had "come up through the ranks" to the pinnacle of government. Some had been senior leaders in the Governor's Party.

I believe that just I and one other Cabinet member were new to California's government and that was the Secretary of the California Department of Rehabilitation and Corrections, the Prisons Chief. He had been recruited from Pennsylvania where he had served as the Director of that state's prison system and had a national reputation of having successfully affected prison reforms.

Shortly following my appointment as Secretary Governor Brown issued an Executive Order creating the Governor's Inter-Agency Council on Veterans and identified my position as Chairperson.

The Order appointed 12 of the 18 Cabinet Members to the Council due to their agencies mission, in part, offered services to veterans. The Order invited voluntary participation by Chairs of the Senate and Assembly Veteran Affairs Committees of the Legislative Branch and from the Judicial Branch he invited the Chief Justice of the California Supreme Court to appoint a representative.

Invitations were also extended to state entities for which the Office of the Governor had no direct responsibility or control or authority; the President of the University of California, Chancellor of the California State University and Chancellor of the California Community Colleges.

I set about scheduling meetings with all of the appointed members, to include all of the invitees, to introduce myself and to welcome them the opportunity to serve veterans. The opportunity to sit and speak with the Chief Justice and the Chancellors' one on one was an honor for me.

Most of the Members were receptive of their new role of focusing on veteran issues but others, in my view, simply saw this as just one more piece of heavy metal on their already heavy plate. I scheduled monthly meeting to hammer out goals, objectives and bench marks with them or their designated representatives and developed some workable avenues to pursue.

I scheduled an annual meeting of the members themselves and all participated as I presided. These were held at the Capitol in the Senate Chambers and televised via closed circuit television throughout all of the state government agency headquarters in Sacramento.

Another once in a lifetime opportunity was bestowed upon me as I was given the pleasure of officiating at a US Citizenship swearing-in ceremony for over 2,500 new American citizens. The ceremony was held at the Sacramento River Rats Professional Baseball Stadium in the City of West Sacramento, a city separated from California's Capitol of Sacramento by the Sacramento River.

Somehow I had been nominated to officials of the US State Department in Washington DC to offer the keynote speech and perform the ceremony to the throngs of citizenship-candidates who had spent months attending classes and preparing to become American citizens. As I recall, 1 they hailed from over 30 countries and all had undergone the requisite application process and approved. Some had been issued the customary "Green Card" years earlier and were anxious to join the other almost 300 million Americans as citizens. Many were actively serving in the US Military and stood proud in their uniforms.

The stadium was filled with over seven thousand family members, friends, neighbors and employers of the candidates. Hundreds had brought bouquets of flowers with balloons as well as whistles and horns. The interior of the stadium was adorned with scores of American flags and red, white and blue banners posted and blowing in the wind. Similar decorations were posted outside.

I had prepared pointed remarks to fit the occasion and made my delivery in just a few minutes as the only thing standing between me and their swearing-in was my speech. I knew full well, they had taken the requisite classes on American history, government, geography, had memorized words to the national anthem, the pledge of allegiance, the Gettysburg Address and the Preamble to the Constitution. I offered my personal thanks and those of the people of the United States for taking the required steps to become citizens of the "Greatest Country in the World" and urged them to vote in every election for the remainder of their lives.

Following my remarks they were requested to stand and take the oath of citizenship which I administered and then it became a very chaotic but joy filled jubilation of cheers and shouts by everyone in the stadium. Since no event is over *"until the fat lady sings"* I restored order by announcing I would lead them in reciting the Pledge of Allegiance for the first time which I did. They then became Naturalized US Citizens.

Upon departing the stadium they passed through a labyrinth of vendors offering for sale American flags of all sizes, sports team banners and a multitude of items adorned with the American flag. The most important tables however were those from the major political parties requesting that the now new citizens register to vote, each Party having several tables. By the time I departed the area the long voter registration lines had not diminished and it was expected that every one of these new American citizens would register.

STATE BUDGET

Prior to my appointment as Secretary I had minimal knowledge on the state government budgeting process. However the Cal Vet staff brought me up to speed very quickly. The Cal Vet budget request had been submitted to the Finance Department a few months earlier, in January 2011, for review. The Governor presented his version of the budget to the Legislature which reflected his priorities and the needs of the state agencies and departments for which he had control.

This version of the budget was then taken to the Senate and the Assembly and each House held hearings, took public comment, deliberated and made changes to the Governor's budget. When this process was done, the Senate and Assembly compared their two versions of the budget and convened a Conference Committee to compare the differences and voted them into one unified budget.

Both Houses then took a final voted on it. Once that was done, the Legislature sent that version of the budget back to the Governor for his approval.

The Governor could not add items back into the budget, but he could "blue pencil" or remove or reduce budget allocations. This was done in mid-May which was called the "May Revise." All agencies were expected to receive some blue pencil, including Cal Vet, since this was my first budget I anxiously awaited the Governor's revision. As expected we received some blue pencil.

The deadline for the Governor to sign the budget was June 30 which would be effective July 1, the beginning of the new fiscal year. The Governor failing to sign the budget by that date then all state expenditures were ceased including pay to the more than 200,000 state employees, the 40 State Senators and the 80 State Assembly Members as well as the various statewide elected Constitutional Officers.

Shortly thereafter the Governor's budget was published with all agency projections and all agencies were anxiously awaiting the Governor's revised budget which is published the second week in May.

The State Legislature recessed during August and reconvened in September for one month. At the end of the month they were out of Session until the end of the year, each returning to their home districts for work there. They returned to Session the second Monday in January and the budget process repeated itself.

While the Legislative Members were on recess and returned to their home districts the Cal Vet staff and I used some of that time to assess our programs and policies and how we were applying our resources to the various parts of the state. I had appointments with various Members at the Capitol and also in their home districts, some requested by me and others by them, to gage how effectively Cal Vet was impacting the various programs in the districts.

CHAPTER 81 FOURTH AND FINAL RETIREMENT

On the statewide election night in November 2014 the Cabinet and senior staff joined Governor and Mrs. Brown at the Governor's mansion for an election night dinner and to watch the returns. There were numerous flat screen television monitors situated in various rooms on several floors. I was impressed that I had the honor of being present when the Governor was going to be reelected (there was no doubt). History shows that he was reelected for a fourth term albeit several years between his second and third terms. Congratulations were in order when the final vote tally was done.

The dinner was served in the mansions' formal dining room on just one elongated dining room table set for 30 with the Governor and Mrs. Brown situated in the center. This accommodated just the Cabinet and senior staff with no spouses. Numerous media trucks and reporters were camped outside.

The evening was dissimilar to the Governor's annual birthday party given for him by the Staff in his suite of offices at the Capitol, including the "horse shoe", the Cabinet meeting chamber, where the plethora of well-wishes spent a couple of hours cruising from office to office each replete with food stations featuring entrees from several countries.

At his birthday bashes, the well-wishers not only included the Cabinet and their spouses but also mid-level staff, friends, legislators (from both Party's), lobbyists, off-duty media, off duty security detail members and many others, including his dog Sutter. Blanche and I always had a good time.

TRANSITION

In January 2015, the Governor began one-on-one meetings with his Cabinet Members to determine whether or not each would be willing to serve him in his final term of office but also to determine if he would reappoint them. I had served four years as his Secretary of Veteran Affairs and had accomplished most of my goals and objectives so I advised him that I would not be serving in his second term of office and submitted my resignation to be effective in a month.

This was a joint decision by Blanche and me, noting that we had maintained two residences and wanted to resettle in Southern California on a permanent basis. I announced my decision to the staff upon returning to the office and began making plans to depart a month later.

Prior to leaving, my competent staff not only gave me a farewell party but a joint party for Blanche as well as she had become a surrogate member and they knew her well and she had become friends with most of them.

I say competent staff because throughout my tenure as Secretary all staff members had not been competent. Governor Brown's governing style was that his senior staff selected and recommended agency Deputy Secretaries to the Governor for appointment and not the Secretary such as me. With this arrangement Secretaries sometimes were saddled with individuals who were charged with assisting them in administering the agency but, in most instances, were previously unknown to them.

This scenario created issues as some were appointed based upon politics and favors as one could expect and the competency of some was questionable. The result was over the course of my tenure as Secretary some of my Deputy Secretaries had finally been removed by the Governor for a myriad of missteps.

This occurred with the Department of Veteran Affairs and other agencies as well. By the end of my tenure however I had a senior staff that was second to none. All were very well educated, possessed the required leadership skills essential for their respective positions and were loyal to carrying out the mission and objectives of the organization.

CHAPTER 82 CAL VET
ACCOMPLISHMENTS

Blanche and I departed Sacramento in February 2015 and returned to our home in Rolling Hills Estates. Now it was time to downsize our living arrangements which we had considered prior to the Cabinet appointment. We listed and sold our home and purchased a much smaller one just about two miles away above the cliffs on the western slope of the Palos Verdes Peninsula in Rancho Palos Verdes. We were home. Securely back in the environs of Southern California we began to review our accomplishments as Secretary and as a Member of the Governors Cabinet and an analysis determined there had been many.

VETERAN HOME OPENINGS

We had opened two new veteran homes, one in Fresno and the other in Redding, to better serve our veterans requiring residential care in those regions. Both of these facilities had been constructed and completed two years prior but had not opened due to budget constraints.

I set about meeting with every member of the Senate and Assembly Veteran Affairs Committees to garner support to fund the operation of the homes. I met with various leaders in the veteran communities around the state and encouraged support from their members to "ping on" the elected officials from the affected communities to take a more active role in making the case for budget allocation.

My then Undersecretary, Brigadier General (Retired) Robin Umberg, and I traveled to Fresno at the invitation (demand) of a very vocal majority in that city to attend what became a contentious live televised community hearing. Although those present were extremely vocal in their denunciation of the Governor and the Legislature for refusing to grant operational funding to open the home there, but also voiced support for opening the one in Redding 400 miles to their north. Though dissatisfied with the slow process of having those doors opened they were aware and appreciative of the efforts that the Undersecretary and I had undertaken.

CENTRAL COAST STATE VETERANS CEMETERY

National Cemeteries around the country are funded, constructed and maintained by the federal government. Individual states, however, also have the option to construct veteran cemeteries which are named as State Veteran Cemeteries. This is done primarily when there is a need for a national veterans' cemetery but one is already located within 100 direct miles of an existing one.

California with its' dense veteran population had a dire need for a veteran cemetery in the Monterey Peninsula area on the central coast which at one time had been populated by several military bases now shuttered. Many military members had retired there which increased the veteran population.

The USDVA had denied several requests to consider constructing one there due to the proximity of the San Joaquin National Veterans Cemetery approximately 80 direct miles east over the mountain in the San Joaquin Valley. With the support of the Congressional Representative on the Monterey Peninsula we secured initial USDVA funding to construct the initial phase of the Central Coast State Veterans Cemetery. The request for this funding had been languishing for many years with no movement until my personal intervention at the request Cal Vet's point person Deputy Secretary for Veteran Services Keith Boylan. More on Keith later.

I was pleased to receive an invitation to attend the ground breaking ceremony shortly following my retirement. Later I received thank you and congratulatory notes from the local Congressman and several of his veteran constituents.

ORANGE COAST STATE VETERANS CEMETERY

With the initial plans for the state Central Coast Cemetery well underway plans for locating a suitable site in Orange County for a Southern California State Cemetery began. Several sites were considered on the former El Toro Marine Corps Air Station now called the Great Park.

I joined in taking the lead in formulating plans for the cemetery with a number of veteran advocates from Orange County led by Mr. Robert (Bobby Mac) McDonald, Chair of the Orange County Veterans Collaborative and Assemblywoman Sharon Quirksilva from Fullerton as well as others. Committees and sub-committees were formed and collaboration was established with the City of Irvine to assist in the funding.

I elicited the support of Governor Brown who came on-board in support of the project and allocated part of the initial funding from state coffers. One of my final treks to Southern California prior to leaving office was to accompany the Governor to the Great Park to attend the ground breaking ceremony. We were accompanied by Assemblywoman Quirksilva and Mr. McDonald.

VETERAN DISABILITY CLAIMS BACKLOG

We assisted the USDVA to reduce their backlog of processing veterans' claims for disability, some having been filed three or four years earlier. It had been reported that many veterans had passed away while awaiting the disposition of their claim. Deputy Secretary Keith Boylan devised a plan whereby Cal Vet would assist by placing California Department of Veteran Affairs state employees in the state's three Federal VA offices to work on eliminating the backlog.

This offer had been made several times in the past but due to the federal bureaucracy policy of not allowing state employees to process federal documents, Keith and I paid a visit to Washington, DC to the Congressional Veteran Affairs Sub-Committee and made a presentation recommending a change to this policy. It just so happened that California had eleven Members on the Committee and a Bill was drafted and approved allowing Cal Vet access to the three federal offices in the state.

Since the technical process of ushering the claims required considerable experience to negotiate the myriad of rules and regulations, we secured funding to hire recently retired, less than two years, and retired federal employees on a temporary basis. They were all from the very VA offices where they were placed but now working as a state employee performing their old jobs. We placed 36 employees in the offices; 12 each in the San Diego, Los Angeles and Oakland offices and within a year the back logs had been reduced to a matter of months.

Several months after that claims were being funded within 45 days. The transaction was so successful that other states made efforts to follow our lead. Deputy Secretary for Veteran Services Keith Boylan's brainchild resulted in thousands of veterans receiving their well-earned benefits.

NEW RESIDENTIAL VETERAN HOMES

We Teamed with Habitat for Humanity and with Residential Enriched Neighborhoods, two non-profit housing groups, to devise plans to construct several veteran villages around the state. These would be self-contained new homes owned by veterans in communities such as Santa Clarita, Sylmar, Riverside, Jurupa, Poway, Palmdale, Lompoc, Sylmar and other communities.

The genesis of this endeavor came as a result of a restaurant meeting in the City of Santa Clarita with myself, Santa Clarita's Mayor Robert Keller, my former colleague from the Los Angeles Police Department, MS Donna Deutchman, Chief Executive Officer of Habitat for Humanity-Santa Clarita-San Fernando Valley Chapter, and architects and developers whom Donna had invited. Blanche was also at the initial meeting and offered sage recommendations and greatly contributed to the discussion.

Donna had the vision, Mayor Keller was offering city land at no cost, I possessed the funding ability through the Cal Vet Home Loan Program and the architects and developers were interested from the business prospective. That was to provide some construction materials at cost as a tax incentive. The Santa Clarita Valley part of the state was a "veteran rich" geographical area.

These were low cost permanent single family housing units with accompanying family services including child care and in some instances counseling services. These homes were financed with a Cal Vet home loan with lower than market mortgage rates.

The overall purchase price for each home would be at approximately 60 percent of the assessed value for several reasons; the land was donated by the respective cities, the developers constructed the homes at cost plus a minimal percentage of profit as a tax incentive and Cal Vet set the monthly mortgage payment at 35% of the monthly salary of the veteran. This was affordable to most first time home buyers.

Homes could be purchased with little or no down payment and a veteran with a family of four, as an example, could purchase a home with a $35,000 annual income. The home owners could resale their home only after ten years of ownership and it could only be sold to another veteran. Meanwhile if the veterans lost their job mortgage payment had the option of being held in abeyance.

The veterans and their families were required to donate 500 cumulative hours of sweat equity. Cal Vet's sweat equity program was unique in that it did not require hammering and nailing by the purchaser but that was an option. The hours were accumulated by the veteran and spouse or partner attending financial literacy classes and if young children were involved the parents were required to attend parenting classes. They were required to attend a veterans' benefit class and teens were required to attend a teen financial management class, all of which were at no cost.

Also all family members could donate personal time volunteering at veteran hospitals and clinics, homeless shelters, women's shelters, food pantries and other community non-profit organizations. By the time each home was completed most families cumulatively had donated more hours than what was required. They also had the option of accumulating additional hours by helping to construct their home.

Each home was purchased as the foundation was being laid and the potential resident and their families are given the opportunity to select some fixed furnishing as the home was being constructed. These included interior paint colors for each room, carpet colors, kitchen cabinets fixtures, lighting fixtures, door knobs and handles.. The homes came with all kitchen appliances.

While at Cal Vet we also expanded the home purchase option to include purchasing condominiums, town homes, modular homes as well as micro farms. This became an option when we learned that many returning veterans had interest in starting their own small farm or agriculture business. Since 1924 when the Cal Vet Home Loan Program was created these opportunities had never been offered. All of this was conceived and implemented by my Deputy Secretary for Veteran Home Loans, Theresa Gunn.

The main street in the Santa Clarita veteran' village complex consisting of 83 homes was named Gravett Place. I had not expected such an honor and was thankful that the Santa Clarita City

Gravett Family at Gravett Place Dedication; Peter, Blanche, Daughter-in-Law Rosalina & Son Mark.

Council voted unanimously for the measure.

VETERAN OUTREACH CONFERENCES

Another success we experienced was addressing the problem of minority veterans not accessing their VA benefits which they had so richly earned as we discussed. To turn this around we held a series of minority veteran forums around the state, open to all veterans, to advise them of these missed opportunities.

Research determined that homeless veterans tended to be male (91%), single (98%) and live in an urban city (76%). Black veterans and Native American veterans were substantially overrepresented comprising a disproportionate number of the total homeless population.

Two Buffalo Soldiers: Robert (Bobby Mac) Mc Donald (Posed as 2LT Henry Flipper) and MG Gravett

Possessing these data we set about abating this by scheduling the forums with the assistance of various veteran service organizations.

We held a Hispanic Veterans Conference in the City of Commerce just outside Los Angeles which was co-hosted by the American G. I. Forum, a Hispanic focused veteran organization. An Asian Veterans Conference was held in Gardena and was co-sponsored by the Korean American Veterans Forum and the Japanese American 442nd Regimental Combat Team. The topics focused on specific concerns of each group. This was the first time that Korean American and Japanese American veterans had ever collaborated.

We held a black Veterans Summit co-sponsored by US Navy and Viet Nam Veteran Robert (Bobby Mac) McDonald, CEO of the Black Chamber of Orange County and Chair of the Orange County Veterans Collaborative. It was Bobby who took the lead by suggesting format and arranged for presentations by national speakers. He also arranged the catered soul food lunch which was gratis for attendees. The event was held at the California State Afro American Museum at Exposition Park in Los Angeles and was the largest of the minority veteran forums with over 300 in attendance, both black and non-black veterans. Bobby had also served as an appointed member of the California Community College Board of Trustees.

The all-day event featured several discussions on a number of topics central to black veterans such as their high preponderance of diabetes, sickle cell anemia and homelessness.

A Native American Veterans' Pow Wow was held in Fresno bringing together veterans from several tribes throughout the Central Valley and beyond. A major discussion was held regarding specific issues which concerned Native American which were referred to the USDVA. These included suggestion that VA Mobile Clinics have a presence at Pow Wows and other community tribal gatherings and selected VA staff attempt to make entry into the veteran homeless camps situated in the mountain regions of Central and Northern California. These camps consists primarily of Native American veterans. Diabetes among Native American veterans was also a major topic of discussion.

All of the conferences were open to all veterans with no restriction in regards to ethnicity, sex or sexual orientation. Service providers were invited to attend to learn how they could more effectively serve veterans.

The Governor's senior staff applauded these efforts for all of the conferences and only questioned why my staff and I would schedule a black Veterans Conference but had no comment regarding the other ethnic conferences.

Obviously they did not understand nor see the total picture. A presentation of the above statistics and the printed program for the other conferences was provided to resolve their concerns.

GAY AND LESBIAN VETERAN CONFERENCE

Since the federal government had officially lifted the ban on homosexuality in the federal military services and the *"Don't Ask Don't Tell Policy"* revoked many military and veteran service members had emerged from the shadows and proclaimed their sexual orientation.

With this phenomenon the USDVA was slowly making specific services available to those members requiring counseling or other benefits. For the first time ever in the nation we held a conference in California for gay and lesbian veterans. We staged the event on the campus of California State University Sacramento with the concurrence of the college administration and with the assistance and cooperation of several lesbian and gay organizations who served as co-sponsors.

The event, attended by over 75 currently serving military and veterans, was coordinated by Minority Affairs Deputy Secretary Mirtha Villarreal-Younger. She and her husband Patrick were both veterans, she a Lieutenant Colonel and he a Major. Mirtha was as passionate as I with the event as both of us knowing full well that lesbian and gay veterans were an underserved group.

Several representatives from the USDVA and veteran organizations attended to gage firsthand the services needed by this group and to measure whether they we being provided. What was critical by the VA was to determine whether these issues were military related.

Many of the veterans brought their concerns to the floor and some voiced their past and on-going issues. The federal government staff and service care providers took notes. At that time the USDVA and the military were not recognizing transgender individuals for benefits specific to their sexual orientation.

Since most returning veterans begin their higher education at community colleges, it was important that these institutions have a place on campus for veterans to gather and share experiences. While in office we dedicated Veteran Resource Centers on 21 of the state's 113 community colleges, many other colleges already having such centers.

Veteran Resource Centers did not require any special budget or funding in most cases. I just encouraged community college administrators to identify and set aside office or repurposed space and furnish them with no longer needed stored furniture. We explained that once the space was appropriated veterans themselves would make it military service friendly by hanging murals, banners, photographs and posters identifying the various services.

In almost all cases this was done and without the red tape bureaucratic nuances of a budget item or a vote by faculty. Once the centers were furnished dedication ceremonies were held with a ribbon cutting scenario. Along the way some Community College Presidents espoused that Veteran Resource Centers were inappropriate for their campus not understanding that they themselves were the beneficiary of the sacrifices made by veterans. Many in this group had never served.

In retirement, I dedicated a student veterans' center at Marymount California University, a four year institution in Rancho Palos Verdes where I was serving on their Long Range Planning Committee. I also donated a portion of my military library to the center.

I served on the panning committee for a Veterans Education and Resource Complex at Cypress College. This multi-million dollar facility would be the first of its' kind in California in that it was being constructed specifically for a center for veterans. This would be a public-private partnership. I had, for ten years, served on the Cypress College Foundation Board.

EL SOLDADO (THE SOLDIER)

During my tenure we raised funds statewide to begin the restoration work on "El Soldado" a monument erected at the Capitol and dedicated to Mexican American Soldiers who had died during World War Two. The monument was originally erected in 1946 but was in disrepair and weathered. Original funds to erect the statue were raised by mothers of the soldiers by selling tacos and enchiladas door to door the year after the war ended.

With the Governor's support a Mexican American Monument Commission was appointed to oversee the restoration project and I appointed my Deputy Secretary for Minority Affairs, Mirtha Villarreal-Younger, as the point of contact for the commission. Although I generated some funding by pitching the project at various veteran events it was Mirtha who generated the lion's share of funding required for the renewal. Following my retirement she arranged and supervised the dedication of the completed project, no doubt successful due to her untiring efforts.

PRESENTATIONS

What goes with the territory of the position of Secretary is speaking at public events and I was frequently called upon to deliver several remarks. These included speeches on every patriotic holiday such as Veterans Day, Memorial Day, Independence Day and Viet Nam Veterans Day. I also spoke at Stand Downs, at dedication of various veterans housing facilities, dedication of college campus veteran resource centers, job fairs, a posthumous and belated Medal of Honor ceremony, veteran service organization conventions, Native American Pow Wow's and others.

During my four years in the position I was called upon to deliver more than 100 speeches. Additionally I sat on numerous panel discussions and swore in a number of veterans assuming office in veteran organizations. I was called before a televised Congressional Hearing and gave testimony on causal factors of veteran homelessness.

It was learned that the fastest growing segment of veterans in the state were women veterans as more positions in the military were being open to women. The overall percentage of women serving in all of the services collectively increased exponentially. Women were also being allowed to serve in direct combat roles. For the most part, women tended to leave the service following just one enlistment period, therefore increasing the overall numbers of women veterans in the state.

To address the growing numbers of women veterans we appointed a Women Veterans Deputy Secretary whose primary focus was to address those issues which directly affected women in addition to those which all veterans faced. Previously women veteran issues were handled as an additional duty by a Deputy Secretary.

The purpose was to have a primary point of contact to not only bring together women veterans but also to bring together government, non-profit and private service providers to address these issues. For example we learned that in some cases women veterans, especially those unemployed or under employed, were lacking in proper attire required for a job interview. With Women's Deputy Secretary Lindsey Sin in the lead, herself a veteran of the US Navy, the need for the donation of various women's attire was communicated to churches, civic and professional women's organizations along with sororities, women college professors, and women state employees. This resulted in the planning and scheduling a clothing donation and distribution drive during the Women's conference.

The event was held at a major hotel in downtown Sacramento which donated space for the staging area at no cost. The request was for women to donate their personal items which had been purchased but never worn and probably would not be, such as new tagged items hanging in their closets or "gently worn" clothing; as Lindsey phrased them.

The specific requests were for dress clothing and accessories. The result was that several thousand items of women's dresses, suits, skirts, blouses, coats, sweaters, scarves, hand bags, shoes, hats, pieces of costume jewelry and other clothing items suitable for job interview were collected.

Additionally, upon learning of the purpose of the event several department stores donated a sundry of personal items of clothing from their new inventory. Deputy Secretary Sin had recruited an army of women volunteers from the above groups to assist.

The hotel mezzanine space was cordoned off into fitting rooms with mirrors and fashion experts donated their time to coordinate outfits. Everything was provided free of charge with shopping bags and clothing bags also provided.

AMERICAN LEGION V.I.P. POST #1

One achievement that brought me personal satisfaction was becoming co-founder of the first ever in the nation American Legion V.I.P. Post #1. This was a Veterans in Prison Post (V.I.P.) organized at the California Women's Prison in Chino. The West Los Angeles Veteran Home Chaplain Rabbi Dov Cohen had the brain-child and I had the resources and means. This was collaboration at its best.

There were a sizable number of women veterans in prisons for a sundry of crimes most of whom will be released at some point. Many of them we learned would qualify for Federal VA benefits upon release. Some were even receiving veteran disability benefits prior to incarceration which, under VA Rules, were reduced to 10 percent once convicted and sentenced but would be resumed at the previous level once released. Many had no understanding that their reduced benefit was being held in trust by the VA to be provided to them upon release, but, only if this was known to them and requested.

In order to establish and activate the Post all of the in-mate veterans were requested to become members of the American Legion, at no cost, and elect officers as all Posts do. A Post activation ceremony was held at the facility, totally supported by the Warden and also by the Secretary of the Department of Corrections and Rehabilitation in Sacramento.

A color guard had been formed by the veterans themselves and conducted several practice sessions. The highlight was the raising of the American Flag in the plaza of the prison with all of the veterans standing at attention in formation just as they had learned to do when serving in their respective military services. Although there was an American flag on a flag pole at the entrance to the prison an America flag had not adorned the plaza flag pole in several years.

The women veterans received great applause from the non-veterans looking on. Following the ceremony a reception was held in the recreation hall sponsored by the Pacific Palisades American Legion Post. This Post also provided the new prison flag, white gloves for the color guard and American Legion caps for all new members. They also paid for the membership fees.

During the process of identifying the number of women veteran incarcerated in the state we learned that the largest number of veterans in the country was still Viet Nam Era veterans comprising over 40 per cent of the total.

HOUSING A HOMELESS VETERAN FAMILY

During my tenure we always wanted to set the example for taking care of veterans. An example of this was when Blanche and I took into our home a homeless veteran and his family. This young former US Marine and his pregnant wife found themselves with no place to live after him losing his job and not having funds to rent.

I learned of his plight while attending the State American Legion Convention alerted by a local veteran advocate. The family was residing in a residential third class motel and would be evicted the next day. He had arranged monetary veteran benefits which would begin two weeks hence. Without missing a step I telephoned Blanche and apprised her of the situation and we agreed to temporarily house the family.

Sight unseen, I telephoned the veteran, who was not at the conference, who in turn telephoned Blanche and between the two of them arranged for him and his family to drive to our home. This occurred while I was out of town attending the convention and was due to take a return flight to Sacramento that afternoon which I did.

They temporarily became part of our family. A few months later after they had moved into their own residence Blanche was invited to the baby shower given for the wife.

"UNBROKEN"

One of my final duties as California Veteran Affairs Secretary was to represent Governor Brown at the memorial service for World War Two veteran and former prisoner of war Lou Zamperini. Captain Louis Silvie "Louie" Zamperini had been a pilot whose airplane was shot down by the Japanese over the Pacific. After surviving 47 days on a raft he was "rescued" by the Japanese and held captive for several years with a harrowing experience. His life and prison camp ordeal was chronicled in the book and later the movie "Unbroken" by Laura Hillenbrand.

Governor Brown authorized a resolution and scroll on behalf of the People of California and directed me to make the presentation at the service which was held at the football stadium of Torrance High School, Lou's alma mater. The framed certificate was presented to his son and daughter. The event was attended by approximately 5,000 citizens.

While in captivity, the former USC track athlete and Olympian was housed in a prisoner of war camp commanded by his Japanese American USC fraternity brother. The American-born student had gone to Japan before the war to visit relatives and was detained by the government when war was declared. He was involuntarily conscripted into the Japanese Army and due to his college education was forced to take a commission and assigned as a POW Camp Commander.

Though he readily recognized Captain Zamperini as his college chum he made no provisions to allow any reduced harsh treatment. As a note when I was attending San Pedro High School as a member of the track team our rival school was Banning High School in Wilmington. The Banning High School Track Coach was Captain Zamperini's brother Pete Zamperini.

NATIONAL VETERANS CONFERENCE

As Cal Vet Secretary I invited my counterparts from the other 49 states and the five territories to California for an information sharing conference on veterans. California had more veterans than in any state and we also had more veterans homes, more stand-downs and more programs directed at veterans. Additionally we had mastered the way to reduce the waiting time for disability payments. The purpose was to share some of California's successes.

With the financial assistance of Mr. Ed Roski, identified earlier, the event was held at the Manchester Hyatt Hotel in downtown San Diego and was extremely successful with almost all of the states participating. Also participating was a full array of staff from the US Department of Veteran Affairs including the newly appointed USDVA Secretary, the Honorable Robert McDonald.

The late February weather was ideal quickly drawing attendees from the east and mid-west. Several attendees were accompanied by their spouses and some brought their school age children for a mid-year vacation. San Diego was the ideal location as it had a large active military presence with the US Navy, the Marine Corps, an Army National Guard Brigade and the nation's largest veteran stand-down was held there annually. Unfortunately San

Diego also was home to the largest homeless veteran population, per capita, in the nation.

I also invited the Secretary's name sake Mr. Robert (Bobby Mac) McDonald, Chairman of the Orange County Veterans Council and member of various other veteran organizations. Bobby had been very successful in designing and implementing county veteran programs and served on California's Community College Board of Trustees when several of the Veteran Resource Centers had been established. Additionally he had been instrumental as part of the team with starting the planning process for the California State Veterans Cemetery in Orange County noted.

SENIOR LEGISLATOR CONFRONTATION

All is not smooth in every job and I can cite at least one confrontational experienced while Secretary and it involved a senior member of the State Legislature. Housing Bond Funds were held by the California Department of Veterans Affairs which, since 1924, had always been earmarked for financing veteran private home purchases. Our bonds are sold on Wall Street and at the time of the incident we possessed a $1.2 billion bond portfolio.

The senior Legislative leader requested that I visit his office to discuss transferring some of the funds to another state agency which financed housing for civilians. I reminded him, politely, that the funds were only earmarked for veterans. In his very heated response he suggested (almost demanded) that half of the money be transferred to the Housing Agency which already had millions of unused funds available to the general public. In his opinion, transferring half the funds would still allow sufficient funds for veterans.

I informed him that the voluntary transfer of funds was not going to happen on my watch and that I doubted the Governor would even approve such a transaction. His remark then was that he was going to draft a Bill for the upcoming election so the People of California could have their say and he did so.

At the next election the ballot measure passed primarily because the political advertisements carried a story that the money was available for civilian housing at no expense to the state but failing to mention that unused funds were available. With the vote, $600.000.000 was transferred with no additional fanfare. This infuriated the Governor, leaders of the veteran community and myself. In that same election the termed out Legislator ran for another office and lost. As of this writing the funds sit idle and have not been tapped as previous funds have not been resourced out.

CHAPTER 83 A REAR VIEW

I had a deep connection with Dr. Martin Luther King where he remarked *"I have been to the mountain top."* While my life in no way compares to his, indeed far from it, there is indeed a connection. I have been climbing my own mountain. Looking down once in a while encourages me to continue looking up.

Since I had no experience in mountaineering and did not possess the requisite equipment to climb the mountain I have depended upon the encouragement of family and friends to assist me to scale that peak. Climbing has not easy and being somewhat out of condition I often rested along the way while even considering discontinuing the climb a time or two but those same family members and true friends offered so much encouragement that I continued on the upward journey. I am not there yet. To quote Nelson Mandela, *"I have discovered the secret that after climbing a great hill; one only finds that there are many more hills to climb."*

RETIREMENT ACTIVITIES

Over the course of my marriage to Blanche we experienced many exciting adventures, especially when celebrating our anniversary. For that we always wanted to get away from the area and several times we were able to do just that. We had weekends at our favorite Bed and Breakfast cottage in the Wine Country, weekends in Las Vegas and San Diego as well as weekends in San Francisco. Several times we rented a beach house in Port Hueneme where we celebrated in seclusion with the nearby waves thrashing about. Weekends in Palm Springs at our favorite resort were always nice during the winter and spring of the year.

In full retirement Blanche and I were able to experience the luxuries of time that had been difficult to grasp earlier. I had been working since I began selling buckets of oranges more than sixty five years earlier.

Blanche had retired after having been a teacher for 37 years as well as serving simultaneously in the Army National Guard nearly 25 years.

What we did not want to do was become so committed to projects and organizations so as not to have time for ourselves. For this reason I chose only a few endeavors. Some of these were to continue my service on the Board and as an Adjunct Lecturer at the University of Southern California's Price School of Public Policy and continue my service on California Marymount University's Long Range Planning Committee.

The others were short term. I was already serving my final term of office as President of the British United Services Club of Los Angeles where I had been a member since 2000 and Blanche since 2007. I continued there and anxiously looked forward to continuing my membership but with no responsibilities of elected office. Also my tenure as an Ambassador and Board Member for St. Mary's Hospital was coming to an end and I was serving in my final term as a Board Member of Vision Quest National.

During my adult lifetime, I have served on the boards of over 25 volunteer, community, non-profit, fraternal and religious organizations, many times serving on several boards simultaneously. I did these things for two reasons. The first was to support the organization by committing my experience and skills for the betterment of their mission, goals and objectives. The second reason was personal and that was to allow me to learn and grow. This has always been important to me. I am always learning.

In order to give the best of me and to exert all of my energies to an organization I made it a personal policy to not serve more than two, sometimes three years with each organization. This allowed me to spread whatever talents I possessed and making it possible for others to give of themselves. Also after two or three years I would no longer have the drive and zeal I would have had when appointed to each respective board.

Retirement allowed me to frequently rerun my favorite movies of all time (too many times according to

Blanche); South Pacific, The Longest Day, God Father Parts I, II & III, Patton, Casa Blanca and others.

I had previously given up golfing and had cashed in my almost one million pennies ($10,000) and gifted the funds to Mark over time. I had begun collecting them at age nine while selling newspapers and most had been in storage vats.

I have a reservoir of over 200 record albums collected over a period of many years. My plan was not to convert them to CDs but rather purchase a record player capable of playing the 33 and a third discs.

Retirement allowed me to resume my Friday mornings coffee klatch with my two good friends Otto and Kenny (pseudonyms), both semi-retired attorneys. Otto specialized in divorces and Kenny specialized in real estate matters. During our very informal discussions developing methodology to solve the world's problems I also heard enough legal discussion to probably pass the Bar Exam without having attended law school.

This informal gathering was proof positive that as Americans we can get along without exercising much effort. Here were three common sense adult individuals of differing back grounds; middle class and upper class: different religions, espousing take to the bank methodology which could solve many existing world problems. Our upbringing and being products of different school systems, public and private, made no difference in our opinions. And although our take on politics and governance differed we always respected one another's opinion and views. To measure whether or not either one of us harbored any desire to make the trio a duo we always expressed that we were looking forward to the next meeting.

UNIVERSITY OF SOUTHERN CALIFORNIA

I earned a Masters' Degree from USC, have been an active member of the alumni association for many years while financially supporting their Army Reserve Officer Training Corps (ROTC) Scholarship Fund. Additionally I had served as Chairman of the Army ROTC Advisory Board for several years and finally being designated as Chairman Emeritus. With this, in 2012, I was invited to deliver the Commencement Speech at USC's Price School of Public Policy Graduate Center in Sacramento, though I had received my Masters' degree from the main campus in Los Angeles.

Following that I had been offered the position of Adjunct Lecturer at that campus which I eagerly accepted. My frequent trips to interact with bright graduate students and share my experiences has been personally rewarding. Most of them were mid-career professional.

VISION QUEST NATIONAL

I have had the pleasure of having served on the Board of Directors of Vision Quest. Vision Quest National is a residential program which serves hundreds of at-risk youth annually. With residential facilities in several states it is rooted in Native American culture and traditions all designed to foster growth and personal responsibility by participants. Equine therapy is central to many of the program locations where each participant is provided a horse, trained to ride and exercise 24/7 care of the equine.

Part of the program includes participating in wagon train rides in various parts of the country. Prior to my joining the board the longest trek was a 2,000 mile journey from Southern Arizona to Pennsylvania. That wagon train itself stretched over two miles including chuck wagons and first class modern support wheeled vehicles. For the most part back country roads and local highways were used.

Shorter treks were designed to teach new arrivals the art and science of equine husbandry. Outfitted in replica uniforms reminiscent of the Buffalo Soldiers of the late 1800's they are often seen in local parades throughout the country.

Our Board of Directors meetings were occasionally held in the wilderness with each member astride a horse or mule and accompanied by spouses. This was similar to what the youth experienced. Blanche and I enjoyed the outings as they were a break from my traditional suit and tie routine. Blanche's personal mount was a mule named Bishop which she enjoyed riding in the Arizona Desert as it was sure-footed and my mount was a horse named Rancho. Blanche was as comfortable in her western outfit as was I. She looked as elegant astride a mule as she did when in the board room wearing an Armani business suit.

Blanche riding "Bishop" in western outfit and boots

I had the honor and privilege of participating in a US Government sponsored ceremonial horseback ride in Montana where we crossed the Little Bighorn River and rode up into the Custer Battlefield. I was totally outfitted in my replica Buffalo Soldier 10th US (Horse) Cavalry Uniform as worn by the Buffalo Soldiers 140 years earlier.

There were two columns of riders, one consisting of US Cavalry Buffalo Soldier rein actors and the other Native Americans riding bare back with only a loin cloth for clothing. This was the first time horses had been permitted on the Custer Battlefield in a century. There were approximately 100 riders in all.

A very interesting phenomenon occurred during the ride. With all of the cavalry riders similarly attired in period uniform including Stetson or Kepi head gear, including a bandana covering the mouth and nose from the dust, it was nearly impossible to determine that one of our riders was female, an accomplished equestrian and daughter of the Vision Quest CEO and ride organizer.

Half way on the ride one of the Native American riders began yelling and pointing at a rider and now for the first time discovered by them to be a female. When this occurred several other Native American riders galloped up to the female and yelled for her to get off of the battlefield. We were not aware that Native Americans considered the area as "Sacred Grounds" and their belief was that if a female rode there it would be disrespectful to their ancestors. With this now known she departed from the march and returned to the encampment. She then drove to the terminus of the ride.

At the conclusion of the trek a monument was dedicated in honor of the Native Americans killed by General Custer and the 7th US (Horse) Cavalry in the Battle of the Little Bighorn in 1876. This was the name Americans gave the battle but the Native Americans called it the Battle of the Greasy Grass, the name coined by the Lakota Tribe to describe the greasy look of the grass near the battle site. The Lakota Indian tribe supported by the Cheyenne and Arapaho tribes fought the battle.

The new monument stood beside a previous monument erected in 1925 honoring Cavalrymen killed in that battle. Finally, after many years of discussion, it was arranged for the tribes to have a monument since they too were Americans.

INTERESTING ADVENTURES

In 2014, Blanche and I traveled to New York City for a week to watch the Macy's Thanksgiving Day Parade and take in shows on Broadway which we did. Over the course of four days we saw four shows and enjoyed them all including the Rockettes' Special Christmas Performance at Radio City Music Hall. Our favorite was the play "Beautiful" which was a parity on the life and times of singer-song writer Carol King, my all-time favorite. I have been known to play her well-known CD "Tapestry" continuously. We enjoyed the performance so much that when it was reprised a year later in Los Angeles we were able to enjoy it in a second performance along with Mark and Rosalina as we had double dated and seen others with them.

It snowed during the Macy's parade but we had prepared for the weather. A hotel executive, daughter of friends, arranged our stay at her first class hotel in Times Square which was a short walk to the parade route. Our tour of Saint Patrick's Cathedral, though under reconstruction, was inspiring as well as were other sites.

In 2015 we traveled to Atlanta to attend the 149th Reunion of the Buffalo Soldiers, the Association of the 9th and 10th Horse Cavalry Regiments and the 27th and 28th Cavalry Regiments, organized in 1866. We able to join friends from across the country who also attended.

PASSING OF TWO BROTHERS

Sadly over the course of several prior years I lost two of my brothers, Charles and Darnell. Darnell, a Viet Nam veteran, passed away in 2001 and Charles passed away in 2009. Both brothers were close to me as they were to all of the family.

Charles was also a military veteran having served in the US Army twice, once when volunteering, serving at Fort Ord, California and again when being involuntarily recalled to active duty during the Berlin Crisis, serving at Fort Bragg, North Carolina. In civilian life he served as a Local President of the Communication Workers of America Union, for Ma Bell and later AT&T.

He was an ideal person to serve as a union organizer and leader as he was a progressive and believed in his causes which was quite often different from mine as a moderate. We very often had healthy discussions on a number of subjects of the day, him staking claim to his beliefs and me taking a more pragmatic approach. All in all we exercised brotherly love and respect for one another.

Charles was just 14 months my senior, so growing up and even in adult life we had some of the same friends, while Darnell, four years younger, had his own set of friends, many of them childhood

Gravett siblings at family event. Seated Alice, left, and Gloria. Standing left to right Phillip, Clarence (Curt), Peter, Leon, Harry, William & Melvin (Duke).

friends and Viet Nam war buddies. He had been employed by two separate utility companies. Both brothers were married with adult children and grandchildren and their loss came unexpectedly and pulled at the heart strings of all who knew them and they are missed. Just as our parents were, both brothers were interred at Green Hills Memorial Park in Ranch Palos Verdes just about three miles from where they spent their youth.

Charles had a knack to paste monikers on classmates, friends, acquaintances and strangers. He was buried along with his signature safari helmet hat which I had purchased for him as a gift many years earlier. This signature head piece always stood him out at the California Interscholastic Track Championship Meet and other sporting events where he wore it. I was disheartened that his very best friend David was not selected as a Pall Bearer. While in junior high school Charles chose to add the letter "e" to the end of his last name which he maintained for the remainder of his life.

Darnell, I often remark, was wounded in Viet Nam and returned home to pass away. My remarks were centered on the fact he and so many other young soldiers serving in that war brought the war home with them in the way of mental, emotional, social and medical scars. So from my perspective they all should have been designated as killed in action and their next of kin so compensated by the federal government.

I can relate some of Darnell's life to passages found in Tom Brokaw's book, "*A lucky Life Interrupted*" where he writes*: "Streams and rivers are like life – they have a source and a destination. They have stretches of calmness and turmoil. No day on the river is ever exactly the same, as it is not in life."* I will never get over losing my brothers and I won't as they will always be remembered.

CHAPTER 84 REFLECTIONS ON A LIFETIME OF WORK

People are gifted in a myriad of ways such as having a musical inclination, excel in sports, lead a union, teach, clergy, become a chef, lab technician and others. My gift was to work at excelling at whatever was expected of me and I consider my achievements are the result of hard work. Through it all like most, I had weaknesses. One was to procrastinate at projects but always meeting deadlines with good efficient results. Much of my success can be owed to subordinate staff at all levels who possessed outstanding organizing skills which allowed everyone to succeed.

As an Agency Secretary in the Governor's Cabinet I made every attempt to allow my Undersecretaries and Deputy Secretaries to address issues within their realm of responsibility rather than becoming personally involved. Most management courses espouse that the manager hire someone smarter than them so they can walk away knowing subordinates can be trusted to do the job and be sure to give credit to whom it is due.

With respect to the veterans that I served, I want to believe in my heart that I made a positive difference in their lives and the lives of their families, at least I made every effort to do so. As they move forward in their lives the future will reveal whether or not this is so.

l am very proud of my personal work ethic and have had some sort of employment since age ten when I was selling oranges door to door for fifty cents a bucket. By age 13, I was selling newspapers on the waterfront. Before age16 I had graduated to washing dishes at a local restaurant after school and on weekends. I held that job until l joined the Army National Guard at age 17 and upon returning home from active duty in the Army a friend assisted me in acquiring a job as a blue printer at age 20.

Upon turning 21 I was appointed to the Los Angeles Police Academy and remained with the police department until retirement at age 43. My law enforcement career was concurrent with service in the Army National Guard. Upon retirement there I returned to fulltime military duty serving at home and in numerous countries around the world before retiring at age 63.

At age 64 the entrepreneurial spirit bit me and Blanche and I formed Gravett & Associates, a small veteran owned business. We focused on emergency preparedness and homeland security planning with business lines in the private sector, especially private and parochial schools and commercial office buildings. Other business opportunities took us to China on two occasions, one to Beijing and another to Shanghai.

With a small staff of four I was quickly joined by three partners. A short time later we merged with Traiden Global Solutions where I served as CEO until age 69. That same year, I was invited by Governor Jerry Brown to serve in his Cabinet as Secretary of the

Brother Curt and his bicycle.

California Department of Veteran Affairs. I served the Governor during the four years of his first term then elected to retire at age 74.

I must confess that the first time I was ever paid for work was when, at about age seven or eight, my oldest brother Clarence (Curt) enticed me to accompany him on his paper route at the handsome sum of a nickel. To earn the nickel I delivered the papers directly on his customer's front porches. While on the route Curt's news paper bag was draped over the back fender of his bicycle which my father had given him on his 13th birthday. Me being very young I suspect that Curt walked the bicycle rather than riding so I could keep up with him while making my short steps.

POLITICS

Along the political spectrum I had always been a moderate and long-time registered Democrat and at one time co-founder of the Los Angeles Harbor Intercultural Democratic Club. Along the way I had worked the campaigns of several Democratic candidates for local, state and national offices however in later years, I found myself drifting away from the planks of the Democratic Party on several key issues which were of primary concern to me.

For example Democrats began espousing the legalization of marijuana for which I was opposed. I had seen the harmful effects of the drug on a few of my childhood friends as a young person growing up in public housing projects. Later, while enforcing the law, I routinely encountered the drug when arresting criminals for illegal possession and others for driving under the influence some causing accidents with injuries. Although some research had indicated that marijuana might be useful in the treatment for pain and some medical uses it was inconclusive.

Once the law was passed authorizing marijuana for medical use history shows there was quick widespread abuse by patients and their doctors writing prescriptions. Due to rising premiums for medical malpractice insurance some medical professionals closed their private practices and resorted to just writing prescriptions for medical marijuana for patients claiming minor aches and pains. This was because the return on investment was so lucrative.

Another plank which I had a differing view from the Democratic Party was its rallying cry to allow undocumented young immigrants, "Dreamers", who were brought to the country by their parents as youngsters, to qualify for in-state tuition and scholarships at public colleges and universities. I was not opposed to this and in fact supported it. But this was at the same time the Democratic controlled State Legislature was denying in-state tuition to military veterans, including wounded veterans in some cases, as well as active duty military personnel recently transferred to California and having been in the state less than a year.

My thoughts were that Dreamers who had spent most of their life here and raised here should be afforded these privileges but they should also be extended to our military personnel and our veterans who have served so well. To not treat military personnel and veterans as equal to Dreamers was irreprehensible.

My parents Clarence and Alice Gravett had always prided themselves in working to support their family and never having been on the dole. California was the leading state in the nation when it came to welfare payments. Welfare was so plentiful in the state that it inhibited recipients from working even though they were able and there were available jobs. Some transients and their families were said to have moved to California for the sole purpose of receiving the welfare rainbow.

The majority Democratic legislature voted annual raises for welfare recipients and provided a special increase in payments to unmarried single mothers when having additional children. This unnerved me. Additionally, Welfare for Work Legislation was routinely defeated in the Democratic controlled State legislature.

Jobs had always been plentiful in California if you wanted to work. For example, in the 1990s the Sunday edition of the Los Angeles Times newspaper classified ad section listed over 5,000 available jobs. Most of these only requiring a high school diploma and many not requiring any education or specialized skills at all. Also, McDonalds and other fast food outlets had signs posted advertising help wanted.

Another plank which the Democratic majority Legislature was moving forward and which I disagreed was proposing Bills to allow undocumented immigrants to apply for and receive a California driver's license or California identification card which could be used to register to vote. There would be no controls nor any system in place to insure that the applicants had insurance to register their automobiles as required by law.

Another measure put forth was to allow anyone to register to vote without producing documentation that they were American citizens. If this was done there would be no need to produce identification at the voting booth which, in itself, was always controversial. Food stamps were always plentiful to almost anyone.

With all of these differences and with my moderate political philosophy I made the personal decision to leave the Democratic Party as it had already left me. I reregistered as a Republican believing that their political philosophy was more in concert with my own. It wasn't long afterwards that the California Republican Party had endorsed almost all of these same social issues themselves.

Whether this was done as a method to garner additional registrants to the Party or to accommodate their base was not known. What was known to me, however, was that there was no standing reason to continue my registration in the Republican Party as society was changing and I realized that I too had to change.

With this I reregistered as a member of the Democratic Party. During the interim I had continued to support candidates for elective office that matched my moderate political philosophy. My reentry into the Democratic Party was timely as the Republican Party was selecting what many viewed as a Far Right Extremist and Racist, nominating him as the Party's choice and who ran and was elected President.

Let justice run down like a river
and righteousness like a mighty stream.
Amos 5:24.

At times, however politics can be non-partisan. At the time I was a registered Democrat I was appointed to a County Commission by a Republican County Supervisor and while I was a registered Republican I was appointed to the Cabinet by a Democratic Governor.

It was interesting to see how members of my circle of Democratic friends reacted upon reading that I was a member of the Republican Party in the Governor's press release upon my appointment. There were attitudinal changes as perhaps some believed, wrongly so, that I supported all of the planks of that Party, that I would vote for any Republican running for office and perhaps also assuming that all Republicans vote for Republicans and that all Democrats vote for Democrats. Perhaps some opined they would offend me if they mentioned anything negative regarding a Republican elected official. Perhaps blood is never as thick as it was thought to be.

Peter's with Vice President Al Gore.

In 1997, I was pleased to have received a letter of appreciation from the French Ambassador to the United States. He was acknowledging my assistance in arranging presentations of a French military decoration to several American soldiers who had served in France during World War One. Some were more than 100 years of age.

In 2000, I had been presented with the Eme' Award by the Black Alumni Association of the University of Southern California. This award is presented to distinguished black graduates who are then inducted into the African American Alumni Hall of Fame. My sister Alice and my brother Command Sergeant Major Melvin supported me by attending.

In 2005, I, along with African American United States Marine Corps Major General Jackson, had been honored by the Orange County Black Chamber of Commerce at the Presidential Library in Yorba Linda for exceptional public

Cornerstone for Redding Veterans Home

service in the military. I again received this recognition in

2013, for exceptional public service in government. Some of my friends attended.

In 2014 Long Beach City College inducted me into their Hall of Fame, along with a five other graduates who had distinguished themselves since graduation. The Honors luncheon was held on campus in the multi-purpose complex and was a grand affair. I was fortunate to have had the support of my family along with my Pastor, Dr. Felton Simpson, and his wife Ozie.

In 2016, I was honored by the California League of Community Colleges as an inductee into the State Hall of Fame. The induction ceremony was held at the Marriot Hotel in San Francisco. Blanche accompanied me there.

Major General Peter Gravett aboard the USS Iowa

Also in 2016, invitations were extended by California State University Long Beach to my siblings and several friends inviting them to attend a ceremonial dinner at the Hyatt Hotel on Long Beach where I was to be introduced as the Distinguished Alum from the School of Health and Human Services and given a place into the University's Hall of Fame. Blanche and I were very much pleased that my brother Leon, his wife Vernette, as well as son Mark and my daughter-in-law Rosalina attended as did 20 of my police, military, veterans and club friends. Some of these individuals and I have been friends for a number of years and we have always supported each other in some way.

Two weeks later, in 2016, and at the invitation of the University President, I delivered the commencement speech to graduates at the University's School of Health and Human Services, the school from which I graduated with a Bachelor's Degree in Criminology.

This was the fourth commencement speech I had delivered at a college or university, the other three being University of Southern California's Price School of Public Policy Graduate Studies Center, Sacramento as mentioned earlier, Compton Community College and Cypress College.

In 2017, The Los Angeles County Board of Supervisors again recognized my life-time body of work during a presentation at a February Black History Month panel presentation. I was honored by the Allied Council of Veteran Organizations in the City of Monrovia where I delivered the key note speech on Memorial Day.

Major General Gravett's Office visit with South Korean Secretary of Defense who Presented Green Vase on Table.

Also in 2017 I, along with 12 other citizens from the Greater Long Beach area were celebrated at the Founder's Dinner of National Association for the Advancement of Colored People Annual Gala. I was recognized with the Ernest McBride, Sr. Award. Mr. McBride has been previously mentioned in these writings and I was deeply honored to have my name associated with him.

In 2018, I was the recipient of the Admiral Samuel L. Gravely Leadership and Service Award presented aboard the Battle Ship Iowa now a floating museum home ported in San Pedro. Oddly enough the location was just three blocks from my former home in the public housing projects across the street. The Battle Ship was now a floating museum.

This award, which is conferred annually, recognizes African American leaders in Southern California who exemplify the trailblazing courageous service of the late U.S. Navy three star Vice Admiral. Not only was he the first African American US Navy Admiral but also the first three star Admiral and Fleet Commander. Earlier in his career he had been stationed aboard the USS Iowa when it was in service.

This honor was very special as several years prior to his passing I had the honor of meeting him. This was in Washington DC at the annual Fall Gathering, a dinner which honors all African American Generals and Admirals. The first year that I qualified to attend him and I had a brief

MG Gravett receiving Admiral Gravely award from Jane Johnson, right, organizer of the event and Blanche Gravett, left.

conversation. The honor was also special as Blanche and I sailed aboard the Battle Ship Iowa when it cruised into the Los Angeles Harbor en route to its final berth.

Admiral Gravely event announcement

Another award recognition in 2018 which I received was the Crystal Eagle Award from the Los Angeles County African American Employees Association (LACAAEA). The Black History Month Celebration was co-sponsored by the Los Angeles County Board of Supervisors and was presented for service to the country and the county.

In general I have been blessed to have had such a supportive family who took time from their personal schedules by attending many of the numerous promotion ceremonies, changes of command events and other military gatherings such as they had support my brother Melvin at his military events. We both have been very fortunate and on behalf of Melvin and myself we offer sincere thanks.

CHAPTER 86 ACKNOWLEDGEMENTS

First, I thank God for all of his blessings and I give all honor and glory to Him. Without Him nothing would have been possible and with Him all things have been possible.

I acknowledge my wife Blanche McClure Gravett who showed me I could love again and who provided the inspiration for me to act and move forward on my inclination to write. Her creative talents as a life-long educator and a senior military officer in her own right encouraged me to codify my childhood and my adult experiences which she had listened to for a few years. Blanche provided the initial and continuous edits and offered welcomed critical comment as I delved into the mechanics of writing.

I acknowledge my son Mark who by his initial writings of poems, prose and verse raised the flame in me to follow his lead. In many respects this book is for him. Mark has been my best friend in life and as noted earlier, that he served as my Best Man when I married Blanche and I served as his Best Man when he married Rosalina. I truly believe no father and son could be any closer. We meet for breakfast frequently and secure our bonding.

I acknowledge Victoria A. Hudson, M.F.A., published author, veteran and veterans advocate who knew very little of my past but repeatedly encouraged me to put pen to paper as we worked side by side on veteran projects.

I especially want to acknowledge John Whitehead, an accomplished computer technician and later a friend, who worked with me throughout the penning of the book and who was always available to quickly troubleshoot and override my computer technical difficulties which were many. John also offered suggestions on format and structure. He became a regular at our home.

Keith Bushey, a friend and author of several books, a retired senior law enforcement official and a retired US Marine Corps Reserve Colonel and combat veteran pointed me in the right direction.

Robert Schriebman, Esq. A Major in the Judge Advocate General Corps of the California State Military Reserve and a personal friend of many years. In addition to being a top notch attorney and one of America's premier experts on taxation in which field he has an earned Doctorate he is the author of over 20 books and manuscripts and he unknowingly supported my efforts by providing copies of his own works which invigorated thought. As an ordained Clergyman Rabbi Schriebman also served as my mentor and counselor.

I especially want to acknowledge and thank Marcia McKeon for her untiring research assistance to uncover portions of the Gravett, Harris and Campbell family's trees with which I had difficulty. Marcia, a friend of both Blanche and mine, was an accomplished and devoted researcher of family histories, an expert actually, and had developed her own personal methods to circumvent dead ends. All of her work in assisting me was of a volunteer nature.

In addition to those mentioned I stand on the shoulders of trail blazers such as the Buffalo Soldiers, Tuskegee Airmen, 555th Parachute Regiment, US Navy Golden 13, Montfort Marines and the 6888 Central Postal Battalion, the World War Two unit of the Negro Women's Army Corps, all whom laid pavement for me to achieve in the military.

Acknowledged also is California's Governor Edmund G. "Jerry" Brown, who selected me to serve in his Cabinet and entrusted me with the leadership of a state agency.

Special recognition goes to the late Los Angeles Policeman Morris Barton Gilmore, Serial #5080, his late wife the late Policewoman Chloe Gilmore, and to his police partner Policewoman Betty Bowden, Serial #7668. All not only coordinators of the LAPD's Deputy Auxiliary Police (DAP) youth program but they also provided superb guidance during my pre-teen and teen years and carefully watched the paths I was taking.

I need to recognize my friends who, without their friendship life would not have been the same. Finally it is imperative that I recognize my siblings, both older and younger, who allowed me to grow along with them as I followed their lead.

So this writing then was an effort to lay out to the reader the full story of Peter James Gravett and to connect the dots to what they knew of me and what was foreign and I hope I succeeded. What the reader should also know was that my success has been my family's success and I always made a point to spread the recognition.

SUCCESS OWED TO MILITARY TRAIL BLAZERS

Colonel Charles Young, the third Black Cadet to graduate from the United States Military Academy at West Point and the first Black US Army officer to hold the ranks of Captain, Major, Lieutenant Colonel and Colonel.

Brigadier General Benjamin 0. Davis, Sr. The first black US Army General Officer.

Lieutenant General Benjamin O. Davis, Jr. The second black US Army General Officer who, after retirement, eventually held the four star rank of General in the United States Air Force, ex post facto .

General Daniel "Chappie" James, United States Air Force. The first black Four Star General in the US Military.

General Roscoe Robinson, Jr. the first black Four Star General in the US Army

General Colin Powell, the first black Chairman of the Joint Chiefs of Staff.

Vice Admiral Samuel L. Gravely, Jr. the first black U.S. Navy Admiral and the first black U.S. Naval Officer to command a U.S. Navy ship and a U.S. Navy Fleet.

Major General Harry Brooks, the first Regular Army black Division Commander.

Major General Calvin C. Franklin, the first black US Army General in the California Army National Guard.

Major General Paul D. Monroe, Jr. the first black Adjutant General of the California National Guard.

Major General Mary Kight, the first female General in the California National Guard, Army or Air, and the first female

General to serve as Adjutant General of the California National Guard.

Brigadier General Hazel W. Johnson, the first black female General Officer in the United States Army.

1LT Phillip Lipscomb, my first Company Commander and the first black US Army officer I served under.

Private First Class Clarence Gravett, Sr. US Army Air Corps WWII, my dad.

Command Sergeant Major Melvin E. Gravett, my brother, at one time the youngest Command Sergeant Major in the history of the 40th Infantry Division (Mechanized).

These fine professional military men and women each had a part in shaping me as a person and shaping my military career, some in absentia.

CHAPTER 87 EPILOGUE

Throughout my years in military and government several national and world milestones occurred. Dare I say a few of them include blacks being given the right to vote in the south, women's rights were legislated, a black was elected US Senator, a black served as Chairman of the Joint Chiefs of Staff and our country went to war an unprecedented number of times. Some wars declared and some not.

Man walked on the moon, man remained in space for weeks, an airplane circumvented the world non-stop, the Boston Red Sox won the World Series for the first time in 101 years and the Chicago Cubs won the World Series for the first time in 107 years.

Other milestones included gays being openly permitted to serve in the military, one US President was assassinated and two others had attempt on their lives and a civil rights icon was gunned down and killed.

Three civil rights workers were kidnapped in the south and murdered by racist law enforcement officers and members of the Klu Klux Klan.

For the first time a woman became a serious candidate for President and for the first time a woman was nominated on a major party ticket for Vice President.

During this time the Los Angeles Police Department allowed women to promote above the rank of Sergeant and blacks to promote above the rank of Lieutenant. It also permitted blacks and Whites to patrol in the same police car eliminating segregation there.

California passed a Fair Housing Law which permitted all citizens, including blacks, to purchase a home in a neighborhood of their choice.

A national law was passed requiring all public schools be integrated and White southern colleges and universities began to allow their sports teams to play teams with black players.

A volcano erupted in the Continental United States for the first time in hundreds of years and terrorist events began to pepper the landscape.

Barak Obama, a black man, was elected President of the United States and a black Ballerina became the principal dancer of New York City Ballet.

Finally, a black General became the first Army National Guard Division Commander in the 225 year history of the National Guard of the United States. The audacity of a nappy haired boy from a public housing project in the Los Angeles Port community of San Pedro believing he could be a two star Army General and later a member of a Governor's Cabinet and attending and graduating from three of the most prestigious universities in the nation would be unimaginable. Only in America.

In the More than almost three years it took in researching and writing this book numerous Interviews were conducted, those meaningful are identified in the bibliography.

My research and travels took me to the Gravette, Arkansas, Little Rock, Arkansas, Scott, Arkansas, Camp Roberts Museum, Camp San Luis Obispo Museum, Los Angeles Police Department Records Archives, Mormon Church Genealogy Centers, University of California at Los Angeles School of Planning Archives-Channel Heights Records Section, collective interviews with former residents of Channel Heights, 40th Infantry Division records and published books and articles.

One of the joys of the writing and research was it that allowed me to reconnect with friends and relations of the past and to understand various events with a clearer view.

Regrets? As vocalist Frank Sinatra once sang, *"I've had a few"* but they pale compared to the fun filled exciting adventures given me in a lifetime of events. Would I have chosen other paths to follow? The answer is a resounding no. I choose not to look in the rear view mirror of life but in the windshield.

My legacy: Various others have expressed to me that *"I have always made a point to lift up others and bring them along with me."*

From The Earth We Rise.
To The Earth We Return.
So Shall I Return to The Earth Soon...
"Walks With Wolves"

I have fought a good fight,
I have finished my course,
I have kept the faith:
"II timothy 4:7"

Epilogue
"Nothing Ever Remains the Same"
-Anonymous

I never forgot where I came from but the trek from East Garrison to the Ranch House was never expected to be quick but also it was never expected to take more than a century and a half. It was daunting. Out of shear curiosity I planned and took a trip down memory lane to visit the two points discussed in the title as well as in the book itself. The discovery was disheartening for one and reassuring with the other. I also connected with the Alexander Plantation in Scott, Arkansas which was discussed.

In reversing my Camp Roberts trek I visited the Ranch House first. Upon driving down Rancho House Road towards the edifice right away I sensed that the area itself had not been well kept as what once had been a narrow country road though asphalted it had deteriorated to the point whereby the thin layered asphalt had loosened to the point that it was primarily gravel. Also large patches of greenery had meandered through the crevasses where asphalt had once been and what remained of the now graveled road was partially overgrown with small patches of wild weed and other indigenous scrub.

Meandering further down the road toward the house the sight up ahead was disheartening as weeds had grown unabated surrounding the house on three sides; the backside patio being concrete but which was had numerous crack lines. The red tile Spanish roof shingles appeared worn and weathered which they were. Several were missing. The wooden window sills were cracked to the point that the mere touch would collect in the hand as tooth picks. Most were hanging carelessly.

Previously when the house was periodically occupied by humans, field mice had always been a problem. After all, it was in a wooded area and the only structure within a few miles to harbor their nesting. What had not changed was the mites were still about but now being very bold by not quickly scattering as humans approached.

Once inside the house the living room furniture which had been installed more than 50 years earlier, during the last remodeling, was still in place though with a very faded appearance with the look of sun-rot. In the bed rooms all of the bedding had been removed and smaller beds stacked in the corners of each room. The place had the look of a movie prop for westerns and only being used when a feature film was being made.

 The daytime visit was essential as all of the power had been shut off as well as the water source though the plumbing appeared to be intact. The 1970's something television set which was encased in a walnut cabinet was still in place. My recollection was that it had never been cable-ready and there were only two or three channels to be viewed on the grainy black and white picture.

I later learned that the Ranch House ceased being used following the earthquake,  centered in Paso Robles about 20 miles to the south, because of structural damage and the integrity of the foundation was questionable. Although listed on the California Historical Registry funds had never been ear marked for its' upkeep and repair by the California National Guard.

This was even though the camp itself had over the previous few years or so been infused with over $50 million of combined federal and state funds which allowed the old World War Two barracks, offices, mess halls and chapels to be demolished and newer ones constructed in their place. This was when the camp once again became a primary west coast Army training center for units and soldiers were preparing to deploy to Iraq and Afghanistan during those wars.

East Garrison on the other hand had never looked better. It was obvious that a share of the funding to upgrade facilities and to construct new ones at Camp Roberts was devoted to the East Garrison.

The World War Two era tents which had housed Colored soldiers and the two-story typical Army wooden barracks which had been constructed to house German and Italian Prisoners of War had long been demolished; the tents during the Korean War in

the early 1950s and the barracks demolished over time between the 1980s and the 1990s.

East Garrison had all but been abandoned from the 1980s forward except for the Material and Training Equipment Site (MATES) and storage facility which was thoroughly discussed earlier. The new East Garrison had recently re-paved roads, new barracks and administrative buildings, upgraded utilities, and what once had been and abandoned airfield for small fixed winged and rotary aircraft had a new look. It was an air field that was functional with all required FAA safety features build in.

CHAPTER 88 PARENTAL ADVICE

Too finally begin to conclude this work I will touch upon the best sage advice my parents ever gave me and advice I gave to my son. First my father and I offer apologies for not remembering the exact circumstances which it occurred.

As a young teenager I recall my father admonishing me to never position myself in a circumstance whereby I could be in jeopardy for being in the wrong place at the wrong time. This would be childhood misdeeds with other young boys which could result in unlawful activity such as malicious mischief which boys my age tended to engage in as a prank for them but had the propensity to wreak havoc, damages or injuries to others. The advice as voiced by him was *"if the house is on fire for me to quickly run out before I got burned."* This admonition has remained with me my entire life.

My mother's advice to me was more pointed and direct. Several times over the years and under the proper circumstances she would recite to me and probably to various others, including her other children, the *"Serenity"* prayer which asks: *"God grant me the serenity to accept the things I cannot change, the courage to change the things I can and the wisdom to know the difference."*

Perhaps she first stumbled across this saying on a greeting card, from a friend or from written document. In any event it apparently meant so much to her and was poignant enough that she memorized it and recited it often, again, when the circumstances were appropriate.

This prayer is often attributed to Reinhold Neibuhr, the American Theologian but actually it dates back to and attributed to Boethius, the Roman Philosopher (480-524 A.D.) and in some quarters it has been attributed to Roman Philosophy Cicero. In more modern times it was used by German military officers in World War Two with the prayer printed on small cards which they were ordered to carry at all times. This was the practice of Canadian soldiers as well.

Alcoholic Anonymous began using it in 1964 as well as various other organizations. It can be seen routinely as passages in management books and found on greeting cards. The phrase is just the first of four verses in the prayer, as identified by an historical record search and has also been codified as the second of five verses in another.

In any event the words have rang true to me over the years. Coming from my mother they were gospel and although my research found otherwise, I consider the words as hers and I have treated them as such. Many times in my professional life I was required to draw upon them for strength. To cite just one reoccurring circumstance the prayer frequently rushed to the forefront of my thinking when making decisions which would affect the more than 18,000 soldiers under my command.

Mark College Bound.

ADVICE TO MY SON MARK: A FINALITY

The best advice I ever gave to Mark was to *"Put a Tiger in your tank."* Although this was not original and probably came from a television commercial advertising a sugar coated breakfast cereal product or another commercial marketing a special brand of gasoline it fit the mood when I was telephoning him nightly from South Korea assisting him with his junior high school home work. I was suggesting that he get a move on and perform more individual research to discover what was required on a specific project and to discover his own answers rather than asking me for them. We reminisce about the phrase often.

Mark should know that for me being a member of a racial minority group growing up and even in adulthood I succeeded partly because I always believed I was the best or among the best and not inferior to anyone though I am not aware that Mark ever harbored these thoughts.

Mr. Mark Gravett

In the DAPs from age 11 to age 17 I rose through the ranks from Sergeant to Staff Inspector faster than any other teenager in my division. In the enlisted ranks in the Army National Guard I was promoted from Private E-1 to Sergeant First Class E-7 in less than 9 years where typically it took a soldier much longer. In the Army upon graduating from Officer Candidate School in a class starting with approximately 750 cadets I was among the 268 who successfully graduated and was commissioned a Second Lieutenant. Among that group I was the third to be promoted to Captain, the second to receive a promotion to Major and the first be to be promoted to Lieutenant Colonel.

By this time, the remaining number of class members had substantially dwindled but of those remaining I was the first to pin on the eagle of Colonel and the first (of only five) to be promoted to Brigadier General and, lastly, the first of only two to reach the two star rank of Major General. From East Garrison to the Ranch House, ah what a journey.

If you look for a book on a subject and you cannot find it, then it

has not been written. Write it.
Toni Morrison

FROM EAST GARRISON TO THE RANCH HOUSE AND BEYOND
SOURCES

- Archives, San Luis Obispo Telegraph-Tribune
- California National Guard Archives, Sacramento
- Camp Roberts Post Archives and Museum
- Camp San Luis Obispo Archives
- Compton, Ruth, *Interviews,* February 2016 & June 2017
- Cunnigan, Jimmy, Photographs, Channel Heights
- Department of Defense Form 214 dated
- Department of Veteran Affairs Benefit Document, File # 549521602, 344/PK dated 3 June 2015
- di Liana, Angela, *Source Document*, Channel Heights Resident, 1945-1947
- Documentary Film, *Prisoners in Paradise*
- Fitzgerald, Edward, *Interview*, November 26, 2016
- Garrison, Alice Mae Gravett, *Recorded Interview* April 3, 2008
- Garrison, Alice Mae Gravett, *Transcribed* Interview, July 31, 2008
- Goolsby, Ken, *Interview, May 27, 2017*
- Gordon, Ronnie, Channel Heights Resident 1947-1952, *Interview* March 15, 2016
- Gravett Sr., Clarence (Late) Interviews, Various Dates and times
- Gravett, Jr., Clarence (Curt) Interviewed December 1, 2017
- Gravett, Harrison, *Interview,* November 24, 2015
- Gravett, Leon, *Interview*, November 26, 20126 and various dates and times.
- Gravett, Melvin, *Interviews,* various dates and times 2016 & 2017
- Gray, John R. *Interview,* November 26, 2016

- King James Bible, *Book of Jeremiah (Leadership Principles)*
- McCoy, Lester, *Interview, May 24, 2017*
- McMaster, Gary, Master Sergeant (Retired), Curator, Camp Roberts Historical Museum, *Interviews,* Various
- Miller, Fred, *Interviews,* Various
- Mormon Church Genealogy Center, Long Beach, CA Stake
- Mormon Church Genealogy Center, Rancho Palos Verdes, CA Stake
- Mormon Church Genealogy Center, Salt Lake City, Utah
- New Testament Missionary Baptist Church, *Articles of Incorporation, May 1937*
- News Paper Clippings, Various
- NGB Form 22E dated 26 March 2002
- Raber, Brian, Interview, November 26, 2016
- San Pedro News Pilot, February 9, 1987
- State of California National Guard Orders #85-153 dated 26 March 2002
- Torgan, Tiffany, *Source Document, Harcourts Prestige Real Estate Properties, La Jolla, CA*
- U.S. Army Training Center, Fort Ord, California, Company A, 3rd Battle Group, 1st Brigade, *Basic Training Year Book, Fort Ord, CA 1959*
- UCLA Urban Planning Department, Channel Heights Historical Documents
- University of Southern California Digital Library
- US Army Corps of Engineers Study, *Describing California Lands, Suitable for the Development of Military Posts,* 1902
- US Army Orders #PO3-280450, 18 March 2002

BIBLIOGRAPHY

- Abdul-Jabbar, Kareem and Walton, Anthony, *Brothers in Arms,* Broadway Books, New York2004
- Bowers, William T., Hammond, William M., MacGarrigle, George L., *Black Soldier White Army, 24th Infantry Regiment in Korea,* United States Army Center of Military History, Washington D.C. 1996

- Brokaw, Tom, *A Lucky Life Interrupted,* Random House, New York, N.Y. Penguin Random House LLC, 2015
- Broyard, Bliss, *One Drop: My Father' Bs Hidden Life – A Story of Race and Family Secrets,* Back Bay Books/ Little, Brown and Company, New York, 2007
- Buckley, Joann H., *African American Doctors of World War I, The Lives of 104 Volunteers,* McFarland & Company, Inc., Jefferson North Carolina
- Bushey, Keith D. *The Many Forks In My Many Roads,* Graphic Publishers,Santa Ana, California, 2012
- Bushey, Keith D. *My LAPD Journey: From Street Cop to Commander,* Santa Ana, Graphic Publishers, 2015
- Calamandrei, Camilla, Director, Documentary Film *"Prisoners in Paradise"*, 2002
- California Governor's *Executive Order 8-32-11*
- Cambridge Editorial Partnership, Michael Young Centre, *The Greatest American Speeches,* Quereus Publishing Plc, 2006, London WCIA 2NS
- Cohen, Janet Langhart, *From Rage to Reason, My Life in Two America's*
- Cole, Harold S. *We Can, We Will, Ready and Forward,* As told to Colonel (Retired)M Dr. Gerald D. Curry, U.S. Air Force, Curry Brothers Marketing and Publishing Group, Haymarket, VA 2016
- Dabbs, Henry E. *Black Brass, Black Generals and Admirals in the Armed Forces of the United States,* Howell Press Charlottesville, Virginia,1997
- Delk, James D. *Fires & Furies: The Los Angeles Riots.* Palm Springs: ETC Publications, 1995
- Delk, James D. *The Fighting Fortieth: In War and Peace,* Palm Springs: ETC Publications, 1998
- Die Starke der Streitkrafte (in German). Bundesministerium der Verteidigung. Retrieved 18 December 2016
- Evans, Robert D. *"Gravette History." Benton County Pioneer 24* (Winter 1979)
- Fannie Lou Hamer, Mississippi Civil Rights Activist, Quote: *"Two things always remember: Never forget where*

you came from or the bridges which got you there", Unknown Date

- Gates, Daryl F. *Chief, My Life in the LAPD,* Bantam Books 1992
- Gates, Henry Louis, *In search of Our Roots,* Skyhorse Publishing, Delaware, 2017
- George, Denise and Child, Robert, *The Lost Eleven,* Caliber, New York, 2017
- Gravett, Peter J. & Edmund "Jerry" Brown, Governor of California, *California Veterans Resource Book,* Sacramento, 2015
- Gravett, Peter J. & Poole, Barbara J. *Promotion and Command Opportunities for Female* Officers*: A Study of the 40th Infantry Division (Mechanized), Published:* United States Army, The Pentagon, 8 January 1999
- Gravett, Peter J. *Commencement Speech, California State University Long Beach, May 20, 2016*
- Gravett, Peter J. *Commencement Speech, Cypress College,* May 2001
- Gravett, Peter J. *New Testament Baptist Church: Feasibility Study Committee Report,* April 2008
- Gravett, Peter J. Poem, *A Tribute To Dorothy,* July 12, 2000
- Gravett, Peter J. *Speech Delivered to Long Beach, CA Black Historical Society: Black Military History (Unpublished), October 10, 1998*
- Gravett, Peter J. Story, *A Word About Dorothy,* July 12, 2000
- Gravett, Peter J. *The New Mafia: Gangs of Los Angeles County,* Master's Thesis (Unpublished), University of Southern California, June 1977
- Gravett, Peter J. *The Valor of Black Soldiers from the Revolutionary War to Desert Storm,* The African American Resource Collection, Burnett Branch Library of Long Beach, California and the African American Heritage Society of Long Beach, California, October 10, 1998
- Gravett, Peter J., *Distinguished Alumni Banquet Speech,* California State University Long Beach, May 4, 2016

- Gravett, Peter, *Street Gangs: An Urban Menace,* Published: Federal Bureau Investigation National Academy, March 1977
- Gravette, Arkansas, Chamber of Commerce (April 3, 2006)
- Gravette: *Yesterday... Today ... and... Benton County Pioneer* 38 (Fall 1993)
- Halbert's Family Heritage, *World Book of Gravett's,* MCMXCIV
- Hudson, Victoria, *No Red Pen - Writers, Writers Group & Critique,* Gutterdog Press 2012
- Jakes, T.D. *DESTINY Step into your Purpose,* Faith Words, New York, 2015
- Katz, William Loren, *Black Indians, A Hidden Heritage,* Atheneum Books For Young Readers, New York et al, January 2012
- Kershaw, Alex, *The Longest Winter,* MFJ Books 2004
- Kraus, Henry, *In The City was a Garden*, Renaissance Press, New York, 1951
- Lanning, Michael Lee, Lieutenant Colonel (Retired), *African – American Soldier From Chrispus Attcuks to Colin Powell,* A Birch Lane Press Book Published by Carol Publishing Group, 1997
- Macy, Beth, *Truevine,* Little, Brown and Company, New York, *2016*
- Mandela, Nelson, *Climbing Hills*
- Michael von Ree, Gravette Historical Museum
- National Alliance to End Homelessness: *Veteran Homelessness*, April 22, 2015
- New Testament Baptist Church, *50th Anniversary Program Book,* 1988
- Nugent, Nell Marion, abstractor, *Cavaliers& Pioneers: Abstracts of Virginia Land, Vol. 3. Richmond State Library, 1979*
- Olguin, Albert "Lefty", Once a Pirate Always a Pirate, Outskirts Press, Denver, Colorado, 2015
- Potter, Lou with Miles, William and Rosenblum, Nina, *Liberators, Fighting on Two Fronts in World War Two*, Harcourt Brace Jovanovich, Publishers, 1992

- Rice, Condoleezza, *Democracy, Stories from the Long Road to Freedom,* Twelve, Hachette Book Group, New York, 2017
- Rose, Robert A., D.D.S. *Lonely Eagles, The Story of America's Black Air Force In World War II*
- Schriebman, Major Robert S., 40th Infantry Division Support Brigade, State Military Reserve, Staff Judge Advocate, *The Posse Comitatus Handbook, A Manual for Commanders and JAG's, 2007*
- Shaara, Jeff, *The Frozen Hours,* Ballantine Books, New York, 2017
- Silka, Henry P. *San Pedro: A Pictorial History,* San Pedro Bay Historical Society, 1993
- State of California, Legislative Analyst Office, *Understanding the Veterans Services Landscape in California,* January 17, 2017
- The Church of Jesus Christ of Latter-Day Saints, *The African American Heritage Society,* February 1, 2003
- The Daily Breeze, *George Peck's Tale of Two Cities,* Sam Gnerre, July 21, 2009
- The Daily Breeze, *L.A. Parks Agency to liquidate trust,* February 28, 1976
- The Fire Ball, *Souvenir Edition, 40th US Infantry Division News Letter, South Korea,* Vol. 2. No. 15, May 16, 1954
- The Los Angeles Times Newspaper, April 27, 2017, *L.A. Riots Ensnarled Athletes,* Bob Nightengale.
- U.S. Department of Justice Grant, *Law Enforcement Assistance Program, 1974*
- Watson, Earl *"The Pearl", Doorman to the Stars*, E & M Publishers A.S.C.A.P. 2012 Revised
- Webster University, United States Department of Justice News Release, *Law Enforcement Educational Program (LEEP),* October 1970
- Wikipedia, *Tuskegee Airmen and the Montfort Point Marine Association*
- WikiPedro/Pedro Pedigree: Stephen M. White, Posted June 1, 2010; John Gaffey, Posted December 16, 2009,

William G. Kerckhoff, posted April 22, 2010 and James H. Dodson, Sr. Posted January 28, 2010

Lieutenant General Herbert Temple, Chief National Guard Bureau and my mentor for many years

Made in the USA
Columbia, SC
19 November 2019